Han Suyin is the daughter of a Belgian mother and a Chinese father who, a Mandarin and scholar entitled to enter the Imperial Academy, had chosen instead at the age of nineteen to travel on a scholarship to Europe.

She was moved by the poverty and sickness she saw around her to take up medicine. She studied Chinese classics and mathematics while waiting for a place at Yenching University. Then, after completing her pre-medical education, she travelled across Siberia to Europe on a scholarship and continued her studies at the University of Brussels. In 1938 she returned to China, married an ex-Sandhurst Chinese officer, who later became a general in Chiang Kai Shek's army, and practised midwifery in the interior during the Sino-Japanese War. From this experience she wrote her first book, *Destination Chungking*, in 1940. In 1942 she came to London, where her husband had been appointed military attache. Three years later he returned to active service in China, leaving Han Suyin to complete her medical studies in London. After her husband was killed in 1947, she spent a year as house surgeon at the Royal Free Hospital before accepting a doctor's post in Hong Kong. There she wrote the Eurasian love story (her own) that brought her international acclaim and success as a writer. The Sunday Times described *A Many Splendoured Thing* as 'an astounding love story ... brilliantly topical, but far more than that, for she handles an eternal theme with power, insight and unfailing artistry.'

Since that time she has written numerous books, both novels and non-fiction. Her combined autobiography and history of China in five volumes, has been hailed as an important contribution to international understanding. Bertrand Russell said of the first volume, *The Crippled Tree*, 'during the many hours I spent reading it, I learnt more about China than I did in a whole year spent in that country.'

By the same author

China: Autobiography, History
The Crippled Tree
A Mortal Flower
Birdless Summer
My House Has Two Doors
Phoenix Harvest

Novels
A Many-Splendoured Thing
Destination Chungking
... And the Rain My Drink
The Mountain is Young
Cast But One Shadow and *Winter Love*
Two Loves
The Four Faces

Non-Fiction
China in the Year 2001
Asia Today
Lhasa, The Open City
The Morning Deluge: Mao Tsetung and the Chinese Revolution 1893–1953
Wind in the Tower: Mao Tsetung and the Chinese Revolution 1949–1975

Han Suyin

A Mortal Flower

China: Autobiography, History, Book 2

**TRIAD
GRANADA**

Published by Triad/Granada in 1982

ISBN 0 586 03738 1

Triad Paperbacks Ltd is an imprint of
Chatto, Bodley Head & Jonathan Cape Ltd and
Granada Publishing Ltd

First published in Great Britain by
Jonathan Cape Ltd 1966
Copyright © Han Suyin 1966

Printed and bound in Great Britain by
Cox & Wyman Ltd, Reading
Set in Monotype Times

The name Peking has been used all through the book for the city of Peking. Although this name was changed to Peiping for the period 1928 to 1948, the inhabitants of Peking never got used to calling it so; the original name, Peking, was restored in 1949.

All Chinese names begin with the family name, the personal name coming second; the inverse is the custom in the West. This reminder appears necessary since in America, after so many missionaries and so many books on China, a majority of people are still unaware of this custom.

Part One (1928–1933)

CHAPTER ONE

Corner-crouched in the train corridor, the train steward's grandfather, black-gowned felt-capped old man, fingers a short rosary of midnight beads. Not the cornelian or jade of the wealthy which keeps finger joints supple; the millennial soothing beads of amethyst rediscovered by New York psycho-analysts for the magnates of computer-technocracy, but common round beans from a kapok tree, strung upon hand-twisted cotton, use-dingy time-killers.

The child hears them click time away, above the train's sneeze and stamp, and sees Apocalypse, holding all Time within gnarled fingers, measuring the midnights and the mornings of the sun. She returns to the magazine, brought by the Englishwoman in the next compartment, also going for a summer at the sea. "You may keep it dear. I've finished with it."

"Say thank you Rosalie," says Rosalie's mother.

The Englishwoman has powder on her face, her lips shine lacquer, her eyes glow blue, she is a shiny-feathered eagle, bright teeth and shoes, hair and eyes glossy. The magazine shines, a lustrous trickle sunpath across its coloured cover photograph of two people standing under a large bell of flowers. Coloured photograph of the wedding of Generalissimo Chiang Kaishek and Miss Soong Meiling, in Shanghai.

Even Rosalie knows about that wedding last December, more than six months ago. Everyone knows. Mr. Hua Namkwei, who is Papa's friend, and his wife Mrs. Hua, who is a Polish Jewess (so Mama says), call the Soong family the compradores of foreign banks. Mama says they are Shanghai bankers. Papa says they are American Chinese. Rosalie knows something about banks, because Papa has an account in one. In Peking the French bank is awesome; the German bank where Elder Brother worked before he went to Tientsin has black iron bars to its windows; the Belgian bank is where Mama, hatted and gloved, collects money sent to her by her father in Belgium. There is a special tone in grown-up people's voices when they talk about banks. The same tone as when they speak of generals and armies. The Big Wedding she stares at on a six-month-old magazine is talked of in the voice used for power, the shoulder-sloping, half-crouched voice,

tentative like a furtive beggar's hand. An eleven-year-old understands that two and two make four. Army and Money add up to
Power. Money is strongest for it buys everything, even warlords
and armies, and out of the marriage of Army and Money, Power
is born.

> The wedding was a brilliant affair. Everybody of import-
> ance was there . . . It unites the all-powerful leader of the
> Nanking armies and the family of Dr. T. V. Soong, brother
> of the bride . . . fully thirteen hundred persons were present
> . . . Sir Sidney Barton, H.M. Consul-General, Mr. S. Yada,
> Japanese Consul-General, Admiral Mark Bristol, Com-
> mander-in-Chief American Pacific Fleet . . . the bride wore . . .
> the honeymoon will be spent . . . it is not known how long
> Generalissimo Chiang Kaishek will be away . . . possibly no
> more than a week, his presence being urgently required to
> consolidate the Nanking government . . .

Oh, we go to the sea, we go to the sea, we go to Peitaiho for our
summer holiday . . . Rosalie and Tiza and Marianne, the three
sisters, and Mama and Papa. Papa will only be two days at the
sea, though in Peking the tiger heat of July registers 103°. Papa
has to keep the trains running. Rosalie is certain trains cannot run
if her father does not sit at his desk, in his cane-bottomed
revolving chair, a beige cushion huddled at his back in the winter.
Papa has trouble. Someone in the railway administration wants
his job. Mr. Chu, the new supervisor, who reads the testament of
Dr. Sun Yatsen, Founding Father of the Chinese Republic, to the
assembled staff every Monday, then makes a speech which ends:
"Long live our noble leader, Generalissimo Chiang Kaishek",
wants Papa's job given to a relative of his, a young man back
from study in the United States whose wife's father is an official
in the new Nanking government. Mr. Chu has wonderful connections, for his brother-in-law is under-secretary to T. V. Soong.
Mr. Chu may displace Papa, send him somewhere down the line,
to a small station on the railway, and give the young relative
Papa's job. For weeks Papa has worried in silence about it; only
last night did he tell Mama he might have to go "down the line"
for a few months, in the autumn, on an inspection tour. The
story of Chu and his relative came out, little by little. Prising
words out of Papa is more difficult than getting blood out of a
stone, so says Mama.

"And you tell me this the day before we go to Peitaiho. How do you expect me to enjoy my seaside holiday with this sword hanging over my head?" asks Mama. She goes on packing and talking. "You always knuckle down to them, you don't stand up for yourself . . . if I were a man, I'd tell this Chu what I think of him – these southerners – all they want is money, money . . ."

Rosalie worries. While Papa is at the sea for two days, will something happen to his job? Rosalie knows that people blacken each other's reputations these days, tell lies which make people lose jobs. Unless one has Pull, or Money for gifts and banquets, it is easy to lose a job. Mama does not call on the three wives of Mr. Chu with gifts, and Papa has no money for banquets. Rosalie daydreams that she discovers a diamond mine in the garden of their house, and gives it to Papa and Mama, who become wealthy, and at last Mama loves Rosalie, because Rosalie was so clever; digging and digging for archaeological remains, and discovering a diamond mine! Holding the shining magazine, looking at the face of the young woman Miss Soong, now Madame Chiang Kaishek, so beautiful, with diamonds in her ears, marrying Generalissimo Chiang Kaishek, the Number One in China, under a huge bell of white roses in December . . . Rosalie dreams. And then it is time to eat.

For train travel eats space, and is also eating time, nearly all the way. Mama may not know what her children are like, she does not quicken to their riddle minds, but she sees to it that they are well fed. And what more can anyone want of a mother? The three sisters munch as beyond the window the barley-coloured telephone poles hurl at them and escape.

The train drums, ululates across the plain, a dry dry world, where heat waves shimmer up and down. The brown mud houses squat in a summer drought; the patchwork fields nurse great cracks. In the great plains, farther west, the peasants are dying because the rains have not come, the wheat is dying a gangrene death of dryness. And not only death but the soldiers shimmer up and down, down and up, five hundred thousand soldiers who must eat and who do eat, plucking the raw seed on its stalk and munching it like locusts. Like locusts in spattering grey clouds falling upon the earth, devouring it, so the armies in the north; and although the warlords have been bought with silver by Chiang Kaishek, although the newspapers scream "there is peace" and "all is well" and "the future is bright", yet all is not so well, all is as it was. At each stop Papa walks on to the platform, looks around, talks with the station-master. At one station

11

about thirty soldiers in grey rags, famine gaunt, spread the smell of danger about them; everyone looks away from, walks far from danger. Some have no arms, some have only one leg; one crawls on four stumps, like a dog. The soldiers are hungry, they beg, or rather demand money from the train, going from open window to window fierce-eyed, scowling, smelly, broken shards in hand, their begging-bowls. "Disbanded men," says Papa. "Crippled." For when a soldier is wounded he is merely thrown out of the armies to beg. But in this gaunt pack are able-bodied men. They try to board the train. The station-master expostulates: "Big brothers, good brother soldiers, all the coaches are full." That is true, the third class is full. At a previous station peasants in rags have tried to climb on to the train roof, and have been beaten off. The soldiers get in, because everyone is afraid. Five climb on the engine front and tie themselves there, above the engine's toothy cowcatcher. The train starts, stamps away.

At noon the train arrives in Tientsin. Tientsin is a big city, a river port, and there are foreign concessions, and foreign soldiers, British, American, Japanese, with bayonets fixed to their rifles. Railways and soldiers. For years there have been foreign soldiers along Chinese railroads; but the new government of the strong man Chiang Kaishek is going to nationalize the railways, take them all back from the foreigners. That is what the newspapers say. But Mama shrugs: "Nothing will be done. The Americans, the British, the Japanese, they are too strong."

Marianne wants a sweet and Mama opens the hamper again. Ham sandwiches, hardboiled eggs, an apple tart, boiled sweets. Beggars immediately materialize, clawing at the glass window-pane, driven away by policemen with sticks. Flies also claw; also magically cluster to bite bare legs and arms, are also beaten away. One fly rushes into Marianne's mouth and she spits it out.

There are two Tientsin stations, Central and East. At the second one Elder Brother appears, peering, short-sighted eyes half lidded.

"There he is," says Mama of her son, "myopic as ever. Why doesn't he wear his glasses?"

Elder Brother looks white and thin in the heat. He wears white shorts, a white shirt, a topee; every European wears a topee in the summer. He says how wonderful everything is in Tientsin. He is teaching at the Jesuit College, making more money than Papa as an engineer after fourteen years on the railway.

"You ought to come here," he tells his favourite sister, Rosalie.

12

"You ought to study here, in Tientsin. Peking is a backward Tartar village. Nothing ever happens in Peking."

Elder Brother stays in a German boarding-house, the Pension Apelt, in the former German Concession. He praises the Germans. "What this country needs is a few Germans to clean it up."

Whistles, the train clangs and clucks, stirs, Elder Brother diminishes, though he is so tall one can see him for a while, until the telegraph poles sail past.

One train journey, and all the train journeys come, crowding back like the locusts which ravage the sun-smoked plains; trains in and out of valley-forked hills, fading in sun-misted horizons, pulsating in rose-washed dawns, screaming at sunsets red with the dust of the dead.

In and out of the stations, with their lice crawl of cankered beggars and crippled soldiers assaulting the trains, beaten off, returning, the Flood, the endless Flood of misery that is China, and the trains, grand, going through it lordly. The owl hoots of engines in the winged night, engines eating coal, drinking water, belching white smoke plumes straight like a general's helmet feathers, trains backing like horses, cantering forward with round enormous eye. Endless, like poverty, like hunger, the talk of the trains, Papa's life, the family's life, Rosalie's life. Whenever Papa's friends come together, Uncle Liu the Lolo, Mr. Hua Namkwei, they talk of the trains, of the wars that cut the railways, of the money the trains make which goes to pay old debts, and of the Great Strikes of the railways, in 1924, 1925.

"Warlord Wu Peifu knew how to deal with wicked Communist workers, he shot them down. Our Leader is just as firm, if not firmer; he will deal with the rebellious workers Communist-inspired, if they give trouble." Mr. Chu has said this as a threat, and Papa has repeated it to Mr. Hua Namkwei, his best friend. Mr. Hua in this summer of 1928 wears a face like an empty railway truck, on a siding, a waiting-for-ghosts face Rosalie calls it. Mrs. Hua is back from France, but their children, Simon and Leila, are still in Europe. Mrs. Hua is writing a book. "A book about what?" Mama asked Papa. "About marriage between a European woman and a Chinese man," Papa replied, looking at his vine.

The train dandles the dreamy afternoon, and the children dream . . . Trains through the land in flood, water soil-brown over all but the train's upraised bed, water twisting lazy brown loll around surprised treetops rearing above its glazed pellicle;

13

quiet water, the lazy silent death of water upon the fields; no houses seen, but in the protruding tree-boughs people, perched like birds, unmoving. The train thunders by them, high on its high embankment, even screams at them. They do not raise a hand, knowing it will not stop for them, nobody will stop for them. They die the lazy death of water, and no one cares. Mile upon mile upon mile of them. Mama opens the hamper; the children eat. All her life, Rosalie will see this, whenever she climbs on a train, all her life; eating and looking at the quiet brown death and the quiet people waiting for nothing but death.

The mirage-making sun draws dream lakes, brown glittering seas, beyond the cracked fields. The child screams: "A flood, a flood." But it is only a dream. "There is no water here," says Papa. "That was two years ago," says Mama, "we went through a flood then, you remember?" Rosalie shakes her head, says no. Lies to Mama, who must not know Rosalie-me.

The plain protrudes a myriad burial mounds, a sky glut of cemetery, the round tents of the dead, each one a foundering of light bones. They, too, are parched. In what subsoil of longing lie these bones which, fleshed, alive, laboured their misery upon earth? And then the sky turns agate. Suddenly, spherical blue, higher than the land, like an enormous grave, at the horizon, a sparkling sapphire dome, a sigh.

"The sea, the sea," cries Mama. Unforgettable this first eye-shock, the blue rainbow spanning the sunset land, unforgettable, the first long-drawn exhalation of the sea. Tiza rushes to the train window, Marianne clutches her pail and spade. Mama puts away the uneaten buns. Evasive white-barked pines slide by, between them the water humps its colossal blueness. "Mama, why is it higher than the earth, why does the sea stand up like a mountain, why is it round like a rainbow?" "Hurry up and don't leave anything in the train," says Mama. "We have arrived. This is Peitaiho."

Out of the train, on the platform, the Chou family, Papa, Mama, Tiza, Marianne, and Rosalie emerge to the muffled music, the perfume and the ecstasy of the sea.

The pension Glauber, our destination, has a porter in uniform at the station waiting for us. There are eucalyptus and persimmon trees, pink peonies eyecatching like a generalissimo's medals, as we ride to the pension in rickshaws.

Mrs. Glauber carries the face of a kind potato above a body

14

trussed in pastel blue. Her pale smooth hair is gathered in a swaying bun. Her prices are reasonable. Mama will later say she serves too many potatoes and not enough meat and eggs. Milk we abhor, being Chinese that way; Mama never tries to make us drink it. "My children have excellent teeth," she says proudly, "real North China teeth, made to last a lifetime. They don't need milk."

Before dinner, Rosalie runs down to the beach, five hundred yards away from the Glauber pension, across a meadow with stubbly grass, lizard glaze slime, and round cowdung patches (the cows are mooing in their byres). The sun is packing itself into an enormous red ball and going down, down, in a desperate slide. The sand is gold, gold to pick, gold to touch; when Rosalie digs at the beach gold to put it in her pail, it turns back to sand.

Many afternoons Rosalie slices away at that gold pellicle the sea has left on the thirsty sand. Gold is money and Papa needs money for Banquets and Gifts to keep his job; always the gold turns back to sand.

At night the restless sea hoots like a faraway train. One can be lonely with breathing sisters, sleeping mother. The sea hums a tranquil railway song.

Mrs. Glauber moves the family. She cannot let them have the room in the main bungalow, but will accommodate them in a smaller bungalow, about seven minutes away, one they will share with an old English gentleman, the only inconvenience being the walk to the main building for meals. At first Mama is upset by this arrangement, but Mrs. Glauber says there has been a mix-up in the bookings.

The smaller bungalow is quite charming, a three-sided box arrangement round an inner garden. One bedroom on either side, a living-room in the middle. We occupy one bedroom, the English gentleman the other, we share the living-room with him. In that living-room, against one wall, is a large glass-paned bookcase, and more books than I have ever seen. I walk up to it and:

"Don't touch," cries Mama, "or Mrs. Glauber will throw us out."

But she walks up to the bookcase, turns the small key left in the lock. The glass doors open. Five rows of large books, smelling musty.

"Now you can read, Rosalie."

People go to the seaside to swim, to get suntanned. There is a small lending library in the little village of Peitaiho, near the shops.

The fee is two dollars per month for the children's books. There is no space fiction, which Rosalie loves.

The bungalow had belonged to an English doctor who came to Peitaiho every summer, when most of his clients were there. He died and Mrs. Glauber bought the bungalow with furniture and books.

The summer visitors in Peitaiho are nearly all Europeans: families of the diplomatic corps, Tientsin businessmen, French, English, American, Italian and German. A few White Russians, a few well-off Eurasian families, a few very wealthy Chinese, who have their own houses and gardens here. The Chinese families in Peitaiho keep to themselves, play mahjong and do not bathe in the sea like the foreigners do. They are so wealthy and important that the foreign diplomats invite them to their houses, and play mahjong with them.

I inherit the dead doctor's books, read them between a trance of sea and sand. Few go to the sea in the afternoons, but we do. We are in sea water twice a day, morning and afternoon. Mama says we must not squander an hour of our precious sea-time, all we have is a month. She sits by the beach hut, matting shading her from the sun, lets the sea wind play over her and is happy. She never enters the sea. "I am resting, I am resting for my life, all these years."

In the evening I read, read the dead doctor's books. At the end I know that I, too, will be a doctor.

But first I acquire, one by one, the diseases I read about. In turn I suffer from scurvy, leprosy and elephantiasis; a short bout of yellow fever lasts a day. I begin to scan others for diseases.

My sister Marianne suffers from scarlet fever; her arms, bitten by seaside mosquitoes, covered in a rash, denote bubonic plague. It is kindest not to tell her, though I worry as I watch her for the more dreadful bubo to develop. Later I discover it is not plague but some incurable African disease. My father, though absent, surely has enlarged tonsils and gangrene of the feet; I pray for him. The only person invulnerable to my imagination is my mother. Yet she has Peitaiho tummy, and runs to the toilet ten times a day. This summer diarrhoea, familiar to all who have been to Peitaiho, is the acceptable, almost fashionable, disease of foreigners at the seaside.

The English gentleman with whom we share the bungalow is a retired businessman from Tientsin. He walks about with a cane in his hand and a fine straw hat upon his head. He makes jovial conversation for twenty minutes after dinner. Somehow or other Mother quarrels with him. "Your mother has a foul temper," he says to me as I read, alone in the living-room, the next evening.

He moves out of the bungalow, and instead of suffocating in a single bedroom – on windless nights under mosquito nets – we have two bedrooms to spread into, which is delightful, for I have read about noxious air, and am terrified of dying from lack of oxygen.

By the end of the first fornight Mama has quarrelled with a few other ladies at the pension. Fortunately she also has friends. There is Mrs. Thassounis of the bakery and pastry shop in Peking. Her daughter Vera is my friend. The Thassounis have a small villa up the hirsute pine-clad hills that ring the bay of Peitaiho. Another friend is Yvette Poh, the wife of Mr. Poh Hungwen who was a student in Europe at the same time as Papa. My mother always speaks of Mr. Poh as "the Bolshevik" because, she says, in his youth he tried to get Papa to follow Dr. Sun Yatsen. Mr. Poh wanted to be an architect but is now an administrator in the railway. He is an enthusiast of Generalissimo Chiang Kaishek, whom he calls the greatest genius of the age. "He is a clever talker," says Mama. Yvette Poh, his wife, is French; Mama says the French pretend to be superior, but Yvette Poh had been a working girl in Paris, a seamstress. She asks Mama's advice. She is unhappy.

When we return to Peking in the autumn, Yvette Poh continues her vists, and they become a calvary for Mama, who never has the heart to be absent when Mrs. Poh comes to tea, although as soon as she is gone Mama burns creosote in a tin and opens all the windows, for Mrs. Poh smells to high heaven.

But the pine-scented wind from the hills, the hot salty tang of the sea, smother the manifest disease from which Yvette Poh suffers; only an occasional whiff (ascribed to her liver) disturbs her conversation with Mama. Mrs. Poh's two sons go for donkey rides with us, up and down the winding stony tracks of the hills. Our mothers linger, plunged in talk, their mouths move, their eyes stray to measure our donkey distance away from them.

Mrs. Poh has a rotting lung, from which at regular intervals the Greek surgeon at the French hospital in Peking drains litres of pus. Mrs. Poh is proud of her lung. "This morning they pumped two litres out of me." She makes us feel that it is normal to have gallons of pus drained out of one's chest, nor can she smell herself. Her husband is in the process of acquiring what Yvette terms "a concubine", a state of marital convenience which Yvette refuses.

Yvette's life is romance thwarted and desolate, but still romance. Mama loves romance, hence their friendship, despite the odour. A beginning in Paris, those enchanted hours when a student from the exotic Orient meets a little seamstress in a French dressmaking establishment, makes her his wife, and now "the other woman", come to break a happy marriage! No such heart-rending domestic tragedy agitates Mama; she now has within reach a sorrow greater than hers, humiliation deeper than the sum of her own, to console and to support. "At least my husband is faithful . . ." Mama begins. Mrs. Poh interrupts, "You see, Madame Chou, I would not care if he beat me, treated me like a dog, but another woman, after all I gave up for him . . ."

It is the end of our month, and Papa comes to fetch us. He stays three days and twice dips his feet in the indolent, sandbank-thwarted sea. Three times he walks to Peitaiho village, where he enters into negotiations with the owner of a shoe shop to acquire a small piece of land, later to build a house for Mama at the seaside. The house built, in 1935, is given to Tiza.

Back in Peking, as Yvette Poh's disease ravages her weekly a little more, her active relish in detailing her tragedy augments. Ecstatically, she unfolds a blow-by-blow recital of what her husband Poh Hungwen said or did to her and she to him. Her hair is now rufous; she has dyed it to recapture the affection of Mr. Poh. "He used to love my hair." Her face is patchy with white powder, her eyes brilliant with fever. On her veined hands she wears more rings. Mama one day, in pity and distress, displays to Yvette Poh her own jewels, standing well behind her as she sprays mephitic ohs and ahs upon the gems. She tells Mama, her eyes dilating, that she inspects Mr. Poh's underwear for traces of you-know-what when he returns at night. She has followed him to a restaurant and stood two hours outside, in the street, watching.

When Papa returns from his office in the evening, Mama reminds him: "Yentung, you must talk to Poh Hungwen about his wife. She is dying."

"It is difficult, it is difficult," Papa replies.

By that time the creosote smell has dispersed.

"I know, she stinks, she really stinks, but I haven't got the courage to tell her."

One day Yvette Poh arrives, radiant with fever, a silver fox round her neck, to tell Mama that she met "that prostitute", riding a rickshaw in the street, and she sneered at her. She ran after the rickshaw, pulled "that tart" out of it, slapped her and pulled her hair. "Now," she says triumphantly, "now!" There was blood in the pus they drew from her the day before yesterday. She adds casually, "I feel so much better, I think I shall be cured as soon as winter is over."

Soon we are all standing in St. Michael's Church on a raw November morning. Mrs. Poh's sons wear black armbands. There are candles, a black-velvet-robed coffin, white chrysanthemums and lilies. Sniffing through the incense and the flowers, my nostrils think they distinguish the fetor of Yvette Poh.

Poh Hungwen marries the "dance-hall girl", who turns out to be a respectable, middle-school teacher. Mama swears she will never receive her, but the occasion for snubbing the Pohs, in loyalty to Yvette, does not arise, for Poh Hungwen goes to Nanking with his new wife and obtains a position as financial adviser there. Mama is very angry: "He does not know anything about finance." She scolds Papa. "Everyone gets on in life, except you. Year after year you go on working like a horse, and no advancement. Having killed off his wife and married that woman, your friend gets a good job. I suppose he will buy himself a motor car now. And send his sons to be educated in America. And what do you do, but put your money into bricks and stones, bricks and stones? And you haven't even thought to ask Poh to put in a word for you, at the top, in Nanking."

A year later Poh Hungwen is back in Peking, fatter, heartier, full of "Our Mighty Leader, Generalissimo Chiang Kaishek". He wears a kind of uniform, he is Chief Secretary to some Military Commission. He gives a banquet at the best Chinese restaurant, the Ho Teh Fu. The brother of our ex-warlord, General Wu Peifu, who once ruled the whole of North China, is working as a waiter in this restaurant. He is a very nice waiter, and has always refused his brother's efforts to raise his condition or to give him money. Hence everyone goes to the Ho Teh Fu restaurant, if only to see waiter Wu, and to talk with him. Poh Hungwen twits waiter Wu, speaks of sending one son to America, the other to France, to "deepen their learning".

"And he *is* buying a motor car. What did I tell you?" says Mama to Papa. "Some get on in life, some don't."

Many years later I, Rosalie, meet Mr. Poh's son, a prosperous businessman, in San Francisco. He wears glasses, looks like his father, has married a Chinese girl from New York who speaks not a word of Chinese. Neither of them want to have anything to do with me, because I go to Peking, to visit my own father. And though Poh Hungwen is also in Peking, his son is afraid even to talk about him, "for the F.B.I. might take my passport away if they knew my father is getting on well in communist China."

There was also a White Russian family at Peitaiho, the Verniakoffs. Other Europeans looked down upon White Russians and so did "good" Eurasian families. White Russians were below us, though not as far down as the Chinese who were only natives, except of course the very rich ones who were really wonderful people, with the most beautiful manners. My mother was different; she made friends, or enemies, according to fancy, without reference to a set social code. Mrs. Verniakoff was the only woman, besides my mother, on the beach in the afternoon, when the wind was strong, the waves loud, and everyone else shopping, tea-ing, mahjonging or donkey-riding. Helena Verniakoff's two daughters, Veronica and Nina, and my mother's three, collected shells, built sand-castles, shouted when the snarling waves came lashing at them, swam in the turbulent surf.

"I love the sea when it is tempestuous," said Helena Verniakoff. My mother and she became friends.

I had a fight one afternoon with a tall statuesque woman in a black bathing suit, who had casually usurped our bathing hut. I arrived, angrily threw her clothes out of the hut in a heap upon the sand. The woman, who lay on her belly, rose majestically, wrapped herself in her bathrobe and started: "Yellow-bellied bastard, half-caste, stinking Chinese." While she walked up and down, sculptured by the wind in her towelling, yelling at me above the sea din, her son threw sand at me. I seized my spade and started to hit him. Helena arrived.

"You have done well, and indeed she should not call you names." This won my heart.

Helena had a white skin with a fine tracery of mauve veins, sea-grey eyes with very pale lashes, pale hair wound under a scarf. There was something distinguished about her profile, Mama said. When she moved one noticed her shoulder stoop, the apology of her hands, then one knew she was one of the crushed ones, as Mama called refugees. "She has suffered, I can tell," said Mama, looking at her own veined hands.

Mama told about a faraway uncle who had lost money in

Balkan bonds in the First World War, and Helena found this an extraordinary coincidence, her own father having lost his money in Balkan bonds. Her lashes came down over her eyes, like the shutters of our bungalow at noon during the siesta hour.

Mrs. Verniakoff would trek with difficult children to collect strange shells among sea-lashed rocks; tell stories at night to difficult sleepers, wade after young children waddling into the sea, and restore them to safety and sand. All she did was with disarming hesitancy, so that it happened without her actually appearing to do anything, and no one needed to thank her.

She took me for walks into the hills, saying: "Come with us. We shall lie in the sun." We walked up the slopes under the pine trees, under our feet the pine needles lay thick and slippery. There was no talk talk talk like donkeys' hooves striking the stones; no suffering of donkeys being whipped; only that squish of pine needles and the wind soughing in the pines. On a hill-top where the sun pushed its way and came down slap upon a patch of rocks, Helena took off all her clothes, and lay on the rocks all naked save for the space covered by the little gold cross she wore on a chain between her breasts; Veronica and Nina also took off their clothes, then I did. The hills were not curious, the silver-barked pines made marvellous patterns, all was delight and a radiance. Why did the nuns insist one must not take off one's clothes, when the wind and the sun were so naked?

Helena lectured on the sun, "It is so good. I worked in a laundry fourteen hours a day, and I never have enough sun." When she rose, the imprint of the small cross was dead white between her breasts.

There was one subject she would not hear about, and that was medicine. Nobody was *really* ill, nobody needed to die. All one had to do was to lie in the sun, and clean one's mind, to get well. Even when Veronica passed a big worm, she said: "That is the sun, it has cured her."

The last day at the seaside was weeping day, taking back boxes of shells, a live crab in seawater in the pail, a starfish which began to stink halfway. "Without doubt," said Mrs. Verniakoff, "I will see you again." For Mama had arranged that I should stay with her that December of 1928, when I was to go to Tientsin, to take my first examination. "Otherwise I would have to go," Mama explained to Papa, "and a hotel is so expensive." So all was arranged that summer at the sea. I would go alone to Tientsin, and stay with the Verniakoffs.

Two hundred candidates from Tientsin's various schools and the Catholic convent sat for the Cambridge Overseas in that December 1928. But our Peking convent school had only one candidate, myself. Hence I had to go to Tientsin to sit for the examination there.

Helena Verniakoff was at the station when I arrived. Long nose very red, mujik boots on her feet, a fur cap upon her head, her pale eyelashes like the wings of a moth in the cold, the train window glided by her and I knocked on the windowpane, but she did not hear or see me. Fifty yards away the train stopped, I pelted down the steps on to the platform. She was walking in the opposite direction.

"Mrs. Verniakoff," I shouted, "here I am."

"And indeed it is you. I have kept Veronica and Nina in bed; they have whooping cough. Have you had whooping cough?"

"Yes, twice."

"That is good, you can share the same bed."

I did not like sharing a bed. Could I get a bed to myself . . . but who would buy a bed for a week? We walked towards the station entrance, I a little subdued, followed by the porter carrying my suitcase.

The Verniakoffs lived on the second floor of a four-storeyed brick house in the French Concession, in a street with many such houses, all alike. The hall, very dark and small, opened on the stairs. There was one large room, the living-dining-room; then up ten very narrow, twisty steps, two bedrooms and a toilet with a washbasin. The flat was dark, but warm. There was a stove in the small kitchen, another stove in the living-room.

Veronica and Nina had become taller since the summer, they were playing cards in the large bed which almost filled their room. They wore long flannel night-gowns and Veronica's hair was plaited into pigtails which reached her waist.

"This is our home, without doubt it is small, but it is comfortable, you will like it. You will be warm at night," said their mother.

"There is Papa and Mama's bed," piped Nina, pointing to the unmade bed in the smaller room. "Papa sleeps with nothing on."

"And now you will eat Russian food," said Veronica.

I had never eaten Russian food, and there was *bortsch* soup and then *pirouskis*. Everything was a little sour, but I was hungry. Then something went wrong. My stomach was not accustomed to this food, perhaps even less to the condensed milk which I

22

drank, and I had to run to the toilet. The next ten days I ran to the toilet many times a day. My stomach hurt all the time, I tightened a flannel belt around it and tried to forget it between visits to the bathroom. And one day I could not stop and soiled myself; Helena washed me and made everything clean again.

We had tea, hot and strong, from the samovar, tea with cherry jam in it. Helena was dreaming, her eyes stared through the single window at the winter afternoon. She asked me if I would like some dinner later at night.

"I would like to get my books out of the suitcase. The examination starts the day after tomorrow."

"Ah yes, without a doubt, well, I will show you tomorrow how to get there. It is in the middle of the English Park that you take the examination."

I was surprised. Would not examinations in the middle of a park in December be a little cold? Could one write with gloves on?

"What happens if it snows?"

Mrs. Verniakoff laughed. "But you are in a building. It is called Gordon Hall, yes, I think such is the name. It is in the Gordon English Park."

Veronica and Nina shuffled packs of cards and taught me to play Russian Bank. Helena tied an apron round herself and announced that she would prepare dinner.

Someone came clattering down the stairs on high heels; there was a knock on the hall door. A woman with curly hair, a felt hat with flowers and a veil, came in.

"Good evening, Madame. Good evening, children."

"Good evening, Miss Gray. Going out already?" said Helena. "Have some bortsch, it's cold outside."

"No, thank you." Miss Gray had slim legs in sheer silk stockings. Her scent came to me through the thicker smell of cabbage and sour cream soup. "Your guest has arrived, I see."

"Yes, we are so glad to have her. How is Miss Hess today?"

"Still not well, you know." Miss Gray's eyes filled with tears. "No, she is not well at all. It is sad, nicht wahr?"

Helena shook her head. "Well, it is sad, especially at this time . . . I hope she recovers, without doubt I do."

Miss Gray's perfume lingered after her. I felt sleepy. Soon we went to bed. The bed was warm and I fell asleep almost immediately.

I woke up in the night scratching. Fire seemed to be racing

23

across my face, neck, stomach. Between my toes I itched so hard that I cried out.

"I itch, Mrs. Verniakoff. I itch."

The light went on, a single bulb, capped in a green silk shade. On the pillow, where my head had lain, bedbugs were scurrying. A few more were on the blanket. Veronica and Nina were huddled together, fast asleep.

"Ah," said Helena, "it is without doubt the bedbugs. Yes, they climb to the ceiling and then let themselves drop on to the bed to bite you. They are very clever."

I began to weep; Mrs. Verniakoff said soothingly: "You must not cry, it will not make them stop. I have some stuff here. I will smear you with it, they will not touch you. One second."

The ointment was sticky, but not unpleasant. It seemed to soothe the itching too; I fell asleep again.

In the morning I woke first. Veronica stretched, yawned. Nina, asleep, ground her teeth.

"Veronica, do you know there are bedbugs?"

"Bedbugs? Yes, of course there are. Where there's a bed there's bedbugs."

"But we must kill them."

"Kill them? How can we? There are thousands of them. Look." She pointed. There they were, studding the ceiling, pick pick picketing it in great patches, some marching down the walls in regular files, like soldiers.

"I thought it was the paint, all those splotches on the ceiling."

"Don't worry, they don't bite us now, they are used to us, soon they will get used to you." And it was true, their skins were smooth and biteless.

Helena said: "I will get some paraffin." She soused the bedbugs with paraffin where she could reach them, which was not very far up the walls. She took the bed to pieces and put paraffin down the joints, and also scalding water. I kept on being bitten; finally became so tired that I slept in spite of the bedbugs, only waking up to rush to the toilet.

After breakfast of hot tea and griddle cakes and boiled eggs and honey on toast, Mrs. Verniakoff walked with me to the British Concession, to Gordon Park and Gordon Hall, where the examination was held.

The streets were broader here, and tarred. "Kiessling's", said a golden sign, and in front of two windows full of mouth-watering pastry I gazed at chocolate shapes of Father Christmas, and

24

angels, bears and ducks. I remembered Elder Brother writing of this shop as the best pastry shop in the whole of China. "We went to Kiessling's" implied social acceptance. Some girls in school, who had been to Tientsin, had spoken about Kiessling's. I looked at the cakes. My stomach hurt terribly.

We came to a building almost like a castle: it had crenellated battlements, all of grey brick, two towers, a large clock. That was Gordon Hall. In the front hall a large notice said: "Cambridge Overseas Examinations". An arrow pointed. Round Gordon Hall a largish square, plots now winter bare winter grey.

Back at the flat, Mr. Verniakoff turned up, a short man with a mop of golden hair, a very friendly smile. He worked very hard, had two jobs, trying to make more money. He came home to sleep late at night, left early in the morning. His teeth were white and even, he spoke in a low voice. The whole family went off to have a bath at the public baths, as it was Sunday afternoon. I would have liked to go, but my stomach was too unsteady.

I was reading the chapter on participles and gerunds in my English grammar book, when a red-haired woman walked into the hall, without knocking. I had forgotten to bolt the door and it was ajar. She was followed by a small Japanese in a grey suit and a green hat and a pair of very large glasses.

"Is Mrs. Verniakoff in?" asked the woman. Her voice was hoarse. "I want someone to tell this guy it's twenty dollars."

"Perhaps I can tell him," I said, "if he understands Chinese?"

"I wonder if he does? Anyway you tell him."

I looked at him: "It's twenty dollars."

The man grinned, showing very white teeth, then he laughed. The woman laughed too.

"Well, anyway, he'll have to pay," she said. "Come on," she pointed, "upstairs."

I sat back to the gerunds, and a little later I heard the Japanese come down. He knocked at the hall door. I opened and he grinned, then dipping in his pocket brought out two pink sweets wrapped in paper. He placed them on the table, in front of me, waved his hand, bowed, and went out again.

That evening in bed I was informed.

"Do you mean," I asked Veronica, "that Miss Hess is a fallen woman? And also Miss Gray?"

Veronica snorted. "Don't be a baby. Everyone's got to live, and you can't live without money. One day they will find nice men to marry. What else can they do? It's life."

25

"But," said I, "doesn't it hurt?"

"Not if you get used to it, I suppose," replied Veronica, in a superior way.

I felt I wanted more details, especially as I was busy catching bedbugs at the time my enlightening took place. But Veronica's great sophistication stopped further questioning. It was some time before I fell asleep, and I forgot to say prayers, even the one especially made up for me by the nuns at the Peking convent, to pass the examination.

In spite of the bedbugs and the diarrhoea, life with the Verniakoffs was strangely pleasant. One took things calmly, it was a rest from Mama, and besides, one knew that it was nothing compared with what the Russians had suffered running away from the Revolution – or so Helena said. "And indeed if my honoured parents could see me now, in this place, they would say Holy St. Anne and Mother of Mercy and all the saints what has our daughter done to deserve this? These things happen, and I have been lucky. Many people died on the road to Siberia; but I did not die. My child did not die. I am very lucky."

Helena had been married in Russia when the Revolution came, and Veronica had been born. Her husband and she, with Veronica, fled, not west but east, because her husband was an official at Cheliabinsk. She always emphasized that he had been a *high* official, and that she came from a *good* family, like Mama. Curtsying, parties, eating ice-cream, long gloves to her elbows, in winter a medallion on a black ribbon round her neck.

They arrived in Irkutsk, and her husband died of typhus. The party in which she travelled was ambushed by some Siberian robbers, the men shot. She managed to escape, carrying Veronica, and continued to trek across Siberia.

"I cannot tell you," she said, "all the things that happened. Sometimes I did not eat for days, but somehow or other I lived, and Veronica lived too."

After a year or more, Mrs. Verniakoff arrived in Harbin, along with a hundred thousand other White Russians. "And there it was worse, the city was crowded with refugees begging in the streets, dying on the river banks, the river smelt bad with their corpses. They would do anything, they would even do the jobs of the Chinese, they fought the Chinese coolies to carry loads and drag carts, and many many had to do bad things." And the worst was that some of the White Russians grew rich on the miseries of their fellow men, opening night clubs, hiring girls to work for them, making children work fourteen hours a day at tanning leather and making matches, and the children died of poisoning and overwork.

Helena nearly fell into the hands of such a brute who beat the women who worked for him in his factory. "And he was a nobleman, an aristocrat from St. Petersburg." She managed to escape and arrived in Tientsin. She went to work in a laundry, and her hands were at first covered with sores, washing clothes. Tientsin also was full of White Russians competing at pulling carts, begging, even foraging in the garbage bins to eat. After a while the stronger men were formed into regiments, because the warlords needed bodyguards, needed private armies. The Japanese also recruited many White Russians and sent them back to fight in Siberia for them. And the British and the French also recruited them, to patrol the Concessions and keep down the Chinese.

Helena stayed in Tientsin, where there was a large foreign population for whom the White Russians catered with bakeries, restaurants, night clubs, brothels and laundries. When the troops of the British, and the French, and the Americans, landed in Shanghai and in Tientsin, business looked up for the White Russian night clubs and the brothels. Mrs. Verniakoff had married again. "Only," she said sadly, "my second husband is a workman, he is not of my class, but he is a good man." He was a Siberian, the son of a peasant. He did not drink or smoke, and it was he who insisted on sending her and the children to the seaside.

She taught her husband to read and to write, sang and recited poetry "to refine his soul". Around the electric light at night, after the table had been cleared from their supper of soup and bread and condensed milk and slices of cold beef and beetroot and cabbage, the father would sit with the children and study with his wife. She taught them all.

Her day-dreaming talent, mixing the real past with the unreal future, enabled her to float above daily miseries. She made plans for the future, which she expounded to me. I listened, occasionally rushing away to the toilet.

"My husband will be an engineer one day, Veronica and Nina will also study; I don't want them to be bad women, on the streets, like others. Without doubt there is no work for girls here except bad work, and many have to do it, but I don't want this to happen to my daughters."

27

One afternoon she appeared with a paraffin can and said to the children: "Come, wash your hair."

"Wash with paraffin?" said I, "why?"

"Because of the lice," she explained. "Veronica has lice in her hair."

I went to the mirror to peer at my hair. Were there any lice?

Afterwards she wrapped hot towels around our heads, then we sat down and played Russian Bank, and drank hot cocoa made with condensed milk, waiting for the smell to go away.

Helena liked to talk to me. "Veronica is my tragic child, but she demands so much. She always wants things, she is always looking at herself. Without doubt she is beautiful, but she looks at herself too much, and it is Nina that I like better, but I don't show it. Nina will study, I am not sure about Veronica. Veronica thinks that she is superior to Nina, and that is bad, they are both my children. I love them both."

The examination was a restful, easy thing. Because of my diarrhoea, when I arrived at Gordon Hall I looked for the toilet immediately and found it, a clean delightful place, at least six seats, all flush, the paper soft, like silk. It was nearly a pleasure to have diarrhoea with this paper, which did not make one sore, like the newspaper at home.

At my desk, the foolscap on which we wrote was glossy under one's wrist. The silence, the bent heads, the gong, the black gowns of the examiners, reassuring.

Outside in the corridors after each session girls used to clutch and ooh at each other, "Tell me, what was the answer to question four? I put three and three-quarters, but Jenny says it is ten." I would never discuss the questions, it brought on diarrhoea.

After the first week, I went to see Elder Brother at his boarding-house, the Pension Apelt.

"What a disgrace, what a disgrace, your being there with these people. And your English is quite terrible. You must come to school here in Tientsin, I'll write to your parents" – he never said "my parents" – about this. It's a disgrace to let an intelligent girl like you get into such a state."

Elder Brother was hurt that Mama had not asked his advice as to where I should stay. He took me to Kiessling's, and for the first time I entered, abashed, tremulous, the marvellous pastry shop, sat in the tea room and ate hot apple dumplings. After that, my stomach was worse than ever, although the dumplings had been delicious. Elder Brother said it could not be the dumplings, Kiessling's was under German supervision, everything was good and fresh there.

Elder Brother took me for a long walk, in the cold, beyond the great iron bridge across the river. We walked for miles, and luckily I had taken some of the good, fine toilet paper from Gordon Hall with me. At night we walked again in the Japanese Concession; there was a great store with a tower strung with electric lights, the Japanese Emporium. Nowhere in Peking was there such a grand multi-storeyed affair, containing so many goods.

"If you come here in the summer," said Elder Brother, "there is a roof garden, with an orchestra and dancing, and ice-cream."

Elder Brother admired the Japanese; he thought they had learnt much from the Germans. Returning to his room that night, he showed me photographs; one of himself, in navy shorts, with a white shirt, standing by some barbed-wire barricade, with his arms folded, a police baton hanging at his belt. He had enlisted in the Tientsin Volunteer Corps to keep law and order, helping the British police to push out the refugees who tried to come into the foreign concessions. There were also photos of British troops patrolling, and French troops; Elder Brother had photographs of them driving people away, hitting them with their rifle butts. And I did not like this, but Elder Brother chuckled, "You've got to teach them their place." He had entirely forgotten that once, a few years back, he had so much wanted to be Chinese.

In the spring of 1929 Mama thought that Elder Brother was right, perhaps my English would improve more quickly in Tientsin, and Elder Brother, in a burst of generosity, wrote that I could stay with him. He would pay half the money for my pension; I would sleep in a small storeroom, off his room, in the boarding-house. The food was good, I would be happy in Tientsin.

This resolve was further strengthened by the fact that I had done well in my examination. The Mother Superior at the Peking convent was a little angry; I had done so well, and now I was leaving, going to the rival convent, in Tientsin.

"You are taking our best student, Madame Chou, I hope you do not regret it."

At first, all went well. I attended the convent in Tientsin. But I could not get used to the method of teaching, the textbooks, the prefect system on an English school model, sports twice a week. In Peking no one bothered with sports, I did what I pleased with my spare time, which meant long walks, time to read, time to dig for archaeological finds, time to construct a telephone out of two cocoa tins ... Here there was no time for anything. And suddenly everyone in the class was to be enrolled in the Girl Guides. That was impossible, Mama would not pay for a Girl Guide uniform neither would Elder Brother. And I did not see any point in being a Girl Guide.

The German pension where Elder Brother stayed was run by Mrs. Apelt, whose husband was dying of kala-azar acquired in Manchuria. Mrs. Apelt, short, fat, sharp-nosed, sat at the head of a long table, her boarders on both sides, except for an English lady with blue-white hair who dressed for dinner and regally walked in after everyone else was seated, bowing gracefully to right and left. The English lady had her own table, where she tinkled a small silver bell so that the Number One Boy would come running, white gown beating his shins, with dishes for her. At another small table was an old man, a professor, who never spoke to anyone, and who the English lady once told me was a dirty old man. "Don't let him touch you, dear."

Elder Brother had a fine central room on the first floor, the best room in the house, with a balcony.

Herr Apelt, the dying man, lived in a large room downstairs, with velvet drapes half across the windows and muslin curtains too, so that the trees outside just managed to show a leafy branch when one sat with him. Inside the room it was always enclosed, dark, smelling of cough drops. The sick man had much blond hair upon his head, and a very big stomach. Elder Brother spoke to him in German. Three weeks after my arrival he died, though from the way he spoke, full of energy, each word heavy like a wooden beam thrown down, one would never have thought he would die so quickly. Frau Apelt wore a black veil behind which she sobbed at the funeral. But the pension went on, the food was the same, and after a while she again sat at the head of the table.

Elder Brother had changed, oh changed so much. He had given up the idea of being Chinese; he now reviled and hated the Chinese and said many things against them. How stupid they were, how cowardly, how ignoble, how lazy. "In the mass they are incapable of order, organization. Here and there a few bright ones, but so lamentably few. Never will they amount to anything. The only way for China is for someone, Japan or preferably Germany, to *drill* them." In the spring he lay upon the carpet of the room, clad only in his underwear, proud of his looks, and talked. "You are not Chinese either, you will not go down into this vulgar, trite mass . . . look at them, all flocking about, cackling like fools and understanding nothing. During the troubles I saw some executions. They catch them by the dozen and take them out to kill them. But even those who are going to die laugh, laugh, the idiots . . ."

At what exact point it all suddenly became unbearable, I do not quite know.

We had been going for long walks, for he had not given up that habit. We walked the countryside round Tientsin. We walked the salt flats outside the city, and I would always remember that ghost-white afternoon. We stood on the bridge over the river, and: "There, that's a floating corpse," said Elder Brother. I looked, and there it was with a round black hole in its cheek, probably a rat had eaten into it.

The big famine that had started in the north the year before, 1928, was going on and on, and millions were dying of hunger. Ten million, said the newspapers. They were being picked up by the hundred in the outlying suburbs of the cities. Of course there were corpses in the river.

Returning in the afternoon, Elder Brother turned upon a rickshaw man parked on the street corner. For no reason he started beating him with the stick he now always carried with him, kicking him in the legs as high as his own legs would go, trying to break the shafts of his rickshaw with his boots, and the rickshaw man, helpless, grappling with him, shouting insults: "F — your sister, f — your sister," looking at me over my brother's shoulder with gleaming eyes and livid face as if I had incited the assault. I would remember his heaving chest, damp, thin, the ribs, the ribs, the eyes and the words, and my brother finally breaking one of the shafts.

It was a terrible tantrum which I threw, a few days later, in the street. I don't know why. My brother started dragging me by the hand, I screamed and screamed, and could not stop. He shut me up in my little room. I sobbed and screamed and wrote a letter to my parents, and my mother came to Tientsin to fetch me back. She took me away, making me pack my suitcase. I remember my brother sitting in his chair, staring at the trees outside the balcony of which he was so proud (best room in the pension),

31

refusing to look at me, refusing to look at her. Now I know that through me he had tried to alleviate his loneliness, which no amount of German pension food and efficiency, of Japanese light effects, no amount of enlisiting in the Volunteer Corps and kicking the Chinese, could really alleviate; for he belonged nowhere, whatever he tried to do, whether he loved or hated, whether he did one thing or nothing, always, always, he was an outcast, always there would be this great black hole in him, and he was a young man, only twenty-one, all alone, and there was no one to care.

My father was a typical non-hero, whose inner life was ignored, whose outer aspect did not arouse controversy. Wit was his, a humour of speech which kept his chosen friends delighted, and a concealed erudition, a seeking spirit, a love of flowers, a texture of fineness enclosed, a lack of worthlessness. He was not a fighter, as his daughter had to become, although it took her a long time to know what to fight for. His whole life could be embodied in his favourite quotation: "The tree would like to be quiet, but the wind is restless."

In any situation where he could have come forward, made a grand gesture, he did not do so. The best friend of his youth had chosen Revolution; and died for it.* My father did not. The Empire crumbled, he read the books of the New Learning, and the New Learning found him adaptable. The Revolution came, and he served on the railways, uncomplaining, faithful, unglamorously painstaking.

If love can be measured by vulnerability, my father was vulnerable to my mother, his wife, except in one thing: the railway. And as she destroyed us, her children, so my father's railway destroyed her. Father worked on the railways all his life, dragging mother with him, on the iron road. He never spared himself, he did not spare her. It was on the railway that six of his eight children were born. It was on the iron road that four of them died.

And because of the iron road, Mother was in China from 1913 to 1948, she did not once return to Belgium in those thirty-five years, although every six months she threatened to go, and a deal of packing was done, only to be unpacked again. Somehow or other Father always contrived to hold her back.

Father only came into his own as an innovator in 1949, in yet another Revolution. It was only then, for all his dimness of out-

* See *The Crippled Tree*.

line, his mildness, the uncomplaining disregard for his life in the diminution that attends the noiseless who have no self-pity, that he suddenly became a hero. A hero of laborious days, of un-shining minute routines, of steadfastness throughout the years, a patriot. A hero in abnegation, in devotion and loyalty to a country redeemed at last, one whose usefulness, neglected in the past, was at last appreciated and rewarded.

If Father now rests upon the Hill of Eight Values in Peking, in the company of great men, many more heroic than he, it is because of what he did after 1949, when he really came into his own. Three rows away from Father lies Agnes Smedley, a great and noble American woman; two rows below him a young revolutionary, executed by Chiang Kaishek. A bourgeois, not a Communist, a technician, not a politician, a Chinese to the end, loyal to his country, who in the process lost his son, his wife, and two of his daughters, my father lies there because, when the time came, he rose from his sick bed, and did what he could.

For in 1949 nearly everything in China had stopped working after so many years of war; railways at a standstill, mines gutted, equipment unusable. Father was called upon to help, and he did. He began to reorganize the Tatung mines, which were destroyed. There he worked for a year, indefatigable, tireless, as he had never worked before, even in his youth. And thus became a Labour Hero, without even thinking about it. And then I knew that I was right to love him.

Perhaps because I was a girl, a female, my father did abandon me to my mother. He did not fight her to put me in Chinese school, or perhaps he felt that a convent school was the best since I was only a girl. He abandoned me to my destiny as a female, which he thought of as marriage, and this was the great wrong that he did to us, his daughters. It took me twenty years to redeem a wasted childhood. I´clung to him, loving him. He brushed me off, because my mother always came first with him. Always.

It was in the year 1929 I lost him as a presence potent to cleave to, as a yearning to love. The last sight of him, as a person not a stranger, was the night of my wine-making incident.

My father had planted a foot of vine in our first house in Peking, the house which I loved so much, in the Manchu quarter. He transplanted the vine to our second, then to our last house. Having read about wine-making in a picture book I decided, in the autumn of 1929, to make wine with grapes from our vine.

Every evening returning from his office, Father walked to the vine, and stood gazing at the hard, shotty green grapes; later they swelled and softened, but lucent plumpness was not theirs. What better suprise than to present Father with a bottle of wine? Borrowing from the cook the wooden bucket in which the live chickens bought at the market were killed and plucked, I placed the unripe grapes in it. Taking off socks and shoes, my sister Tiza and I trampled upon the grapes in the fashion of the picture book. We poured the liquid into a bottle, and since there was remarkably little of a brownish fluid, added water.

Papa, the mild, silent one, whom Mama, always splendid at nicknames, called The Dumb One, for once stormed, became enraged, shouted, broke a plate. Mama defended her children. Not Tiza, this time, who wept easily, but I, retired to the bedroom to weep out my heart, to hear the bottle of wine flung to splinter against the garden wall . . .

That night there was an electric blackout. Blackouts were numerous, the small electric power plant serving Peking in bad repair. Papa went to bed, holding a lit candle. I watched him, staring with the eye of love for the last time, already turning, closing upon the vision to become meaningless snapshot. The departing candle speared with hollow flame quavered on its way to the other bedroom, where Mama was. Papa ceased that night to be a need for me, though for some years we continued to live in the same house. He no longer had the power to make me happy or sorrowful. Only in 1956, in the New Order, did I find him again, and knew my loving him was right, and knew my love restored.

Father had refused to be converted to the Catholic religion when he married my mother in Belgium in 1908, and yet in the winter of 1929 he was converted. That year the railways were again overrun by warring armies, for the peace and unity heralded in 1928 had quickly decayed into more power brawls, and Chiang Kaishek and his Nanking government were no more effective than any previous warlord reign had been. My father went up the railway line to inspect the damage, to rescue part of the rolling stock from some local commander. He returned in a flurry of icy weather, the wind like a razor slashing at cheeks and tearing at lungs. He brought back a small dry cough which turned to broncho-pneumonia. He lay in the large iron bed, under my mother's crucifix, tended by my mother and our Greek

34

doctor. Mother was directed to apply hot compresses to his chest. She tore soft large handkerchiefs, dipped them in boiling mustard and water, laid them on him. They scalded him deeply, the wounds became infected, suppurated. His temperature rose to 105°, and one day he was removed, delirious and near death, to the French hospital. Mother wept, offered God her own life in exchange for his.

Daily we children went to the hospital, prayed in its chapel for our father. I knelt there, but no feeling inhabited me, except a strong desire to laugh. I constantly remembered a friend of mine, Ina Jones, whose father had died. I saw myself in her black dress and black stockings, telling with icy calm of my father's decease. The idea of father dying evoked only an astonished amusement. My knees ached and I wondered how long before I could give up pretending I was praying and go back to skating. There was thick ice on the Peihai lake and I was learning to skate.

In came a nursing Sister of Charity to light more candles. I looked at the candles wavering, choked on a laugh, managed to turn it into the sound of a sob. The blue serge robe rustled, a gentle hand, a breath were upon my bowed head, a white starched bird's wing, the sister's coif, hovered within the horizon of my left eye.

"Hush, my child, do not weep. Pray to God."

"But my father is going to die."

"Pray to the Holy Virgin, who can perform any miracle."

She thrust a picture into my hand, the Virgin of the Compassionate Heart. I went home and with a pin transformed the heart into a small sieve.

The next morning Mama, distraught with grief, told us that my father was going to be baptized. "He is dying." At eleven in the morning the priest, in a white cassock, with a Chinese choir boy holding the implements of Extreme Unction, my mother, the Greek doctor, myself and my sisters, assembled in Father's hospital room, to witness the first and the last sacraments of the Church. The Superior in charge of the hospital and two nuns knelt on the linoleum floor.

Thus was Father made a Catholic, and given the name of Dionysius.

Then he became better. Everyone said it was a miracle, except the Greek doctor, who thought it was his skill.

When Father recovered, I tried to speak to him about his conversion. Marianne was being prepared for Holy Communion. I was told to make her recite her catechism. By asking questions loudly, making her say the answers loudly, I tried to catch Father's attention. I wanted him to be interested. Perhaps then we might argue, together study the unanswered illogicalities of the catechism which had begun to worry me. But Father kept silent. He attended church, even made his Easter Communion, and one day at lunch said matter-of-factly, "It is all supersitition. We don't really know that it happened." "What," said Mama, "you don't believe there is a hell for sinners?" "No," said Father. After six months he dropped all pretence of belief. And though to please my Mother, from time to time, he still went to church, it was with such a distant air, so obviously thinking of something else (probably the railway), that he still managed to be absent even when corporally in our pew.

And I, in my first tooth-and-nail-sharpening assay, tried the unanswered on Father O'Connor, the Irish priest whose Chinese sermons were unintelligible. Hell, limbo, animal souls, unbaptized babies . . . not to speak of the Ascension, the Conception, the Assumption, what an array of things to believe! But what was belief?

"Father O'Connor, about the Host . . . How ever do we *know* that it is the Body of Christ?"

"Why is it that babies who are not baptized and who die can't go to Heaven? It is very unfair. After all, no priest is around to baptize them."

Father O'Connor started to explain. I did not really listen, I let him talk. My mind was on the quaver of the candles, they moved like shy music. "And Limbo is most unfair. These babies should not be born, or else God should arrange for a priest to be near them when they die . . . And why should animals not go to heaven, why shouldn't they have souls? I think God is very unfair; animals suffer so much, is it not wicked to make animals suffer?"

Father O'Connor became upset. "My child, you must not say God is unfair. This is blasphemy against the goodness of God. God may hear you and punish you."

"Anyway, I don't think it's fair." Off at a tangent. "I don't think going to church makes anybody a good person. If God is everywhere, one may as well pray at home. And why is it a mortal sin to eat meat on Fridays and not fish? Fish live just as much as chickens do . . ."

Coming home from school, passing by the church, one Friday in Lent, I saw again the blind children, standing, sitting, round the church gates. I discerned their rags tied with string. It was afternoon, not the time for Mass, but the blind were there, because of the Way of the Cross, because there was a patch of sun near the gates to warm them, a stone ledge to sit on. The time had come to announce my decision at home. "Mama, I am going to be a doctor."

"Wash your face, you have dust all over you." The big dust winds of March were blowing, engulfing the city in sand.

"I am going to be a doctor, Mama."

Mama counted the stitches in her knitting.

Papa returned from his office, the soup was placed on the table. "Papa, I am going to be a doctor."

"A doctor? It's very difficult to be a doctor if you are a woman."

"She is making up stories as usual," said Mama.

"I am not dreaming," replied Rosalie-me. "I am going to be a doctor. I don't want to go to church, I don't believe there are miracles, not with all those blind waiting, waiting, and they can never see. I am going to be a doctor and I will do something, so they won't be blind, they will see." Then Rosalie-me burst into tears, and Papa sighed irritably:

"One moment laughter, the next moment tears, there is no peace in this house."

And Mama: "It's the growth, she is nearly twelve." She said this because Tiza, though younger than I, was already grown into her periods, painlessly. Month after month I expected something, but it never happened. Mama had bought a nerve tonic because I was so nervous. Everyone said I was a jumping jack, a bundle of nerves. It was very hard on Tiza, on Marianne.

"They do not believe me, they do not believe me. One day they will have to believe me."

I looked at them, my parents, each other's hostages, now both my enemies. I understood Elder Brother, his resentment, his attachment, his pitiful efforts to retain his parents, even at arm's length, and his efforts to tear them out of him . . . And now love's rope was worn out at last and I gave up. I clamped down on the surprised absence of any feeling. Father had died, candle in hand, on wine-making night. Mother the day I was born. And now "my parents", the couple in whose house I lived, went to their burial

37

in my mind. I was twelve years old. I was going to be a doctor, and cure the blind . . .

> My First Daughter is shallow and easily temperamental, always changing her mind . . . my Second Daughter is much like a Chinese woman, quiet and subdued, affectionate and devoted . . .

Father wrote thus of me and of Tiza to my Third Uncle, and Third Uncle gave me this letter along with all my father's letters of that period, when I returned to Szechuan in 1939. I keep it, it does not hurt. Not now, after the Last Judgment of the Revolution, which changed so many, and also changed us, my father, myself.

It was not until after 1949, after the Revolution had transformed the whole background of our lives, and forced us to a new understanding of our passions and torments, that we rediscovered each other. Of all his children, I was the only one to return to him. He died happy because of that. And I, knowing he died happy, am well content. In the end, Life had not cheated him. And in this thing at least, Life has not cheated me.

Go through twilight, shadow between the sun and self; go between the star load of a thousand eyes.

She, Rosalie, is I, Rosalie-no-longer. I am twelve years old, and I have changed my name. I have changed Rosalie.

It is a new name, superseding Rosalie; I want to be another, not hamstrung Rosalie. It is the beginning of being a doctor, changing one's name.

I announce it casually, as casually receive my defeat. "I want to be called Josephine from now on. I don't want to be called Rosalie." This, in the morning, courage to the fore like a mast, mouthful of eggs with buttered toast in a thick paste swung from cheek to check, self ambushed behind the words and the mouth full of food and the sticking up daringness of heart beating in the middle of my stomach.

And it all slithers away with one remark from my mother, who never sits down to breakfast. For she is the worker, slave of her family, up the earliest, getting us up; dressed and ready for the brawl of words, her day.

O brawl of words how I know you, dread you, urge you on, wait for you and miss you, in the agony of finding always another

38

yet no one there, perpetual hunt for what is me, what do I want? A mask, a wall, this side of to become.

"I don't want to be called Rosalie any more. From today I am Josephine."

Mama seizes the blessed events, the disaster-making phrase upon which to hang her day of episodes. A burst of great laughter gusts the breakfast table, the hahaha laughter which listens to itself.

"Josephine, Josephine! Why that was the name of my servant, my maid, Josephine."

Then I remember those evening-round-the-lamp tales that stick, clammily, to the memory of me-before-twelve. I see Josephine, the maid of my mother's youth. Rather I see her varicose veins, great lucent grapes, juicy grapes of the vine of her dolorous days, pulsating blueworm coiled bags of standing hours and climbing from sub-basement to attics in the narrow dark house with its window-peeping mirrors, in Belgium, in my mother's happy childhood house. I have started my day casting a pebble, and it is the wrong one, but I must go on to the end of the day.

"I *like* the name Josephine."

Tiza and Marianne now sing it, rubbing their buttocks on the chairs that creak.

"Josephine, Josephine the servant, your name is Josephine the servant."

Chew, chew Josephine-Rosalie, as you chew bread, chew this away. Jolt the word as you wish, you cannot clutch it back from the listening morning.

CHAPTER TWO

Yesterday, but a grief ago, I was thus bereft of love, to be enlarged into a world of living. Stronger than consciousness or intelligence, deprivation is gain; the urge to change a name a symptom of this striving to mutate, chrysalid seeking urgent maturity in a beckoning dimension – and the dimension was the world of China.

The world of China – and China then but a world of beggars, moribund continent, carrion land; yet the cadaver refused to perish. So often I heard China's doom pronounced: "China is finished." "This is the end." "There is no hope for China." And yet its anticipated death throes became the quaking of new life; the unburied dead hosted the new-born; and we, the semi-blind who sought the light, long deluded by false promises and lying prophets, have lived to see the transformation which in turn transformed us.

Today the look backward is not a look of regret but a measure of the distance achieved, the distance still to go for millions of others in the Universe of Mankind. The reckoning past distils order from the inchoate, sifts the misleading moralities which swaddled monstrous crimes; and we who ought to have known remain aghast at our own ignorance. Thus my class, the possessors, abdicated the right to lead; we were not only overthrown, we also overthrew ourselves; today I discover a similar process repeating itself, on a much larger scale than in yesterday's China. History, the winnowing wind, never halts. We see the chaff rise, forget the waiting grain, seed of the future, fallen to the threshing floor. We never learn, but live on, silt-narrow as if our living were a pencil line traced upon paper, behaving as trapped denizens of a flat world hemmed in by the bigoted horizon of our own making. Yet the meaning of living is a pushing back, a pulling down of the great walls and domes of fear and ignorance, is relinquishing the nest for the sky, ignorance for understanding. The look back is also a look forward.

I look back to that time in 1928, when my Uncle Liu the Lolo, his great laughter shaking the windows, shouted: "Only a handful of bandits in the wildest mountains of Kiangsi . . . their names are Chu Teh and Mao Tsetung." I hear, as if it was but yesterday, his voice stunning the windowpanes.

Chu Teh, Mao Tsetung: names that have changed a world of beggars into a world of men.

When my Uncle Liu spoke of them, these names were laughing puns; only the name of The Leader, The President, the Generalissimo Chiang Kaishek, on all lips, revered, hailed as China's salvation, anchor securing our ship of hope. Though neither Uncle Liu nor my father liked Chiang Kaishek, they too believed in him; for all of us were afraid, afraid mainly of revolution, which meant our peasants rising and taking the land for themselves. All of us said we wanted orderly progress, reform, but as slowly as possible. Timorous, always ready to compromise, uncertain and turncoat, we believed Chiang would redeem the land, save our people, build the railways, and pay our salaries, and all without really changing the Old Order. Did not his portrait, with serious unsmiling face and direct look, his hands with white gloves resting upon his sword hilt, hang above our heads in all the railway offices? Did not the generals and the officials click their heels, or straighten their bodies, and observe ten seconds' reverent silence when they said : Our Leader? Since so many called him great, he must be great . . . The western newspapers lauded him; the bankers told us that our future was bright in his white-gloved hands; eminent intellectuals praised his enlightened mind; missionaries praised his Methodism . . . our lives, our properties secure in those gloves, those gloves which stick through the years. For a decade I was to have nightmares about these white gloves, for I too had to wash white gloves, keep them pristinely immaculate, while all around the country foundered in decay.

I lived under Chaing Kaishek and his government, the Kuomintang government, for many years, in contact and proximity since my husband was for a time in Chiang Kaishek's "Follow and Obey" Service, which meant that he belonged to his praetorian guard named the Blueshirts, and modelled on Hitler's S.S. During those years much happened which I could not write down, because China was at war, and the wife of a Chinese officer must be loyal to the nation and its Leader for the sake of unity in wartime. One does not denounce the head of the government in a national emergency, unless one wants to be shot as a traitor, or disappear.

Today, free from any allegiance except to truth, I can write the facts, write of Chiang Kaishek, not as an immortal, not as a Leader, but as a human being whom I neither hate nor revile. For he but did what his class, history's processes, and his own choice decreed that he would do. The instrument of forces he did not understand; the object of options, he pursued a humbug of personal grandeur, which betrayed him, as surely as so many were betrayed to die on the execution grounds every Saturday, during the years of his rule.

Chiang Kaishek was born in 1886, the same year as my father. In his days of strength legend wound tight vagueness round the certainties of his life. Before 1928 there were well-documented stories about his connections with the secret societies of Shanghai, but later this talk disappeared, blanketed by edifying anecdotes of devotion to his mother, promises of his childhood, conversion to the Methodist faith, and his triumphal marriage into the Soong family. In this he is no different from many another public figure for whom hagiography replaces biography, and authenticated events are removed from the files of history.

The son of a landowner of Fenghua county in Chekiang province, some claim he was adopted. This is not derogatory in China, where adoption is common. Those who say so add that his name was Tseng, his father and mother were peasants from Honan province, parted during a famine. His father died, his mother remarried, which, if true, shows that she had great spirit, for it was extremely ill thought of for a widow to marry again. However, Chiang Kaishek when he came to power and began to resurrect a gallery of old feudal virtues, extolled women's chastity so that a widow's remarriage remained almost a crime, and I remember this particularly because some of the wives of his junior officers were occasionally forced to starve themselves to death, or to commit suicide, as an example of the great, pure, and chaste revival of Virtue which the Leader promoted as the Way of Salvation for China.

One of my most vivid quarrels with Pao, my husband, was when he tried to make me swear I would kill myself should he die in battle. Since he was never allowed to fight the Japanese, but was kept in reserve, as were Chiang's best troops, to fight the Communists after 1945, my husband did die in battle, fighting against his own people, and I did not kill myself as a virtuous widow should.

One day in the summer of 1941 a policeman from Honan province, named Tseng, walked into Chungking, temporary capital of Free China during the Japanese war, claiming that Chiang Kaishek was his younger brother. He had come to see his "small brother" who had done so well. He was immediately lodged for some years in a sequestered place, far away in Kweichow province, and held incommunicado, his wife and children being sent for and also detained there. After Chiang left in 1949, Tseng the policeman returned to his original village in Honan, where he now lives, still claiming to be Chiang Kaishek's blood brother.

In Fenghua county, where the young Chiang Kaishek lived, he was known as a bright and attentive student. In 1905 he was sent to Japan, but could not enter any school there and soon returned to China.

In 1906, then twenty years old, he entered the military academy in Paoting, the same academy which my Third Uncle attended, approximately at the same time. This military academy was the pet project of Yuan Shihkai, at that time Commander-in-Chief under the Manchu dynasty. Yuan knew that the Manchus could not remain in power very long'; he wanted the Empire for himself, and consequently trained, at the Paoting Academy, young officers loyal to him personally, later to be his henchmen in the power scramble. In 1907 Chiang was sent to Japan on a military scholarship, one of four outstanding students personally chosen by the Commander-in-Chief, Yuan Shihkai. He stayed two years in Japan studying field artillery. My Third Uncle remembers Chiang Kaishek going to Japan, though coming from another province, Szechuan, Third Uncle did not mix with the students from Chekiang such as Chiang. "Chiang had another name at the Academy, Chinshih, he only changed to Kaishek in 1910, while he was in Japan," said Third Uncle.

Personal name-changing is frequent and common in China. We all change, or add, new personal names, at different periods of our lives. We thus have milk names, school names, official and unoffical names, courtesy names, book names, genealogical names, sickness names (to cheat the demons of disease), style names, studio names, names on taking a degree or high office or being honoured, post-humous names; poets adopt fresh names to suit their moods, or even when moving abode. Only the family name, which in China always comes first, and not last as in the West, cannot be changed.

Chiang Kaishek's change of name was not surprising. For it was probably in 1910, in Japan, that he joined the Revolutionary Party of Dr. Sun Yatsen. Hence a new determination and a new name.

In 1909 Sun Yatsen, that stout-hearted and grand-visioned Chinese revolutionary, with a good deal of money collected from the overseas Chinese in America, arrived in Tokyo. There a man named Chen Tsimei, who was his supporter, introduced Chiang Kaishek to him. Chen Tsimei was actually a very important secret society man, and secret societies, like the freemasonries of Europe, were deeply concerned in political manœuvres of all kinds.* Chiang, through Chen Tsimei, also became a member of the secret society with headquarters in Shanghai.

In 1911, Chiang returned to China and went to Shanghai. He

* See *The Crippled Tree*.

did not take part in the Wuhan uprising of October 10th, 1911, which led to the Revolution of 1911 and to the overthrow of the Manchu dynasty; but under Chen Tsimei took part in some local fighting and disarmed the Manchu troops of the local garrison in Hangchow.

Chen Tsimei soon died, and Chiang, through his secret society connections, entered the business world of Shanghai in the capacity of a broker, or middleman, the term connoting not only brokerage in the accepted sense, but an intermediary in all kinds of transactions. It was 1913, the Revolution of 1911 had failed, Sun Yatsen had fled, many revolutionaries were being killed by Yuan Shihkai, the ex-Commander-in-Chief of the Manchu armies, who now established a military dictatorship, tried to become Emperor, and died in 1916.

Shanghai in those years was a fabulous gangster city; the biggest and wildest free-for-all, unparalleled by any other metropolis. Beside it the Chicago of Al Capone was a staid, almost pious, provincial town. The festering, restless, brutal and relentless conglomeration of sickening misery and dizzy wealth was actually run, by arrangement, between the police of the foreign settlements and the Chinese secret society gangs, and this ensured protection for the wealthy and utter debasement for the poor. Chiang became acquainted at that time with a man named Huang Chingyung, the head of the French Concession C.I.D., who was also the head gangster and secret society member with this area under his double jurisdiction, legal and illegal, an unsurprising symbiosis. The perpetration, then the detection of crime, the capture and quiet liquidation of "political undesirables," were Huang Chingyung's outstanding specialities. One applied to him, the specialist, for such jobs as the removal of some too noisy Chinese journalist, or the recruiting of a batch of young fresh virgins from the countryside for a party, or the breaking of a strike with no count of bodies to be buried or dumped in alleyways. The police looked the other way. Chiang Kaishek became an adopted "grandson" of Huang Chingyung, in the secret society hierarchy. He thus enjoyed a semi-filial relationship which had many advantages in the business world of the Gangster City, Shanghai.

It was during the decade 1913 to 1922 that Chiang established his lifelong friendships and loyalties. Most of his colleagues also belonged to the secret societies, and continue in this relationship to him until today. It was then that he became intimate with

44

Chen Kuofu and Chen Lifu, the nephews of his late patron Chen Tsimei. The CC brothers, as they were to be called later, were to become important members of the Nanking government.

Another friendship, with a man named Tai Chitao, dates back to their years in Japan together. It is averred by some that Chiang Kaishek's second son, Chiang Weikuo, is actually Tai Chitao's son, given for adoption and in token of friendship to Chiang. Tai had all the talents of a king-maker, exerted much influence on Chiang Kaishek's thinking, and always showed great devotion to his advancement. Tai was known as an extreme leftist in 1918; so radical were his emotions that he then called himself "Authority's Foe," and swore to kill every foreigner he met. When he began the usual slide from Left to Right, he changed his name from "Authority's Foe" to "Traditional Wisdom", and ended up in Formosa, where he died recently.

The friends that Chiang made, either in Japan or Shanghai, became prominent or influential members of Chiang's government in Nanking when he rose to power, thus fulfilling the oath of brotherhood of the secret societies: "When there is good fortune share it as between brothers."

From 1913 to 1921, Chiang prospered in Shanghai and was reputed a financial success as a broker. However, in 1921, a crash on the Shanghai money market occurred; Chiang became impecunious. It was then that, urged by Tai Chitao, Chiang Kaishek decided to reattach himself to the Revolutionary Party, and to try his fortunes once again with the star, now recrudescent, of Sun Yatsen.

The stir of history is never done. For China the watershed between Yesterday and Today began on May 4th, 1919. All my generation date ourselves from that year and day, which means nothing to the Western world, but means everything to a quarter of the world's humanity. For it was the day on which China's intellectuals turned away from the West, because the Western democracies killed democracy that year and thus condemned themselves and their own system to the decline and fall in Asia we see enacted as we breathe.

The First World War had ended on November 11th, 1918. What was so obnoxious about the end of that war, and the peace treaty of Versailles of 1919 which followed it, that it precipitated a crisis in China?

Writers of that period, such as Maynard Keynes, E. J. Dillon and others have described the atmosphere of the Peace Conference. "From the rank soil of secrecy, repression, and unveracity sprang noxious weeds . . . no such bitter draught of disappointment was swallowed by the nations since the world first had political history." And thus, lamentably, history unfolds its monstrous paradox.

For China, the story began a little earlier, in 1915, when, profiting from the inter-European massacre, Japan presented Yuan Shihkai, then in power, with an ultimatum called the Twenty-One Demands, which gave Japan Shantung province (previously Germany's sphere of influence), sole rights in Manchuria, and concessions which represented a virtual hand-over of Chinese sovereignty to Japan. To frighten the pusillanimous Chinese of 1915, these demands were drawn on paper watermarked with dreadnoughts and machine-guns.

But all did not work as smoothly as expected. Chinese protest was so vehement that it subdued somewhat the Japanese. In 1917, then, Japan made a secret agreement with America, in which she obtained "special consideration" for her rights in China, because America at the time wanted Japan's navy as a buffer to the German U-boats in the Pacific. Secret treaties with Great Britain, France, and Italy quickly followed, all at China's expense. By 1919, when the Versailles Peace Conference started, everything had already been arranged, in secret; and thus the League of Nations was doomed from birth.

China was an ally, having entered the war in 1917 on the side of England and France, on the understanding that the unequal treaties of the nineteenth century would be revised, Shantung province returned to her, and that she would regain tariff autonomy and other rights of a sovereign independent country. When war ended on November 11th, 1918, the jubilant Chinese declared a three-day holiday, sixty thousand parading in joy through the streets of Peking. The League of Nations, with its solemn and piously moral announcements, seemed to augur a new era of international relations, based on justice, respect for the rights of nations, and an end to exploitation . . . How disillusioned the Chinese were to become!

China in 1919 was a semi-colony, everyone's prey, no one's responsibility. In India, the British at least *had* to keep things running; but in China no such duty existed, and all who could swooped upon her, to grow fat and wealthy upon her carrion misery. There were all kinds of extraterritorial rights and privi-

46

leges for foreigners; within her territory spheres of influence, spheres of special interest, war zones, leased territories, treaty ports, concessions, settlements, quartered her independence and despoiled her of authority. The foreigners maintained their own law courts and post offices. Even the Chinese who had lawsuits with foreign residents were subject to foreign courts; there were any number of special privileges granted to the Great Powers in respect of commercial and industrial rights, railways and mines, loans, and currency. Two of China's chief revenue sources, the maritime customs and the salt tax, and their administration, were completely under the control of Western diplomats posted to China. Their proceeds, as well as other revenues, were pledged to meet fixed charges on foreign loans – loans in most cases concluded by warlords for the financing of personal struggles for power. And worst, perhaps, in the financial stranglehold upon China was the fact that she had no way of fixing her own tariff rates. These had been fixed by the Great Powers and made it impossible for China to compete against foreign imports. Firearms and narcotics were smuggled in and dumped on the Chinese market at will. In many strategic places within China, considerable bodies of foreign troops and warships under foreign command were stationed. "China was a geographic term instead of a foreign state, a market instead of a nation . . ."

The Grand Illusion nourished by millions in China, who believed ardently in President Wilson's fourteen points and the war aims so nobly declared, was dispelled as soon as the Peace Conference opened on January 18th, 1919. Soon it was known that Japan would be taking over the German territory of Shantung province in China. China's chief delegate Dr. Lu Chenghsiang, a Belgian-educated diplomat (later to become a Benedictine monk), was frightened out of his wits; another delegate was at that time engaged to the daughter of a pro-Japanese militarist and inhibited from displeasing his prospective father-in-law. Other members of the delegation were openly in the pay of Japan. In full session at Versailles, the Japanese delegate bluntly revealed that five of the assembled Great Powers, America leading, had signed secret treaties with Japan, and thus revealed the League of Nations' declarations as so much bunk.

It was on the United States that China had counted most; on President Wilson, the man of peace, on his fourteen points. America was the emergent power, unshattered by war, the wealth of the world in her grasp. All over China the intellectuals asked:

"What is Wilson doing?" The answer: nothing. For President Wilson, alas, was as muddle-headed and lacking in purpose as any Chinese delegate. To Maynard Keynes we are indebted for a portrait of the American President and his peculiar lack of lucidity: "His thought and his temperament were essentially theological not intellectual"; he could, while doing the utmost violence to tenets of international morality, utter pronunciamentos of astounding self-righteousness. "The President had thought out nothing . . . his ideas were nebulous and incomplete . . . he was . . . ill-informed . . ." Computers notwithstanding, history seems to repeat itself today.

Conceit was also a component of the American master-mind. The President could never appear to have made a mistake; the United States and its President *must* appear omniscient, omnipowerful, never lose, never withdraw. Yet the Fourteen Points announced with so much fanfare were not even discussed at Versailles. The seeds of World War II were planted even before World War I was terminated.

When the intellectuals of China understood what was happening at Versailles, they became very agitated. All over China discussion groups formed, thousands of telegrams were sent, not only by students and professors, but also by merchants, shopkeepers, businessmen, associations and guilds, and overseas Chinese communities. Some of the poorer students at Peking University saved on food to pay for their share of the telegrams sent; so urgently, so seriously, did the Chinese people consider that Versailles was the testing point, the watershed; that it was democracy on trial. Were the Great Powers really going to behave as they said they would, or let China down? This was the crisis, the point of no return.

Then came the terrible news. All demands by China for readjustment of the unequal treaties and for tariff autonomy had been brusquely rejected. Shantung province was allocated to Japan as her "sphere of influence". In short, China, an ally, was treated as an enemy. The news leaked out on May 1st, 1919, in the Peking newspaper *China Press*. In spite of the censorship it was in all other newspapers by May 3rd.

"China, who had looked for the dawn of a new era, saw that no sun would rise for her in the *west*; we realized that the western democracies were great liars; then we knew that another world war would come, and *that a great war would be fought in the east* . . ."

American observers in China were discountenanced. Paul Reinsch, American minister to China, wrote: "Nowhere else in the world had expectations of America's leadership been raised so high . . . The Chinese trusted America."

On May 4th, 1919, in one stupendous tidal bore, one hundred thousand of China's students and intellectuals rose in a gigantic demonstration in Peking. Immediately following this, in two hundred and twenty cities of China, demonstrations surged, in which twenty million people participated. The May 4th movement affected not only intellectuals and students, but merchants, shopkeepers, and even the peasants of far-off Szechuan, who knew nothing about the First World War, but knew that "wrong has again been done to our country by the foreigners".

Of course there were arrests and shootings; but things were not the same. Though on the surface everything went on as before, already the future was groined in the present, changing it even as it was being lived.

From that day in May 1919, for many Chinese intellectuals disillusion with the West was complete.

A Federation of Students' Unions was formed on May 6th, to become one of the most powerful organs of revolutionary ferment and patriotism in China. In every university and middle school, the students' unions organized a militant vanguard to fight against imperialism; thirty years later, these were to find their culmination in another revoltuion.

Societies for the study of Marxism now sprang up everywhere; in this atmosphere many of today's leaders, including Mao Tsetung, received their shaping.

From that year all classical writing withered, a cultural revolution occurred, which led to a new, colloquial writing style, and the extension of literacy to all now became possible in fact as well as in theory.

From that May, co-education became the rule rather than the exception in China's universities. Until then only one small Christian college in Canton was co-educational. After that May, representatives from the girls' schools sat in all the students' unions; the first admissions of nine women to Peking University were announced. The movement for the emancipation of woman had truly begun.

From that day, Peking University became the centre of left intellectualism, and all China's intelligentsia were influenced by its galaxy of brilliant minds. Two years later, the Communist party

49

of China was founded in Shanghai with several of Peking's University intellectuals as its first members. Among them was also Peking University's former assistant librarian, Mao Tsetung.

From that year the Chinese learnt the principle of mass action. The success of the massive demonstrations, paralysing economic life; of the boycott of Japanese goods, which made Japan back down; of the strikes of textile workers, printers, railwaymen, civil servants, bus lines, and even the police (who refused to arrest demonstrators), were an unforgettable object lesson which influenced profoundly the strategic thinking of China's leaders. This principle of mass action has now become an essential component of the struggle for national liberation, taking place today all over the world.

May 4th, 1919, was the first purely political and patriotic demonstration in the history of China. It had no aim of material benefit; the strikers made no demand for higher wages. The significance and heroism of the workers, who demanded nothing for themselves, escaped the attention of Western reporters; but did not escape Mao Tsetung, who was to draw attention to it in his writings, later.

On the date set for the signing of the Peace Treaty, June 28th, 1919, Chinese students, workers, and overseas Chinese in Paris surrounded the headquarters of the Chinese Delegation and the residence of Dr. Lu Chenghsiang, the chief delegate. When French guns boomed, announcing to the world that the Versailles Treaty had been signed, the Chinese delegates were still immured within their quarters by a living wall of protest. China did not sign the Peace Treaty of Versailles.

On July 25th, 1919, Leo Karakhan, the Foreign Minister of the new U.S.S.R., issued in Moscow a declaration, abrogating *all secret treaties and other unequal treaties concluded by the Tsar's government with China*, and relinquishing all privileges and interests without compensation.

This cable was delayed for eight months. It reached the Peking militarist warlords in March 1920, was denounced as a forgery by the Western Powers, but was made known through the Chinese newspapers to the Chinese intellectuals. In April 1920 the Federation of Students' Unions of all Chinese universities acknowledged its existence and thanked the U.S.S.R. for this gesture. The popularity of the U.S.S.R. assumed enormous proportion. The study of Marx also boomed.

In 1922, America brusquely cancelled her 1917 secret agreement with Japan, and refused to recognize the negotiations. But it was too late.

It was probably due to this tide of revolutionary fervour, which caught even the most obstinate reactionary in its patriotic overtone, that Chiang Kaishek decided to rejoin Sun Yatsen. For Sun was back in the limelight if not in power: millions turned to him as their only hope.

Sun Yatsen, in 1921, was no longer the idealist of 1911. In 1911 his dream, the overthrow of the Manchu dynasty, had been accomplished, yet by 1913 he was fleeing from the assassins of Yuan Shihkai, the military dictator and strong man so well thought of by England and America in those not-so-far-off days. Sun Yatsen's adherents were hunted down everywhere, but managed to retain a foothold in the city of Canton, at the extreme south of China.

In 1916 Yuan died. China was split into the factions of numerous warlords, provincial and within each province, all contending for power. Three main groups emerged: the warlords of North China, those of South China and those of West China. But within these groups the change and shift of power and personalities was to continue, a bewildering kaleidoscope of intrigue and war, for the next twenty years. In the hiatus between these local conflicts Sun had already, in July 1917, emerged from exile in Japan, arriving in Canton on board a Chinese naval vessel, the admiral being his friend. The navy was progressive and anti-warlord, it would remain Sun's staunchest adherent till his death.

Sun organized a government in Canton, reserving the civil power to himself and relying on the provincial warlords for armed protection; but there is a world of difference between giving orders and being obeyed, especially when the power of the gun is not in the hands of the one giving the orders. As a civilian Sun could pronounce and revoke laws, sit in a contrived parliament, vote recalcitrant generals out of office, but actually the feudal warlords, just as today the military juntas of many states, did what they pleased because they had the guns.

Once again Sun was defeated, and the navy which had brought him, and which always kept a ship well stoked, engines purring, ready to take away the President they had brought, sailed him away in the spring of 1918.

The fury over the Versailles Treaty in 1919 brought the unsinkable, undaunted, marvellously courageous Sun sailing back to Canton in 1921, optimistic as ever. His China-wide popularity now frightened the Western diplomatic corps, which was in control of the Chinese customs and the salt tax. These main sources of China's revenue had been in the hands of foreign powers for nearly twenty years, for the servicing of previous loans and war indemnities. The Western diplomats now denied Sun *all funds from the customs duties levied at Canton, or anywhere else in China, reserving the money uniquely for the coalition of northern warlords in Peking*.

This final lesson in indignity made Sun Yatsen realize that never, never would imperialism give up its prey, that release could only be achieved through bitter fighting, inch by inch. "The vampire will not give up its bloodsucking. Economic oppression is more severe even than political oppression. Even the First World War, the holocaust and the millions of victims, has taught the whites nothing. *They cannot learn from history. Henceforth we turn our faces away from the West*."

And now Sun also saw that the instruments of foreign imperialism *inside the country* were the warlords, the militarists, all those who sold themselves to the West for money or power, and were then called "strong men".

In June 1922 Sun's life was again in danger in Canton and the faithful navy again conveyed him away. Indomitably he collected funds, and in 1923 was back in Canton, once again reorganizing his party. This time there was an important difference. In the words of Tang Leangli, the historian of the Kuomintang Party: "Sun now viewed with keen interest the experiment in Russia."

Already Lenin had begun to correspond with Sun, and had sent his secretary Maring to China. Maring wrote that "Sun is the only person in China who has principles and a programme."

Sun decided to obtain help from Russia. He also realized that what his party needed was its own army, its own guns, instead of relying on devious, corrupt and unreliable warlords. To establish his own army, he needed a military academy to train officers.

Sun therefore decided to send a young man of worth to Russia, to study what Americans would now call "his project implementation."

And now, at hand, there was Chiang Kaishek, trained in artillery in Japan, devoted, to all appearances, to Sun Yatsen's cause.

Chiang was sent to Moscow in October 1923 and returned in 1924. During his stay in Russia he had interviews with both

Stalin and Trotsky, and on his return, as pledge of his good Marxist faith, he sent his elder son, Chiang Chingkuo, to Moscow. Chiang was highly regarded by the Russians, and his speeches of the period abound in professions of enthusiasm for the Soviets; no one could fault his revolutionary zeal.

In January 1924, in Canton, Sun assembled at last the First Congress of his Party, now named the Kuomintang or Nationalist Party. This was his hour of triumph, for which he had laboured forty years. Under his directives the Congress passed three important resolutions: an entente with Russia; the admission of Communists to the Kuomintang Party; a thorough reform plan for the livelihood of workers and peasants. Implicit in these resolutions was a programme for the reunification of China. The right wing of the Kuomintang Party, though voicing no open objection, immediately became apprehensive, But Sun was too popular, no one dared to oppose him. Chiang Kaishek became the Director of the Military Academy, situated at Whangpoo, ten miles outside the city of Canton and later known as Whangpoo Military Academy. Thus, almost casually, enormous power was placed at Chiang Kaishek's disposal, the same power and of the same kind as Yuan Shihkai had wielded. Thus came into being a nucleus of young officers, bound to their military commander and leader by the ties of teacher-student loyalty, by the esprit de corps of a military clique.

Besides Chiang Kaishek as Director of the Academy, a young man back from France, where he had founded a French branch of the Chinese Communist Party, became the dean of the political department. His name was Chou Enlai. Another, a quiet, tall, soft-spoken peasant from Hunan province, named Mao Tsetung, became alternate member in charge of the propaganda department of the Kuomintang Party. Chou Enlai's friendship with Mao Tsetung dates from that time in Canton. Later Mao was to be put in charge of training peasant cadres in Canton; he never lectured or taught at the Whangpoo Military Academy; nowhere is there any record that Chiang and Mao ever actually talked to each other in those young days.

Chiang's diary makes no reference to Soviet direction in organizing the academy, though there were forty Soviet advisers besides Borodin, the Chief Adviser to Sun Yatsen; many were engaged as military instructors, including General Galen, personally selected by Chiang as Chief of Staff.

According to Kuomintang historians, Chiang early voiced his

dissatisfaction with the Soviet advisers, writing to Sun's close friend Liao Chungkai, the Minister of Finance of Sun's government, that the Kuomintang would not be able to co-operate permantly with the Chinese Communist Party members, and complaining that Sun Yatsen did not have full confidence in him. He implored Sun to trust him, to believe that his actions were not influenced by motives of "personal gain." In the midst of all the intrepid fervour and the clang of revolutionary phrases, this letter sounds our of place.

The right-wing faction of Sun's Kuomintang party, opposed to co-operation with the Communists from the very start, became restive as the months wore on. As long as Sun lived there was no open rift, but in November 1924 he departed for Peking, and never returned.

The reason for Sun's trip was the following: he had received an invitation from the militarist then in power in Peking, Marshal Feng Yuhsiang, a warlord outstanding in that lawless age for his integrity and the discipline of his soldiers. Sun eagerly responded to this invitation. His dream was reunification, and if only he and Feng Yuhsiang could agree, North and South would be united without bloodshed. But Sun Yatsen died in Peking of liver cancer in March 1925, and soon after that, in a warlord tussle, Feng Yuhsiang was defeated and withdrew from Peking.

Now the rift between Right and Left in Sun's Canton government came out in the open. Liao Chungkai, Sun's close friend, was murdered in August 1925, and this was the prelude to an assault on all left-wing members. But at first it looked as if the Left was winning, for in the conclaves of the Kuomintang Party the voting in favour of left-inspired resolutions was in majority. Ostensibly, the Right operated a strategic retreat. Our erstwhile left-winger Tai, "Authority's Foe", first tried to promote a "Body for the study of Sun Yatsen's theories." Now renamed: "Traditional Wisdom," Tai and some other right-wingers withdrew to the Western Hills in Peking, there to organize themselves, and to bide their time. Chiang Kaishek now held the balance, as arbiter between the factions, and appeared to condemn the right-wingers. Actually, as is now known, he and Tai had an entente, and Tai's withdrawal was a tactical move.

M. N. Roy, an agent of the Third Communist International sent to China by Stalin at the end of 1926, later wrote bitterly about all these manœuvres. The Chinese Communists were taken in by the ultra-radical speech-making of the petty bourgeois.

It was obvious that since 1925 Chiang and his friends had begun preparation for eventual betrayal of the Revolution. Chiang Kaishek did not try to fool the Communist party, they should have known what he was up to. But those directing communist policy failed to press for a bold approach to the social problems, on the pretext of maintaining the united anti-imperialist front. They capitulated to the Kuomintang.

Chiang, playing his arbiter role, now propelled himself to supreme power with left-wing help.

The Second Congress of the Kuomintang, in Canton in 1926, was packed with right-wingers; many masquerading as left, and others who had now returned under cover of "unity." There were T. V. Soong, and H. H. Kung, both scions of the Americanized, missionarized and Christianized Chinese middleman class, both brothers-in-law of the late Dr. Sun Yatsen; at that time T. V. Soong was only a modest erstwhile executive of the National City Bank, New York; he had many contacts, however, and these were to be very useful later to his future brother-in-law, Chiang Kaishek.

Chiang moved ambiguously, steering that tortuous, deft course to power in which he was to excel, playing off one man against another, one clique against its opposite clique. It was an art he has persevered in, and it has stood him in good stead, to maintain himself all these years in Formosa, against all American intrigues to remove him for a more compliant figurehead. In March 1926, suddenly, he attempted his first coup against the Communists, in Canton itself. Suddenly he disarmed and imprisoned junior naval officers, as well as Russian advisers, trade union leaders, and some Communists including Chou Enlai. The militia of the labour unions was dispersed, the workers' guards disarmed. The coup was enacted so swiftly that everyone was taken by surprise. This should have warned the Communists about Chiang, but the Central Committee leadership, insisting on "preserving unity at all costs," accepted a "restoration of order" by acquiescing in many restrictions upon themselves, including the permanent disarming of the workers' militia. Chou Enlai, released, went to Shanghai, where with his wife Teng Yingchao he began to organize the factory workers. After that it was obvious the Right would win.

Things were patched up. The left wing, believing it could win over the right by restraint, forbore to go too far in their programmes for workers and peasants. The peasantry were promised twenty-five per cent reduction in land rent, uniform taxation, abolition of illegal levies, no collection of rent and taxes in advance, a distribution of waste lands, and the limitation of usurers' interest rates to twenty per cent. This palliative blueprint, which would never be attempted, pleased no one. By this vacillating indecision, the left wing lost the psychological impetus of revolution, and the right wing was immensely encouraged.

The Northern Expedition, so called because it would proceed northwards from Canton to reunify all China, was launched in July 1926, with Chiang Kaishek as the Commander-in-Chief of the army. The army was officered by the first batches of cadets from Whangpoo Military Academy, some four thousand of them. No one seemed to realize that the Whangpoo young officers were already in danger of becoming the personal army staff of Chiang. In the initial cadet corps of five hundred recruited in May 1924 a man called Ho Yingchin, a student returned from Japan, a friend of Chiang's, had been enrolled; later he would be Chiang's Minister of Defence. Already the officer corps was infiltrated with Chiang's supporters, and thus the feudal pattern of personal allegiance to the Leader was being set, and national issues would take second place to personal lust for power, to be settled by force of arms.

In the six months from July to December 1926, the Kuomintang armies of the Northern Expedition swept from victory to victory. In September Wuhan, the Triple City on the Great River, where the Revolution of 1911 had begun, was captured by the Kuomintang. By accretion of warlord troops, fighting with the intensity of feather pillows and gladly surrendering on sight with their officers, the armies of the Kuomintang increased in size, but their worth succumbed. Swollen to ten times their original numbers, they were corrupted by the feudal mercenaries. And now it became painfully obvious that most of the bloodless victories had been won because the countryside had already been infiltrated by the propaganda squads of the Communists. Whole districts, both in the cities and the countryside, had risen against the warlord armies and put them to flight. Enormous demonstrations had occurred inside the Triple City, hundreds of thousands joining in them, and taking over the British Concession there. Wisely deeming it risky to maintain a small piece of land against a nation in revolt, the British, counselled by Eugene Chen, an overseas Chinese, born in Trinidad, who had joined Sun's Canton government and become Minister of Foreign Affairs, voluntarily gave up their concession in 1927. This was the second foreign enclave in China recovered by the Chinese people (the first being the Russian concessions returned in 1919); and it exalted the prestige of the Kuomintang.

Two million workers in trade unions, ten million peasants in peasant unions, had now been organized by the Communists, and they hailed the Kuomintang armies as liberators. Battles became walkovers, the people themselves doing the work of disarming and killing the officials, and all this became increasingly disturbing to the Kuomintang, and even to many leftists. Now the peasants began to organize their militias, and everywhere started to seize the land on their own and to share it. They fought the landlords and administered their own justice; this intensely frightened the young officers of the Kuomintang army, many of whom came from landlord families. Things were going too fast, they said; there was disorder, and anarchy.

The Kuomintang government now moved from Canton to Wuhan, the Triple City, in November 1926. From here the reunification could be pursued far more easily than from the southern tip of China. The Russian advisers now suggested temporary consolidation. Roy writes that Chiang Kaishek was disinclined to "take Shanghai" too soon, for he did not wish to displease the imperialist powers and forfeit the sympathy of the Shanghai bourgeoisie; he therefore established headquarters at Nanchang in Kiangsi province, and for a while nothing happened in the field. All through December 1926, January and February 1927, mysterious negotiations between Chiang's headquarters at Nanchang and certain individuals from Shanghai went on.

To take or not to take Shanghai first? Or first proceed north-wards, along the railway, to take Peking? Within the city of Shanghai itself, a Left movement was already organizing the workers. Chou Enlai and his wife Teng Yingchao had arrived in Shanghai from Canton after the coup operated by Chiang in March 1926, in which Chou Enlai had been imprisoned for a while. By February 1927, in preparation for the arrival in Shanghai of the Kuomintang armies under Chiang Kaishek, the communized trade unions had taken over sections of the Chinese part of Shanghai, and established their own municipal council.

But there was undoubted panic in the International Settlement and the French Concession, in those parts of Shanghai under Western control, where to be a Chinese was to be barred from the Park, the good hotels and restaurants, unless one was a top warlord, a top gangster or a top banker, these three professions being also interchangeable.

British, American, French and Japanese troops, forty-five thousand in all, were assembled here with gunboats patrolling. "We must preserve the Settlement at all cost." A Volunteer Corps to defend Shanghai, boned and fleshed with five thousand White Russians, drilled on the Bund. Meanwhile delicate negotiations went on, unknown to the public; the man who, at these secret talks, represented the British and American authorities in the Settlement was Yu Chiach'ing, a banker-landlord-secret society man. Later, for his services, a street in the International Settlement, the erstwhile Tibet Road, was renamed Yu Chiach'ing Street.

The record of an American, J. B. Powell,* editor of a newspaper in the International Settlement, is remarkably forthright on the events in Shanghai during that spring of 1927. They also form the subject of André Malraux's powerful novel, *Man's Estate*.† "For a long time," Powell writes, "the complete story of the Shanghai war between the right-wing Kuomintang and the left-wing radicals and communists could not be told, because the methods that were used could not possibly be revealed, while those who were suppressed did not survive to tell the story." (*sic!*)

The bulk of the Kuomintang armies, with Chiang Kaishek, was still some hundreds of miles away, at Nanchang, Mr. Powell tells us. Shanghai and the seaboard were under the "protection" of a warlord, Sun Chuanfang, whose bodyguard executed people on the streets if they wore a red muffler, or had anything red on them, be it notebook or pencil. The troops of General Sun Chuanfang numbered two hundred thousand. There were strings of fortifications round the International Settlement and the French Concession; barbed-wire barricades, garrison posts, patrols, the inhabitants thus insulated from contact with the native sectors.

A certain newspaperman (perhaps Powell himself) found that the French Consul-General "knew more than he was willing to admit, and that the French had already established contact with

* 25 *Years in China*, by J. B. Powell (Macmillan, New York, 1945).
† Methuen, 1948.

58

Kuomintang officers." Actually there were several negotiations going on at once, some with the French, some with the British. An interview was arranged in the French Concession between two Kuomintang generals and "some American pressmen." The French municipal police opened the gates in the barricade to allow them in. The two were Ho Yingchin (the Whangpoo cadet later Minister for Defence in the Chiang Kaishek government), and a Commander Li Shangchen who would play an important role in eliminating the Shanghai workers. Both were envoys of Chiang, and assured the American pressmen that the Kuomintang had no intention of attacking the foreigners, and would take steps to restore order in the native areas about Shanghai.

"This assurance was greeted with much relief," writes Powell. For in late March, the vaunted two hundred thousand men of Sun Chuanfang had simply melted away. They had been undermined by the Communist propaganda squads. There was no questioning the fact that prevailing sentiment among the students and labour groups favoured the leftists and their programme of social reform.

The letters of Liu Yuanlung, a student, later an official under Chiang Kaishek, to Anna Melissa Graves, the American writer, describe the prevailing sentiment:*

> *February 19th.* There is a general strike of the Shanghai General Labour Union as a protest against the dispatch of foreign troops to China.
>
> I went for a walk in the Chinese city and also in the Settlement; I saw many sympathizers going from shop to shop explaining the purpose of the strike. So far neither the Chinese authorities nor the foreign authorities have interfered, which is curious, considering the fact that newly arrived troops are encamped at various points within the International Settlement, and curious also because Shanghai is still supposed to be in the hands of Sun Chuanfang. The authorities, Chinese and foreign alike, have always taken strong measures in dealing with a situation . . . but there is no sign this time. The strikers have NO ARMS WHATSOEVER. The Kuomintang armies are several hundred miles from here. I can't account for it at all. A friend of mine is connected with the Kuomintang Party says that there is some

* *The Far East is not Very Far* – Letters from Liu Yuan-Lung to Anna Melissa Graves (private printing).

understanding between the Party and Sun Chuanfang's adherents here . . . but even if it is so, how about the foreigners, who always clamour for peace, order, and trade and what not?

March 18th. The general strike was called off on February 24th, but after HUNDREDS OF INNOCENT WORKMEN, STUDENTS AND OTHERS were killed without trials or questioning! You remember I said that the International Settlement authorities were acting splendidly, THIS WAS TRUE OF THAT ONE DAY, but after that they were not; they themselves did not kill, but they connived at the killing; they let the Chinese police and soldiers do their killing for them and they let them come into the Settlement for this special purpose. This might have been excusable if the strikers had been violent or disorderly, but they were not; they in no way molested foreigners, and it has not even been reported that any foreign property was destroyed or in danger during the whole of the strike. It was one of the most peaceful and orderly strikes we have ever had . . .

The situation has grown tenser and more serious since the strike was called off . . . The foreign troops, British, French, Japanese, American and Italian in the last few days have been stationing themselves outside their Settlement and Concession and digging trenches wherever they are stationed. And not a word from these self-entitled patriotic Chinese authorities! I am much discouraged in my work these days for my chief does not allow me to say what I want . . .

March 27th. Sun Chuanfang has been completely done for. There are rumours that there will be another strike. The city is quiet, except for assassinations almost every day, in most cases, foremen in the factories . . .

May 6th. You must certainly have heard of Chiang's suppression of the communist elements . . .

What happened between March 17th and May 6th, 1927?
The warlord Sun had fled with such celerity that the railway rolling stock and all the available shipping on the Yangtse river had been utilized by him. "Chiang's troops might be delayed," mused Powell, now eagerly awaiting Chiang, whereas he had previously execrated him. "In the interregnum the Left might take over . . ." It was then that Shanghai was saved for the foreign vested interests by a man Mr. Powell calls the Benevolent Gang-

ster, a secret society man of the same brotherhood as Chiang Kaishek, Dou Yuseng.

Dou Yuseng, later to be listed in China's *Who's Who* (1930) as a banker, philanthropist and welfare worker, had started his career in the Shanghai French Concession as a fruit pedlar. Later he peddled opium and herion and "familiarized himself with the racketeering, hijacking, and other practices prevailing in Shanghai." He emerged as a controller of opium dens, gambling and brothels, and became so powerful that he actually combined and then controlled the two rival factions of the secret societies in the International Settlement. He thus shared honours with the grandfather-by-adoption of Chiang Kaishek, Huan Ching-yung, policeman and gangster, King of the French Concession. Dou held more chairmanships on directorates of Chinese bank and business houses than any other man in the city. He had his own private army of plainclothesmen, numbering fifteen thousand or more. He had his reserved suites in the best foreign hotels of the Setllement, including the Majestic, where Chiang's wedding was to be celebrated later that year. Operating under him was a man called Ku Tsuchuan, known as the "Big Boss" of the waterfront, whose brother, Ku Tsutung, was a Whangpoo cadet and one of Chiang's underlings. Later, as General Ku Tsutung, I was to meet him in Chungking, and to remember him chiefly for his massacre, in 1941, in the middle of the Sino-Japanese war, of the Communist New Fourth Army.

Stirling Fessenden, the American chairman of the International Settlement, popularly known as the Lord Mayor of Shanghai, complements our knowledge of the events with the following story:

In late March the French chief of police phoned me. I went to the address he gave me, I was suprised it was a Chinese residence, with armed guards at the front gate . . . the large entrance hall was lined with stocks of rifles and, sub-machine guns. I heard voices, the French official entered with Dou Yuseng and an interpreter. We got down to business immediately. Dou went to the point. He was willing to move against the Reds, but had two conditions: first he wanted the French to supply him with at least five thousand rifles and ample ammunition, then turning to me (Fessenden) he demanded permission to move his military trucks through the International Settlement, something which the Settlement authorities had never granted to any Chinese force.

Dou got this permission from Fessenden.

"It was at this point that the shooting began, and continued without stop for days," Powell tells us, with admirable restraint.

About eight thousand workers, trade unionists, labourers, and students were slaughtered by the gangsters of Dou Yuseng, Ku Tsuchuan, and Huang Chingyung. Their arms and ammunition were supplied directly from the foriegn authorities in the International Settlement and the French Concession. Ammunition depots were installed, manned by British, American and French soldiers, who handed the material to the gangster battalions. Dou Yuseng toured these depots, where he was treated like a visiting Commander-in-Chief. "The Communists could not stand up against the experienced gunmen of Dou Yuseng," Powell concludes.

On the night of April 7th, raids against the trade unions began, with the second division under a commander Liu Chi of the Kuomintang army aiding the gangsters. Liu Chi called upon the trade union leaders, invited them to a friendly talk and a friendly feast at the North railway station; he had come with orders from the Communist Politburo to the workers to disarm, as he would protect them.

Liu Chi was not lying entirely; the capitulation policy was on. Not only the Central Executive Committee of the Communist Party, but certain of the Russian advisers, quite out of touch with what was happening, still believed that "unity" must be preserved at all costs.

On April 12th, Chiang Kaishek arrived with the remaining troops, and completed the work of "re-establishing peace and order" begun by the gangsters and the second division of his army under Liu Chi.

In some areas, workers still held out; some of their militia posts greeted the troops like deliverers, only to be mown down by machine-guns. Another eight thousand or so were killed in the next week. Six thousand women and adolescent girls, wives and daughters of workers, were sold into the brothels and factories of Shanghai.

Dou Yuseng, the deliverer, became a hero to the European women of Shanghai. He was also decorated by Chiang Kaishek, acclaimed a pillar of society. As a philanthropist, he cashed in on all the money collected for famine and flood relief and with it continued the narcotics trade on a larger scale. During the war with Japan in 1939 he moved to Chungking; Chiang asked his help to break the local secret societies, the Kelao, which were a different gang from the Shanghai ones, and which controlled the opium of Szechuan province which Chiang's Blueshirt organization coveted for itself. In 1949, Dou arrived in Hongkong with the fleeing Kuomintang. There he lived quietly in extreme comfort. Dou's funeral in Hongkong in 1950 was a modest affair; the local newspapers wrote reserved epitaphs, calling him a philanthropist and a businessman.

The Shanghai massacre was Chiang Kaishek's consecration; henceforth he was in the clear; he qualified for further patronage by Big Business. On April 18th, 1927, he established a military government at Nanking, defying the legal government now installed at Wuhan. Immediately the foreign press began to laud the Nanking government and to call the Wuhan government "Red". Legal and parliamentary measures, relieving Chiang of all his posts, were published by the Wuhan government; but nothing could affect Chiang, the army was his, and the money bags of Shanghai.

The China Year Book of 1928 states : "No governmental group in China started under better auspices than that which composed the Nanking government . . . the Shanghai bankers and merchants were willing to support and finance it, on condition that the Communists should be suppressed."

By May, there were two rival "governments" of the Kuomintang; one in Wuhan, one in Nanking. Legally speaking, Chiang had seized power by a military coup, thus doing exactly what Yuan Shihkai, his first patron, had done. From this basic conflict between the civil authority and the military, the civil did not recover. It never does.

The "legal" Kuomintang government in Wuhan harboured various tendencies; dubbed "Red," its Left consisted of four men : one was Sun Fo, the son of Sun Yatsen, a morose nonentity; another was Wang Chingwei, a brilliant but petty, intriguing and unprincipled intellectual, who had a great beginning, throwing a bomb at the Regent of the Manchu dynasty in 1909, and a murky end, as puppet to the Japanese in 1938. The third of these "leftists" was none other than our Shanghai banker T. V. Soong, brother of the future Madame Chiang Kaishek. What Mr. T. V. Soong was doing there remains an unwritten tale. The fourth, the most honest of all, was our candid Victorian, the overseas Chinese from Trinidad Eugene Chen, whose best service was the negotiation over the surrender of the British Concession, and who found Chinese politics, in their delicate swift wheelings and duplicities, sometimes utterly confusing. These men denounced Chiang, demoted him, took away his rank, called on the army to rise against him; and all this meant absolutely nothing, since Chiang had the backing of the foreign interests, the bankers, and the guns. American and British gunboats patrolled the Yangtse River and blockaded the Wuhan government; there was no rice, no oil, no coal, and no money. This was done to cause the Wuhan government's surrender to Chiang Kaishek.

And now both Nanking and Wuhan had to proclaim a continuation of the Northern Expedition against the warlords of the North, and the reunification of China. That meant getting to North China; but neither could move, without fear of the other. It was obvious that a third, another ally, another army must be found.

The key to North China, the best army there, was the army of General Feng Yuhsiang, the Christian General, whose troops so often sat astride my father's railways, whom my father had come to know well, who stayed with us when we were on the railway, and who ate my mother's macaroni without complaint.

In a gallery of warlords, Feng stands out, a social phenomenon, for he was an honest militarist, a man of peasant patriotism, remarkable in his total lack of personal avidity. "Feng is the only man I shall never be able to buy," Chiang Kaishek said. "The only way to get round that rough country bumpkin is to touch his heart."

Feng had enlisted as an ordinary soldier at twelve because his peasant family was utterly destitute. He rose to become a divisional commander under Yuan Shihkai in 1911. In 1915 he was sent by the latter to Szechuan, where the military governor had revolted against Yuan's pretensions to become an emperor. Instead of obeying, Feng too revolted against Yuan.

Feng always kept a great sense of justice, a hatred of wrong-doing, but was too conservative to favour a revolution, and believed that a paternalist, personal rule could renovate China. He did not fleece the people, and his ideal was Cromwell.

After Yuan's death Feng served under another powerful warlord Wu Peifu, but turned against Wu and in 1924, in October, took Peking, and for a time ruled us there, kicking Puyi the abdicated Manchu Emperor out of his Imperial Palace, and opening the gardens to all the people as a park. Feng's rule over Peking was a time of great simplicity which I remember well, for he sought to emulate the Roundhead government of Oliver Cromwell. No one was allowed to have large banquets; three dishes were enough; all salaries were cut, but the cost of many goods also fell. No one could wear ornate jewellery, and there was much chorus singing, and many soup kitchens functioned for the beggars. My father twice went to pay a call on Feng Yuhsiang and found him in a bare room clad in a cotton uniform in mid-winter. Though the students liked Feng, Feng was afraid of "leftism." He had married a Y.W.C.A. worker, one of the few emancipated women in the 1920s, called Li Techuan, a cheerful, energetic, and capable woman, who for ten years was Minister of Health in Peking, and is now a vice-president of the People's Political Council. Feng was a champion of women's rights, as Mao Tsetung is, for emancipation of women and social progress are linked in China. Feng's army, well clothed, fed, paid on time, and kept in hand, were regularly lectured by him and hosed once in a while in a speedy baptismal ceremony invented by himself while they paraded in front of him. "When they went through a village at night, no child woke, no dog barked," said the peasants. "I'll cut off your head if you dare touch a woman," shouted Feng at his soldiers. On their armbands was written: The People's Army.

It was this man, in 1925 driven out of Peking by another warlord, who retired to the north-west, and waited. Times were hard and he had little money, and then his luck returned. Already, while in Peking, he had made advances to Sun Yatsen, and the latter had responded, but unfortunately died in Peking while Feng himself was driven out. In 1926 he again made overtures to the Canton Kuomintang government; when the Northern Expedition reached Wuhan, in September 1926, Feng seized the opportunity to place himself in a strategically important position, by occupying the western section of the Lunghai railway, my father's railway, for which Feng seemed to have a particular affection. He encamped at Chengchow, a city on the Yellow River at the junction of the Lunghai railway, running east to west, and the Peking-Hankow railway, running north to south. Both these railways were built with Belgian loans; on both my father worked. And that was enough for us to follow every move.

We did not know Wang Chingwei or Chiang Kaishek then, but we knew Feng Yuhsiang. Here at Chengchow he was in a commanding stronghold; he could stop all troop movements, northwards, eastwards or westwards, from this one single vantage point.

Both Chiang in Nanking, and Wang Chingwei and company in Wuhan, now flirted with Feng. A delegation from Wuhan went to Chengchow to meet Feng and to parley. He soon arrived, riding in a cattle truck "since my brother soldiers also travel like this," wearing a worn-out uniform; extracted from his pocket a hunk of dry, coarse millet bread, and began to munch it with much relish.

There followed two days of chatter. "They do nothing except eat and talk small talk, such as how many flies there are in China . . ." wrote one witness. Actually Feng was shrewdly studying his guests, and the conclusion he came to was that they did not mean what they said. He was right; already the Wuhan government was taking action against the very peasants and workers who were supporting it against Chiang. For the fear of revolution was stronger in them than anything else. Wang Chingwei, in fact, let out that the peasants were getting "too upstart," a judgment with which our conservative Feng agreed. But this did not prevent him from despising them for their hypocrisy. He also realized that their power was being frittered away in internal squabbles. "There is no difference between Wuhan and Nanking," Borodin was to say, "they all want the same thing: *Chow*." *Chow* is an ubiquitous Chinese word meaning money, good jobs, bribes . . .

After two days of courtesies Feng re-entered his cattle truck, with most splendid promises of co-operation and harmony, which for a time fooled even these wily men. They returned to Wuhan, deciding to throw the Communists to the dogs and reorganize. Some of them, to make *chow* more secure, immediately sent messengers to Chiang Kaishek in Nanking . . . but Feng Yuhsiang was swifter than they.

His cattle truck sped along the Lunghai railway, eastward from Chengchow until it reached Hsuchow, the town on the east section of the railway where my sister Tiza was born. There, waiting for Feng, was Chiang Kaishek, and further abstemious feasting. Chiang had taken the trouble to study Feng, and set out to charm him. And he could, and for a long time, with many

66

others, did persuade and charm. Astutely, he cast himself in the posture of an earnest, sincere suppliant, a younger brother, uncertain, asking Feng's advice, a man who wanted to leave the "heavy burden" of power and retire to meditate, to paint, perhaps to write a little poetry . . . Feng Yuhsiang was taken in.

The two militarists exchanged solemn oaths of brotherhood; Chiang insisting on calling himself "small young brother" to Feng, and begging for his advice. They made a joint announcement to the nation, that their troops, to obey the sacred behest of the late Dr. Sun Yatsen, would wipe out all imperialism in China, and accomplish the mission of unification in "revolutionary" style.

Feng, always kind-hearted, now sent a private telegram to the Wuhan government, advising that their leftist elements should take trips abroad for rest and study, or else join Chiang Kaishek. As for the Russian advisers, they would be well advised to leave, for the sake of their health . . .

This moved the odds in favour of Chiang Kaishek; made it posssible that Peking should come under the rule of the Nanking government in 1928. Feng Yuhsiang was to regret bitterly this step, and eighteen months later revolted against Chiang. "He fooled me," he said. "Nanking is full of corruption. It is no different from the past."

The Feng-Chiang agreement made it possible for the Terror to be unleashed quite openly; hundreds of thousands of "Communists" were jailed or killed in the following months. Actually, from 1927 to 1937 the Terror never really stopped in China, and three million people must have been slaughtered as "Communists".

The Wuhan government, seeing the game was lost, decided to make terms with Chiang. In August 1927 a delegation headed by Wang Chingwei agreed to a Unity Conference. But because Wang and Chiang hated each other, and due to other personal intricacies, a "face-saving" farce was played. Chiang Kaishek retired apparently under a cloud, actually with his friends well placed to watch his interests. He was "relieved" of his command, knowing full well that this was only a prelude to greater triumph. Modestly, Chiang declared his purpose accomplished; he had no personal ambition but to study and improve himself, and he was now proving to the world that he was sincere in abandoning power when it was in his hands. It was then, Chinese sources say, that Chiang received a thirty-million-dollar bonus from the Shanghai bankers to help him in his studies abroad.

Chiang away, Wang Chingwei started the Unity Conference with a palaver designed for a patching up. "The present meeting," he told the Nanking government delegates, "is my heart's desire. Both our sides (Nanking and Wuhan) have committed errors, the Nanking brothers having been too hasty and somewhat careless, and the Wuhan brothers *too slow in suppressing the Communists*, thus giving rise to misunderstanding . . . now all is well, and it is time for me to retire . . ."

Upon which, having neatly handed over to the Nanking government (to Chiang *in absentia* and to his military clique) the civil and legal apparatus. Wang Chingwei also withdrew for rest and study, receiving a paltry million dollars.

Chiang Kaishek had resigned in August; sailed to Japan in October, and returned to Shanghai on November 10th 1927, declaring that the pressing instances of his friends had made him desist from his cherished purpose of quiet retreat, and meditation on the sages. Much against his will he must now take up the heavy burden of power again. Chiang became Generalissimo of the Kuomintang army, and on December 1st married Soong Meiling, sister of the Shanghai banker T. V. Soong, the one who had been so bravely left-wing the previous year. And now all that remained was for Chiang Kaishek to march north, in concert with his "brother" Feng Yuhsiang, to take Peking from the warlord then in power, Marshal Chang Tsolin, and to rule over all China.

In January 1928 the liquidation of all Communists in China was ordered. From then on, in Shanghai, every Saturday, the "Communists" caught in the International Settlement were handed over by Pat Givens, the Irishman in charge of the police, to the Kuomintang to be executed, and from 1928 to 1936 there were twenty thousand of them. Pat Givens afterwards wrote that the only Chinese he respected were the Communists, because they knew how to die.

The Northern warlords, big and small, were now abandoned by the foreign powers. Chiang was far more efficient and ruthless, he had proved his supreme ability by suppressing the Communists.

This was Chiang Kaishek's finest hour. It was followed by a further triumph when, in July 1928, before an enormous conclave of "friends and brother generals," he saluted the coffin of Sun Yatsen, which had been lying in the Western Hills in Peking waiting for burial. There Chiang wept, hugging the coffin, and the mantle of Sun Yatsen was refitted to envelop Chiang Kaishek.

From December 1927, Chiang's month of triumphal accomplishment, crowned by a wedding which, like the grand marriage alliances of the European Middle Ages, consolidated his position as successor of Sun Yatsen, Father of the Republic, Founder of the Party; to December 1936, when in a provincial town of northwest China called Sian, he was kidnapped by his own subordinates, and forced to reverse his policies, Chiang Kaishek was to create by his own choices the very conditions which would bring about the triumph of the adversary he tried so long, so hard, so strenuously to destroy – the triumph of communism, under Mao Tsetung.

The grand marriage alliance accomplished by Chiang Kaishek deserves further elucidation. By marrying into the Soong family, Chiang Kaishek proved himself remarkably astute; but not, as the newspapers reported, or as the general impression was created, because the Soongs were wealthy; they were affluent, but vast wealth only came to them later. Chiang did not marry for money, but for more subtle reasons.

We must begin with Charlie Soong, the Chinese Methodist preacher, converted to Christianity, who at nine years old was sent by his family from Canton to Boston to help his maternal uncle, the first tea and silk shopkeeper to emigrate to America. The uncle was without a son, and Charlie was to inherit the family business; but he ran away at fourteen, became a Christian, received an American University education; and adopted the profession of a Methodist preacher. He returned to Shanghai in 1886 and married a Miss Nyi, also a Protestant Christian. She was a descendent of Su Kuangki, who was converted to Catholicism at the end of the Ming dynasty (seventeenth century), and was a friend of the Jesuit Matteo Ricci. Some members of this family, in the twentieth century, had switched their allegiance from Catholicism to Protestant Christianity. By his wife Charlie had six children: three daughters, the renowned Soong sisters, Eling, Chingling, Meiling; and three sons, of whom Tsevun, later to be known as T. V. Soong, was the most famous.

Like so many overseas Chinese, imbued with American democratic fervour, Charlie Soong became enthusiastic over Dr. Sun Yatsen's cause. The overthrow of Manchu despotism, the founding of a democratic republic of China, appealed to him; besides, Sun Yatsen was also a Christian (although not an orthodox one). The Soong home in Shanghai in the French Concession (Avenue Joffre) became Sun Yatsen's home; Soong Eling, the eldest daughter, was for a while Sun Yatsen's secretary. Eling, educated in America (as were all the sisters), married a young man called Kung, later to be known as H. H. Kung. Kung claimed to be a direct descendant of "Master Kung", no less than Confucius himself, and this claim is fully validated by research. His family was a banking family of Shansi province, and the Shansi bankers had been bankers to the Imperial dynasties for many centuries. However, by the twentieth century, modern banking methods, and flight of capital to the foreign banks in Shanghai, destroyed the old-type banking set-up (which was on a credit system throughout the Chinese empire), and the Kung family turned to trade, and also invested in Shanghai. A company set up by these descendants of Confucius was the sole agent for the Asia Petroleum Company, an American-owned corporation, in the province of Shansi, and dispensed paraffin for the lamps which were utilized there right up till 1949.

H.H. Kung was educated in a Shanghai missionary school, and was converted to Christianity; whether his ancestor Confucius was troubled by this is not recorded. He then went to the United States on a fellowship and there in 1905 met Sun Yatsen for the first time. Like so many other young Chinese, he was fired by the idea of overthrowing the Manchu dynasty and restoring China's rights; but he does not seem to have done anything very actively about this. In 1909 he graduated from Oberlin College, came back to Shansi, and started a middle school; in 1910 he went to Japan and became Chinese secretary-general of the Y.M.C.A. in Tokyo. It was there that he met and married Soong Eling, who was then Sun Yatsen's secretary. Upon her marriage to Kung, Eling gave up her secretaryship but introduced her sister, Chingling, to take over. Dr. Sun Yatsen promptly fell in love with Chingling, and married her in 1913.

Due to this marriage between Sun Yatsen and Soong Chingling, the Soong family acquired much importance within the circles of Sun's revolutionary Kuomintang; T. V. Soong, brother-in-law of Sun Yatsen, became a member of the Canton government. He too, like his sisters, was educated in America.

He had worked in the National City Bank, and though described as a banker, was only in a minor position then.

It was into this close-knit web of family connections, with its American-Christian missionary influence, that Chiang Kaishek sought admission, by marrying the youngest Soong sister, Meiling and thus also becoming brother-in-law to the now defunct Sun Yatsen, on a par with H. H. Kung and T. V. Soong.

Although H. H. Kung and T. V. Soong, together with Sun Fo, the son of Sun Yatsen, were for a brief period, as members of the reputedly Left government at Wuhan, in opposition to Chiang, in September 1927 a reconciliation was effected, and Chiang left for Japan that October, returning to marry Soong Meiling in December.

Who actually in the Soong family decided to put this "grand alliance through marriage" into effect?

More than one report credits this move to Soong Eling, Madame H. H. Kung. She was always the matchmaker, planner and builder of the family wealth. Would it not be a brilliant coup to marry off her youngest sister, Meiling, to the powerful Commander-in-Chief of the Nationalist armies? "We can use this man," she said. And immediately went about convincing the recalcitrant Meiling that such a marriage would be in the interest of all, especially the House of Soong.

On the part of Chiang Kaishek, it was not so much the person of Meiling herself that counted (he already had two official and one unofficial wives), as the fact that Meiling was the sister of Chingling, now widow of Dr. Sun Yatsen.

For it was Chiang's ambition to succeed to Sun Yatsen; only by thus establishing a family connection, by becoming brother-in-law to Sun Yatsen, accepted in the latter's family circle, in the good old feudal way, would he have the right to speak in the name of Sun, the right to occupy his position . . . otherwise many another disciple of the late founder could claim, with equal justice, a share of Sun's influence.

There was, for instance, Wang Chingwei, Sun Yatsen's favourite; present at his deathbed, he had been credited with the drafting of Sun Yatsen's will . . . "Chiang aspired," says the historian Tang Leangli, "to the *undivided* succession of Sun Yatsen's heritage, notwithstanding the fact that this heritage had been put into perpetual commission, in June 1925, by the terms of Sun's will . . . As a first step to this end he made a matrimonial alliance with Soong Meiling, sister of Madame Sun Yatsen,

71

having to turn Christian and to dismiss his third wife (and divorce his first wife – Author's note) to do so. For this marriage, which took place in December 1927, he hired the biggest hotel in Shanghai, the Majestic, inviting all the available foreign authorities, including the commander of the British Expeditionary troops at Shanghai, and spending some hundred thousand dollars on the show . . . He had amassed a huge fortune during the Northern Expedition, which enabled him to buy up the Central Kuomintang Organization, the Nanking administration, the allegiance of several militarists . . ."

This reference to a huge fortune covers the thirty million dollars in silver bullion Chiang received as his reward for the April suppression of the workers in Shanghai. Noticed among the guests at the wedding at the Majestic was the gangster Dou Yuseng.

Both T. V. Soong and Madame Sun Yatsen (Chingling) opposed the marriage strenuously; Madame H. H. Kung backed it; as did her husband. Since Charlie Soong was dead, the final acceptance of Chiang into the Soong family rested with Charlie Soong's wife, the Christian Mrs. Soong, and she too had been opposed to Chiang on the grounds that he was not a Christian and did not lead an exemplary life. Mrs. Soong was in Japan, resting at some hot springs; thither Chiang Kaishek betook himself when he went to Japan in October 1927; and there he won her consent by promising to adopt Christianity, but only after the marriage, in order to keep face, and not to appear coerced into it.

The grand alliance by marriage thus took place; and Chiang was converted to Christianity; the news of the impending wedding and conversion were bruited about by the Japanese press much before the event occurred.

This marriage also raised the status of T. V. Soong and H. H. Kung, both Christians, both connected with foreign interests; and it immediately provided the necessary middlemen, all within one family, for the most ambiguous financial transactions possible.

Both H. H. Kung and T. V. Soong thus became useful as "go-betweens," or compradores, in the transactions between Chiang Kaishek and the foreign powers. It is often thought that Chiang was manipulated by the House of Soong; but actually, all through his career, Chiang was both manipulator and puppet; he utilized both his brothers-in-law to obtain money from the Americans, the British, and any other group. In the years to come there was always to be an alternance between T. V. Soong and

H. H. Kung; the one in favour when the other was in apparent disgrace; replacing each other, almost as regularly as clockwork as Finance Minister, or Minister of Commerce or Industry, or in some other capacity in the Nanking government which made possible the begging and obtaining of large foreign loans. Actually everyone knew that Chiang Kaishek preferred H. H. Kung to T. V. Soong. The latter was far less subservient to him, far more brilliant, and less unscrupulous. It is a pity that his great gifts could not have been put to better use.

The Christian connection became most useful of all. Already the missionary influence upon American politics, which had started with Goodnow, American adviser to Yuan Shihkai, and still goes on today, was shaping public opinion in America as regards China. Glowing reports, exalting the Christianity of the linked Kung-Soong-Chiang family complex, and the beautiful Christian home of Chiang Kaishek, made it easier to extract money than would otherwise have been possible.

Thus, the House of Soong entered upon its destiny, as "the great and mighty compradore family, in greed and might and glamour to rule" . . . The real promoter of the family personal wealth all through remained that clever woman, astute for herself blind to her country, Soong Eiling, Madame H. H. Kung. From that time on, she amassed money; while her brother-in-law, Chiang Kaishek, amassed power. T. V. Soong, though not loath to make money, remained a pawn to Chiang's ambitions. Cleverly, Chiang manipulated the Houses of Kung and Soong, to obtain money from America and England; but the only one he could never sway, the one he dared not touch (though he put innumerable detectives and spies to watch her every movement), was the widow of Sun Yatsen, his sister-in-law, Soong Chingling.

Soong Chingling, who is now vice-chairman of the People's Republic of China, in Peking, is, of all the Soong family, the most remarkable, yet the most modest. She is the bright pure flame, who has always adhered, irrespective of her own self-interest, to her husband's principles, sacrificing comfort and fame, spurning her wealth-grabbing family in a great dedication to her country and to the future of the Chinese people. She raised her voice in 1927 and denounced Chiang Kaishek and his betrayal, and all through the years she maintained this uncompromising upright-ness. Self-effacing and shy, she will one day be recognized as one of the world's most courageous women. Round her and her importance as Sun Yatsen's widow her family spun their intrigues;

it was through her position they attained their power and grabbed their millions during the years of misrule. But she would have none of it; she refused the slightest benefit from this ill-gotten wealth and remained unsullied, unbending to their wiles and the only true Christian of them all.

CHAPTER THREE

All this we knew, yet did not know; we saw the executions, and accepted them. From every newspaper came the chorus: "The future is bright with Our Leader Generalissimo Chiang."

Uncle Liu and Mr. Hua Namkwei hoped there would be no more civil wars; and that the railways would now run on time. "Only a few, a handful of Communist bandits, in the mountains of Kiangsi and Hunan . . ." Their names? Chu Teh, Mao Tsetung.

One evening in March 1965, I was at the University of Columbia Library of East Asian studies in New York. There, upon the steel shelves, were the publications delineating the beginning and the growth of the Chinese Communist Party. With almost hysterical passion, with an ecstasy of hatred akin to love, the American experts on China seek to document China for themselves. China is an abiding passion with them, they scarcely talk or think of anything else. And the phenomenon, so unexpected, of an Asian nation driven to the depths of abject misery, and rising again so swiftly, against all the rules and maxims of their expertise, is a frustration "which makes them foam at the mouth," as my friend Colonel David Barrett writes. "We can never forget that we lost China, we're going crazy about it, we're half insane, like people who kill what they cannot possess and then commit suicide."

On the shelves were the weeklies of those early days, 1918, 1919: among them the *Hsiangkiang Review*, the magazine founded and edited by Mao Tsetung. The first number was dated July 14th, 1919. It sold five issues of five thousand copies each before it was banned. There also were *New Youth, Labour's Voice*, many others, fifty years of Chinese political journals. The man in charge of the library, a Chinese scholar who had left China in 1948, told me:

"We have everything, everything here. We collect from everywhere. We have our sources in Hongkong, the Jesuit Intelligence Service for example. Newspapers are smuggled out to us, from many parts of China, even today. Everything we can possibly lay our hands on." He lifted tenderly one of the older magazines, pointed to an article signed by "TWENTY-EIGHT STROKES GENTLE-MAN."

"Mao Tsetung's pseudonym. There are twenty-eight strokes in his name. I did not think it possible then that Mao could become what he is today . . . but his Chinese writing is superb, of course. His style is good . . ." He pointed: "See, Mao always put the date when he finished writing something, at the end of his essays, that's not Chinese. He was scolded for it by his teacher, when he was young." "It's a habit everyone ought to have," I replied. The hands of the scholar touched the print, his eyes lingered on the pages . . . Unlike him, I am no scholar, self-pleased and fortressed in lore. Only a stubborn, patient plodder, tenaciously pursuing traces of the past to fit into my present. I could only perform in retrospect my own Long March to this hour, catching up with time in order to understand the future, because the future had, for so many of my generation, begun here, with these reviews, these words upon a page: Twenty-eight strokes. The whole world of China had already been changed by someone who called himself "Twenty-eight strokes."

"We've got everything, all his writing, every bit," repeated the obstinate scholar.

As if by owning this they owned Mao Tsetung himself, clutched his mind in their fingers.

Well did I remember the first time I heard the name of Mao Tsetung; from Uncle Liu the Lolo, his stentorian voice making our windows quiver in their frames.

Uncle Liu and his first wife, my father's eldest sister, had come to our house. Soon after the visit my aunt died, giving birth to her thirteenth child. Uncle Liu married again, a squat, tough northern woman who gave him four sons, so that he now had fourteen sons and three daughters. Of these, only one, the eldest, is abroad, a diplomat in the service of Chiang Kaishek. All the others are in China, as doctors, engineers and technicians.

Since 1949 Uncle Liu, like my father, has continued working on the railway and has been four times mentioned as a Labour Hero. At eighty-two, today, he still does half a day's work, though he is getting deafer.

All through 1929, 1930 and 1931 Uncle Liu and my father

would get together, sometimes with Hua Namkwei, my father's best friend, also an engineer, and talk of Chu Teh and Mao Tsetung, Mao Tsetung and Chu Teh. The reason was not that they liked communism, which was anathema to them, but that Chu Teh was a Hakka Szechuanese, like my father and all our family, and Mao Tsetung was from Hunan, which is next door to Szechuan. They had gradually become disenchanted with Chiang Kaishek; they found the names Mao Tsetung, Chu Teh, alluring.

Chu Teh was the son of a Hakka tenant farmer. A clever child, his schooling expenses were paid for by his clan, in Hakka fashion. After graduation he chose the military way, as my Third Uncle had done. He took part in the revolt which Szechuan began against Yuan Shihkai in 1915, and his valour earned him a great name. Later, caught in the web of provincial feuds, he began to degenerate, found himself fighting for one warlord against another instead of fighting for righteousness. And suddenly one day he gave it all up, wealth, position, wives, and the opium habit, and became a "Red". Hence the fascination with which we talked of Chu Teh, "one of ours," who had done what he thought was right, like the great heroes of childhood legends. Uncle Liu and my father did not forget that their ancestors had been poor, pedlars of salt and other goods, then tenant farmers in Szechuan, like Chu Teh's parents. Who climbs up a mountain can tumble down again; who is down can come up; here was Chu Teh from Szechuan, with this man Mao Tsetung from Hunan, shut up in some mountain fastness in Kiangsi, and years had come and years had gone and it was impossible to finish them off, though time and time again they were said to be dead. Sometimes, in the newspapers, we read of the prices on their heads, one hundred thousand silver dollars, dead or alive . . .

"Chiang won't be able to beat Chu Teh, he is a Szechuan man," said Uncle Liu proudly. Though he disliked communism, he disliked the Shanghai bankers more. "And Mao Tsetung is from Hunan, the Hunan people are also good fighters." Hua Namkwei would add, "Hunan and Szechuan people both eat red peppers." They would chortle.

With Mao Tsetung, today, hagiography is also perilously near to replacing biography; as the years of his triumph heap their victorious arches above his head, books which are exercises in devotional litany thicken. This is nothing particular to communism, it occurs elsewhere. Fortunately we have Mao's own unpretentious autobiography, his own writings, more revealing

76

of his development than anything else. There are his poems, their classic restraint cloaking the tumult of new creation. There are films of his days in Yenan, showing him, a tall, gaunt man with dream-filled eyes, talking, expounding with that unemphatic gesture of his half-open hands, which he still uses today.

Mao's father, by great exertion, had come to own three acres of land, which made him "middling prosperous", and soon engaged in a small grain trade which Mao Tsetung repudiated. Very early on the young Tsetung roamed the country-side in rain, wind or tiger heat, walking and dreaming. The love of long solitary walks, the love for water and swimming, the love for the harshness of weather, and the ruggedness of the land to pit himself against, all these came to him and stayed with him. He would swim the coldest November river, frost on the ground, wander through a summer's heat from village to village, staying with the peasants, listening to them, eating what they gave him to eat. He became steady and patient in great pacings among the plains and the mountains of his province, in the solitude nourishing to long-reached thoughts. Today's Mao Tsetung has preserved the habits of youth. On a cold day in February 1964, at the airport in Peking, all his contemporaries, Liu Shao-Chih, Chen Yi, Chou Enlai, wore coats in the freezing dawn weather 15° Centigrade below zero. But Mao Tsetung, in cotton garb and without gloves, strode his six-foot frame round and round the airport, swinging his arms, laughing, irrespressible. At sixty-eight he swam across the Great River, a mile and a half of water, at seventy he plunged into the reservoir built near the Ming tombs; at seventy-two he has been swimming a few lakes; anything that looks deep enough he cannot resist. As a result, a whole nation of six hundred and fifty million landlubbers, traditionally taught to beware of water-demons, now jump into lakes, rivers and ponds in all weathers.

Even when hunted by a million Kuomintang troops, in Yenan, Mao would still, whenever he could, have contact with water. In Yenan's loess caves, where after the Long March he led the remnants of the Red armies, the visitor can see the light, low wooden tub Mao used for his daily bath, a habit which astounded the northern peasants, who wash as little as possible in winter. "Whatever the weather Chairman Mao would have his bath winter or summer, and he would work or write all night."

He was bright at school, with a talent for clear-cut, incisive exposition of ideas. In 1911, he cut off his queue and joined the

77

local army against the Manchus, a solider at seven dollars a month. He carried buckets, cooked, wrote letters for other soldiers, for "there was little fighting"* and by February 1912 it was all over. He then began a period of self-education and travel on foot, interspersed with spasmodic attendance at a teachers' college. It took him six years to graduate, but by then he had read enormously, everything he could lay his hands on, from Greek tales to English geography, from logic to law, from Montesquieu to Darwin; he read faster than most people, and today at seventy-two can "see" a whole page at a glance. This devouring of books he supplemented by newspaper-reading. Mao Tsetung could never take things easily, and whereas others forgot great issues when their own personal lives were affected, always he would carry an extra weight and depth of feeling, a conscious exhaustive search for facts, forgetting himself in the process. "Myself is my smallest being; the universe, my greatest being." He is actually a universalist, such as the Renaissance produced, a spirit both scientific and artistic, capable of scientific analysis and new creation. His talents were at first not appreciated, for he was shy when young, and consequently taciturn; slow to make up his mind, slow to talk, though swift and unswerving in execution. "Understanding must precede decision. The truth alone is valid; all the rest is claptrap."

One thing the Communist leaders in China have in common is their love of debate. "We argue continually, we debate everything," said Chou Enlai to me in 1956, as I had raised this point with him. And indeed it is Mao who has given the Chinese people, who did not know what debate was, the habit of discussion meetings, endless discussion meetings till all is sifted, chewed over, revised . . . Mao was stating sober fact when he wrote: "The evil feudal practice of arbitrary dictation is so deeply rooted in the minds of the people and even of the ordinary Party members, that it cannot be swept away at once – they have no liking for the bothersome democratic system." "Men's minds are fettered by circumstance and habit, from which even revolutionaries cannot always escape." The "habit" of free speech does not come easily; it took England a good many centuries to evolve it, and China has possibly more democratic debate today than she has had for her last four thousand years of history.

This habit of debate began for Mao when, in the summer of 1917, he advertised for "young people interested in patriotic

* The quotations are from Mao Tsetung's own autobiography and writings.

78

action," to form a New Citizen Society, a kind of debating society for young men, like himself avid for learning, for disputation, and also for positive action, for with him discussion always leads to active decision. He gathered seventy to eighty members, among them some who were later to become Communists and follow him.

In 1918, Mao went to Peking with some Hunan students, who were planning to go to France.

The "work and study scheme" under which young Chinese went to France had been started in 1914 by some revolutionary students of Szechuan province.* Embittered at the failure of the 1911 Revolution, and to escape the tyranny of Yuan Shihkai, they went abroad to train themselves for the salvation of China. The dearth of manpower in France during the 1914–18 war led to the intensive recruitment of Chinese labourers and students, almost two hundred thousand of whom went to man the factories, mines, and public utilities of France. A good many of today's Communist leaders, Chou Enlai, Chen Yi, Teng Hsiaoping, thus went to France, where they not only worked and studied, but also established, in 1921, a branch of the Chinese Communist Party in Paris.

Mao Tsetung did not accompany his Hunan fellow students to France: "I did not want to go to Europe. I felt I did not know enough about my own country." He remained in Peking, and worked as assistant librarian in Peking University, the germinal centre of intellectual and political thought in China. There a nucleus of brilliant, bold minds were assembled; their mainstay and core was Li Tachao, the librarian, China's first Marxist, who gave Mao Tsetung his job and became with him one of the twelve founders of the Communist Party in Shanghai in July 1921. As assistant librarian Mao read voraciously, enrolled in many classes; met some of the great intellectuals of the day, among them Chen Tuhsiu, who was later also to become one of the founders of the Chinese Communist Party. It was at Peking University that for the first time Mao tasted the arrogant disdain of the Chinese intellectual mandarin. "To most of them I did not exist as a human being," said Mao, measuring the arrogance of the literati, their blindness and contempt for the servant, the menial, a state of things still present in many places, such as India, where brilliant left-wing socialists with the latest *New Statesman* in hand will discourse with passionate fluency on the things that

* See *The Crippled Tree*

should be done to elevate the monstrously poor of their land, but without a glance brush off the beggars crawling to touch their lofty Brahminical feet. Mao the peasant early recognised the single enormous failing of these intellectuals: their overweening vanity. When the time came he would deal with this as well.

Mao Tsetung's words describe his living conditions in Peking.

I was paid eight dollars a month. My office was so low that people avoided me. I tried to begin conversations (with famous intellectuals) on political and cultural subjects, but they were busy men. They had no time to listen to an assistant librarian speaking a southern dialect . . .

My own living conditions in Peking were quite miserable, and in contrast the beauty of the old capital was a vivid and living compensation. I stayed in a place called Three Eyes Well, in a little room which held seven other people. When we were all packed fast on the *k'ang** there was scarcely room for any of us to breathe. I used to have to warn people on either side of me when I wanted to turn over.

But in the parks and the old palace grounds I saw the early northern spring, I saw the white plum blossom flower while the ice still held solid over the North Sea Park. I saw the willows with the ice crystals hanging from them and remembered the description by the Tang poet who wrote about the winter-jewelled trees.

In 1919, at the time of the demonstrations against the Versailles Peace Treaty, Mao returned to Hunan and went to Changsha, the provincial capital, where he founded the *Hsiangkiang Review*, which I saw in Columbia University. By now the need for liaison between various student groups in Hunan and with the other provinces was obvious. Mao travelled to Peking and Shanghai on behalf of the student groups, and since he had attended courses on journalism in Peking University, became head of a student news agency. In Shanghai he met Chen Tuhsiu again, "he had influenced me more than anyone else." He also saw Hu Shih, the scholar-philosopher who died in America recently. Hu and Chen in 1920 were accounted the most brilliant intellectuals in China; joint leaders of the intellectual renaissance movement, they were politically divided into the inevitable Right and Left. Mao discussed plans with Chen Tuhsiu, who encouraged him to

**K'ang:* stone platform, heated from below, which serves as bed in North China.

organize workers as well as students; he returned to Hunan and began to set up unions of workers of the An Yuan mines; it was the first time Hunan workers were thus organized. By the summer of 1920 he had become "in theory and to some extent in action" a Marxist. In April 1921 he went to Shanghai, where he worked in a laundry, washing clothes, and later keeping accounts. On July 21st, he founded with eleven others, including Li Tachao and Chen Tuhsiu, the Chinese Communist Party, at number 108, Wang Chih Road, a quiet street in the French Concession of the Gangster Metropolis.

These twelve represented fifty-seven Marxists, the total number in China in 1921. By July 1922 there were one hundred and twenty-three members, and by 1927 fifty-seven thousand were said to be enrolled; but the figure is suspect. Twenty-five thousand left the Communist Party within the first three months of Chiang Kaishek's first bloody purges, which began in the spring of that year.

In that same 1921, Chou Enlai, in France as a student worker since 1920, founded a Chinese Communist Party in Paris together with Li Lisan and some others. I remember Mrs Hua Namkwei dictating to me, in 1931 in Peking, her fictionalized account of this founding for a novel she was going to write. She had met these young students in Paris; had possibly followed with great enthusiasm their activities; but when she recounted this episode to me the Terror of Chiang Kaishek was on and it was not healthy to be even a liberal. I marvel at her courage still.

In that same year Chu Teh, the ex-warlord seeking righteousness, was in Germany on his quest for truth, and there founded a German branch of the Chinese Communist Party. Other small parties were founded elsewhere; unaware of each other's existence, they floundered on their own, until their founders returned to China, and the various branches met, and coalesced, into one unified Chinese Communist Party.

By 1922 the Hunan branch of the Communist Party, founded by Mao Tsetung on his return from Shanghai, had organized more than twenty trade unions, but "most of the work was among students and workers, very little was done among the peasants," Mao recalled later. Already he felt, obscurely, that neglect of the peasantry which was to lead to the debacle five years later. His logical mind had grasped the essential flaw in the Marxism as interpreted and applied by Chen Tuhsiu, now become the head of the Central Executive Committee. In a country like

China, where there were one million industrial workers and three hundred and eighty million peasants, how could the workers, backbone and vanguard of the Party, supply that sufficiency of manpower necessary for ridding the land of its feudal militarism with its ramifications in every village?

Among the twelve founders Mao was the only one with a peasant background who remained in close contact with the peasantry.

Chen Tuhsiu, of mandarin family, was city-bound and auto-cratic. "He was," says O. M. Green, "nauseated by the noise and reek of common folk." He found the Chinese peasantry particularly repulsive, and this fear of the peasant was very obvious later in his actions to curb what he called their excesses.

Mao, on the contrary, liked to stay with peasants, to walk in the small paths in the unending fields. His talk was of harvest and planting; of seasons and locusts, of drought and taxes; his speech remained Hunan-accented, though his sentences were drawn from the classics. It was he, and not the city-bred Chen Tuhsiu or the brilliant French-returned Li Lisan, who would acclimatize Marxism to a country of rice and millet growers.

From the very beginning Mao's strength was that he looked for China's salvation not *outside*, but *inside* China. And strength within China meant China of the peasantry, the ninety per cent on the soil, who carried the most enormous burden of suffering, deprivation, and exploitation upon their shoulders.

In 1923, Mao Tsetung left Hunan for Canton, to attend the Third Congress of the Communist Party held that June. Already it was known that Sun Yatsen was turning towards Soviet Russia. Soon, in 1924, Sun would advocate co-operation with the Communists. The Communist Party decided to co-operate with Sun's party, to form a United Front against the warlords, and to achieve China's reunification. Mao Tsetung now had two roles: one, as a Communist member of the Central Committee of the Party; the second as member in the Executive Bureau of the Kuomintang. His work was co-ordination and liaison between the Communist Party and the Kuomintang; he had been successful in Hunan, though somewhat criticized as a right-winger because of his moderation, so that this pivotal liaison work was entrusted to him. He thus came in contact with Wang Chingwei, the volatile left-wing bomb-throwing intellectual who was to end up as a puppet of Japan, and many other left-wing intellectuals, all of whom were to slide so swiftly into reaction.

Mao records how "previously I felt that only students were

clean, but after living with workers, peasants and soldiers, I felt that such intellectuals had many unclean places in their minds, and the cleanest people were peasants." He also records how his sense of smell changed. "At first only the students and intellectuals smelt good to me, later on it was the peasants who smelt good . . .

"If you want to know the taste of a pear, you must eat the pear . . . if you want to understand something, you must practise it . . ." Justice needs the evidence of all our lives. Mao conceived, in his contacts with these pseudo-revolutionaries, a deep contempt for them. But he listened more than he spoke, and few regarded him as anything but a useful committee worker. So far he had always gone back to his province from Shanghai to put into practice the theoretical conclusions which Chen Tuhsiu, and other leaders of the Communist Party, proposed. In work dangerous as it was difficult he had tested these theories and found them lacking. In his liaison work, at a desk job in Shanghai, in Canton, he was away from the true material of revolution that he knew, the peasantry. Around him were the Shanghai and Peking intellectuals, "returned students" looked upon as "leadership material," all intellectuals talking brilliantly. Mao the practical dreamer began to smoulder, for he alone knew in his bones the peasant's great silence, his fight against hunger and flood and drought and injustice . . .

Many of the returned students spoke German or French, and took part in discussions with the Russian advisers; they held forth at length on revolutionary theory. These therories were based on conditions in Russia and France rather than on conditions in China.

In November 1924, the very month when Sun Yatsen left Canton to go to Peking, at Feng Yuhsiang's invitation, to try for reunification of China without bloodshed, Mao Tsetung fell ill in Shanghai and returned to Hunan. In January 1925 he was voted out of the Central Executive Committee of the Communist Party, a demotion; and that was when his career really began.

What happened to him during that year of liaison work in the cities of Shanghai and Canton? The jobs he handled must have been multifarious, and frustrating. Forever trying to co-ordinate the incompatible, dealing with all the pettinesses of petty opportunists, he probably was aware earlier than most that the façade of unity was but a façade. He must have watched the beginnings of the split between Right and Left, but kept his own counsel, for would he not be accused of sabotage, were he to spread rumours of rift? He must have witnessed all the job-hunting and power-climbing; his co-workers made derogatory remarks about him. Many years later, Edgar Snow, the famous American correspondent, was to ask Mao Tsetung: "In your political life, what was it you found most difficult to cope with?"

And Mao replied: "The internal struggle, right from the beginning." Within the Party there must have been chicaneries, malice, gossip, slackness, sabotage, disregard for the real interests of the people when unscrupulous men were engrossed in ambitious rivalries. Mao later was to comment on this. "To say nothing to people's faces, but to gossip behind their backs . . . intellectuals have become talking-machines, fogetting their duty which is to reconstruct and to create . . ." So off he went, back to his province of Hunan. "It was then that I organized the nucleus of the great peasant movement of that province," said Mao Tsetung. The future had begun.

Destitute peasantry, in open revolt against the established social order, had been the basis of many uprisings in China, the last being the Taiping uprising in the 1850s, which had drawn its greatest strength from the central provinces of Hunan, Mao's province, and adjoining Kiangsi. Many of the peasants there still remembered those twelve years of Taiping rule, then they shared the land, abolished taxation, and women unbound their feet. In the 1920s the peasants were still singing the songs of the Taiping times, for the peasant has mother-root memories, spanning the centuries.

A Kuomintang historian, Tang Leangli, enlightens us on the peasantry in China in the 1920s. "Landlords in China are also merchants, usurers, and administrative officials as well. Landlord-usurers are landlord-merchants, and landlord-politicians. Many are also military and civil officials and tax-farmers; they possess grainstores, oilmills, warehouses and shops." In these words, Tang Leangli expresses what is difficult for many in the West to visualize: despotic feudal power, the personal, direct rule of the many by the few. In this system there is no division between public finance and private wealth. The officers of the state, from high to low, belong to a few powerful families, or land-owning clans, and these have near absolute control over the region, or province where they live.

At every turn the peasant is dominated by the landowner; police, judicial, education systems are all built upon the landlord class, and the taxation system is also run by tax-collectors who are the agents of the landlord-officials. Poor peasants failing to meet their obligations are imprisoned and even tortured by the landlord-official; peasants owning small farms cannot secure credit from the banks, run by landlord-usurers, whereas big landowners can command the trade and usury capital of the locality. The rate of interest on loans is around thirty-six per cent per annum, but when money is tight (as in time of drought, flood, poor crops), reaches sixty per cent. The rate has even reached seventy-two per cent per annum in some provinces . . . The big landowners take advantage of the poverty of the peasants.

Because rents and taxes are chiefly paid in kind (as in Szechuan, Hunan, and Kiangsi provinces), the entire surplus agricultural production accumulates with the few landowner-official-usurer-militarist families who are *also* the provincial authorities, and who thus exercise a complete monopoly over all so-called public funds, derived from taxes, which become their private treasury.

At every turn the burden of taxation, a burden so monstrous as to seem unbelievable, fell on the peasant.

Eighty per cent of the peasantry did not own their land, but signed tenancy agreements for land which was held patriarchally by the clan of the landowner; in appearance therefore there was no individual large landowner; in appearance therefore there was no individual large land-owner, but a joint family, or clan, owning large estates. The land-tax was collected by the tax-farmer, who happened to belong to the same family or clan, or an allied family or clan, as the landowner.

The land-tax, supposed to be assessed only once a year, was sometimes collected two or three times; it varied from ninety-six to three hundred and eighty-seven dollars, gold, per acre a year, and the tenant-farmer paid three-quarters of it, smuggled into his rent in kind.

On top of that were extra taxes to be paid by the tenant-farmer: tax for release from corvee, or forced labour; tax for release from military service; taxes for local grain transport, upkeep of roads and dykes, patrol of highways (by the landlord's privately recruited retainer armies), construction and repair of walls, fairs, markets, support of schools (these schools being built by benevolent landlords, the schoolmaster being one of the landlord's cousins). There was a bandit eradication tax, pacification tax, door and window tax, roof tax . . .

Here are some of the forty-four taxes payable until 1949, in the one province of Kansu:

kettle tax	"purification of countryside" tax
stocking tax	army mule tax
bedding tax	kindling wood tax
wheat bran tax	skin overcoat tax
water-mill tax	miscellaneous expenses tax
copper tax	temporary expenses tax
flour-shop tax	soldier enlistment tax
extraordinary tax	circulation (of money) tax
hog tax	hemp shoe tax
penalty tax	troop movement tax
wealthy house tax	soldier reward tax*

After Chiang Kaishek came to power, none of these taxes was repealed; on the contrary they were increased, both in number and in amount. There was even inaugurated in certain areas a "happy tax," for the purpose of promoting happiness on the day taxes were paid. By 1943 the number of taxes payable in Szechuan province varied between forty and one hundred and forty-eight.

Everywhere in the small towns could be seen the high, square towers of the landlord-pawnbrokers, looking like fortresses, and so they were. These pawnshops were given benevolent names: The Compassionate Palace; The Venue of Mercy. Here the peasant might, by mortgaging his crop, borrow money at thirty-six to seventy-two per cent interest per year.

Since the peasant worked with primitive tools, his productivity was very low; the exploitation he endured not only took away the whole agricultural surplus, but even expropriated a part of the necessary labour, so that he became poorer and poorer, and this factor alone prevented China's entire agricultural and industrial production from ever making progress. The abject poverty of the

* From the list given by O. E. Clubb in *Twentieth-Century China* (Columbia University Press, New York, 1964), p. 187.

countryside was not relieved, but increased after 1927, and *went on increasing up till* 1949.

As a result, the land under cultivation actually *diminished* in size between the years 1921 and 1949; while the population increased, and the amount of peasant exploitation *increased*. By 1949, in some areas, the peasants had paid taxes, collected several times a year instead of once, forty to seventy years in advance.

This was the exploitation which the young Mao Tsetung saw in his own province of Hunan.

"Formerly I had not fully realized the degree of class struggle among the peasantry." And then, in May 1925, due to shooting incidents, the British firing upon and killing demonstrators in Shanghai and in Canton, the Hunan peasantry suddenly became very militant. This is what Mao says; and he was well placed to observe these manifestations. He then began to work in earnest among the peasants studying them closely, organizing peasant unions. The provincial governor sent troops to arrest him and he had to flee back ot Canton in July 1925. He records that "an air of great optimism then pervaded the city and the Kuomintang . . . Chiang Kaishek had been made Commander . . . Wang Chingwei was Chairman of the government, following the death of Sun Yatsen (in March of 1925) in Peking."

For Mao Tsetung, emerging from a deep-sea plunge into the abysses of China's peasant misery to go back to Canton, a city by contrast sophisticated, and now glibly revolutionary, must have been a strange experience in contrast. Few, I think, wanted to listen to his talk of the woes of Hunan peasants, and if they listened, it cannot have seemed to them as important as what was happening in Canton at that time: the marching and the parading; the arming of workers' militias; the speeches, the flags, and especially the enormous strike then taking place in the neighbouring port of Hongkong, a British colony. This strike had been called because of the shooting of students in Shanghai, and the machine-gunning of demonstrators in Canton, by British troops.

The strike was to paralyse the port of Hongkong for fully sixteen months; one hundred and thirty thousand workers of Hongkong, downing tools, left the British colony and flocked to Canton, where they were given heroes' welcome. Any time now, it seemed, the British would leave Hongkong, steam away . . . but after a few weeks things became difficult in Canton. This was because the customs revenues and the salt revenues were all controlled by the Western Powers, who withheld all funds from the Canton government; it became difficult to feed and to pay so many strikers, both in Canton and those remaining in Hongkong.

Mao was now put in charge of training organizers for rural areas; a disused temple was turned into a school for cadres, and he trained three hundred and eighteen of them. At the same time, he became editor of a journal called *Political Weekly*. This was a Kuomintang journal, and thus again Mao filled a double, or liaison, role. "I was writing more and more, and assuming special responsibilities for peasant work in the Communist Party."

On the basis of his previous sojourn and observations among the Hunan peasantry, in the first half of 1925, Mao now wrote the extremely important document: An Analysis of Classes in Chinese Society. For the first time Marxism was used to analyse the social structure of feudal, semi-colonial Chinese society. And the analysis is so fundamental to the subsequent development of the Chinese revolution that no modern student of history can neglect it.

This essay was written in March 1926; "there were then two deviations in the Party," says Mao. One, represented by Chen Tuhsiu, the secretary-general of the Communist Party, was the capitulationist, or right-wing deviation; Chen himself was extremely anxious to co-operate with the Kuomintang bourgeoisie, and being a city-bred intellectual and a mandarin, found it easy to forget all about the peasantry. It was this line which was almost to destroy the Revolution, and sacrifice thousands of lives, by disarming the workers for the sake of a non-existent and impossible unity with the right-wing bourgeoisie of the Kuomintang. The other line was an extremely Left one, concerned only with armed insurrection, launching attacks and capturing big cities. It likewise forgot the peasantry.

In his "Analysis," Mao Tsetung demanded a radical land policy for the peasantry, "our chief ally in the Revolution."

It was the first time since the inception of the Chinese Communist Party in 1921 that a creative application of the principles of Marxism to the concrete problems of the Chinese situation was being made; it was to remain an example, to all future party members, of how to ally theory with practice. "No talking without investigation first."

Mao's study, needless to say, was not welcome; Chen Tuhsiu opposed the opinions expressed in it, denied that a radical land policy, and the vigorous organization of the rural areas under the Communist Party, was a necessity; and refused publication of the essay in the Central Executive organs of publicity.

The Analysis was published in the *Peasant Monthly* of Canton, this being the magazine of the school where Mao taught and trained cadres for work in the peasant movement. "I began to disagree with Chen Tuhsiu's policy about this time, and we drew further apart."

And now it was March 1926, a year since the death of Sun Yatsen. In that month occurred Chiang's first coup, the trial balloon of counter-revolution, when he arrested naval officers, Russian advisers, and Chou Enlai, thus testing the mettle of the Communist Party and its head, Chen Tuhsiu. The latter in his concern for unity allowed the trade union militias to be disarmed; upon which an ostensible reconciliation, on Chiang's own terms, occurred. Chiang was now on his way to power; the Northern Expedition began, swept headlong to the Great River, and everywhere, without waiting to be told, the peasants rose and started their own liberation. Mao, in Canton at the time of the coup and later, was ordered back to Hunan province, to dampen down the ardour of the peasant movement, which, Chen said, was threatening the "good relationship" he felt was imperative with the Kuomintang, and getting out of control.

In December 1926 a conference of peasant delegates held at Changsha passed several resolutions; confiscation of land from the landlords began on a large scale; the peasants formed their own militias, courts of justice, protection units. In that autumn Mao, his mind prey to conflict, was ordered by the Party to "curb and bridle" the untameable peasantry. Already, the previous year, he had begun to express his doubts in a poem:

> Stark autumn, northward flowing stream
> Past Organge Grove isle; ten thousand hills
> Crimson with forest-hiding leaf.
> Fair the green river racing a hundred boats;
> Eagles sky-poised, fish shallows-still,
> All under vast heaven vying in freedom.
> I stare at the wholeness, bewildered:
> "Which is the path Mankind must follow?"
> Lo, the crowded turmoil of gone years,
> When with many friends I first came here!

Friends talented, audacious in talk,
Impassioned of our mountains and rivers,
Wealth and honours to them worthless as dust.
And memory stirs,
Of the rapid water straining, straining,
While our boat swept past.

In Mao's mind must have been gnawing doubt, travail; what he felt was right for the Chinese Revolution, and the theoretical bureaucratic, and capitulative directives he received from the Central Executive Committee were becoming ever more different approaches to revolution. He must have felt that much of all the word-spinning which went on counted very little in front of the vivid realities, the rebellions of flesh and blood, the enormous exhilarating excitement of these masses of peasants, the many-millioned, downtrodden as the grass, suddenly rising and demonstrating this tremendous power of change, overturning heaven and earth, building a new world; before the inventive strength and essential justice of the peasant unions he must have felt carried away, in a great leap of cognition. And this springs out of his next study, the famous: "An investigation into the peasant movement in Hunan", which is a poem of peasant revolution:

> I saw and heard many strange things, of which I had hitherto been unaware . . . All talk against the peasant movement must be *speedily* set right. All the wrong measures taken by the revolutionary authorities concerning the peasant movement must be *speedily* changed. Only thus can the future of the revolution be benefited.

What were those "wrong measures"? They were based on Chen Tuhsiu's assessment that "if the bourgeois-democratic revolution loses the assistance of the bourgeoisie, it will cease to have any social basis in the revolutionary cause." Not to antagonize the bourgeoisie, Chen had taken care to water down his peasant programme, promising not land reform, but only *alleviation* of land rent and taxation. As a result, there had been no real programme for the peasantry. Now he again ordered that the peasant unions stop the peasants from going too far.

Mao, exalted, passionate, wrote:

> The present upsurge of the peasant movement is a colossal event. Very soon several hundred million peasants will ride

like a mighty storm, like a hurricane . . . no power, however great, will be able to hold them back.

There are three alternatives for every revolutionary comrade: to march at their head and lead them; to trail behind them, gesticulating and criticizing; to stand in their way and oppose them.

EVERY CHINESE IS FREE TO CHOOSE, BUT EVENTS WILL FORCE YOU TO CHOOSE QUICKLY.

This prose poem, penned in the heat of the peasant uprising, shows that Mao realized that he was witnessing the most important thing occurring in China, more important than anything he had seen in the cities, which so impressed others. Here, here was the heart of the matter, here was the immense hurricane power, ready to destroy, rebuild a new heaven and earth.

The gentry say: "It's terrible." But this is a marvellous feat, never before achieved, the rural forces of democracy overthrowing the rural forces of feudalism, and this is the REAL OBJECTIVE OF THE REVOLUTION.

To reject them (the poor peasants) is to reject the Revolution. To attack them is to attack the Revolution.

One can imagine the effect this had upon the Central Executive Committee and its elegant secretary-general, Chen Tuhsiu. "Insubordinate, saboteur," he must have shouted.

Mao's investigation was thrown out by the Central Executive Committee at its Congress in May 1927. "I was very dissatisfied with the party policy then, especially towards the peasant movement. If the movement had been better organized and armed . . . there would have been an earlier and more powerful development of the revolutionary bases throughout the country."

At the Congress, Mao was deprived of the right to vote. With its only spokesman muzzled, the peasantry was now betrayed in order to "appease" the Kuomintang; the Congress passed some placatory phrases in its "resolutions," but this in no way satisfied the peasants, and neither was the right wing placated. It had already tasted blood in that April's Shanghai massacre; it had its leader, Chiang Kaishek; it had money and guns. Fourteen thousand workers had been slaughtered, twenty-five thousand more were to die swiftly in various cities that summer; and still Chen Tuhsiu spoke of unity, and still he ordered the peasant militia to be co-operative, and deplored their "violence" and enjoined them to lay down their weapons, if any . . .

In May 1927, on the outskirts of Changsha, a mass of about twenty thousand peasants previously disarmed by their own leadership, were pitilessly machine-gunned. In late June, the so-called "Red" government at Wuhan began to vie with Chiang Kaishek's Nanking government as to who would kill more Communists; as Wang Chingwei later was to explain: "Our only fault in Wuhan was that we did not get rid of the Communists sooner."

In this race as to who could kill more, the Nanking government easily won in the cities; then the armies of both Nanking and Wuhan got together, and did some more slaughter everywhere in the countryside of the provinces under their sway. Meanwhile, in other provinces, where there had also been sporadic peasant risings, the feudal landlords were now back; they began to revenge themselves on their hapless tenants; in Szechuan, too, the old warlords and the young officers, who had been frightened that Revolution might come their way, now vied with each other in "mowing down the grass."

No one will ever know how many were thus slaughtered.

In his autobiography, Mao says: "Many Communist leaders were now ordered by the Party to leave the country, to go to Russia, or to other places of safety . . . I was ordered to go to Szechuan. I persuaded Chen Tuhsiu to send me back to Hunan instead."

Hunan was, at the time, perhaps the most unhealthy province in China; it was riddled with Kuomintang armies; it was in Hunan that the peasants had been most militant; and it was there that the killing was at its worst. Mao himself tells of a narrow escape he had; but he still went back to his own province, Hunan.

Chen Tuhsiu, seeing things fall apart, now suffered from acute vacillation, gave orders only to rescind them. "After ten days, Chen ordered me hastily to return." This was an order to Mao to return to the Party Politburo, now in hiding in Shanghai. However, on Auust 7th, at last, Chen Tuhsiu was deposed, and the whole line of the Party was changed officially; unofficially, it had already been broken. "I was active in this decision (to depose Chen and to change the Party line)," reports Mao. "A new line was adopted, all co-operation with the Kuomintang was given up – and now the long, open struggle for power began."

CHAPTER FOUR

On August 1st, 1927, Chu Teh with Chou Enlai and other Communists led an armed uprising in the city of Nanchang. This action, though it failed, had great importance, because it was a clean break with Chen's policy of giving in to the right wing, and it was also the beginning of what was to become the Red Army.

In September we had succeeded in organizing widespread uprisings through the peasant unions of Hunan, and the first units of a peasant worker army were formed; recruits drawn from the peasantry, the miners, and insurrectionist troops which revolted against the Wuhan government when it surrendered to Chiang Kaishek . . . this we called the First Division of the First Peasants' and Workers' Army.

This was the beginning of the famous Autumn Harvest uprising in Hunan, which took place between September 5th and 18th. But the Terror was on. Everywhere, in a flood, the armies of Chiang Kaishek closed in upon the pitiful small bands of the Communists. Mao got together nine hundred men, and started to retreat.

The little army moved southward through Hunan . . . it had to break its way through thousands of troops and fought many battles, with many reverses; discipline was poor, political training low, there were many desertions.

Throughout that September, repudiated by the Central Committee, surrounded by Kuomintang armies, Mao wandered through southern Hunan. He was dismissed from the Politburo and from the Party Front Committee; the Hunan branch of the Committee also attacked him, calling his men "the rifle movement". "It seemed they preferred a wait-and-see attitude," said Mao, ironically.

Later many of his detractors also went over to Chiang Kaishek. Mao did not lose his head, nor his heart. "We held our army together, feeling certain that we were following the correct line ."

And so, leading the nine hundred, Mao retreated through Hunan, along its borders with Kiangsi province, following the foot-hills of a massif of mountains called Chingkangshan, or Well Ridge Mountain, a name now become famous in revolutionary history; there he was to nurture back to life and to decision the Communist Party of China. There, later, Chu Teh and many others were to join him; there the policy of the Red bases was formulated, and Mao began to move in the direction, completely his own, which made it possible for the Chinese Revolution to rise from wreckage to triumph.

"Of course we follow him. If he had been wrong we would not have followed him, that autumn, when we climbed Chingkangshan mountain."

And, perhaps not so strangely, the concentration of the defeated and scattered forces of Revolution took place in the regions which had also seen various campaigns during the Taiping peasant revolutions,* in the mountainous country on the border of Hunan and Kiangsi provinces, a massif well known for its colossal stronghold qualities and desolate seclusion.

Mao's selection of Well Ridge Mountain was not fortuitous. It is safe to surmise that he must have heard about it in his wanderings, when on foot he covered the entire region. Handed down by oral tradition, the places where the Taiping had fought must have been a topic of peasants' tales in the evening, all labour done.

In Chingkangshan Mao founded the first Red base and incidentally saved the Communist Party for the next revolution. It was there that he began to develop the theory of revolution in a peasant society, and wrote: "a single spark can light a prairie fire." The big tree of the Revolution of 1925–7 had been felled; its seed sprouted again, in Chingkangshan mountain.

Mao wrote:

> So it came about that a sudden attack was perfidiously launched against the Chinese Communist Party and the people, and the great dynamic and vigorous revolution was crushed. Thereupon unity was replaced by civil war, democracy by dictatorship, and a China full of brightness by a China covered by darkness. But the Chinese Communist Party and the Chinese people were neither cowed nor conquered nor exterminated. They picked themselves up, wiped off the blood, buried their fallen comrades and went into battle again.

* See The Crippled Tree.

To Chingkangshan, Well Ridge Mountain, I went in the rainy October of 1964, to see for myself the place where Mao Tsetung and his small band had gone to earth in the rainy October of 1927; the very month when Chiang Kaishek went sailing to Japan, from whence he was to return in November to marry Soong Meiling, to become China's Generalissimo, and to begin ten years of war against Mao Tsetung.

To reach Chingkangshan, I first flew to Nanchang, the capital city of Kiangsi province. There, on August 1st, 1927, Chou Enlai had led a clean and splendid fight, making a thorough break with the vacillating leadership of Chen Tuhsiu and some of the foreign advisers "more attuned to conditions in Russia or France than in China." The hotel where Chou Enlai, Yeh Ting, Ho Lung and Chu Teh resided when they planned this feat is now a museum; all is kept as it was, the outmoded furniture, the beds with their mosquito nets, the copper washbasins. In one room, on the wall, is an enlarged photograph of Chou Enlai when twenty-four years old, on the boat which took him to France in November 1920. Who would have thought such a darkly handsome, romantic face would become that of a revolutionary? Behind him only the sea, and the ship's railing.

Actually the uprising was based on orders as unrealistic as Chen Tuhsiu's commands had been, but whereas Chen was afraid to fight, the new line was at the opposite extreme. There was, at the time, a dominant idea that the capture of cities was of the utmost importance. Nanchang was captured and later abondoned, but Chu Teh and the other Communists were set to assault other cities, with great loss of men. Finally this extreme policy also had to be abandoned.

The next morning, in the fluffy autumn rain, we set off by car from Nanchang, crossing the Kan river by ferry to Chieh An, where Mao Tsetung had arrived one October day in 1927, with his little troop of men, exhausted and hungry.

Along the road were camphor trees, new cotton fields, pilot fields of alfalfa to improve the red earth which bedevils a good part of Kiangsi province; earth rich in iron oxide, poor for crops. Here were the work-and-study university colleges; trekking along the road long lines of middle-school students, boys and girls, carrying their bedding and luggage on their backs, going to labour in the commune fields. Upon the slopes the tea shrubs, yielding tea oil for cooking.

Now a wide good motor road runs to the mountain massif which housed the spark of revolution, Chingkangshan, though in 1927 only a pathway existed. Our car climbed amid a tumble of hills, eroded soil and weathered rock. And now the fog rolled in upon us, smothering us. We got out to walk a little to get the taste of what it must have been like, climbing in the rain. The ground was pure glue underfoot, clawing, clayey mud, bronze and red, slippery and dangerous. "I climbed this in straw slippers, that's the only way," said Ko the writer, who was with me, and had been a twelve-year-old in 1927, when he joined the Red Army at Chingkangshan.

Steep cliffs tumbled leprous rock, thick forests clustered behind wood-hiding trees. The rain soaked us through in a few minutes and undrifting milk strata of fog clotted the sky upon us. We stood at a certain point called Huangyangchieh, where Mao had had lookouts posted, watching the wide plain. The massif was a huge citadel made up of mountain chains overlapping each other, about twenty-five miles wide and a hundred and sixty miles in circumference; its name, Well Ridge Mountain, was apt, for it consisted of spurs and crests in the shape of an irregular circular ridge in the centre of which lay a sunken plain, somewhat like the enormously enlarged crater of an extinct volcano. In this basin bottom, or plain, was a hamlet called Tzeping, the headquarters of Mao for some months, The highest of the many peaks in this mountain knot was 5,500 feet above sea level. On the last day I was there the sun came out at last and I could see the ranges rearing away like wild horses, their slopes forming five long and narrow gullies, tortuous passes to the surrounding plains. Inside the massif more paths wound, north to south, east to west; they had been used by salt smugglers for centuries, and were to be used by Mao and his men, giving them a far greater mobility than was apparent. In fact, from Tzeping, the centre of a five-pointed star, Mao could control his surroundings for forty miles each way; and thus early on the stronghold became the centre of a network of poitical agitation, and for the collection of information, in all the surrounding counties.

When Mao reached Chingkangshan, it was already occupied by two groups of peasants turned bandits, numbering six hundred men. How these bandits and their chieftains were incorporated into Mao's small Red troops must be a lively example of the persuasion technique which forms part of Mao's belief in man. "Education, not slaughter – persuasion, not liquidation." "The two chieftains became regimental commanders and I was Army Commander," Mao contents himself with noting in his autobiography. They later reverted to banditry, unfortunately, and were dispatched by their own men.

The total number of inhabitants within the five passes of Chingkangshan was about two thousand; they were among the most miserable in China. They used flints to obtain fire; they carried everything on their own backs. They lived in small straggly hamlets, in huts with bark roofs and mud walls of clay mixed with split bamboo. The hamlets clung to small rocky platforms among the tortuous valleys. No wheel had come here. In the mountain caves were tigers, boars, leopards, jackals and wolves. On the lower slopes were herbal plants, and at the mountain base rice, beans and groundnuts were grown. Among the two thousand a good many were ambulant carriers, going up and down to the plains and back again to the villages. Mao mentioned that most of the inhabitants of this mountain massif were Hakkas; settlers of the Guest people, extending in a wide band across the central provinces, part of that migration* which came too late, when the best land had already been settled, and therefore had to make do with poorer mountainous ground. The system of salt peddling, from which my own family derives its origin, is actually salt smuggling, due to the government monopoly of salt, and Chingkangshan was a main pathway for the traffic. The clan spirit is strong among these disinherited, all the inhabitants of one village bearing the same family name.

This was an ideal hideout, on the border between two provinces, at the intersection between six counties, four belonging to Kiangsi province and two to Hunan province.

Said Ko, guerrilla turned writer: "We chose our revolutionary bases at the frontier or borders of two provinces; when we had to run from one place to another we always chose to run along the border line. The provincial and warlord troops avoided the borders; most of them were concentrated to hold warlord power round the cities, in the plains where there was food and loot. Border fighting might lead to actual collission with the troops of another warlord, something to be avoided if possible. The jurisdiction of the magistrate-landlord was weaker at the fringe of their counties than in the centre. We benefited from all these weaknesses of our adversary. All the Red bases were established in wild, mountainous regions, difficult of access, where jurisdic-

* See *The Crippled Tree*.

tion was weak and open to dispute, where we could always, should the troops of one province be mustered against us, escape into another province."

The problem of food supply was solved by the villages at the mountain foot, where fertile rice plains lay. Transport up the mountains could be organized by the Hakka carriers. In this transport of food both Mao Tsetung and Chu Teh took part. Chu Teh's bamboo pole for hauling rice sacks is preserved in the mountain museum at Tzeping.

The five passes could easily be defended by outposts, manned by a few men, overlooking entire sections of the valleys and the tree-denuded fields.

We stood in the hamlet of San Wan, where the central massif begins, and looked at the pathway, winding its way across the plain. "From that direction Mao came walking," said the old peasant, now in charge of what had been the clan house, and for a time the hospital for the Red Army's wounded. "I saw him, he was so tall, very thin, those days. He came to me and hailed me: "Old cousin, what is your name?" It was morning time, they walked by night, then, and in bad weather. He settled here in San Wan, to rest for ten days or more. There were many wounded men, and all were very hungry."

"Out of defeat, we shall grasp victory. Out of calamity, pluck forth good luck."

Thus did Mao speak to the discouraged men who had followed him. And there for the first time he enuniciated his thought, not to the intellectuals of the Party, but to the peasants. "It is not the cities that are important now, it is the countryside."

They must have stared at him, out of the depth of their despair. About two hundred of his nine hundred men left him, shaking their heads: "The Revolution has failed. Each on his own now."

But Mao went on. Every day he talked to those who remained. He drew up a plan for survival. This was called: "The readjustment at San Wan."

For now he was to start the most important work of all: the restructuring of the Chinese Communist Party, ideologically and physically, testing and then carrying out what he thought was the correct line: the organization of a Red Army, made up chiefly of peasants, that enormous reservoir of manpower. And the work done at Chingkangshan is of such tremendous significance today, because it not only laid down the basic groundwork for the Chinese Revolution, but it applies also to all the peasant revolutions now brewing and simmering and about to burst, in Asia and Latin America, and later in Africa.

For today the thoughts which Mao expounded, beginning at Chingkangshang, are extending on a global scale. Two-thirds of humanity, still deprived, still exploited, are the new peasantry of the world; above them lord the affluent, exploiting metropolises, the cities, of the remaining third. The theme of Chingkangshan, the meaning of Chingkangshan, revolution in the countryside, bases for revolution in the countryside, the countryside surrounding and finally winning the cities, is beginning to govern the history of the century to come, to shape the lives of our descendants, as ours were shaped by what was done at Chingkangshan.

There is something almost biblical in the evocation of Chingkangshan, Mao's high mountain, compelling us to memory of other passions, illuminations of other dreamers going into high mountains, untempted by all the kingdoms of the world, to find a new way of life for humanity.

Mao Tsetung, being of this scientific age, a modern in a fuedal country, not only meditated, but made Chingkangshan a laboratory and testing ground, measuring there, with scientific objectivity, the dimensions and limits of his reshaping of China.

He began by giving regular lectures, half classes, half debates, carried out untiringly almost every afternoon, models for those discussion meetings which later took place at every level in China after 1949. Western writers have indicted them with culpable ignorance, calling them brainwashing. They were actually the beginnings of education in democracy. For in a country where there has never been democracy, where people have never been allowed to discuss anything openly, nor to believe that one could persuade and change man by word of mouth, that one could conquer hearts by persuasion, exhort and finally change spirits by talk, this was done by Mao Tsetung. And one day people will say that it was Mao who taught the real meaning of democracy to China and gave a voice and a platform to the millions who were never heard before.

From word to action, Mao went on. He proceeded to educate his band of peasants, deserters, and bandits, not only into a disciplined army but into a legion of apostles of revolution. His writing shows the clearness with which he tackled the problem of turning such riffraff into disciplined, honest, educated and ardent revolutionaries.

> The proportion of vagabond elements is large, and there are great masses of vagabonds in China, especially in the southern provinces. Some want to expand the armies by recruiting almost anyone. But we must intensify education, to counter the vagabond outlook, draw active workers and peasants experienced in political thought into the ranks of the army to change its composition and deepen the agricultural reform.
> We must not have a roving bandit army, but a truly revolutionary army, every man a revolutionary.

The reorganization of the army into cells, units, regiments, was done in minute detail by Mao himself.

"He would drill the men, then talk to them; he sat on this stone, a book in his hand, always a book about him, and watched the men being drilled. In the evening, again, he would talk to them." When he was not drilling or talking, he was "sitting on a stone, reading a book, or in his room, writing." He forgot to eat. His gaunt tallness was seen everywhere. Some of the soldiers called him "old cousin" and would ask him to hold their gun for them when they carried rice up the mountain. He would do so, standing there, holding their gun for them."

Mao laid down that the Red Army must be a politically educated army, and not merely a careerist instrument of war. He built cells at the lowest level; each consisting of three, not two, party members. "The officers do not beat the men, they receive equal treatment; soldiers enjoy freedom of assembly and speech; cumbersome formalities are done away with; the account books can be inspected by all . . . these measures are satisfactory to the soldiers."

Later, in encounters with the Kuomintang who massively attacked his mountain bastion, he was to receive deserters, take prisoners.

> The newly captured soldiers in particular feel our army and the Kuomintang are worlds apart; though in material life they are worse off in the Red army than in the White army, spiritually . . . they are liberated. The same soldier, not brave in the Kuomintang army yesterday, becomes very

brave in the Red army today, because of the impact of *democracy*.

For this was democracy, the only democracy possible for the Chinese soldier, a peasant captured while at work by kidnappers, pressganged, starved, beaten, fighting not knowing why. He responded to it, gave himself body and soul to it, to this new heaven and earth, where he was, at last, a man, not a beast to be maimed and left to die.

The average soldier needs six months or a year's training to fight, but ours, recruited yesterday, fight by courage alone.

In China, not only the people need democracy, but the army needs it too. The democratic system in an army is an important weapon for destroying the fuedal mercenary army . . .

Mao held that an army is an ideological and spiritual force which must destroy the old and build the new. To achieve this, each man had to be utterly convinced not only that what he was doing was right, but that he was completely involved in it, whatever the sacrifices he personally had to make. All new ideas, including Christianity, have advanced only because they mattered so much, to men and women so convinced of their validity, that they died to uphold them.

Mao split his men into small groups, set them to carry out in practice his theory of a revolutionary, Red, army, both a fighting unit and an ideological weapon. Guerrilla activities and revolutionary activism are inseparable."

Since nothing is worse for an army than inaction, the troops were soon put to work. They planted rice, or went down to help the peasants, or to work on abandoned lands. Mao established courses to teach them to read and write.

In November Mao attacked Chaling, the district capital of one of the six districts in Kiangsi. Chaling was easily taken, the first Red government was then set up. At first, it did not work well. "Mao himself was not there; but stayed at the centre, in Tzeping. As a result, some of the troops, too raw, did not behave well. It was hard for them, accustomed to the fuedal system, to the "roving bandit" habits, to start applying the lessons Mao had drilled into them for a fortnight. They soon reverted to bad habits; requisitioned large houses, called the merchants' guild which ran the economic life of the agglomeration and notified the merchants of their requirements in food and money, behaved in the typical 'feudal' style, hallowed by time and custom."

Mao heard of this and immediately dissolved the "revolutionary committee" which the troops had organized. He ordered that a "revolutionary government of workers, peasants, and soldiers" take its place, and set out to reorganize the soviet in Chaling.

Chaling was therefore the first "experiment" for the new type of army, a type unknown till then in China. About seven weeks later, the warlords of Hunan province, where Chaling county lay, turned their attention to it and started an offensive. About fifty thousand men were mustered for this. The Red battalion retreated up the mountain in December 1927.

From the experience of Chaling, Mao reinforced his army code.

When fighting the landlords, get money from them, do not pressure the chamber of commerce; for the small and middle merchants, being less well protected, have to pay up the bulk of the requisition, the big ones go more or less scot free.

Never take anything from the people, not even a sweet potato.

Indoctrinate, organize the masses, to establish the power of a worker-peasant-soldier government.

When confiscating from the landlords, give everything to the people, keep nothing for yourselves.

He redefined the three main tasks of the Red Army: political indoctrination, social and military action must be combined and performed *at once and together*.

In January 1928 Mao went to Suichuan, another county within the scope of his mountain stronghold. His army propaganda units spread into every hamlet of the district. But the people were afraid and did not dare to approach the army. "You speak well, but how can this be done?" they said.

This time Mao himself was with the troops. "We must not only talk to the people, we must convince them by action." The Red Army led the people in the fight against the landlord-usurer-magistrate. But even when led to the granaries of their former master the peasants did not dare to take any grain. The propaganda units distributed the grain, taking nothing for themselves, but the peasants refused it; they were afraid of retaliation. "What

102

will happen to us when you leave us?" they said to the Red Army.

The propaganda units sometimes carried the grain, secretly, by night, and such food as pork, chicken, etc., to the peasants' homes. "And at depth of night, sure that no one would see and carry out revenge on them, the peasants accepted what we brought."

Slowly the soldiers began to understand what it meant to be a Red Army man; slowly confidence was built up, and the peasants, instead of fearing the army, began to look forward to the troops' arrival. After a time they gathered enough trust to follow the soldiers to the landlords' houses, though at first keeping well at the back; a little while later they would wait, with baskets and bags, "when they saw us come with the red flag, the crowd would gather, even the children. They knew that after the talking we would go on to the landlords' houses and requisition the grain."

"Thus did we train the people here to justice. Before that they had been so oppressed and terrorized, they did not even dare to hope for justice."

At Suichuan a peasant named Wang was appointed as head of the local government. A militia brigade was established for the county. The revolutionary work spread, organization of women's and youths' units, so that in every hamlet there was now a small nucleus of Red power.

Again collecting data and summarizing experience from this second test of his theories, Mao announced the six basic principles of the Red Army, which later were to become eight principles:

1. Put back all doors when you leave a house (doors are wooden boards, in China used as beds, to sleep on).
2. Rice-stalk mattresses must all be bundled up again and returned.
3. Be courteous in speech, and help people when you can.
4. Give back all borrowed things; even if only a needle.
5. Pay for all things broken, even if only a chopstick.
6. Don't help yourself and search for things when people are not in their houses.

Two more were to be added later, by Lin Piao, now Commander-in-Chief of the Red Army.

7. Pay for all you buy.
8. Be clean, establish latrines away from people's houses.

And now the winter was over, the first winter of Chingkang-shan. Food supplies, communication lines were assured for a while. Spring was beginning, and Mao got ready to receive a visitor, a guest, the Hakka from Szechuan, ex-warlord, ex-opium smoker, Chu Teh.

Chu Teh, with Chou Enlai, had led the Nanchang uprising of August 1st, memorable because it was a clean break with the previous policy of defeatism and moral surrender. Nanchang was held for a week and then given up. Chu Teh then led the small, outnumbered troops, taking and losing cities, hunted by thousands of Kuomintang and feudal troops, encircled time and again; he succeeded in taking Canton in December but could not hold it. Fighting his way through enemy territory, in an epic so far inadequately covered, Chu Teh finally went to earth in a border area, and strove to plant a Red base there. And now, through Mao Tsetung's brother, who acted as courier, he decided to link up with the base at Chingkangshan. Picking up what was left of his soldiers, fighting in true guerrilla style, eluding all attacks against him, by forced marches, he reached the Well Ridge Mountain on April 28th, 1928.

On a flat plain in front of the Dragon River which runs by Ningkang, one of the six counties accessible to the Red base, Mao and Chu Teh met, prelude to a friendship and partnership of thirty years. "Because they both eat red peppers," my Uncle Liu would have exulted. But it was more than a liking for red pepper, it was a comradeship in dedication to the cause of Revolution. Chu was forty-two, Mao thirty-five, at the time they met.

Actually Chu Teh arrived first, and waited for Mao, who was not there at the time, and who then walked to meet him, crossing the small wooden bridge over the Dragon river. On May 4th, a large "joy meeting" was held at Ningkang. Here was inaugurated the Fourth Red Army, with Chu Teh as Commander-in-Chief, Mao as Party Representative. Including cadres, recruits, and other personnel, twelve thousand attended the meeting that day.

Thus started the Red Army, named at first the Fourth because there were supposed to be three others, in other parts of China. "And also to make the enemy believe we were stronger than we really were," said Ko the writer to me as we paced the historic plain, and the Dragon river near by purred mildly over its stones. It was nowhere near army strength; consisting then only of the 11th, 12th and 13th regiments. A humorous and (at the time) slim young man, a Szechuanese returned student from France, named Chen Yi, who had joined the Communist Party in Paris, was in command of the 13th regiment. Today he is the Foreign Minister of China, and portly, though still full of that infectious gaiety which makes him such exhilarating company. The tales of his personal adventures and mishaps on Well Ridge Mountain, when he was officer commanding the 13th regiment, are full of zest and hearty mimicry, like Szechuan opera. "I had eight hundred men, armed with bamboo spears which we pretended were rifles. But there was not one rifle among us." Later, in the cold comfort of Yenan, after the Long March, Chen Yi would convulse glum audiences with his parodies of Chiang Kaishek orating, and other Nanking government pundits.

On the worst days at Well Ridge Mountain, Chen Yi's natural sense of fun must have helped to lift spirits. "He used to buy a little red pepper and cook Szechuan dishes for everyone, unfortunately all other ingredients except red pepper were missing." Other troops than Chu Teh's also began to straggle into the mountain sanctuary. "But with so many more people to feed at the Red base, living conditions in Chingkangshan became bad. By the winter of 1928 the soldiers had no winter clothes, and food was scarce. The soldiers shouted: "Down with capitalism and eat squash," squash made from sweet potato being the gruel fed to pigs, which was the only available food. The economic blockade by the Chiang Kaishek forces became very harsh. There was a great dearth of all necessities, as well as cash. "Salt, cloth and medicines have been scarce and dear," wrote Mao in October 1928. "The Red Army has to fight the enemy and to provision itself at one and the same time. The soldiers are undernourished, many are ill, the wounded in the hospitals are worse off."

The Red Army had now swollen to twelve thousand men; but of these four thousand were not in a fit state to fight, so that only eight thousand were actually fighting men. Their equipment consisted of two machine-guns, one mortar, and about six hundred rifles. Mao spent much time at the temporary hospitals, set up in ancestral sanctuaries and clan houses. He wrote to the Hunan branch committee for medicines and medical officers; but all supplies had to run the blockade and few reached him.

None the less, after Chu Teh's arrival a cadre school was organized on the same lines as had been organized by Mao Tsetung in Canton. Drilling of troops began in earnest, Mao and

Chu consulting on the strategy to be followed. The troops were taught night fighting, body to body combat and other tactics of guerrilla war. Emphasis was placed on speed, the lightning attack. In one such onslaught upon a county feudal army the troops ran about fifty miles in under a day, and scored a significant victory over a too confident feudal commander. Three tobacco leaves, a pair of straw sandals were rewards for the swiftest, the ones who ran and fought best.

Towards the population Mao enforced a policy of moderation, refraining from burning and killing. He also ordered and saw the order obeyed that in battle the wounded enemy must not be ill-treated or killed, or harmed in any way, and this rule has since been a very strict one, rigidly enforced by the Red Army. "The foe must be re-educated. Mao Tsetung never liked killing, he never liked to shed blood, and when he had to fight, he preferred that the enemy should surrender, and be re-educated. That is why he taught us always to allow an opening, a way out, that the enemy should repent, rather than die. These words, almost biblical, were uttered by Ko, who had lived under such a rule and to whom it was habit. "Even criminals condemned to death nowadays have a two-year reprieve. But it was not so before Mao Tsetung taught us."

None of Mao Tsetung's political oppenents have been put to death; today in Peking the men in the Party who most opposed him, who were responsible for grievous losses, are still there, in positions of security and comfort if not in power. Even Li Lisan, and others, who demoted Mao, or punished him, go about freely, still members of the Party. And it is this personal magnanimity which must be understood if any objective account of Mao the man is attempted. His advice to the Algerians, when Ferhat Abbas came to see him to ask for help, was the same: "Do not kill needlessly; do not kill so much, wanton killing is not a good weapon in revolutionary war."

"Whenever enemy forces are captured, they are divided into those who wish to stay, and those who wish to leave. The latter are given travelling expenses, and set free." This policy gradually shattered the Kuomintang propaganda that "the Communists kill everyone on sight." Mao instituted the practice of soldiers giving "farewell parties to new brothers." Which meant that they gave farewell parties to prisoners of war they released to go home. And this made the Kuomintang soldiers weep, for they were not accustomed to any kindness.

Mao now summarized the experiences gained in battle in his famous dicta, the basics of guerrilla war:

> The enemy advances; we retreat.
> The enemy halts; we harass.
> The enemy slackens; we attack.
> The enemy retreats; we pursue.

Mao lectured on the art of war. He made the soldiers practise the "wave" assult tactics, the "biting the enemy's tail" tactics, the mass agitation tactics, the "fishing net" tactics, many of them based, it is said, on the guerrilla art practised by the Niens, those mounted peasant warriors of the nineteenth century.* A committee was set up to study land reform; upon its findings, and the experiences of land reform accumulated at Chingkangshan. Mao based his further socio-economic writings. He now drew up distinctions between poor, middle, rich peasants and landlords, analysed the errors committed in the previous years, and definitely instituted a policy of benovolence and unrestricted trade towards the merchant class.

The Party Central Executive led a precarious underground existence in Shanghai, and so did the provincial branch of the Communist Party in Hunan. But now the precarious unity between Chiang Kaishek and the apparently reconciled warlords was breaking down, and the Communist Executive thought this a propitious time for counter-attack. The Hunan Committee issued orders to Mao Tsetung and Chu Teh to come down from the mountain, to attack and capture the city of Changsha. The mania for "city taking" was not spent; mulishly, the "Left" line went on, organizing pointless uprisings, and this led to reprisal executions of hundreds of hapless workers and peasants, so that instead of winning support, reluctance to obey the orders grew.

Mao in his mountain retreat, apparently unmoving, seemed to these foolhardy Communists as "needing directives"; he was "isolated", they said, unaware of trends . . .

The Party constantly sent Mao reprimands, because he did not do enough burning and killing, was too moderate and lenient towards reactionaries. Mao wrote: "In March 1928 the representatives of the Huanan Special Committee criticized us for leaning to the Right . . . for not having done enough burning and killing. As regards our plan of action . . . the Hunan Committee

* See *The Crippled Tree*

107

changed its mind *three times* within a few weeks in June and July . . ."

Faced with the order to take Changsha city, Mao recorded that the Kuomintang forces in the province were strong; that the hold of the landlords and the landlord-officials on the peasantry there was stable; he envisaged much peril in the undertaking. But two party members came to Well Ridge Mountain, bearing a formal order from the Central Executive. Mao was absent, and under the orders of the two messengers, three thousand of the eight thousand healthy fighting men of the base marched down the mountain to fight in southern Hunan. They suffered a severe defeat, and were almost annihilated. A few hundred straggled back to the mountain. Mao's pointed letter of November 1928, blaming the Hunan Branch Committee for this disaster, and calling it military adventurism, goes on to expand further his thinking on the development of the revolutionary forces. "It is absolutely necessary to build up and expand Red political power in bases . . ." he wrote. And what was crucial, to protect the base areas, was the protection of the industry and commerce of the national bourgeosie, and not their heedless destruction.

But the Kuomintang intelligence knew that grievous loss in manpower had weakened the Red base at Chingkangshan. A counteroffensive was prepared. On August 30th, 1928, another extermination campaign against it began, a first having been routed in the early part of that year.

This was the famous battle of Huangyangchieh pass, so called because the enemy tried to overcome the defences at this point.

The description of the battle was given to me by a Hakka peasant, who became an activist in the peasant militia in 1928. When he was six years old his father had died and he worked in the fields. "For ten dollars my mother had borrowed we paid thirty cents per month in interest, and we paid for ten years; in 1928 no longer did we pay, for the Red Army had come, and the landlord had run away. I was thirty years old when Chairman Mao first came to us here, in this hamlet. I joined up, and in June of that year, when Chu Teh had come, he gave me a shotgun, as leader of the militia.

"In August my elder brother and I went to gather intelligence as carriers, with empty baskets as if to buy rice. Because that was how we were organized; we Hakka carriers spread in all the hamlets, carrying loads for people, and we kept our ears open and our eyes, and came back with all the news. Thus we found out that people in the plain were being requisitioned to carry things; and someone who was careless told us it was for an attack on Chingkangshan. So we returned that very night, climbing the mountain with the news, and told our Red Army; thus the defence preparations were started in good time.

"We made bamboo spikes, one hundred per person, everyone helping, and we sowed these spikes on all the pathways leading to the mountain. Then came the troops, many of them, and for two days surrounded the mountain; on the third day they were going to attack. At first there had been mist in the valleys; when it lifted we saw the enemy, but they did not see us for it was summer, thick the trees and bushes on the mountain slopes. The enemy troops opened a barrage of fire, pounding the slopes and the pass at Huangyangchieh, and we did not reply, for we had so few guns. But our militia crept under the bushes, nearer and nearer, nearer than the barrage so that the shots went over our heads. I had crept so near I could hear the gurgle of water in their Maxim machine-guns.

"Three times, four times, their fire raked the slopes and then stopped, and we felt they were going to assault. Then our one and only mortar was made to shoot; it had only three shells, and we fired one shell. This shell fell right among some soldiers and wounded or killed no more than six, but it was so unexpected that it created confusion, for until then we had kept perfectly silent, not even moving a stone. And now, suddenly and all at once, we raised an enormous racket, with gongs and drums and firecrackers, and shouting and also screaming, and as we were so near them, so much nearer than they thought, they ran away." The old man was now pensioned, sitting all day in the sun; he pointed to the stone, the house, the tree, where Mao had sat, lived, shaded in the hot noon. "Here it all happened. And in 1929 when the Red Army left, the Kuomintang came and five out of nine were killed in my family. I ran away and became a hired porter in the plains." In 1960 he had seen Mao again, been invited to Peking to receive at last his reward, a medal.

To celebrate the victory, someone had written the song of the battle of Huangyangchieh:

> I stand above Huangyangchieh, looking at field and valley,
> Suddenly a confused shouting of men and horses from below.
> My eyes pierce the distance, gazing afar,

There are the warlord armies of Hunan and Kiangsi!
They come because they know there are only poor peasants
  here,
Who do not know much about fighting,
And because our main troops are gone . . .

Please do not hesitate, looking to right and left,
Your hearts undecided, O gentlemen;
For here is no ambush, and no soldiers hurry to the rescue,
Only poor peasants, who bid you welcome!
Here in store for you, sweet melons and glutinous rice.
Sweet melons, glutinous rice, especially for you.
Come, come, come,
Come up our Well Ridge mountain, and taste immortality.

Mao and Chu were now in closer partnership than ever,
their critics silenced by the defeat at Changsha, the victory at
Huangyangchieh. In December 1928 the Sixth Congress of the
Communist Party, held in Moscow, reversed all previous erron-
neous lines, and Mao was thus vindicated. He had composed his
report, "The Struggle in the Chingkang Mountain", in November
1928 sent it directly to the Central Committee, thus asserting
his resolve no longer to obey directives of the imbecilic Hunan
branch of the Committee . . .

But the Central Committee was as riddled with adventurism
as its branches, and continued to insist that the progressive
qualities of the urban city workers made them the class pre-
destined to lead the Revolution. They concluded, by a strange
logic, that *therefore* cities were still to be taken, the countryside
treated as an adjunct. Although Chou Enlai pointed out that
party membership was changing in composition, that far fewer
workers were joining it (sixty per cent by 1930), this myopic
city-bred left line was to persist right up to the Long March in
1934. How many lives it cost one will never know.

A third campaign was now launched against Well Ridge
Mountain, with eighteen regiments, by the Kuomintang armies
combined with feudal forces. Under extreme pressure Mao and
Chu left Chinkangshan, and for a while roamed, turning to
guerrilla warfare; finally they arrived in Juichin, another border
area in south Kiangsi province, and established a base there.

Throughout most of 1929 Mao was to expand and consolidate
the Juichin area base, and also to create a base in Fukien province.

Chingkangshan, temporarily lost, was retaken in June 1929.

110

In the early part of 1930, there were altogether fifteen Red bases in China.

In December 1929 Mao Tsetung's writings expose another phase of his development. According to certain authorities, the acutely sarcastic "On the rectification of incorrect ideas in the party" is his first essay in purely ideological debate, and is an indirect attack upon the Li Lisan leftist line. Hitherto Mao had written on peasant movements, on military strategy and tactics, on social problems, on partial errors, but he had not engaged in fundamental polemics. Now, it seems, he went about it in his usual thorough manner, exposing the various unhealthy tendencies present among the cadres and Party members in the Army under his command.

> Some comrades, disregarding the subjective and objective conditions, suffer from the malady of revolutionary impetuosity . . . they will not take pains to do minute and detailed work among the masses, but riddled with illusions, want only to do big things . . .
> In the Red Army there are quite a few people whose individualism finds expression in pleasure-seeking. They always hope that their unit will march into big cities. The last thing they want is to work in the Red areas where life is hard . . .
> Blind action . . . inadequate and irresolute application of the Party's policies for the cities . . . acts of house burning . . . the practice of shooting deserters and of inflicting corporal punishment, both of which smack of putschism . . .

In February 1930, the area under Red control had greatly increased, covering a large part of two provinces; more and more of the rank and file in the Communist army were now turning to Mao Tsetung. His prestige was growing, fed by his successes.

Meanwhile Chiang Kaishek had not been passive. Mao's wife, Yang Kaihui, daughter of a professor at Peking University, and his younger sister, were seized in Mao's native village and executed. The wives of his two brothers were arrested.

In 1930 civil war on a larger scale than even during the "warlord decade" prior to 1927 broke out between Chiang Kaishek's Nanking government and Feng Yuhsiang and other warlord factions; actually, during the period 1928 to 1931 six civil wars occurred. The peace we so longed for never materialized and the

111

bright prospects heralded by Chiang's advent had thoroughly dimmed.

At this juncture Li Lisan, in June 1930, ordered yet another attack on a city: Changsha; this also failed in the end, and at last Li Lisan's city-taking line was revoked. This probably saved the Red Army from a catastrophic attack on Wuhan, which Li Lisan was demanding.

All the time Mao had opposed Li Lisan's theory that there was "a great new upsurge"; he had estimated, shrewdly, that the factional quarrels between Chiang and the warlords, however intense and widespread, would be patched up fairly quickly. "These attacks are not necessary," he maintained. "The enemy is actually making preparations for a great drive against us . . . this is not the time for possibly disastrous adventures . . ."

In November 1930, at a Congress in Moscow, the Li Lisan line was officially abandoned. But the Nanking government was now thoroughly aware of the growing revolutionary potential of the Red bases; it did hasten to make peace with the warlords, and Chiang Kaishek now prepared to annihilate the Red bases by more than local campaigns.

The First Extermination Campaign launched by Chiang Kaishek began in December 1930. One hundred thousand men were involved, and began an encirclement of the Red bases, advancing along five routes.

The Red Army by then had increased to between thirty to forty thousand men. Mao Tsetung now had an opportunity of trying out his tactics of war; by January 1931 the campaign was over, the Nanking government forces retreating in defeat.

In February 1931 a Second Extermination Campaign was launched, this time with two hundred thousand men.

It was led by Ho Yingchin, the Minister for Defence. Ho moved his troops along seven routes, going very slowly, burning and destroying the villages in his march. The Red Army let the Kuomintang columns advance into its territory, then suddenly attacked, concentrating their forces on one route after the other, isolating and destroying enemy formations one by one. "In fourteen days we fought six battles," recalled Mao Tsetung. Ho Yingchin withdrew, and Mao wrote a battle poem:

> Our Army has marched two hundred miles
> Along grey rivers and blue mountains;
> And the enemy troops are swept away

112

Easy as rolling a mat.
Someone weeps, woeful for his lack of speed . . .

And indeed Ho was weeping, for Chiang Kaishek was scolding him for his "slowness". In April 1931, without a pause, Chiang Kaishek started the Third Extermination Campaign and this time he had three hundred thousand men. "I shall finish off this bandit Mao," he roared. "My head upon it if I fail."

Chiang moved rapidly, forcing the pace of advance up to twenty-five miles a day. Everywhere he used scorched-earth tactics. "Rather kill one thousand, than let one Red escape."

The Kuomintang troops penetrated deep within the enemy territory, and now their lines of supplies were extended. This brought about the very conditions under which the Red Army fought best with its guerrilla tactics. In five battles within five days, giving the Chiang Kaishek troops no rest and no pause, the Red armies swooped down from right and left, before and behind, throwing Chiang's divisions into confusion, isolating them and exterminating them piecemeal. It captured in this campaign massive replenishments in guns, ammunition, equipment of all kinds. "We have never had so much booty."

By the end of August 1931, it was obvious that the Third Extermination Campaign was as much a failure as the previous two had been.

While the contestants paused, poising for yet another round, another danger came up.

For it was in that autumn of 1931 that the Japanese started their long career of aggression in China, beginning with Manchuria in September 1931.

Chiang Kaishek withdrew from the assault upon the Red bases a week before the Japanese, in a sudden strike, occupied Manchuria on September 18th, 1931.

And we in far-off Peking, reading the newspapers, hearing whatever filtered through despite the censorship, and counting the years and the lost hopes and the disillusions since 1927, had by now begun to feel that Chu Teh, Mao Tsetung, were supermen, genii, like the wind, ungraspable, immortal.

"It is because they eat red peppers," Uncle Lui would remark.

Menacing, upon the horizon, yet another alien conqueror; and though the name of Chiang Kaishek still covered the sky

113

above us, like a tent pulled about our heads, we felt the night it kept us in long, long, and in the stultifying darkness were beginning, fearfully, to wonder, to look, to hope for another star . . .

CHAPTER FIVE

In December 1930 my education was over.

"We have nothing more to teach her, Madame." Mother Superior looked patiently at my mother, whose brown gloves became restless. She obviously wished that Mama and I would thank her and walk away. But with her difficult daughter Rosalie out of school so soon, Mama was worried. Rosalie was too young to work, and what would she do at home but quarrel and shout? Could she not stay at school, perhaps, to coach other students, to teach, to earn a little money? "No business or bank will take a girl of not quite fourteen to work," said Mama. "Of course, for a factory girl, it's different. They take them at eight. What shall I do with your daughter now?" She was speaking to Papa, and always said "your daughter" when she spoke of Rosalie.

The last year at school had been good to me, chiefly because of Mother Joseph Helen, who was half-Indian, with marvellous sombre-lashed eyes, a golden skin, small hands. She made lace and I fell in love with her clever fingers and low voice.

During that year I had bought tiny bouquets of violets and forget-me-nots, laid them on Mother Joseph Helen's desk. Rising early, to walk the unpaved misted street with its dust and potholes, I saw the morning throwers of water spray the dust down as I walked to the flower shop, money clutched in my hand. With six coppers I also fed a dog which lived near the flower shop and now it waited every day for me. School had been happier than home. Now school was over, childhood over.

For a fortnight in January 1931, Mother Superior allowed me to return to the classroom, to sit at the desk I had sat at the last year, doing the things I had done, reading through the same books, for without school I was lost. But one morning Mother Joseph Helen told me not to return.

I was at home all that day. The next day I went back to school, walked outside it, lingering in the icy street, entered the courtyard to chat to former classmates; trying to see Mother Joseph Helen. Then I saw her.

"You must think of other things, now, of getting married one day, for instance. You should help your mother."

"But I don't want to be married, Mother."

"Nonsense, unless you want to be a religious, you must get married."

Mother Joseph Helen said: "a religious". She clipped sentences off, in an economical Indian way.

I wanted to say: "I want to be a nun." It was so much a lie I could not say it. I went again to visit her, pretending to inquire about the signs and symptoms of a vocation, almost hoping for a vocation, thinking that her interest might be aroused. But instead Mother Joseph Helen was a little angry and said shortly: "Mother Superior does not like your coming in because it disturbs the others." I went to the toilet to weep, then walked away, remembering as I walked down the tiled corridor to step from orange to orange square. In front of the chapel the green-robed angel to one side of the door had protuberant eyes; carefully I walked, not stepping on the lines between the squares, watched by his painted gaze.

Twenty-six years later, in the summer of 1957, I passed the gate of my school, saw again the fake granite front with its grey statue of Christ, went up the steps (how small the courtyard now). The door opened oillessly, a lay sister in grey, with a shrinking manner, stared suspicious, but let me into the parlour. There was the same corridor, with the orange and white and black tiles now worn, sagging in places. On both sides of the chapel door the painted angels with their trumpets; I looked at the angel with the green robe on the right side, and he was just the same, exophthalmic, his trumpet a long-stalked lily. Into the parlour came a nun, equivocal, evasive, reluctant, nervous. Not Mother Joseph Helen.

"Yes, we are going on teaching, but only the children of diplomats . . . yes, we do teach French and English still, but only the children of diplomats . . ."

She had not known Mother Joseph Helen, never heard of her. One more thing done, one more meticulous reordering, fitting a piece of the unquiet past into its place. No more.

Perhaps one day, having relived everything, done with the quest which each has to do, all pursuit spent, and things allotted their true and proper places, I shall be able to let go, at last, to let go.

As I went out, I was careful to step on every line that separated the orange, black, and white squares.

Now I was home. Mother and I fought each other every day all day. I would go out, dragging my bicycle out of its shed, cycling until the hard fierce words would uncoil, unshapen, flaccid, dead tired. I would return, put the bicycle back on its rack, sit at table, eat supper. Read.

In March my father suggested that I should study typing and shorthand and accounting, and try to get a job as a secretary. I was growing a fine crop of forehead pimples, but they became discouraged and left me almost as soon as I began to study again. I was still flat and thin, still wearing Tiza's clothes, for Tiza was taller than I was, and already known as a young beauty. Papa received visits, in his office, from the fathers of sons of eighteen or twenty, and even from a wealthy older man or two, all of them eager to secure Tiza.

"There will be no trouble getting that one settled," Papa said, crinkling his eyes. He too considered daughters as only fit for marriage.

There was no school in Peking where one could study typing and shorthand and accounting. Secretaries were European or Eurasian girls; they came from Tientsin or Shanghai, or went there to be trained. But my mother had become acquainted, at the seaside, where we had gone again in the summer of 1930, with a Mrs. Heyward, and American. Her son, Don Heyward, had had a Chinese father, now dead; his mother had resumed her American name. Mrs. Heyward taught at the American school in Peking. There were more and more Americans teaching in China, most of them missionaries. On our return to Peking Mrs. Heyward did not forget us, but invited us to a children's party, the parquet glistened, the cushions shone, the resilient settee bounced, and never had I seen so many different kinds of "cookies", cakes, and everything so prettily done. I drank Cola-cola, but did not like it. Then we played games, which after a while became boring.

Through Mrs. Heyward I was introduced to typing and shorthand. Some American Catholic nuns were newly come to Peking, to open a girls' college, part of the American–Chinese Catholic University called Fujen University. My father, at great expense,

116

bought a second-hand Royal typewriter. I learnt typing, and Gregg shorthand, with a patient American nun. I was a very bad student, careless, absent-minded, sloppy; a great trial to the sweet woman who taught me without ever losing her temper. I was beginning to grow out of childhood, and beginning to feel unreal to myself. All the time the consciousness of being double was fast upon me, a thick gooey otherness between myself and others, a molassy non-grasp. It would be years before I would understand that this was part of growing up; meanwhile I was terribly frightened that it meant I was going mad.

The American nuns had baths every day and did not think it a sin as the French convent nuns did. They approved of dancing, and rode bicycles. Two of them were trained doctors. If a nun could be a doctor why could not I? My mother said Americans were different, everyone in America was terribly rich. "Of course they can do anything they like."

Every day I walked from home to the American nuns' temporary college, behind the North Sea Park, and back again. It was the mule track I trudged, the one in front of our house, and the white dust came up to my ankles, filling my tennis shoes. Passing over the great marble bridge in front of the park I would linger to see the white thirteenth-century pagoda, crowned with gold, commanding the mirror lake. The willows become green-swathed and supple in the patchy spring, and my parents debated where I could apply for a job: to the Belgian bank? or the French bank? But my job was decided, not by them, nor me, but by my friend Hilda Kuo.

Hilda takes an anormous amount of space, though so little time, in my adolescence. Even today, her memory stirs me; I long to see her again. She was three years older than I, and for a short while all I wanted to look like, sound like, dress like. She was the only girl I knew who told me I wrote excellent letters. She made a picture of me, at sixteen, which I have still. She and I were nearly killed, falling off a hillside road in her small car. Hilda was so full of life, I cannot believe her dead.

I met her in the street, I walking, she riding a Mongolian pony on the pavement, and that was Hilda all over. She stopped the pony and we talked. I told her I needed a job. "Why don't you apply where I work, at the P.U.M.C.?"

I said: "What is that?"

"It's that big hospital there, you goof." She pointed with her riding-whip to the green-tiled roofs that rose high above the low grey houses and shops. "The Yu Wang Fu," I said, giving it the Chinese name. "Rockefeller Foundation." I was awed.

The massive marble and pillared palace had been the residence of the Emperor's uncle, now acquired by the Rockefeller Foundation, and turned into a hospital and a teaching school called the Peking Union Medical College. When anyone said "Rockefeller Foundation" there was even more reverence in their voice than when they said "Generalissimo Chiang Kaishek".

The day after meeting Hilda I wrote a letter to the Rockefeller Foundation, applying for a job.

Neither Father nor Mother thought I would get in. "You have to have pull. It's an American thing, Rockefeller Foundation. You must have pull."

Mother said: "That's where they do all those experiments on dogs and people." All the Big Shots of the Nanking government also came here to have medical treatment, and sometimes took away a nurse to become "a new wife".

It made sense to me, typing in a hospital; I would learn about medicine, since I wanted to study medicine. And as there was no money at home for me to study, I would earn money, and prepare myself to enter medical school. I had already discovered that a convent-school education was not at all adequate, and that it would take me at least three more years of hard study before being able to enter any college at all. Science, mathematics, Chinese literature and the classics . . . with the poor schooling given to me, it would take me years to get ready for a university.

"I will do it." But clenched teeth, decision tearing my bowels, were not enough; there was no money, no money, my mother said it, said it until I felt as if every morsel of food I ate was wrenched off my father's body.

"No one is going to feed you doing nothing at home." Of course, one who does not work must not eat unless one can get married, which is called: "being settled at last." But with my looks I would never get married, I was too thin, too sharp, too ugly. Mother said it, Elder Brother had said it. Everyone agreed that I should work, because marriage would be difficult for me.

Within a week a reply came. The morning postman brought it, and I choked over my milk and coffee. "I'm to go for an interview. At the Peking Union Medical College. To the Comptroller's office."

Father and Mother were pleased. Mother put the coffee-pot down and took the letter. "What good paper, so thick." But how could we disguise the fact that I was not fifteen years old? I had claimed to be sixteen in the letter. In fact, said Papa, it was not a lie since Chinese are a year old when born, and if one added the New Year as an extra year, as do the Cantonese and the Hakkas, who become two years old when they reach their first New Year (so that a baby born on December 31st would be reckoned two years old on the following January 2nd), I could claim to being sixteen.

"You *look* sixteen," said Mama, "all you have to do is to stop hopping and picking your pimples. And lengthen your skirt."

What dress should I wear? I had two school uniforms, a green dress, a brown dress, and one dress with three rows of frills for Sunday, too dressy for an interview. I had no shoes except flat-heeled schools shoes, and tennis shoes. There was no time to make a dress and in those years no ready-made clothes existed. Mother lengthened the green dress, and added her voile scarf. I squeezed two pimples on my forehead, then went to the East market and bought some face powder, Butterfly brand, pink, made in Shanghai by a Japanese firm.

The next morning, straw-hatted, with powder on my nose, I went with my father to the gates of the hospital.

"It's not this gate, this is for the sick. It's the other gate, round the corner," said the porter.

The Yu Wang Fu Palace occupied a whole city block. We walked along its high grey outer wall, hearing the dogs scream in the kennels, and came to its outer gate which was the Administration building gate. It had two large stone lions, one male, one female. We crossed the marble courtyard, walked up the steps with their carved dragons coiling in the middle, into an entrance hall, with painted beams and intricate painted ceiling, red lacquered pillars, huge lamps. There was cork matting on the stone floor.

"I'll leave you," said Papa. "Try to make a good impression." And he was gone.

I found the Comptroller's office easily, there was a messenger in the hall directing visitors. An open door, a room, two typewriters clattering and two women making them clatter.

I stood at the door and one of the women came to me. She had the new style of hair, all upstanding curls, which I admired, a dress with a print round the hem; she was very pregnant, so that her belly seemed to be coming at me first. She smiled. "Hello what can I do for you?"

119

"I have an interview."

She took the letter from my hand. "Glad you could come. Now, just sit you down. No, sit down *there*. I'll tell Mr. Harned you've come."

The office had two other doors besides the one to the corridor, on one was "Comptroller", on the other "Assistant Comptroller" That was the one she went through and returned from.

"Mr. Harned will see you now."

Mr. Harned was very tall, thin, a small bald head, a long chin, enormous glasses. I immediately began to quiver with fright. His head was like a temple on top of a mountain, like the white dagoba on the hill in the North Sea Park. I could not hear a word of what he said. A paper and a pencil were in my hand, however, and Mr. Harned was dictating to me, giving me a speed test in shorthand.

I went out of his office and the pregnant secretary sat me in front of her own typewriter. I turned a stricken face to her. "I couldn't hear. I couldn't hear what he said . . ."

"Wait, I'll tell him." She bustled off. At the other desk was a blonde, thin girl, who had thrown one look at me and then gone back to clattering. The pregnant one reappeared, a pink sheet in hand: "Now just copy this on the typewriter, best you can."

I hit the keys, swiftly; the typewriter was the same make as mine, a Royal.

"My, you are fast. I'll tell Mr. Harned."

And Mr. Harned came out, benign behind those enormous goggle glasses. "Well, Miss Chou, we've decided to take you on as a typist, at thirty-five local dollars a month. To start Monday. Is that all right?"

I nodded, unable to speak. Had he said ten dollars I would have accepted.

The kind secretary said: "Now take your time, and wipe your face. How old are you, by the way?"

"Sixteen, nearly."

"Is that all? Why my eldest is bigger than you, and she isn't through school yet. I told Mr. Harned you were shy and upset, and that's why you couldn't take dictation. He's all right, just takes getting used to, that's all."

"I couldn't understand his English."

"Oh, you'll get used to it. Now, I won't be around on Monday, I'm going to have a baby. It's your letter that got them interested in you, you wrote such good English, better than all the other letters we've had. Mr. Harned will give you a try." She whispered. "I put in a good word for you."

"Thanks, thanks a lot . . . I need the money, I . . ."

"Yes, dear, we know." Obviously she wanted her typewriter back, and her chair. I was still sitting on it. "Well, toodledoo for now, hope you enjoy yourself in this job. I've been here six months and I've enjoyed *every minute*. Don't let Mr. Harned worry you, he's really great, once you get used to him."

I had a job, had a job, had a job . . . I walked home treading on air, I could not have sat in a rickshaw. Outside our house was the mule track and opposite the house was the well, a well which nestled under a tree. All the creaky squeaky water-carts of the quarter come here to fill their barrels from this well. The well winch was turning, clear water, the beautiful clear spring underground water of Peking gushed out, one by one the water-carts lined up, the men naked to the waist, wiping their sweat, and spitting. While her husband drew the well water the well woman sat as usual by the stone margin, breasts exposed, feeding her last baby.

Oh, how wonderful life, happy like this water, gushing out so clean and so cold, ice-cold in the June heat! I smiled at the well woman, who had wonderful teeth, and though she was so filthy her skin was always clear and smooth; she never combed her hair, she was a real northern woman, slovenly, unkempt, though she and her husband owned that beautiful well. Mother hated her, and the well woman laughed at Mother, laughed deliberately, standing well back on her planted hips and legs, carrying her large baby across her stomach, breasts hanging like two melons on either side of her open jacket; rippled with well-water laughter.

The more Mama shouted at the well woman, the more she laughed, and her husband who turned the handle of the well-beam and made the water gush stared at Mama, and in his drawling Peking burr said: "Now what is she angry about on this beautiful day?" And the water-carriers chuckled. I smiled at them now. I had a job, a job, gushing money like water from a well . . .

At home Mama was not happy.

"Thirty-five dollars a month! You should have asked for more! Thirty-five silver dollars . . . Why, Mrs. Heyward pays her amah fifteen dollars a month . . . Thirty-five dollars. Thirty-five miserable dollars . . . I suppose they thought you were Chinese . . ."

Papa also was disappointed. "I heard Mr. Yew say that it is usually fifty for a typist . . ."

121

Thirty-five dollars, and the cost of everything going up and up; even eggs were quite expensive . . .

By nightfall, Mama was reconciled. "Well, in three months' time, you can ask for a raise. If you work well, they will give it."

"The P.U.M.C. is a good place. It's American, it has a good reputation," said Papa, who sometimes had not been paid his salary six months on end; and now again there was civil war; he might again not be paid for many months.

I went to work on the Monday at nine o'clock, and since it was no longer necessary to pretend, I wore my school uniform, to save the other dresses.

I arrived too early; only the cleaners were there, washing the cork matting with soapy water, and the water was not even dirty after they had finished. All the cleaners wore starched uniforms, and they also washed down the marble courtyard which gleamed, white and beautiful. At eight-twenty-five Mr. Harned, wearing a hat on top of his small head, came in. "Morning, *beautiful* morning. You're early." It was a good beginning.

Since the pregnant, kind secretary was gone, there was only Miss Pillman, the thin girl at the other typewriter, and she was also leaving to get married. Her ring flashed when she typed; she looked so clean with a pleated green skirt and a big white sailor collar. At a third small table, with a typewriter on it, sat a Chinese clerk, Mr. Yeh; quite fat, with a crew-cut, a big stomach, glasses, a long grey Chinese gown. Then something buzzed, and Miss Pillman said:

"That's for you, two rings. Mine's one ring. Take a pad and go in."

Again I could not follow the dictation. So Miss Pillman told Mr. Harned, and then told me: "You'd better type for the first three or four days, till you get over your shyness." I was now tearing my handkerchief to bits, expecting to be fired immediately.

Three rings, Mr. Yeh went in. Mr. Yeh did not do shorthand, only typing; Miss Pillman chatted about her fiancé, about Peitaiho the seaside, about films. She gave me things to copy; then I went for a college health examination, and an X-ray; the college health physician was a blond Englishman with very cold hands and a little moustache, his office was reached by crossing over an elevated marble terrace. All the buildings had green tiled roofs. There was a large grey chimney belching smoke; the Chinese said corpses were burnt in it. I was given little boxes for specimens, and when I came back Mr. Harned again gave me dictation, and this time I could take it. It was about accounting for six chairs, and it was only a few lines.

The telephone on my desk rang. It rang again.

"Go on, pick it up, answer it," said Miss Pillman.

"But I don't know how to listen to a telephone," I said. There was no telephone at home. When I wanted to say something to someone I wrote a letter or walked to their house to see them. I stared at the black ringing phone, with its ominous downturning double knobs.

Miss Pillman sighed, and took the telephone and the message. "Come on, you try again," she said. "You'll have to answer the phone when I am gone."

It was Mr. Yeh who gave me my first telephone lesson. He said: "I teach you," and rose. He seemed to roll on his black slippered feet, rather than walk. He went out of the office and my phone rang.

I picked it up, and said: "Assistant Comptroller's office," as Miss Pillman had done. Mr. Yeh's voice said:

"My name is Yeh. Can you hear me?"

"Yes." I was astonished that I could hear.

Mr. Yeh returned, beaming: "There, it is very easy."

"Oh, thank you, Mr. Yeh." Everyone was so kind to me that I went to the ladies' toilet to cry.

Lunch time came and Mr. Yeh went to the Chinese canteen; Miss Pillman went to lunch with her fiancé; I had forgotten to take any money, so I went to the ladies' room and lay down on the long armchair, and drank water out of a paper cup, as Miss Pillman had done when she had shown me the ladies' room.

A fortnight later Miss Pillman left to become a married woman. Mr. Yeh and I "held the fort", as Mr. Harned described it, for a whole day, and then arrived Miss Radley, a red-curled, freckled English girl, with fine long legs. Those legs were her downfall.

Miss Radley was cheerful, starting the morning with a smile, a brisk, jovial manner. She said righteeo and toodledoo. She told me that Peking was ever so much fun, with so many young men around to go dancing with, and pony-riding with to the Western Hills.

The third day she was there Miss Radley told me that a young man was "pashy" on her, and she was only working to pass the time away until he could return from home leave and marry her. He was on furlough in England, but would soon return to his bank in Shanghai. She had come up from Shanghai to see Peking, and taken this job to pass the time.

The week after, she wasn't sure whether she would marry this young man from the bank, or another young man who was in Peking in a business and was absolutely pashy on her, and had a sports car.

Miss Radley was paid three hundred and fifty silver dollars a month, ten times as much as I was. For the first week I thought her competent; all white people, of course, were competent, able and superior; for the remaining three, I waited for her to be fired.

Mr. Harned did not like Miss Radley. She was always having trouble with her typewriter; she banged the keys, she erased; Mr. Harned loved immaculate letters, he made me recopy many of Miss Radley's efforts.

I was also working an hour a day in the filing room in the basement with Mr. Yeh, who had now been sent back to the basement as filing clerk. He had been allowed upstairs merely as a filler-in, while all those changes of secretaries were taking place. Mr. Yeh always wore the same long grey gown. He told me he had six children, and had been working ten years in the Filing Department. His salary was now thirty-five dollars a month, the same as mine. He typed, he could do accounts, but he would never get more than thirty-five dollars a month.

After a week in the filing room, Mr. Yeh one day grasped me awkwardly round the shoulders, whispering: "Oh, you are nice." I pushed him off. He never tried again, and somehow I felt sad, as if I had done him wrong. He was so ugly, and looking at him I felt that life was very unfair to Mr. Yeh. The thought that in ten years' time perhaps I too would still be here, at thirty-five dollars a month, frightened me . . . Oh, no no no, not even for three hundred and fifty, although that is more than Father gets, after years and years on the railway . . . I'm going to be a doctor, I'm going to be a doctor . . .

Miss Radley brought her silk stockings to mend in the office, and put her feet on the desk. "I'm faddy about my shoes," she said gaily. Her hair was shingled, bobbed in a point which came down the back of her neck, where a knob of bone stuck out. She was freckled all over, which aroused Mr. Yeh's inquiries. He asked me why she was thus made, and I could not explain.

By the third week Mr. Harned was very fidgety. If his letters were not ready by four-thirty he would appear in the outer office, going out with a sheaf of papers, returning with the same sheaf, producing an attenuated tornado effect by grinding his heels into the cork matting as he turned his body.

Miss Radley ate chocolates, mended stockings at her desk, and every day came with a new pair of shoes. Hilda gave me a box of chocolates she did not want. Craftily I gave them to Miss Radley. "Oooooh, I *love* chocolates"; immediately Miss Radley seized one. Mr. Harned came out just as she was popping it in her mouth.

One afternoon Mr. Harned gathered courage to say: "Miss Radley, are my letters ready?"

"All but the last two, Mr. Harned."

"Well, could you please do them now? All this delay cramps my work." Miss Radley said he was very rude.

She then swivelled her chair to make me admire her legs with their coquettish shoes. "This is my fourteenth pair, all hand-made by the little shoemaker in Suchow Street."

Mr. Harned erupted into our room while Miss Radley was holding up her leg to make me admire it and her shoe.

Two days later Miss Leuter came. She had light-brown eyes. I knew she was Eurasian, though she was very beautifully dressed in a blue linen suit, with a little brown hat with feathers. Her face was long and thin and her nose too, but the width of the cheeks and something in the sideways look said: half-Japanese, and a look at her legs confirmed it; short for the long body. She was ushered into Mr. Harned's room. Then she left. An hour later Miss Radley was called into Mr. Harned's office and came out with cheeks blazing. "I've been fired." Then she turned on me. "It's your fault, you little yellow bastard, you keep on talking and stopping me from work."

I kept quiet. "Yellow bastard" only brought me back to the day on the beach, an afternoon with waves like prancing horses, little blue-green horses, a wind blowing their white manes, and the fat Russian woman, wind-sculpted in her towelling robe with bizarre blue moons and yellow suns all over it, walking up and down in front of me: "You dirty shit of a Chinaman, you yellow bastard . . ." I was perfectly happy. Miss Radley would go. Miss Radley left, and Miss Leuter came.

Her mother was indeed Japanese, and her father, now dead, had been a German businessman, so that she counted as German, through her father's nationality, as I was a Chinese, through my father. Miss Leuter was incredibly neat and systematic. She made me clean my typewriter, which had not been cleaned since my arrival, and I began to learn what being a secretary really meant. All the time I knew her she seemed evenly happy, and only later did I find out that she too had her share of tragedy. But no one could tell from her placid face, her calm manner. She was good to me in a kind, detached, cold way. And it was because of her that in November I was raised to fifty dollars a month.

First she extracted from me my real age, and was shocked. "You are actually only just fifteen?"

"I am fifteen, Chinese fashion; soon I will be really fifteen."

"When were you born then?"

"1916," I said, rapidly calculating.

"Let me see, 1931. Yes, that makes you just fifteen. And they are paying you . . . thirty-five dollars a month?" She shook her head. "That is too little," she said decisively. "It is true you do not know much, but you type well, and you can follow Mr. Harned's dictation. Not many people can. You must ask for more."

I went to Hilda, who was working in the Accounts office, and asked her opinion, and she said I must ask for more. She had been getting one hundred and twenty, but would soon be raised to European level, three times as much, because her passport had just come through. "I applied for naturalization as a British citizen and I've just got it. It'll make all the difference." It did. She was now an English national, entitled to European pay.

Mr. Bradfield, the Comptroller, returned from furlough. He was a short, stocky man, always cheerful. Miss Leuter was Mr. Bradfield's secretary, and I was Mr. Harned's secretary.

"Now the office is getting in much better order," said Miss Leuter.

With fifty dollars a month Mr. Yeh's attitude towards me changed. We had been on more or less equal terms, but we were now unequal. I was making fifteen dollars a month more than he did. I had crossed the "Chinese" line, I was on my way towards "Eurasian" pay, though a great deal below European pay. I never would attain the latter, unless I married a European, perhaps.

The subtle well-ordered differences in status and in pay even among Eurasians, where it depended upon being more, or less, Chinese, I learnt about during the two years I was a secretary at the P.U.M.C. But I had no sense of personal injustice because I was not there to stay, I was there to earn money while preparing myself for the University. I did not fight for fair wages, I merely

126

found two extra jobs to do in my spare time, to increase my study fund quickly.

When Miss Leuter had been a month in the office, it looked very different. Instead of untidy files sitting on top of the cabinets, everything had been neatly stored away. Miss Leuter used to announce, mouth pursed, her intention: "I am going to fix this." It was done. She stayed after hours to fix. My desk now had two trays, one marked In, one marked Out. The worn telephone cord was replaced. The messenger who had sat in a corner of the room, and who took letters to the various departments, was moved into the corridor and provided with two very sharp pencils, which he had to keep sharpened. A geranium appeared, and sat on the little table where Mr. Yeh had typed. Mr. Yeh disappeared for ever into the filing room downstairs. Two cushions were provided, one for each swivel chair. The window screen, which had hung askew, was replaced.

Mr. Harned was delighted; he came out quite often now, padding softly, like a toy giraffe. No longer whirlwinding. He made little clean jokes. All his letters were neat and ready for him long before half past four. By now I knew his little quirks and foibles. He dictated at top speed, but his vocabulary was extremely limited. His letters consisted in the assemblage, diversified according to requirement, of about twenty key phrases, and once these key phrases were known to me, with their set pattern, I evolved a code sign for each of them, so that instead of writing each word down, I only had to know the first one to type down the rest. And all his letters began with a present participle, of which he had only three in store: "referring to", "thanking you for", or "confirming our conversation".

Miss Leuter went downstairs to inspect the filing which Mr. Yeh and I had done, and said it was no good, we would have to do it all over again. My idea of filing had been to put all Mr. Harned's letters under the opening present participle. As a result I had never found again the carbon copy of the correspondence about the six chairs, the first letter I had typed under Mr. Harned's dictation, because, wonder of wonders, it was one which started: "Agreeing to." However, Miss Leuter found it.

When the files were done it was November and Miss Leuter announced that all the cockroaches would be killed in our office. They were.

And when that was performed, Miss Leuter's Japanese passion for order abated, and she announced that she was taking a fortnight's holiday to get married; but she was not giving up working, she would return.

She came back from being married looking just the same, although now known as Mrs. Bürger. Searching anxiously her face for the "difference" which marriage was supposed to make, and not finding any, was surprising. She had come back with a toothache, four teeth having been filled or extracted during her honeymoon, to save time going to the dentist during office hours. Now she was furnishing a house, and departed promptly at five every night; her husband, blond Mr. Bürger, a German, came to fetch her in his car.

Of the thirty-five dollars a month I had earned, fifteen went as a voluntary gift to Mother for board and food, for Papa after the first month had said: "You ought to give some money to your mother," and Mother specified how much she wanted. Then I found that the money was used to make dresses for Tiza, and I became angry.

"Your little sister needs dresses," said Mama, defensive.

"I need dresses too," I cried. Her look, the look of a woman once beautiful, and now fighting to repossess that beauty through her daughter, Tiza, I shall never forget.

Thus began my corroding resentment of Tiza, eating away my love for my sister, a love itself corrupted with jealousy from the beginning, not only because of the distinct preference shown by my mother, but also because, in all ways, Tiza was a much nicer, kinder, more attractive child than I could ever be.

This grievance festered; upon it piled others; a root of hatred ineradicable through my mother's lifetime which grew into a tree of withering shade. It shrivelled all of us. Only after Mother's death at eighty, in 1965, could I begin to reach again towards the lost childhood love for Tiza. And by that time it was too late.

And so, as in a dreadful nightmare sequence, my mother's preference of Tiza, her resentment of me, not due to anything I had done, but a reaction to the mad gesture of a doctor's wife, closing her door to my mother and her dying child, warped all of us.* Such frivolous pain, all the more horrible for its triviality. And though I was the one to be resented, the real victims became Tiza, the loved one, and Marianne, our youngest, the neglected one. I escaped, or so I believe.

The immediate lesson in economics I derived from this my reluctant gift of fifteen dollars for food and board, was that I only

* See *The Crippled Tree.*

128

had twenty dollars a month left, of which ten dollars went to pay a Chinese teacher whom I hired in August of that year. When I was raised to fifty dollars, in November, I said nothing to my mother, for I did not want to pay more. I put the extra money in a savings account, called it "money to study with", and after a while it began to accumulate.

In August 1931, then, I began to study Chinese again. Teacher Wu came home three times a week and thus slowly, painfully, I started to make up for the silly, totally inadequate education I had been given. In December I decided to renovate some of the furniture at home as a Christmas present to my family. The table on our veranda sagged in the middle; its paint had worn off; six dollars went to renovating the table.

Meanwhile I was also taking on two extra jobs. And now all at once I was in a great hurry. There were so many things to learn, and I was afraid that if I did not hurry, I would be too old, and one's brain degenerated with old age. The fear of losing my brain was very strong. I had read a book called *Races of the World* the year before. It began:

> There are four races in the world; white, yellow, red and black . . . the white race is distinguished by the characteristic that its BRAIN WEIGHT is the highest; the brain of the average white man weighs one thousand six hundred grammes, that of the yellow man one thousand four hundred, the red man's brain weighs one thousand three hundred and forty and the black man round about one thousand two hundred . . .

This account was illustrated by pictures, front and profile of skulls; with captions calling attention to "width of brow". There were a few lines on mixtures. "Racial mixtures are prone to mental unbalance, hysteria, alcoholism, generally of weak character and untrustworthy . . ."

"Oh God," I prayed, "don't let me go mad, don't let my brain go, I want to study." I hurried, cramming myself with everything I could lay hands on: good and bad, injurious and helpful. If I survived, it was precisely because I was raised on the strong poison of my mother's dislike, and like Mithridates, had grown immune and would survive. I am grateful to my mother, more grateful every day, because in the crucible of her dislike I was staunched always to seek a beginning in joy.

CHAPTER SIX

I typed at the P.U.M.C. from June 1931 to July 1933. All that time I was in the Comptroller's office, working for Mr. Harned, the Assistant Comptroller, occasionally taking dictation, if a secretary fell ill, from others; thus I worked for Davidson Black, the anthropologist, George Barbour, the geologist, Mr. Bradfield, the Comptroller, and Ida Pruitt of the Social Welfare department.

My salary increased from thirty-five dollars to fifty dollars, later to seventy-five dollars. "What else do you want? You're doing fine," said Mrs. Bürger. "And soon you can find a nice boy and get married."

During those two years I became fragmented into many contradictory selves; and that was very good, that was survival. I resurrect these, incredulous that there should have been so many, so disparate, pulling in so many different directions, but this lack of cohesiveness undoubtedly saved me.

During those two years I grew from a child into a young woman. I fell in love, or so I thought. I was both crazy and sober; I learnt to drink, and to hate drink; to smoke, and have continued smoking. I made many friends, and left them when they stood in my way. Nearly broke with my parents and was nearly broken by them.

What went on round me affected me much, with immediate response. The young are imitative. The voracious I, clamorous, all-demanding, made of the pinpoint me a total universe. Yet at the same time there were other urges and demands, I was aware of other lives, other potential me's than the life I was leading and the me I was, and I reached for all I could guess at with savage ardour. The world was made into separate watertight compartments impenetrable to each other. But could not I penetrate them all? And which one would be more truly mine? When I seemed most adapted to that half-world, so cheerful and self-satisfied with small conceit, where the Eurasian lived, clinging to the arrogant white world whose dominion and privileges in Asia were never questioned (except by the Chinese, but they did not count in this small half-world of ours), I was already preparing myself to leave it. I would hear, unperturbed, the vilest insults hurled upon the Chinese; but the next day or week, I would insult in turn,

130

blindly, some European or other. Thus I was to make the wife of a Belgian banker and her daughter complain about me to the Belgian Consul; and yet, at the same time, I would be impatient and short at a Chinese coolie. Only in one thing was I steadfast, my indignation at the Japanese. And I had enormous quarrels with almost all the other secretaries, including Mrs. Bürger, because of my talk about Japan. Though I had no precise idea of what was happening, I became hot and cold when I thought of the fighting going on, and I followed what was happening between Japan and China. Yet I did not belong to any Chinese group, student or other, and had no clear consciousness at the time of belonging to China. I refused to go to church, and argued with the priest; yet when Hilda Kuo talked about the evils of the Vatican, I pointed to the seventy churches being built in France to provide employment in the depression which was hitting Europe, as a great saving gesture. In short I was a sum of contradictions, and the only unbending resolve in me, holding me true, this urge to study, the fire in my heart in spite of the tacking waywardness, the confusion.

I was still unaware of sex, yet I was to have my first love affair at sixteen, out of this desperate determination to learn everything, grabbing at life the sooner to grow into all-knowing.

Of this turmoil, medley, confusion, memory of externals remains, rather than of inner states, since the latter were a transient assemblage and in retrospect, however imperative their demands, assays of mobility. I am not fond of this adolescence stunted, ferocious and hamstrung, that self before seventeen. I merely record it, for it was my worst time, incoherent, fuzzy, restless, passive, aggressive, dispersed, odd, candid, misrepresented, a stretch of chaos in which no pattern is all patterns.

There was the diminutive society of the office, replacing school; the Peking Union Medical College and its secretaries, dominated for me by my friends Hilda Kuo and Olga Hempel.

Hilda's dominion over me I doubt she ever knew. I was looking for someone to imitate, and Hilda was the main colour of my jumbly heap, though not the only one. I was never to be entirely possessed by any one person, all my personal favours for ever diluted by that incomprehensible striving towards the future, a becoming which preserved me from any absolute offering. The more I tried to be like Hilda, the less I was, but the imitation had to be performed, as a way of finding myself. The fact that she

131

was riding a pony on the pavement when she told me to apply for a job, and that I got the job, alone created in me a reverence, a gratitude.

Hilda's mother was Scottish, soft-voiced and charming; she divorced her Chinese husband and reassumed her English name, and Hilda acquired British nationality; which enabled her to rise in the salary scale as a European.

Hilda and her sister were examples of the rule that in a mixed marriage the siblings can differ greatly from each other, both in appearance and in mind. Hilda was small, dark-haired, thin; Gladys was taller, golden-haired, blue-eyed, and one of the most beautiful girls in Peking, with slim wrists and slender body. Hilda managed, however, to look more striking than Gladys in all her classic beauty. Her hair, cut short and curly, gave her a waif-like agelessness, her Chinese eyes were belashed and mascaraed until they looked enormous. She dressed with casual grace; she could be French, Italian, a Celt; she whitened her face with witch hazel. For a short while both Gladys and Hilda had been at school with me; and there Hilda had shown herself very rude to me because she had been to England with her mother, and anyone coming from Europe or America was automatically superior, which I had questioned. "Shut up you!" she had screamed at me. But that was years ago, now all was well, we were both secretaries at the P.U.M.C., and great friends.

Olga Hempel was German and, in our secretarial hierarchy, definitely number one. The Hempel family ran a butchery shop on Hatamen Street and had three daughters. Mama bought meat at their shop. They owned a house in Peitaiho where we had stayed in the summer of 1929, for they had spare rooms and took paying guests and Mama did not want to return to the Pension Glauber. Olga Hempel was reputed most clever, and she was a hunchback. Her deformity was due to tuberculosis of the spine, an affliction far more common then, even among the whites, than it is now. She was secretary to Davidson Black, the anthropologist, famous with his friend, Teilhard de Chardin, for the discovery, by their combined team of archaeological workers, of the skull of *Sinanthropus Pekinensis*, or Peking man, at Choukoutien, not far from Peking. The discovery had been made in 1929, and actually had led to some resentment in the local Press, for it was a Chinese workman who had espied the skull bone projecting from its million-year-old fossil bed. But the Western Press had given all the honour of this discovery to Davidson Black and to Teilhard de Chardin. The latter, however, always disclaimed this, and made it clear that the discovery was due "to the whole team".

In the Anatomy and Anthropology department, under glass, were the fossils from Choukoutien. Olga, who ran the department allowed Hilda and me the awesome privilege of looking at them through the pane. Like all secretaries, she was immensely possessive of her boss, Davidson Black; Hilda would go to Olga's department, and talk with Davidson Black, quite unconcerned, while I was so shy that, when he appeared in our office one day with that wide smile he distributed round him, I could only lower my head and type furiously, too embarrassed to smile in return. When Davidson Black died in the spring of 1934 Olga was grief-stricken, and wandered about red-eyed for many days. She felt that the P.U.M.C.'s chief achievement was Davidson Black and *Sinanthropus Pekinensis*. Nothing else counted for her.

Père Teilhard de Chardin I also met occasionally, when he visited the department. He was a thin-visaged, long-jawed man, full of mild jokes. He teased Olga, which made her eyes shine like stars.

In winter Teilhard de Chardin's big nose was red, and he sniffed, because he often had a bad cold; he stooped a little, and had a muffler round his throat and a French beret; I do not remember exactly what he said but I remember a sensation of laughter, of wit and easy, immediate pleasure in his talk, full of observant irony. And this impression of my youth is confirmed as I read him today, for Teilhard de Chardin was more keenly aware of the pulsing thoughts in the Chinese people than most Europeans; and this not because he was a political thinker, but because he was human, interested in the development of the human being. The hominization of the earth, as revealed by the discoveries of palaeontology, led his thoughts to man's further development. "Humanity is still in its infancy," I heard him say at one of those amiable sessions of talk while drinking Olga's coffee; and later the phrase leapt back at me from the writings of Mao Tsetung. I feel that Chardin understood what was happening in China, though he did not predict what would happen. "The Chinese definitely have the self-awareness, if not the capabilities, of a modern nation," he wrote in April 1931 . . . and added: "It means an end to (Western) privilege . . ." And again, acerbic and sad: "The European in China is *engrossed* in the business of commerce and religion. This arrests him at the lowest intellectual level . . ."

After seeing Teilhard de Chardin I read a book on palaeontology and also tried to pick up archaeology. Olga and Hilda talked so knowledgeably about *Sinanthropus Pekinensis*, and I was envious of their superior erudition. I was to discover that many women have a facility for picking up bits of information, stringing them together, a butterfly talent, which saves one the actual work of acquiring facts and forming a solid education, as reading book-reviews passes for book-reading; thus Hilda picked splinters from Davidson Black's talk and overwhelmed me with her brilliance. I went home flayed, gnawed with jealousy of all that others knew and did, while I was so stupid.

This small coterie, to which I clung, because it was the one that condescended to have me standing there, wide-eyed, respectfully silent, was good for me. Olga and Hilda did enlarge my horizon. Only one thing they did not encourage, nor understand, and that was my pig-headedness (Olga Hempel's word) in wanting to be a doctor. "You'll never make it, you'll never make it, you just haven't got the brains," she chanted. In most things I would listen to her, and to Hilda, and also to Mrs. Bürger, but not in this. For this was mine, all mine.

Through Olga, Hilda and Mrs. Bürger I made entry into another group, which for a little while provided me with a convenient niche: the world of the Germans in China of the 1930s.

Germany had lost the war of 1914–18, lost all her concessions in China, lost Shantung province, her sphere of influence, to the Japanese by the Treaty of Versailles. Because of Germany's defeat, the only concession made to China at Versailles had been to remove the privilege of extraterritoriality which all foreigners enjoyed, from the Germans (and the Hungarians). As a result the Germans were more popular in China than any other whites, not excluding Americans. Germany had suffered through a terrible blockade, starving her people needlessly, months after the war had ended. They too had been humiliated, and as a result, and also because Chiang Kaishek early on began to use Germans to train his army, by 1928 the Germans were back in China with their briefcases and their blue eyes, sweating in the summer, cheerful in the winter, smiling and wanting to do business. The mighty monopoly of Krupp had weathered the war, and was once again forging the weapons for another war, and Chiang Kaishek bought from Germany. The Germans did not act superior like the British, nor did they mouth religion like the Americans; they had no soldiers in China, but they had military advisers and technicians training the armies of Chiang Kaishek, and drawing plans and selling machines for everything from electric cables to opening new airways. Because they did not have extraterritorial privileges, they behaved prudently, since they could be tried by the Chinese for breaking the law, whereas other foreigners were exempt. The German Club and the German School in Peking were most energetic. The Lufthansa, the German airline, had obtained permission to fly to Peking, to Urumchi, via Lanchow across Siberia, and was trying to establish an air route to be called Eurasia, from Peking to Berlin.

Hilda acquired a German boy friend, Leo Bielfeld, a gangling, tall young man with a large mouth and a loud voice, almost pathologically exuberant and cheerful.

By early 1932 I was looking for a teacher in science, and of course it was also a German, Mr. Vogel, who agreed to teach me physics twice a week, but I was to pay him thirty-six dollars a month. The German School was the only one equipped with a good science laboratory; the convent had none. Thirty-six dollars was a great deal, but I managed it. At first Mr. Vogel did not really believe I wanted to study. He told me so, when I was paying him his first thirty-six dollars.

"Why did you ask me to teach you?"

"I want to learn, I want to go to university."

"Nobody believes it. Nobody believes that I am only teaching you..."

"But so it is."

Mr. Vogel did begin to believe me, and taught me well. He had a wife, and it was rumoured he also had a girl friend, a Miss Stenner, who thought him marvellous. He did not want more complications in his life, and that was fine. But I was a Eurasian, alone with him in a laboratory twice a week; who could, indeed, believe that nothing happened? But I had to go on, doing what I wanted to do.

Besides physics, I studied Chinese three times a week. Teacher Wu was a small, prim little woman of about forty, in looks a sprig of lavender tidily pressed, spinster all over but with no quirks or frustrations. She had not withered but simply dried up, and was now incorruptible, immune to decay. She was quiet, patient, immensely serious, giving of herself in such a self-effacing way that she disappeared into the lessons she tried to instil. Her skin was evenly pale, her hair black, tidily bobbed, as was the custom then for unmarried and educated Chinese women. She wore the neatest grey dress, her white stockings, black shoes, were childish and clean. And beneath all this mild, satisfactorily muted, well-bred air, behind this small neat-featured face, there was fierce dignity, passion and persistence, without flourish or demonstration. She, too, was in mute agony over what was happening in China, for scarcely a month after we began our lessons, Japan invaded Manchuria. It was she who put this seed in me, the habit of learning "current events". And although, at that time, the tumultuous volcanic seething of my exuberant and maladroit growing up smothered this curiosity among a hodge-podge of other inquiries, yet it persisted, even if spadmodic.

Teacher Wu must have thought me indifferent, however, for there was little I could say, there was so much I did not know. She brought the newspaper with her, and with a preoccupied look, would make me read some passage. This usually occurred at the end of our lesson; and later, she would stay longer, and talk, tell me what was really happening. But often she must have felt disappointed, for I absorbed, but nothing ever welled out of me, not in her presence. I had too much greed of life and too little discernment, unable to separate the important from the trivial, and those with whom most of my time was spent – like Hilda and Olga – were not like Teacher Wu. Had they heard her they would have laughed, or called her names, like "Red", or "hothead". So that I constantly had to readjust myself, as I went to and fro between Teacher Wu's world and the world of Olga and Hilda. And yet it was towards Teacher Wu's world that I was moving, slowly, so slowly, so imperceptibly that even I did not know it. On the surface I was becoming a typical, well dressed, good-looking, empty Eurasian; avid for a good time, parties and boy friends. At bottom, I was going in a diametrically opposite direction. "You have no small talk," said Hilda loftily, catching me one day talking of the loss of Manchuria. And that was more damning than anything else. Teacher Wu was part of the seabed motion, deep, strong, enduring, which in my many-levelled life would, in the end, efface all shallow tumults, and carry me in the strong current back to China, a China not of the past, not dead, but of today, alive. Perhaps that is why I want to find Teacher Wu again, to grasp her small dry hand, the nails always cut so short and clean, to say: "Look, Teacher Wu, you did not waste your time . . . Look, I am here . . . I have not forgotten you and your words."

The first two months Teacher Wu came to our house to teach

me. I would find her, at five thirty when I returned from the office, waiting for me. In the third month, November, on one appointed afternoon, she was not at home. At supper I had the usual argument with my mother. Quarrels rose, rocketed over nothing and everything; in between our fights Mother would buy fruit I liked, prepare some beef tea to make me stronger, trying her best to overcome that aversion, neither her fault, nor mine. And I, shrivelled with remorse, would vow to behave better; but it did not work. At least she did not suffocate me with loving pretence and leave me perplexed and anxiety-ridden, wondering what sin I had committed; I always knew what was the matter; it did not maim me in secrecy. But over Teacher Wu's absence she remained silent, and though I wondered aloud what had happened, she did not explain.

The next morning, in my office, I received a letter from Teacher Wu. By that time I was proficient enough in Chinese to read it. Catching up on a language that I should have studied from the age of six, but which was not taught to me after eight, was not easy; and I was always laughed at by some of my friends, like Hilda, who thought it very funny that I should want to learn Chinese. Olga would add: "You'll never do it, Eurasians can't. They're mentally *blocked* up there." Hitting her forehead, almost obsessively. Olga prided herself on her Peking accent, which was excellent. I think seeing me so obstinate enraged her, for she liked to subdue others to her views.

When I had read Teacher Wu's letter I went to Olga, eyes blurred with tears. "Olga, my mother seems to have kicked out my Chinese teacher, what do I do?"

Olga's heart-shaped face turned to me. Her misshapen body was always wrapped in a white overall; she frowned: "Your mother doesn't like you, do you know that?"

"Of course."

Olga did not like my mother because at Peitaiho my poor mother, suffering from Peitaiho tummy, had soiled a bed sheet. It was no use arguing with Olga, one could never argue with her.

"What shall I do about my Chinese teacher, Olga?"

"What the hell do you want to study Chinese for, anyway?"

"I want to get on. I want to go to university, I want to be a doctor."

She snorted. "My dear girl, you're nuts. Real crackers. You *won't* be able to do it. Even if you tried for ten years. Studying Chinese is already bad enough. But what about the rest? Physics,

137

mathematics and chemistry. You haven't got the brains. I've watched you and I know. Why don't you just settle down and give it up? You'll go batty one of these days."

I went to the ladies' room and wept it out, then went back to type. Mrs. Bürger was buying new curtains and talked about the beautiful silk one could get for curtains at the Cloth Store.

Teacher Wu was waiting at the entrance gate with the two stone lions. She walked with me in the cold, and came straight to the point:

"Your mother made it clear that it was not convenient for me to sit and wait for you in your home. As I admire your determination, I would like to continue teaching you. But I can no longer come to your house to do it."

She then suggested that at eight o'clock in the morning three times a week she come to the P.U.M.C., and we would study in the auditorium. The auditorium was a rectangular edifice, across the street from the entrance. There were tables with magazines and newspapers, chairs, it was very convenient, provided we stopped before nine.

Said Teacher Wu: "We shall continue our studies."

And so we did. Punctual as her own watch, a prim affair of steel which she took out of the inner pocket of her gown, Teacher Wu was there.

Thus we went on, till the summer of 1932, when suddenly she gave me up, announced that she had to go away. And now I am afraid that Teacher Wu was in trouble, for she was a fierce patriot, perhaps she had to hide, to escape . . . I never saw her again.

After that I had another teacher, a man, a Mr. Wang who taught Chinese at the American school.

For my lessons with Mr. Wang I had to go to the compound of the American-Chinese school, which was rather far. He took me on at six in the evening, twice a week. "I shall teach you better than anyone else," said Mr. Wang, exaltedly. Immediately he put me to the works of Liang Tsichao,* the great reformist of the nineteenth century. His monumental volume of political philosopy *Yin Pingshih*, which can be translated as: "The Pavilion of Iced Beverages", was a classic, written in the most elegant style of *fin de siècle*; the contents of the Pavilion of Iced Beverages totally undid in me whatever knowledge and whatever contact with the reality of the Chinese situation I had acquired, so late, with Teacher Wu. "You are now at about that level in your Chinese,"

* See *The Crippled Tree*.

138

said Mr. Wang. How wrong he was. Liang's style, he said, was "easy to comprehend". It was nothing of the kind. Today, in China, Liang's style would not be read or understood by many, it would be about as current as Chaucerian English in 1966 London.

Teacher Wu had stuck to colloquial, plain Chinese, and I was just getting proficient at it, when this large dose of gothic verbiage was flung at me, dazing me and making it impossible for me to be sure, when I read the newspapers, what I was reading. I still have "The Pavilion of Iced Beverages" in my library, and now I can read it with ease, but how laughable and archaic the turns of phrase, how long-winded and abstruse the arguments, how tedious and unreal the whole political philosophy of parliamentarianism for China!

Liang Tsichao was a devotee of parliamentary democracy, and there is nothing wrong with that, except that China in his days was neither a democracy, nor able to practise it. It was being invaded and cut up, yet, Liang asserted, China would never be able to do anything worth while until she became a democracy; and it was the democracies who were doing the evil. Liang praised the rule of law, admired the rule of law in England and France, yet these countries had trampled on us, and no law had held their troops back! He admired Japan, and there were we, in 1932, being thoroughly mauled by Japan. He was gloomy about China, asserted that the Chinese should do things gradually, and not try to hasten matters; yet we all felt we had waited long enough, and must do something. In short, Liang was a grandiloquent, well-meaning old man, and in that summer of 1932 his recipes for China sounded uncommonly like Marie Antoinette when she recommended a diet of cakes to her starving peasants.

Mr. Wang was devoted to democracy, and after the lesson would talk at length of what was wrong with China. There was plenty, and Mr. Wang waxed pessimistic, shook his head, spoke of moral reform, of the virtue of the sages. "Students should not indulge in politics, they trouble the spirit of learning." In "The Pavilion of Iced Beverages" there were sentences he repeated enthusiastically: "Alas, our people are like sand, our institutions are effete, the land is overrun with incompetence . . ." He also advised me to read Dr. Hu Shih, another grandiloquent pessimist. "Dr. Hu Shih is the greatest intellectual in China," said Mr. Wang. I did all he told me, since he was my teacher, and rapidly lost ground in Chinese again.

And now I was often tired; I was growing fast, going to many more parties, studying and working. I sometimes stumbled in a daze, out of touch with myself, too tired to know it. My mental confusion was intense, I could feel myself a sum of separate vortices, each whirling its own restlessness, separate from others. Perhaps in the end it was good that my mind was not affected by the melody of Liang Tsichao; and thus the vague, diffuse, semi-liberalism which Liang and other nineteenth-century reformists had dabbled in, so singularly inappropriate to conditions in China, remained to me an insipid and tedious cacophony. The concrete situations of power, rather than subtle theses of government, were always to weigh more with me; and there were going to be plenty of such situations in my life later.

Fortuitously, I met the great man, Dr. Hu Shih himself, that year; looked at him with trepidation, remained conscious of the tuft of hair that stood upon his head, giving his long face the lugubrious benevolence of a camel.

And since in 1932, 1933, it was treason to feel heart-rent at what was happening in China; since it was forbidden to discuss current affairs, and to advocate resistance to Japan was to be a Communist, perhaps Mr. Wang was merely being very careful, reading these enchanting phrases in praise of democracy, and never hinting that at that very moment the democracies were once again letting China down.

CHAPTER SEVEN

No single crisis shapes a generation; but a succession of events, each one bringing its shaping blows to bear; all my contemporaries, and myself, were finally solidified into action, catalysed out of dubiety, by the onslaught of Japan on China which began in 1931.

And now that another onslaught is being prepared, it is time for the new generation to turn their look back and to learn what it was like; to recognize the lineaments of the future as the old world is battering itself down in the same imbecile and sordid schemes which led to so much slaughter in the past.

My generation hated the Japanese for what they did, but we do so no longer, though the portents are that they may repeat their folly. I can now care for this gifted people, so near to us, so near that it is a tragedy they are being manœuvred into war again. This relinquishing of resentment towards Japan I do not owe to Chiang Kaishek, nor to a vague humanitarianism, but to Chou Enlai, Prime Minister of China.

Chou Enlai was meeting a Japanese delegation in Peking three years ago, and the delegation was apologizing, as is the custom of the Japanese, for the evils of the past. Many of us in Asia think it more dignified to apologize, than to go on, as America is doing, losing not only face but honour, and gaining the world's contempt for the death she rains down upon an unfortunate small country, Vietnam, because America, so large, so wealthy, is unable to admit to a mistake in judgment.

When the Japanese delegation apologized, Chou Enlai said to them: "Please do not apologize, it is we who must thank you. Because you made war on us, you hastened the crumbling of our old feudal system, and through the national war against you, the Chinese people found themselves, became conscious and united, and won out to the bright promise of a new China."

In 1962, by accepting an invitation to visit Japan, I was also atoning for having hated the Japanese in the past. I hoped they would never again, misled by the death-wish of their militarists, be made the instrument for an even greater militarism than Japan ever practised. The future of Japan is in friendship, equality, and peace with China. There is no other way for Japan.

The time is October 1962. I sit, legs folded under me, on the *tatami* floor mats of a luxurious Japanese-style restaurant. Mr. Osaka of the Far East Section, Ministry of External Affairs, and his two aides, Mr. Okura and Mr. Yamada, sit opposite me. We all smile happily. We have discussed Malaysia, South-East Asia, the golfing ability of "smart guy" Lee, prime minister of Singapore; we now come to China.

"Yes," says Mr. Yamada, who is clever, subtle, going at topics with a slight peer of his bespectacled eyes, like the good golfer that he is, gauging the sweep of his club: "We Japanese are obsessed with China, always obsessed, because we share the same culture, but I believe we are getting away from this now. We want to know, though, whether China is still worried about us?"

"Ah," says Mr. Okura, who has a very strong American accent, and is keen on baseball, "some people say they cannot tell a Japanese from a Chinese, but I think one can, seeing the way they walk in the street; the Chinese steps with a loose gait rolling, as if

141

he'd just enjoyed a good dinner; he looks, but he does not see, he doesn't pay attention; while a Japanese walks carefully, holding himself tight, and his eyes take in everything, like a camera."

This is a typical Asian conversation, proceeding by indirection, metaphor, circling the core of fire – the question of relations with China.

On either side of me kneel the two finest geishas of this most luxurious restaurant; a new geisha, who had not been in circulation before, comes and dances a few steps in front of us, utters a few melodic screams. The geisha on my left pours *saké* into my cup. I smile at her. I smile at the geisha on my right. My knees hurt, kneeling on the floor. The new geisha sits by me, I have three women surrounding me, attentive to my wine and food. A great honour.

Always at these moments of high and delicate courtesy, of nimble diplomatic innuendo, I put my foot through the floor; today is no exception.

"I remember, when I was a child in Peking, in the 1930s, your soldiers had just invaded Manchuria. I remember it so well. I was walking near the East Market in Peking, with the ambulant sellers of food, noodles and soup steaming, the itinerant barbers with the zing zing zing of their iron forks, the wooden clappers of the pastry men; and in the middle of all this students were passing in a double file, waving flags and chanting: 'Down with Japanese imperialism, boycott Japanese goods . . .' "

The three faces in front of me remain completely passive; Japanese diplomats are very well trained. The geisha on my right forgets herself and hisses; stares at me with round eyes; the white and pink powder on her face, however, remained uncracked. I continue.

"I was educated to cry: 'Down with Japanese imperialism', and yet I have always thought it was a great pity, that if Japan and China could have remained friends, as was the wish of Dr. Sun Yatsen, things could have been better, much better, all round."

"Yes," says Mr. Yamada, "but perhaps our diplomacy was not too subtle," and by this superb understatement he nearly wins this uneven match between us.

I face Mr. Osaka: "Tell me, Mr. Osaka, do you think that in the future, at any time, it might happen again, that Japan will again try to invade China?"

Mr. Osaka laughs heartily, laughs long. Mr. Yamada replies

for him: "I don't think we Japanese want to commit suicide."
And that is the end line. Curtain. I leave Japan tomorrow.

We all drink, toasting each other. Perhaps I should have toasted
the co-prosperity sphere, Pan-Asia, tongue in cheek. Perhaps I
have insulted them dreadfully. I humbly apologize, and shall
delegate myself to beg forgiveness, but I cannot withdraw my
meaning. Japan's future is in Asia, as a friend of China. But
whatever happens, I cannot hate the Japanese again, for now I
know that they too are victims; yes, even Mr. Osaka with his fine
American tie; Mr. Yamada, Mr. Okura with their golf and
baseball pitches; they are victims, not free; they are bondsmen,
and I have seen, when calling at the External Affairs office, who is
the master; sitting at the desk, okaying every letter in English
that goes out of this office, the languid, insolent stranger.

Contact with the West was as fraught with pain for Japan as
for China. As in China, merchants and Jesuit priests, learning the
language, made a favourable beginning as individuals. But this
soon changed. Edicts prohibiting Christianity followed. The
Japanese also decided to confine, as did the Chinese, the entry of
foreign ships to one harbour, and managed to keep aloof for two
centuries. By the nineteenth century, however, while China
suffered defeats and humiliations, Japan had decided on a different course. Her feudal society was crumbling, leaders with a
far-sighted nationalism realized that change was essential for
survival. By 1853, when the American squadron under Com-
modore Perry sailed to Japan with an ultimatum, warning that
unless trade relations were opened he would be back "with a
larger squadron the following year," the Japanese had ample
time to digest what had happened to China when she had
resisted the opium trade enforced by war with Great Britain.
America wanted a coaling base in Japan for her ships going to
China; she was competing against England, and at a disadvantage
against Hongkong, Britain's base in South China.

For already in the 1850s America had begun to dream of the
conquest of Asia; since then she has been on the march, designing
to reign first on the Pacific, then in Asia, later – who knows? The
Monroe doctrine was not isolationist, but exclusivist; it eliminated all other influence than hers from the Americas themselves,
and later an Asiatic Monroe doctrine would extend her supre-
macy across the Pacific, right up to the Himalayas, the Indian
Ocean . . .

In this Grand Design Japan was to become America's most important base, to control the Asian mainland, and principally China.

Japan's leaders had hastened Japan's industrial revolution by herding the peasantry into factories, in the same fashion as Victorian England; then imitating the West further, she made successful war upon China in 1895, and this aggressive conduct hoisted her to a position of prestige among the other, similarly aggressive, powers. The indemnity levied from China paid for another decade of industrial development in Japan.

But once a capitalist state, Japan's industrial complex needed raw materials, needed markets; the course of exploitation is ever the same, whichever country practises it. Her dream of imperial destiny now took shape, and it was to beat Britain, or even to do better. Japan won a war over Russia in 1905; an action much praised in England, at that time dominated by paranoiac fear of Russia. And though it was the beginning of the erosion of white prestige in Asia, which the Second World War, the Korean War, and the two wars in Vietnam (the French, and now the American) are completing, no one saw it at that time. No one knew that Japan was determined to supersede all other Asian powers in their zones of exploitation in Asia. But for this she needed to conquer China, that immense source of manpower and of raw materials. "Who conquers China conquers the world." But meanwhile other powers were gorging on China's inexhaustible capacity for producing wealth for others. "The vampires are feasting, we may be too late," wrote a Japanese statesman in 1898.

But after 1900, Japan's ambitions were given stimulus by her alliance with Great Britain. The latter, uniquely obsessed by her nightmare of a great Russian advance into India, supplanting British mastery there, and reaching the warm and ice-free Indian Ocean, found it expeditious to befriend Japan as a pawn to play against Russia. British expeditions into Tibet were designed for the purpose of establishing there a buffer state between British India and the Tsar's sprawling Asiatic conquests of Siberia. Japan was to be manoeuvred, counterweight to Russian expansion; and if it meant giving her a portion of China, who cared? China was to pay for these games of power, in suffering and exploitation, but whoever thought of China and her people, in that ferocious era which is not yet ended today?

When Japan struck at Russia in 1905, destroying the Russian navy without a declaration of war, *The Times* exulted: "The Japanese Navy has opened the war by an act of daring which is destined to take its place of honour in naval annals . . ." Yet nine years later Germany was denounced as barbarous for invading Belgium without a declaration of war. . .

The Anglo-Japanese alliance lasted till 1921; it had clauses recognizing Japanese interest "in a peculiar degree" in Korea, and giving her a free hand to block Russian advance elsewhere. In 1921, when America suddenly became aware that Japanese plans of domination in China might interfere with her own plans, she forced an end to this alliance. And now Japanese statesmen lamented that Japan had lost her opportunity. "Perhaps it is too late." Yet they had tried, tried especially during the First World War, when in the absence of Western powers, engaged in slaughter, from Asian markets, Japan had made great industrial advance; and had thought the time ripe to present an ultimatum to China, the Twenty-One demands. But this unsubtle diplomacy had failed; then again, at the Peace Conference of Versailles, Japan, by secret negotiation, had won the ex-German sphere of influence, Shantung; but this was brusquely repudiated by the United States in 1921. Meanwhile, despite the militarists in Japan, there was a growing alliance between Japanese and Chinese intellectuals; mutual sympathy, and understanding of the idea of friendship and alliance between the two countries. Dr. Sun Yatsen had many friends in Japan. He had often delivered lectures on the necessity for China and Japan, as two Asian countries, to become friends, and for Japan to give up being "the hawk of western rule of Might" and to become instead "a tower of strength for the peoples of Asia".

This vision of a United Asia, the cornerstone of which would be friendship between China and Japan, had been repeated by Sun Yatsen in his last lecture, only three months before his death, at Kobe in December 1924. "This is the choice now before the people of Japan: A pawn of the West, or a free and great nation of Asia."

Sun Yatsen's speech, his vision of the choice before Japan, remains still valid today. Still today Japan has to choose; will she become an Asian country, in an alliance with China, or will resurgent militarism serve to confirm her as a satellite and war base to an America seeking to dominate the heartland of Asia?

Alliance and friendship with China, or a second Hawaii to America; which will Japan chose?

The effect of giving Shantung to Japan upon the Chinese people was one which the West had not reckoned with. It was the famous May 4th, 1919 movement, turning point in China's history*. When it became obvious that China's intellectuals were all veering to the Left, when Sun Yatsen bitterly said: "We no longer trust the West," in 1921, America brusquely rescinded the secret agreement she had concluded in 1917 with Japan, and also pressured England not to renew the Anglo-Japanese treaty of friendship. And Great Britain, indebted, impoverished and weakened, slowly expelled out of Asia by her own exhaustion, gave way.

By 1922 it was obvious that Japan would lose out in the race for markets, *unless* she could, quickly, assume dominion over China. Russia was busy with her Revolution; and temporarily out of the running. America played a waiting game, for she was herself, after the First World War, in a crisis, anxious for a period of retrenchment and consolidation. The nine-power treaty of Washington in 1921 and 1922 was designed for a realignment and a reapportionment of markets among the principal powers which had intersts in the Pacific. It declared that where China was concerned, the nine powers would *always* act together, and would *refrain from taking advantage of conditions* in China, to seek special rights or privileges which would abridge the rights of subjects or citizens of friendly states.

The treaty was described as "a covenant of self-denial" among the signatory powers, "deliberate renunciation of any policy of aggression which might tend to interfere with the development of China," wrote Secretary of State Stimson. That is a pious hypocrisy. The Western Powers needed a pause, the rebuilding of shattered economies; they were not ready for immediate hostilities on this question of markets. It was now obvious that no one power alone could keep China down. The agreements concluded at the time of the nine-power treaty were designed to ensure a *collective system* for maintenance of the status quo, nothing else.

In the next few years America, England, Japan, and France were to disembark many troops, repeatedly, to protect their privileges in China, and none of these privileges were given up; in 1943 some were conceded, at last; but the most important,

* See page 49

tariff autonomy, was not actually abolished till 1949.

All through the 1920s Japan's problems increased. She had long coveted Manchuria, with its deposits of coal, iron, and gold, and its strategic position. She had first tried to make Manchuria a separate regime under her control in 1911.

When the Revolution of 1911 had occurred in China, Kawashima, head of Japan's secret service (Manchuria section), advised the Japanese General Terauchi to let Sun Yatsen have South China, but to guarantee to the Manchu dynasty North China, and to erect independent regimes in Mongolia and Manchuria. Arms were smuggled in for this purpose, but when Kawashima went to Tokyo, in 1912, expecting to receive official aid, he was told that the policy had changed. The Japanese were entering into the International Consortium, lending twenty-five million pounds to Yuan Shihkai, which enabled Yuan to defeat Sun Yatsen and to crush the Revolution of 1911. This also ended the first attempt to create a separate Manchuria.

A second attempt was in 1915, included in the unsubtle twenty-one demands. Again Kawashima came to the fore. In Manchuria a military commander later known as Marshal Chang Tsolin was groomed as Japan's puppet. But the Japanese did not succeed in winning him over completely. He took their money, but also held out against them. Many attempts to kill him failed, though three thousand men, from 1915 to 1928, were to be employed in the job of assassinating him. It was not till June 1928, when Chiang Kaishek, in alliance with Feng Yuhsiang, was advancing towards Peking, that the Japanese succeeded in blowing up Chang Tsolin at last.

In 1927 all the portents of a crisis for Japan were there: imbalance of payments, bankruptcies of small and later bigger banks, increasing power of extreme right-wing militaristic groups. In the spring of 1927, two and a half years before the Wall Street crash and the Great Depression, thirty-five banks closed their doors in Japan. The military party, akin to the hawks of America today, used this financial debacle to force the moderate-minded Prime Minister, Shidehara, out of office.

Prime Minister Tanaka who took office on April 20th, 1927, a week after Chiang Kaishek's April 12th massacre of Communists in Shanghai, was committed to a get-tough policy.

"Manchuria is Japan's lifeline, we must settle this problem, otherwise there will be war."

147

In the autumn of 1927, while his friends kept his seat warm for him, Chiang Kaishek went on a visit to Japan. Besides visiting his future mother-in-law, Madame Soong, at a Japanese spa, he also stayed in the house of Toyama Mitsumi, now head of the Japanese Secret Service. What converse they had is not known, but from Chiang's subsequent docility to Japan, it became clear that he had agreed to Japan having "special rights" in Manchuria, most probably because he was more afraid of Russia and communism than of Japan. But his docility did not satisfy the hawks; a boycott of all Japanese goods following the landing of some Japanese "protection troops" convinced the militarists that no time was to be lost; nationalism was rising "at a terrible pace" in China, and even if there was internecine fighting between Right and Left, Kuomintang and Communist, this nationalism would continue to demand that all sovereign rights be restored to the Chinese people. Moreover, when Chiang married T. V. Soong's sister, Soong Meiling, he was tacitly entering in an alliance with American finance, and this was not to Japan's liking at all.

In May 1928 a third attempt to seize Manchuria ended in failure; for at this point America sent a warning reminder to Tokyo, to "apprise the United States in advance, if they intended to take any action in Manchuria."

Fear of a clash with the United States made Tanaka pause; general mobilization of the Japanese troops in Manchuria had already started, but was countermanded.

Chang Tsolin was blown up in June 1928; Chang Hsuehliang, his son, known to all the world as the Young Marshal, now became ruler of Manchuria. He proved even more recalcitrant than his father; approached for some railway projects, he not only refused, but actually started to build his own line. Wooed by Chiang Kaishek, who used with him the same mellifluous persuasion as with Feng Yuhsiang and became his "brother" (they exchanged blood to seal their brotherhood oath), he proved patriotic, In December 1928, the Kuomintang flag flew in Manchuria; the Young Marshal accepted a high post in the Nanking government. China seemed unified at last, even to its furthermost provinces in Manchuria.

Angered, the Japanese hawks searched for a suitable puppet, and remembered Puyi, the last Manchu emperor, who for some years now had been living in the Japanese Concession in Tientsin under protection.

In his autobiography* Puyi described his unhappy life as Emperor. Placed on the throne in 1908 when three years old, the Revolution of 1911 had forced him off it; for two weeks in 1917 a warlord put him back as Emperor in Peking, then he was off the throne again. He lived in the Forbidden City on a two-million-dollar pension served him by the government, until Feng Yuhsiang in 1924 threw him out and bade him become an ordinary citizen. His eunuchs disbanded, he went to the Japanese legation, was conveyed to Tientsin, where he lived quietly, visited by Japanese officials.

When Tanaka came to power in April 1927 "my hopes of restoration grew stronger," wrote Puyi.

Meanwhile Chang Hsuehliang the Young Marshal sat uneasy in Manchuria. He knew the Japanese were angry with him, and he hated them for killing his father. His unease was vividly described to me by my friend Malcolm MacDonald, who travelled in 1929 from Kyoto, where he attended the Institute of Pacific Relations Conference, to Mukden, the capital of the Young Marshal. Chang Hsuehliang was taking his mind off his troubles by playing golf. Every time he was going to putt, Malcolm asked the Young Marshal: "What do you think Japan is going to do next?" and watched him miss. "The poor young man was a victim of drugs at the time, first opium, then heroin. But he was great fun, and he had great character. He later cured himself of the habit. He was most intelligent; he stood between Chiang Kaishek and the Japanese, and trusted neither. His first enthusiam for Chiang had cooled; he realized Chiang made use of people. And he knew the Japanese were grooming Puyi to make a comeback as Emperor in Manchuria."

In the summer of 1931 a Japanese officer paid Puyi a visit in Tientsin and handed him a fan with a symbolic phrase upon it. At the same time Puyi's brother, Puchieh, who was studying in Japan, was told: "Chang Hsuehliang, the Young Marshal, has been behaving disgracefully to us and something may happen soon in Manchuria. Please ask your brother *the Emperor* to take care of himself, and not to lose hope."

Again the Japanese pressed Chang Hsuehliang for concessions and privileges; Chang neatly referred the matter to "the central government in Nanking," i.e. Chiang Kaishek. The Chinese

* From *Emperor to Citizen*, by Aisin Gioro Pu Yi (Foreign Language Press, Peking, 1964).

were already opening coalmines to compete against the Fuhsin coalmine, a huge open pit owned and developed by the Japanese (and where, in 1947, my husband Pao was to fight his first and last battle against the Communists). They were also drawing plans for a port to rival the Japanese port at Dairen.

In spite of Japanese attempts to encourage Japanese immigration into Manchuria, by 1930 there were thirty million Chinese, two million Manchus and only eight hundred thousand Japanese in Manchuria, and this in spite of the fact that with special privileges, the Japanese could settle at will and without passports.

In 1929 Prime Minister Tanaka resigned, the Army accusing him of weakness and indecision over Manchuria; the depression increased, aggravating Japan's problems.

Britain and America now got together in another conference, as their financial crisis was also becoming more serious. An attempt to cut down spending in capital ship building was made.

The Japanese navy viewed this with grave misgivings. They had already been frustrated with the settlement forced on Japan in 1921, limiting her to a ratio of three ships for every five of America or England. By virtue of this treaty Japan had to be content with a navy which could never engage the American Fleet in Far Eastern waters; though it could wreak havoc on China. The increasing depression was forcing America and Britain to retrenchment of capital spending on sea and land, and they sought for their own safety to bring Japan within a limit too. But Japan feared that once the crisis was over, England and America might become allies to put her, Japan, out of the running for the conquest of China. A desperate course of action followed.

On September 18th, 1931, Japan, on a pretext, seized Manchuria. Her timing was perfect. On September 22nd, 1931, London went off the gold standard; in 1929, the New York stock market had crashed. Depression was in. Japan had calculated well. This was her best hour.

CHAPTER EIGHT

Oh, the pellucid autumn of Peking, when clouds strut so high in the air that to look up is another vertigo. Autumn in Peking is nearly paradise, and the season when the people are proudest of their city, for then the yellow of the imperial palaces' tiles glows more yellow, the purple walls more splendid and the evening flush above the autumn crimson of the Western Hills is a glory which makes one shout. At night the moon's image freezes in the flowing water of the Jade Fountain, surpassing precious stones in radiance. The birds fly in their cohorts, crying desolation; in the streets people stop each other to say: "How good the autumn is!"

The willows trail their long sleeves in the lakes. The honeyed heat of noon is still summer for them. Nights and days are equally long, and the main roads fruit-sided, as pedlars put their trestles up and arrange fruit in baskets, in rows, in heaps and pyramids: every size of grapes – green elongated mare's nipples, seedless lucent pale jade, round moonlike pearly, all the tones of magenta to amber; apples too, of all kinds, and pears by the gross, big and small, smooth or rough-skinned, brick-brown to primrose; quince and melon of so many kinds and from many places. Standing behind their bounty, lovingly, the pedlars sing:

"Oh, gentlemen and ladies, and you young sirs, young damsels, pray look, look your fill, for where else, where will you get such happiness of eye, to gladden the heart within you? For my fruit is the best in the city, renowned of all, fresh plucked, borne this morning in hampers from beyond the city walls to you. Look, the bloom is on it yet. And all this basket for a dollar, a mere silver dollar, four hundred coppers."

And though it is still summer for the noon willows, by three o'clock the limpid cold sets in, catching summer by its morning throat and evening feet. At night, walking to smell the hint of frost, one comes upon the aroma of chestnuts tossed on the outdoor stoves, roasted in big iron pans, shovelled in fine dark sand and a little honey. The chestnut merchants sing their chestnuts mellow, golden, fresh, half the night through.

Then comes the autumn festival; for a whole fortnight, in all the markets, the mooncakes in orderly armies parade their roundness in all the food shops, light, feathery, moon-white, with pink markings to indicate their stuffing, dates or honey or sesame with crushed fruit, bean with rose petals, ginger with quince, delightful to look at and better to eat; a Peking childhood is forever ravished by mooncakes. Mooncakes I wanted to eat during the years abroad, mooncakes the first thing my father bought for me when I returned to Peking in 1956. Only Peking mooncakes have that air and flavour, that whiteness of the moon and that manner of disappearing on one's tongue. Nowhere else, not in Szechuan nor in the south, are mooncakes made with the smell and feel of moon substance.

And besides them, like golden giants, are piled the fruits of the moon, pummeloes and oranges and tangerines, ample-bellied and full-faced as the goddess of Mercy herself. Above them hang the unnumbered lanterns of the moon, lamps of silk and paper; and like ten thousand mirrors, in scarlet and gold, emerald and turquoise, riding upon tigers and hippogryphs, lions and moon dogs, the hare monarch of the moon ranges upon the open shelves in the East Market. All the children know that a hare lives in the moon palaces; on clear nights his white-pink face, his red and green and gorgeous garments can be espied. He often dresses as a general, the flags of his office in a quiver at his back. Every child buys at least one Moon Hare gentleman; there are large ones, half a child's size, tiny ones, to carrry about in one's folded fist, and all of painted clay.

All is abundance at the Moon Festival, even if armies rampage, and food is scarce, and fear is about, and the Japanese are coming, have come. The Japanese are beyond the Great Wall, they are in the land, they have come – and already in Peking the families hoard rice, make fast the doors against pillage and rape. But lest the children weep, it is not good to show sorrow before sorrow comes.

In the Central Park are rows of chrysanthemum pots, and the scholars and old men walking their birds in birdcages, swinging their birds in the honey warmth, go to enjoy them, and in small groups, quietly, ask each other what will happen now? Along the front of our house, in the mule- and donkey-cart dust road, the porters shuffle at dawn, swinging loads from the ends of poles, loads of chrysanthemums, white and pale mauve, pale pink, yellow golden, and bronze; big and small chrysanthemums, some are so heavy laden with bloom that the stem is supported by a bamboo stick, chrysanthemums large as a fist, small as a violet. In the East Market the wine shops set out their best jars, and little cups of porcelain, and wooden benches, for tasters to sit and sip a little autumn wine.

So was the autumn, lovely in 1931. In Peking so quietly, beautifully, autumn came; and those who did not know the hearts of men, who did not want to understand the secret darkness where ripen the thoughts of men, said that all was well.

"Why, these people couldn't care less – about the Japanese, or about anything."

152

"Just give them a bowl of rice, they'll be content."

The children of Peking went about, clutching their hare monarchs and their lanterns. In the Peking Union Medical College, the secretaries talked of Jeanette MacDonald and Ramon Navarro.

In the reluctant owl-light evening going home, I could see the people standing, blueclad, immobile, standing to read the newspapers posted on wooden boards. The wind blew from the north, and their eyes were cold.

That was all there was to see, in September 1931, when Japan suddenly came down upon Manchuria, our north-east, and took it away.

On that autumn day, September 18th, 1931, a small detachment of Japanese soldiers patrolling the Japanese-owned railway in Manchuria found that a bomb had detonated, and ripped thirty-one inches off the steel rails. Yet the express train that was running that day went over the gap without harm, and later investigation could not reveal a damaged rail. But this specious excuse was enough. Japan invaded, bombed, strafed, and started the occupation of Manchuria. Fifty thousand troops, with tanks and aeroplanes, marched in.

Two years of protest and talk at the League of Nations came to naught. It soon became clear, as the *Cambridge History of the World* puts it:

> "that neither collective nor individual action against Japan would be taken . . . in fact, for the first four years the U.S.A. continued to supply Japan with *two-thirds* of the war materials she required for her war of aggression against China, a state of affairs brought to an abrupt end *only* by the Japanese attack upon Pearl Harbour on December 7th, 1941."

At home, the "hawks" of Japanese militarism had gained control. Political assassinations, as plain or as ambiguous as that of Kennedy, disposed of those who stood in the way of militarists and their will to war.

Abroad, Japanese diplomats were busy; they inculcated in Western governments the notion that once Japan was given her *Lebensraum* in Manchuria, she would be satisfied, and would guarantee equal opportunities to Great Britain and the U.S.A.

153

Great Britain on the decline in Asia was not anxious to come into conflict with Japan, so long as she believed that in Manchuria Japan would keep open the door for British products This she found it expedient to believe.

On January 7th, 1932, the American government's note to Japan, described as "stern," actually encouraged Japan to further attacks. Since September 1931, the American government, which though not a member of the League of Nations was obviously the only nation that could stop Japan, had not taken or recommended any action in advance to that of the League; indeed it had exerted a restraining influence, for instance with reference to sending a commission, or fixing a definite date for the withdrawal of Japanese troops.

The substance of this fateful American note was actually to demand of Japan an assurance that the "international policy relative to China," that is, the open door policy, giving equal rights and privileges to all nations, would be maintained in Manchuria. And this dishonest core was not lost upon the Japanese, who immediately gave this assurance.

"It is agreeable to be assured that the American government are devoting, in a friendly spirit, such *sedulous* care to the correct appreciation of the situation."

Japan's satisfaction was exquisite; she was getting away with her bold coup; heady with victory, secretly contemptuous of the white powers' faintheartedness, she proceeded to further attack.

On January 28th, 1932, she attacked Shanghai.

On February 18th, 1932, the independence of the Manchurian provinces was proclaimed. Puyi was conveyed from Tientsin to Mukden to become the Chief Executive of the new state of Manchukuo. Meanwhile, where was Chang Hsuehliang, the Young Marshal, whose bailiwick was Manchuria? He had retreated with his one hundred and seventy thousand troops into North China, dissuaded by Chiang Kaishek from offending the Japanese.

And this was the greatest puzzle of all, at least to us; a puzzle which at first stupefied us, and later roused us against Chiang Kaishek: his policy of non-resistance to Japan, carried out with incredible stubbornness, in the face of a rising tide of national demand for resistance against aggression.

"Why is nothing being done, why is nothing being done?" Teacher Wu read the papers, her mouth quivered: "If you want to learn Chinese, Miss Chou, you must also learn what is happening." "Yes, Teacher Wu, but why is the government not doing anything?" "The Nanking government say that it would be foolish to resist the Japanese as China is too weak . . . although many of us do not think this . . ."

The students of Peking University paraded and demonstrated as winter came closing in upon Peking. I saw them march, carrying banners; in the cold they boarded trains, to go to Nanking, to plead with Chiang Kaishek to stand up and fight . . .

But Japan was now bombing Shanghai; forty warships, and sixty thousand men disembarked, occupied the Chinese sector and began massacres. An Englishwoman, Mrs. Mills, the mother of Hayley Mills the actress, recently told me how, sixteen years old at the time, she saw some of the victims of the Japanese: thirteen men, tied to stakes, dead, their genital organs stuffed in their mouths.

Nanking was also bombed; Chiang Kaishek moved his government to Loyang. Then something quite extraordinary occurred. One Chinese army, the 19th Route Army, under a general called Tsai Tingkai, stood up and fought, against the wishes of Chiang Kaishek, fought in Shanghai against the Japanese.

Tsai Tingkai and his 19th Route Army under Chiang's orders had been used in the Third Extermination Campaign against the Red bases of Mao Tsetung. Through the summer and autumn of 1931 they had fought the Communists, very reluctantly, and lost badly. The 19th Route Army had then quartered near Shanghai to recuperate; an action which had caused unease in the foreigners. It was they who now fought the Japanese, fought as they had never fought before; certainly as they had never fought the Communists the previous year. And the whole of China watched them, and they were heroes, to all of us; but not to the foreigners, nor to Chiang Kaishek.

Even today, my throat gets stuck, my eyes prick when the emotion of those days wells up from me; and oh, the quarrels with the other secretaries, with Hilda, when I lashed out proudly, so proudly with the 19th Route Army stand in Shanghai, because what they were doing redeemed China from shame, from dishonour. "What is the use," shouted Olga, "the Japanese are too strong, you wait," It was not that the Europeans were all on the side of the Japanese; in fact, later they became worried that the Japanese would go "too far," which happened when the Japanese in later years occupied Tientsin and Peking, and the Japanese

155

sentries made the British take off their trousers in public, and bow to them in their under-pants.

But a Chinese army standing up and fighting disturbed the pet prejudices of many Europeans: "They are just making a show, soon they'll bargain for some money, and they'll let the Japs do what they like." Others said: "Tsai Tingkai is a Communist."

The Japanese bombed the Commercial Press in Shanghai with its priceless library; bombed a camp of eight thousand Chinese flood refugees established in Chapei by the International Flood Relief Commission. They increased their troops to one hundred thousand in Shanghai alone. The International Settlement was used by them as a base for landing troops and operations. The British and Americans allowed them in, as they had allowed the gangsters of Dou Yuseng in 1927 . . .

Chiang Kaishek was angry, not with Japan, but with the 19th Route Army for disobeying his orders. "Non-resistance to Japan, fight communism first," said he and his Defence Minister Ho Yingchin. Chiang finally halted the heroic 19th Army by refusing Tsai Tingkai ammunition and supplies for his troops. The 19th Route Army had to withdraw.

On May 5th a truce was signed between Chiang and the Japanese; it was actually a capitulation. China had to agree to a "neutral zone" around Shanghai, which meant the Chinese would evacuate the area but Japanese troops remained to garrison it.

In the West, public opinion was becoming restive, but the Japanese government then evolved the famous "domino theory", which is now being used by the United States in her war in Vietnam.

If Japan withdrew, the Western nations were told, Bolshevik Russia would take over Manchuria. Bolshevization of Manchuria would produce bolshevization of Korea and of China; the whole of the Far East, as a pack of dominoes falling, would fall to communism . . .

Japan's "mission in Asia", which she was to shoulder, manfully, although she had no territorial ambitions, was to stop the "Red rot." Japan had in mind great plans for the welfare of the Asian people, once the threat of communism was purged and freedom (under Japan) could reign: so went the propaganda.

Actually the Japanese could not have held out in Shanghai. In the Japanese-owned factories and textile mills of Shanghai, the foremen were armed with pistols and whips, to beat or to kill the

156

recalcitrant workers. Though most of these were women and children, working fourteen hours a day, there were the beginnings of strike. The big boycott of Japanese goods was going on, in spite of Japanese pressure. In Manchuria guerrilla bands, in small numbers, were beginning activities in the countryside. Japan found that she had to send in more men. The troops withdrawn from Shanghai were syphoned into Manchuria for anti-guerrilla operations, and never went back to Japan.

In May 1932, as soon as the truce was signed, and while the battle areas of Shanghai were still a pile of rubble and corpses, Chiang Kaishek announced his Fourth Campaign of "extermination of Red bandits" in which he used five hundred thousand men. The students who had demonstrated were cowed with beatings and jail; "Fight the Communists, no resistance to Japan," and "Leave it to the League of Nations," said the Nanking government.

But the clamour against Chiang Kaishek's policy of non-resistance to Japan was becoming more audible.

Though the students who had agitated were quelled, other voices took up the protest; among them, the most outstanding, that of Chiang's sister-in-law, the sister of Madame Chiang Kaishek, Soong Chingling.

Soong Chingling had made it clear since 1927 that she disapproved of Chiang's actions. She had enormous moral influence, not only because she was the widow of Sun Yatsen, but in her own right. She now led the protest; and with her many writers, intellectuals, and such political figures as Eugene Chen.

Chiang had to explain himself. In June he called a conference at Lushan near Nanking. There he held a series of lectures to explain his policies. Some were open; others secret; the secret ones were addressed to his officer clique, old and young militarists, graduates of Whangpoo Academy, Blueshirts and secret police, the chief support of his military dictatorship.

"Civil war is more important than war against Japan" was the gist of Chiang's arguments. "This is the most important thing, to stamp out communism. We live or die by these anti-communist campaigns."

He harangued some scholars and intellectuals, called to listen to him, including among them the famous Dr. Hu Shih. Hu Shih felt greatly affronted by this. "He spoke to us as if we were soldiers, ordering us to march," he said bitterly. When I saw Hu

Shih he was still full of acerbity against Chiang for being "un-democratic"; but he could not make up his mind to lend his name to the nation-wide demand for resistance to Japan. "We are too weak, we cannot stand up to them," he maintained. He was alway a confirmed pessimist, and easily swayed by titles.

Chiang secretly toid his officers at this conference: "Don't worry, the day will come when inevitably Japan and America will clash; for America wants Asian markets, just as Japan does; and both will be fighting over China. So all we have to do is to sit back and let Japan do her worst; America will fight her; and then we shall cash in and be able to establish our rule."

In October 1932, from his Red mountain bases, Mao Tsetung called for resistance to Japan, accusing the League of appeasement. His statement was of course censored by the Nanking government.

Feng Yuhsiang, the Christian warlord, who had now become anti-Chiang, joined with fourteen others in a joint telegram to the nation, asking Chiang to abandon his policy of non-resistance to Japan and to form a common front of patriots.

Chiang refused. The Fourth Extermination Campaign utilizing five hundred thousand men started in October 1932; in November an edict, forbidding, under pain of capital punishment, any criticism of the "non-resistance to Japan" policies was promulgated; as a sop to the intellectuals, a "democratic" Constitution was also promised for the next year, but it was postponed again and again. On the contrary, a witch-hunt now started, and many intellectuals went into hiding.

In this Fourth anti-communist campaign the Kuomintang troops practised a scorched-earth policy, about one hundred thousand peasants were massacred in a devastation of the provinces where Mao Tsetung had his bases. A rigorous economic blockade was enforced. The German advisers of Chiang Kaishek began to take operations in hand. To keep the restive population under control a system of collective responsibility was established. Should any member of one clan, village, or district behave "in a subversive manner," the whole clan or village was held responsible, and likely to be annihilated.

Where did the money for these enormous anti-communist campaigns come from, when there was so little money for anything else?

None of the reforms promised by Chiang Kaishek had been

achieved; none of the social and economic injustices eliminated. Kuomintang historians themselves are unanimous on this point, although they aver that Chiang Kaishek never had a chance "because of communist penetration and the Japanese invasion." The answer is that he simply could not have started on any reforms at all without cutting off his own support. He was the victim of his own treachery.

True, the feudal landowning classes, in the provinces, did have conflicts of interest with the new Shanghai-based industrialists and bankers, whose representatives, T.V. Soong, H. H. Kung, and other relatives and stalwarts of the Nanking government supported Chiang Kaishek. These wanted certain modernization, chiefly in the internal taxation structure, and uniformity of currency. But this was in order to benefit from an increased and stable market for exploitation by themselves. China's chief problem, China's peasants, the question of land, the agricultural poverty, was never tackled. And yet awareness of this question was present. Many an American expert went round China writing reports on land reform, and there were "model farms" and many other glamour "projects"; and nothing was done.

In 1932 the financial situation in China was worse than in 1912, and though show pieces in the cities made visitors feel there was "progress", the countryside was worse off than ever.

To begin with, all China's demands for abrogation of the nineteenth-century unequal treaties, and the restoration of her sovereign rights, for customs control and tariff autonomy, had either been rejected outright, or dragged through lengthy conferences and finally bypassed. The single most important demand, tariff autonomy was nominally achieved in February 1929, but it was an empty victory. And as long as China did not have tariff autonomy and control of her own revenue, she was as helpless and dependent on the Western Powers in 1932 as in 1902.

According to the treaties forced upon her through war, China could not herself change the tariffs imposed on foreign goods brought into her territory. Her customs were under foreign control; the customs revenue earmarked for repayment on loans of the past. The tariffs were fixed at an arbitrary rate of five per cent, and no Chinese government could ever budge this rate. In addition the internal taxation revenue, such as the *likin*,* or road transport taxes, and the revenue on salt which was a government monopoly, were also hypothecated to repay China's war debts

* See *The Crippled Tree*.

and loans and the interest on them; her railways were similarly mortgaged, their profits disappeared in repayment of loans and interests. With no control over her revenue, no control over her customs, no control over her railways, no right to have her own troops in foreign concessions (but rights were granted to foreign troops to garrison in China), it was impossible for her to modernize or to industrialize *except* if such industries were to be owned by foreign capital in China, and thus became simply branches of Western industries, the enormous profits benefiting from China's cheap labour remitted back to the West. No strong national bourgeoisie could develop in these circumstances or find the capital to create independent industries, or found that middle class, both managerial and technical, which developed in Europe, and which would have launched China as a bourgeois, democratic modern state.

The only capitalism possible to China under such Western financial thwarting was the kind called "compradore capitalism", dependent on foreign investments; and the only bourgeoisie possible was a denationalized one, which would be oriented towards the West and also keep its money abroad, a "compradore" bourgeoisie.

In 1929 the granting of a new surtax tariff of two and one-half per cent over and above the tariff fixed and controlled by the West since 1842 was hailed as a triumph by the Nanking government. But it was nothing but a minor concession, for it only applied to certain imports, and not to the most needed. The Inspector-General of Chinese Customs remained a foreign national, a Britisher until 1943; in 1943 an American took over till the Communist Revolution of 1949.

The abolition of internal taxes such as the road transport and salt taxes which hindered trade were favoured by the Shanghai compradore capitalists, as well as by foreign bankers; because they envisaged an expansion of their products once these were abolished. But here lay the contradiction: at the same time as the foreign bankers and diplomats were loudly calling for a modification of China's internal tax system, the revenue from these internal taxes was essential to finance the provinces and their internal economies such as they were; otherwise it was impossible to pay even the local county clerks.

Chiang could not enforce abolition of these internal taxes because the provincial authorities and the militarists financed themselves out of these, and their support to Chiang's govern-

The author (aged 12) in the Forbidden City

Family group, 1928 (author at left)

Chinese children working in a Japanese-owned mill,
Shanghai, 1936—12 hour day, 7 day week, £1 a month.

Tiza and Marianne in the Forbidden City

Dr Sun Yatsen, founder of the turbulent Chinese Republic

Mao Tsetung—the revolutionary

Mao at Yenan, rear base of the Chinese Revolution

Chou Enlai today—Prime Minister of People's China.
Photo taken by the author in 1965.

Chu Teh—warlord-turned-guerrilla

ment (such as it was) was conditional on his allowing them to pay themselves, since he was unable to pay them. The Nanking government did nothing about revising the internal tax structure *except to add its own taxes to the already existing ones*. As a result the taxation burden upon the peasantry – eighty-five per cent of the population – and the small trader and petty bourgeoisie multiplied; it was from eleven to forty times as much in 1943 as in 1928. The road transport tax was not abolished till 1949, although it had been ordered to be abolished in 1929.

A Disarmament Conference was held by Chiang Kaishek in 1928 and again in 1929; the purpose was to cut down the two million armed men under the various warlords. But the warlords at this conference soon realized that Chiang, eager that they should cut down their armed forces, did not propose to cut his own; those wily men were not going to relinquish armed power and then be butchered. They were not as naive as the Communists had been.

As a result the armies were never cut down, they went on expanding; from two million men in 1929 they expanded to five million in 1939.

The railways were nominally back under control of the Chinese government by 1929; but the long-standing debts on railway loans and servicing were still to be repaid; and such monopolies as the Belgian Société Générale, which had loaned money for two railways in China, pressed hard for repayment. No new loans for building more sorely needed railways were therefore made available in 1931, the burden of railway debt was *one thousand three hundred million dollars*. Since after Chiang's accession to power civil war rapidly broke out again, the railways returned to the same state of chaos and disrepair, with warlords straddling them and taking the rolling stock away, as they had been before the advent of Chiang Kaishek.

Since its inception in 1927 the Nanking government had lived on loans from the bankers of Shanghai, loans given to Chiang who had proved so brilliant at putting down the Communists. But in order to obtain more money, he had to go on proving himself anti-communist and a good servant of foreign interests rather than of his own people's interests.

In 1929, due to the recrudescence of civil war, the actual revenue collected by the Nanking government came from only two provinces adjoining Shanghai's Kiangsu and Chekiang; the other provinces were financially autonomous, their internal revenues going to their own militarists. In May 1929 the Nanking government was already indebted to the bankers for one hundred and twenty-six million dollars, at an average interest of 9.5 per cent per annum. Since the customs revenue and the salt revenue were already mortgaged for the servicing of previous foreign loans, this interest was secured by the revenue derived from the two and a half per cent surtax on customs granted as tariff autonomy to China in 1929! This was indeed giving with one hand only to take away with the other.

The actual income of the Nanking government from these two provinces was five million dollars a month, but the expenditure in these two provinces alone, for the upkeep of troops against Communist infiltration, was nine million dollars a month.

The West, which had held out tempting offers of loans in 1927 and 1928, when the Communists were being slaughtered in their hundreds of thousands, now made it a condition for help that there be pacification of the country, reduction of military expenditure, centralization of national finance, curtailment of the power of provincial warlords.

To demand this was like asking Chiang to turn mud into gold. It could not be done without huge amounts of money, and Chiang could not get money unless he fulfilled their conditions; in this appalling dilemma, tangle of contradictions, Chiang Kaishek was enmeshed, paralysed, unable to do anything but promote show pieces, mouth slogans of "non-resistance to Japan, internal pacification first" and obtain hand-to-mouth loans from America for anti-communist campaigns. In his own Nanking government there were two contradictory trends; these two allied to demand their pound of flesh from China, but fought against each other for their share of the meat. One clique was the pro-Japanese militarist clique, with Chiang's own Minister of War, Ho Yingchin, at its head; the other was the pro-American clique, made up of the financiers, T. V. Soong, H. H. Kung, and his own wife, Madame Chiang Soong Meiling.

In a 1931 a conference for the stabilization of finance was held by the able T. V. Soong. There were at the time fifteen currencies in circulation, not counting that of the Red bases, which had their own paper money and postage stamps. T. V. Soong calculated that taking all sources of revenue together, both internal and external, the total (hypothetical) revenue of the Nanking government was four hundred and fifty million dollars. Of this sum that year, three hundred and eighty million dollars was necessary for the total expenditure upon military items, leaving seventy million for everything else, which was not enough even to pay the interest on the foreign loans contracted, which amounted to near three hundred million dollars, let alone arrears, or repayment of the principal. Taking the average over the years 1928 to 1934, the principal items of expenditure were: military fifty-one per cent, servicing of loans and repayments thirty-nine per cent. leaving a bare ten per cent of China's total receipts to finance the running of the country . . .

However, by launching the anti-communist campaign, a loan of fifty million dollars was negotiated by T. V. Soong (urged on by brother-in-law Chiang Kaishek). But this was not enough. Direct loans from banks, at onerous interests, and from American private enterprises, such as Rockefeller, were also negotiated; but these palliative measures could not redress the fundamental deficit in the balance of payments.

Due to the depression in the West credit was very tight. To cover the permanent imbalance of payments, and to balance the budget, two large national bond issues were floated between the years 1927 and 1936; the first brought in one thousand one hundred and forty-one million Chinese dollars, the second two thousand two hundred and sixty-eight million Chinese dollars. Almost all of these issues were bought up by the various banks in Shanghai, at a forty-four per cent discount; the net result was to drain the interior of the country, and the provincial towns, of solid silver dollars which accumulated in the vaults of the banks of the gangster metropolis.

And now occurred the Great Silver Exodus, one of the less honourable episodes in the history of financial manipulations.

China's currency was pegged on silver; and silver, in gold-standard countries, was a commodity which did not affect their currency exchange value. China's currency was in a peculiar position; to begin with, it was vulnerable to fluctuations in the price of silver, and secondly, because of foreign control upon its sources of revenue, the economic stranglehold upon the disposal of its resources through the extraterritorial privileges of foreign companies and banks, the Chinese government had extraordinarily little control over the value of its own dollar. Manipulations on the silver market in London and New York, where silver was a commodity, affected not only the value of the Chinese dollar, but also all her internal economic structure: the prices of her products, and the values of her exports.

With the depression since 1929 world prices of all commodities fell; and so did the price of silver, which had already begun to decline in 1926. From 1926 to 1931 silver prices declined by fifty-three and forty-nine per cent respectively in New York and London. This depreciation tended to produce inflation in countries on silver standard, of which China was one. And this inflation actually, for a short while, benefited China's internal economy; as prices of commodities rose, more money came into circulation, there was a stimulus to trade and industry, and adjustment of domestic prices and cost to a higher level in terms of silver. This reflected favourably on her trade balance; the deficit began to shrink. But the effect was short-lived.

As soon as England and America went off the gold standard, the price of silver began to rise, in terms of the pound sterling, rupee and yen and the American dollar (though in terms of gold it continued to decline slightly until the end of 1933). "But the silver market was dominated by political interests and manipulations," writes Dr. W. Y. Lin in her book, *The New Monetary System of China*. "From 1932 to 1934 there was a steadily increasing outflow of silver from China, almost entirely from Shanghai."

By 1932 a large amount of China's silver was deposited in the foreign banks of Shanghai. Shanghai, with its centres of industries, dominated by foreign capital, which also controlled tariffs, customs revenues, and through extraterritorial rights enjoyed almost unlimited freedom as regards financial activities, acted as a big sponge, soaking up all the silver from the interior. A wide net of smuggling, and other illegal dealings, went on: had there been political stability and normal conditions, however, and had the price of silver remained more or less constant, silver would have gone back, through normal trade channels, into the interior cities of China. But the situation was not stable; the aggression of Japan in Manchuria and in Shanhai accelerated a process of bullion accumulation into Shanghai bank vaults and decreased the outflow into China proper; the increase in the price of silver abroad determined an export of the metal from Shanghai. Silver was sold by Shanghai banks and companies, and as the price rose more and more of it went out. From ten million dollars going out in 1932, the amount rose to two hundred and sixty million in 1933, and twice that amount the year after. It is reckoned that over one billion taels of silver bullion were stored in Shanghai and that seventy per cent of the metal was to go out of China in the next five years. And this process was directly related, in its intensity of outflow, to the monetary policies adopted by the United States of America.

For America in 1933 now began a process which was equivalent to stockpiling silver; she announced in early 1933 that she would take repayment of debts in silver as well as gold. It is said that this new and unprecedented rise, on an already rising market, was due to certain "bi-metallic experiments," to quote Maurice Collis, in progress in America, which required the import of a large quantity of silver. This experiment, to describe it, was to bolster American currency on a bi-metallic base of both gold and silver; later this was abandoned for stockpiling of gold alone.

In December of that year newly minted American silver was set at 64.6 cents; a jump of 25 cents; in early 1934 the U.S. Silver Purchase Act was passed, and resulted in another rise, the price of American domestic silver jumping to 71 and then to 81 cents. "The Nanking government expostulated with the U.S. government, but the much feared *artificial* efforts for higher prices of silver did materialize . . . the abrupt advance, largely engineered by speculative operations, had a distrous effect on China's economy . . ."

China's balance of international payments could not support this advance in the price of silver, which proved highly unfavourable to her exports. "China's exchange was governed by factors outside the fields of trade and finance, subject to irrational changes arising out of political manœuvres . . ."

The export of the metal went on, in spite of pleadings and repeated attempts at control; it accelerated, all representations to the American government to "refrain from action causing the silver drain" proved ineffective. While the country's economy was affected, however, certain individuals in the Nanking government personally profited, and joined in selling the metal; fabulous deals were made by relatives of the ministers, including members "of the highest families in the land . . ." i.e. the great houses of the compradores, Kung and Soong.

The consequences of this drain were a most serious decline in prices of China's exports, and an increasingly serious deficit in trade balance. From 1931, in spite of the economic difficulties, Chinese exports had managed to cover in values sixty-three per cent of the imports; but in 1935, owing to the fall in price of export commodities, only forty-five per cent of her purchases abroad were covered by her export payments. Between 1931 and 1932 the excess of outgoing payments over incoming increased from five hundred and eighty-four million dollars to seven hundred and forty-six million dollars, a jump of one hundred and sixty-two million dollars; from 1932 to 1933 the deficit jumped to eight hundred and seven million dollars. By 1934 economic chaos was in; China was on the brink of total bankruptcy.

In order to meet certain immediate contingencies, especially American demands for repayment and servicing of loans, China was now forced to sell gold; one hundred and eighty-seven million dollar's worth of gold went out in 1933, but only partly offset the imbalance.

The American Silver Purchase policy, carried out without regard for China's economic difficulties, causing a fall in domestic prices, depressed trade and industry, produced a greater disparity between prices of agricultural products and industrial (mostly foreign-produced) goods. The heaviest blow was once dealt to China's farmers; the price index of agricultural produce fell from 100 in 1926 to 57 at the end of 1933. This reduced even more the income, and therefore the purchasing power, of China's peasantry.

In 1935, upon the advice of the British economic adviser, Sir Frederic Leith-Ross, China went off the silver standard. A monetary reform took place: silver was nationalized; legal tender restricted to three main banks, government-controlled; the Chinese dollar pegged to the pound sterling at the rate of 1s. 2½d. per dollar. Dr. Lin says that "repeated wilful attempts at interference occurred," but there was a sudden decline in the price of silver and "withdrawals of American purchases in the world market of silver." However, to meet urgent needs, another fifty million and sixty-four million ounces of silver were sold to America, at 65 cents per ounce, and thus some U.S. foreign exchange was acquired by China; the Chinese dollar now had the backing of both the pound sterling and the U.S. dollar. But this made the Chinese economy even more vulnerable to foreign pressure than ever before, and in no way managed to overcome her permanent state of deficit budgeting. By 1939, the Chinese dollar was worth 3d. instead of 1s. 2½d.

A contemplation of the "finances" of the Kuomintang period leaves one bemused . . . How was this possible, one asks; yet all this time the compradore bureaucracy in power, supporting Chiang Kaishek, acquired private wealth, sent their money abroad for investment and did well for themselves; the ministers and their wives, the gangsters and the generals, grew rich out of the economic chaos generated by their own actions at the time. And in this they were abetted by foreign interests. One wonders at the incredible gorging, the plunder, the rapacity of great nations, such as the United States. Today the same processes are being enacted, in a welter of the same corrupt practices, in other parts of the world; where regimes with nothing to commend them but their dishonesty are kept in power by "loans" and handouts which beggar their people, provided these regimes launch so-called "anti-communist" drives. But, the very opposite result to that wished for was produced in China, and no doubt will be repeated elsewhere . . .

CHAPTER NINE

The winter between those terrible years 1931, 1932 was very cold; the wind moaned and raved at night; and it began to freeze hard in the black cold of December. There was a tremendous famine going on due to floods in Middle China, and every week four thousand corpses were picked up in the streets of Shanghai. In Peking too, along the city wall, the beggars in their rags died by the dozen, watched by the silent sway of crows, drifting in the ashen sky clamped upon the city like a casque of lead. I found dead babies on the street pavement as I walked in the morning, deposited parcels wrapped in newspapers, which the wind blew open to show small wrinkled faces with their frozen grin. Small children begged, and they too were wrapped in newspapers and died of the cold, standing in the corners of the dust-suffocated hutungs. And all of us were so used to this we did not see it any more, it went seeping through us and out again, like the dust that seeped in through the windows. . .

I was growing fast, and looked with satisfaction at my develop-ing chest, My coat was too small, I bought cheap silk stockings, Japanese ones, but they laddered quickly. Hilda said: "You must buy American stockings." But they were too expensive. In the ladies' room at the P.U.M.C. where the secretaries congregated, I listened to talk about dresses, parties, drinks. The secretaries made up their faces in front of the three-paned dressing-table mirror. They mentioned husbands and boy friends, pony rides and skating and dancing and cars. One girl shrieked one day: "Honestly, after two white ladies, I couldn't do any more." And I puzzled about this incomprehensible sentence for a week. I would also look at myself in the mirror, wondering how the others kept their faces smooth in the winter. I would never be glossy, smooth, beautiful, well dressed, knowing all the important things, like dancing and what to wear. Two of the secretaries were American, they received five hundred dollars a month, part of their salary was paid in American dollars. I knew that the pound was not as good as the American dollar, after that terrible September when the Japanese had taken Manchuria, because there was a Depression. But now, even in America, people killed themselves because they had no money. In the films we saw long queues of people being fed in New York. So many things were happening in the world, and I wanted to know everything, learn everything. There was the library, discovered one day through Ida Pruitt. Ida Pruitt was in charge of welfare work and came into the office at times to talk to Mr. Harned. One day the word "library" dropped out of her mouth as she was leaving. I heard it. "Is there a library here?" I asked. "Of course, but it is not exciting," said one of the secretaries. I discovered the library, it was on the other side of the Yu Wangfu palace, past the hospital buildings. Marvel, delight, quiet penumbra; books, books in rows, waiting to be opened. The librarian was a heavy blonde Scandinavian, very kind; when she heard that I worked in Mr. Harned's office, and I was studying for the university and wanted to read, she said I could come any time and read in the library, but I could not take books out. It was warm in the library and I could buy some food or pack some bread and ham, eat in the ladies' room, come here and read. I learnt so much, reading in the P.U.M.C. library; I read everything I could, without selecting, cramming himself, I started on the Encyclopedia too, but did not get very far with it.

"I just don't think I'm going to be a secretary all my life. I want to study," I told Hilda Kuo.

"I want to be a doctor," I told Mrs. Bürger.

"I'm not going to be a secretary all my life," I told Miss Ferguson. She was trying on a new winter hat, brown, with a yellow feather. Miss Ferguson was about fifty, a spinster, on the administrative staff, and American.

"Here, you try it," she said, handing the hat to me. "Oh, it

168

suits you better than me." She went on, "My dear child, of course you won't be a secretary all your life, you'll probably be getting married." She took back the hat and again put it on, pushing her hair under the brim.

"But I don't want to get married, Miss Ferguson. I hate men."

Miss Ferguson laughed. "Another year or so and you'll also be having a boy friend," she said.

"I shall never marry, I hate all men. And I want to be a doctor." So many books, so much to learn – so many things happening in the world, all life, out there, to be grabbed. Where could I start?

Fredi Jung was the first young man who took me out. Our friendship remained platonic. We never even kissed.

Fredi was half German, half Chinese; he had two brothers, Eugen and Julius, and a sister Anna. He worked as a typist in the Accounts office, and was two years older than I. Fredi's German father had died, he and Eugen worked, their sister Anna sang Chinese opera in the theatre of the East Market, and since no other Eurasian anywhere in Peking could do this she was quite famous. At that time no Chinese woman sang or acted on the stage. Women's roles were always taken by men; and Mei Lanfang, the most famous female impersonator, was drawing enormous crowds. Anna was a courageous woman. When she sang, dressed in the heavy embroidered clothes of the stage, no one could tell she was not Chinese, though out of her clothes, her figure was on the massive side, especially her hips. "She has a Chinese actor's face on a German hausfrau body," Fredi said of his sister. But he was proud of her, even though "good society" at that time looked down on all actors, and Chinese opera singers.

I met Fredi at an annual pre-Christmas tea-party given to the staff of the Peking Union Medical College; he walked me home, speaking of himself, his family, and after that we met, and walked together, fairly often. Fredi was looking for "where I belong" and did not know what to do with his life.

"I want to be an engineer, I don't want my life to be spent as a small clerk. But there is no money at home."

"How much do you get, Fredi?"

"Forty dollars a month, and I've been working eighteen months."

I kept quiet. I had been raised to fifty dollars, already I was dreaming of asking more; because with fifteen dollars for Mama, ten for Teacher Wu, only twenty-five dollars were left, and soon I would be paying Mr. Vogel thirty-six dollars a month for physics. Of course I made an extra twenty dollars by teaching, but it was difficult to save, for there was so much I wanted to buy. And I ate in a restaurant, because going home every day in the winter was too exhausting.

Fredi walked a little in front of me, large-gaited, stepping fast, wrapped in his black overcoat. In the evening haze of six o'clock winter, his voice sounded blurred, he was seventeen years old, he said: "You know, you know . . ." We went to the park, sat on a bench in the icy cold and talked and talked, each his own dream wrapped around him.

Fredi bought me my first hot dog when he took me to see the ice hockey match one Sunday night at the skating rink of the French Club. The French Club was in the Legation Quarters, and had a library with magazines from France, most of them pornographic. An habitué of the library was a certain Mr. Doriau, the father of eleven daughters, all extremely devout; Mr. Doriau was always at the club turning the pages of the magazines, and recommending them to me. At Mass on Sundays, unctuous father of a large family, surrounded by his anaemic and ugly daughters, he looked round at me, his dark protruding eyes rolling.

Outside the French Club library were tennis courts, in winter converted to an enclosed skating rink. I skated usually in the North Sea Park where the lake froze deep in winter, and where an old eunuch of the Empress Dowager still gave exhibitions, using old-fashioned wooden skates. When Fredi took me to the ice hockey it was the first time I had seen an indoor rink. A good many of my ex-schoolmates were there looking very pretty in bright sweaters and dark skirts, some with white leather skating boots on; it was the fashion that year to have one's hair long to the shoulder, the girls threw back their heads and their hair went a-swing behind them as they whirled round the rink. The lamps glowed, the ice sparkled. French officers, American marines, Italians, leaned on the fencing round the rink, the girls slowed, to talk with them, tossing their hair. I leaned on the fence, and felt I was like everyone else, now that Fredi had brought me there. For the ice hockey match the rink was cleared, water poured on which froze instantly. Fredi and Eugen, in leggings and shirts with a big D, the insignia of the German Club, trailed in with other Germans and German Eurasians. And then it started, the ursh and fling of bodies, colliding, harsh, rasping, the shouts, the whistles, the thud of hockey sticks, the speeding crouch and pounce and hit, the screaming. Around the fence the viewers screamed, louder than the rest. The French team wore green shirts with white socks and green stripes. "Come on," shouted the girls, "come on . . ." There was Amanda, an ex-schoolmate of mine but who had left school suddenly. She had a long pale face, arrogant hands, her Chinese father was very important, in the government. Amanda wore a fur coat, and if anyone said anything to her she replied: "I'll tell my father, he'll cut off your head." She had very thin lips, a very pale skin; I thought her exceedingly beautiful, her mother was French. She was friendly with a girl who wore slacks, a man's suit, and that was why she had left the convent. Gossip said she had been seen on top of the city wall in a compromising situation with certain French officers. But since it was Mr. Doriau who said this, no one knew whether it was true. She was bending forward. shouting, her eyes dilated, and her hands opened and shut, opened and shut, like dreadful flowers, beautiful, predatory.

The ice flew, the skates crunched and slithered, water glistened on the rink surface and the players' skins and breaths smoked in the air. The game was over.

Fredi, sweating, a towel round his neck, was taking off his skates. All the men were now sitting panting, putting on their sweaters.

"Come and have hot dogs with us, at the Y," said Fredi. Off we went, a large group of Germans, some girls and me. I stuck close to Fredi. I ate my first hot dog with mustard; closing my eyes. So this was hot dog. We walked home; Fredi and I, his skates on his shoulder. On the way along Hatamen Street, Fredi hummed to himself, very pleased, because his team had won. He told me the French were no good. "They can never beat us. We're the best team. We're soon going to Tientsin, to play the Italians and the British. Some very pretty girls in Tientsin. Girls there dress up very smartly, better than in this little burg." Then he talked again about his sister Anna who sang in the theatre. Papa had taken me to the theatre and I liked it so much I had been again by myself. The gongs, the violins, the high shrill singing, the hum of talk, the towels thrown about, the hot tea. "Lets' go together, Fredi." "Yes, but my sister's voice will soon be going, she likes beer, and she's too popular, she goes out to too many parties" . . . visions of scores of men, all rushing forward to

171

escort Anna to eat hot dogs at the Y.M.C.A., almost over-whelmed me. How could I compare with such glory?

We went, Fredi and I, to the Chinese theatre at the back of the East Market to hear Anna sing the opera *Snow in June*. In 1961, thirty years later, I was to go back to the same theatre, now enlarged and much cleaner, to hear an opera, and to remember Anna. Where is she now? In Germany, managing a Chinese restaurant. That night of December 1931 she was not at her best, she played too fast, her hands shook, and her voice shredded raw. People went away, scarves about their necks and herding their children gently along the passage-ways. But a clique of Anna's fans cried "Hao, Hao" (good, good), the drums covered her voice and the violins wailed. I ate a pound of hot salted peanuts during the opera and Fredi muttered: "You see, she's tired, too many parties."

After the opera we went backstage to Anna's dressing-room. The painted face was Chinese theatre, a mask of pink and white with painted eyebrows like slanting bamboo leaves and a string to hold taut the skin around the brow. The face was purity itself, infinitely noble in its immobile beauty; at the neck the paint stopped and Anna was perspiring in spite of the cold dressing-room. She had only a white blouse on and a skirt, embroidered slippers on her feet with pompons of silk floss flopping gracefully; she turned her face away and her marvellous red hair flowed down to her waist like a wig. The hair was incredible, it belonged to another opera, a Wagnerian tragedy, nothing to do with China, with Peking, with the precise falsetto and ritual of the painted face and embroidered costumes. It was truly terrifying, that splash of barbaric hair alone by itself in a Chinese theatre dressing-room. There was a glass of hot tea on the table; the violin player sat behind Anna, who tried her voice, her back to him as is customary. She said to us: "I'm tired," and we sipped a few mouthfuls of hot tea given us by the dresser and left.

After six weeks of winter walking and watching hockey matches Fredi palled on me. His flow of conversation was even; he was always cheerful, he never made advances. He wanted our friendship to be pure. "You know, I could never take a girl, like that. Like all the others do, and then talk about it. I want the woman I marry to be pure, like me. I want to keep myself for her." And we had a semi-solemn compact, that both of us would remain pure, not like the others. "That's the most impor-

172

tant, for us Eurasians," said Fredi. "You know, they all look down on us, the others, the whites and the Chinese too, say we're just good for sleeping with, girls and boys . . . I want to be different, I want to prove myself." And it was true, even I knew that. That as Eurasians we were *expected* to be just for sleeping with, and that whatever we did people always brought that up. Sex was supposed to be our availability, and if a Eurasian was seen out once with a boy, everybody assumed she slept with him and immediately that she was available for anyone and everyone. It was different for the whites, they could do what they liked, get drunk, beat people, smash things, sleep with anyone, no one said anything; they seemed to have a right to do what they liked. And many Eurasian girls were brought up to think that going out with a white man was an honour, and they often did not dare to say no if, at the end of the dinner, he made advances. He just had to say: "Oh come on, you're not being a sport," and the girls felt they had to do it, to show how smart, how modern, how European they were. And also to be taken out again. "We'll never do that," said Fredi. "We won't," I said.

My appointment at the hairdresser's was at five thirty.

"I have a ticket for you, for the musical evening at the German Club," Mrs. Bürger had said to me a few days previously. The proceeds were to go to relief for the flood victims, and there were five million of them in that February of 1932. "It will be a nice party; decent people you will meet."

This was my first grown-up party. What would I wear? Mother advised pale-blue wool with collar and sash of white silk; the little tailor in Eight-side Tumble Street made the dress with a swinging skirt, a big hem, in case I grew taller. I bought a pair of silk stockings; on Hilda's advice, a long pair, American, but as I did not know about girdles they were held up with elastic garters. Underwear was a complication. Shoes were a difficulty. They must be high-heeled for such a grown-up party. The problem was solved by purchasing second-hand high-heeled shoes from Annabelle Lee, an American-Chinese secretary who was to marry a doctor and generously parted with a pair for six dollars. A Tangee lipstick, some Pan-stik make-up, recommended by Hilda. Mrs. Bürger had her hair set and curled for parties and I must do the same; at the Beauty Salon on Hatamen Street, where a Max Factor beauty counsellor, newly arrived that winter, gave lessons in make-up. "Try it, it's plush," said Hilda, who now

173

arrived in the morning with a faint tinge of powder, lipstick, eye shadow; and with her expensive suede-brimmed felt hat achieved a haunting look. But it cost something like ten dollars to have a complete lesson in make-up; and I could not afford it. "You should have a manicure," Olga advised, but this also was beyond my means. I would have my hair done, and dispense with manicure.

The dress cost me twelve dollars; the shoes six dollars; a slip four, panties one dollar sixty cents, altogether twenty-nine dollars and sixty cents, or three-fifths of my month's salary, for one grown-up party. The hairdresser would be an adventure: first step into womanhood. I recapture its swivel chairs, the tang of hot irons, the smell of burnt hair, the permanent clips hanging from corkscrewing wires overhead, the sneezy soap-water smell, the reek of ammonia. And clinking around the past image, seven silver dollars, bright and round, to put some curls into straight straight hair, for a grown-up party in aid of five million peasants famished in China's plains . . .

"Ja," said Mrs. Bürger, "you will look nice with curls."

Wind-ragged snowmounds piled unmelted on the sidewalk; the stones were slippery with ice. The hairdresser's window had a haughty wax face with a pompadour, a corkscrew curl loping down the neck, staring at the Chinese street below gold lettering proclaiming it the Elite European Hairdressing and Beauty Salon. Some beggars shivering with cold were picking a garbage bin. I pushed the outside door with its mattressed inner protection, and then the inside door, for in Peking's winter two doors kept the bitter cold out. The White Russian assistant looked like the wax head, even her hair the same gold. Her beauty completed my overthrow.

"Yes?" The glance went from my flat boots, warm stockings, up my coat to my unmaxfactored face with chapped lips. I stammered that I had an appointment.

She flicked the pages of a book, "Miss Suzy, shampoo and curl for this lady." Then to me: "Take a seat. We aren't ready for you yet."

Around me, beautiful European women sat under the driers or under clips firmly gripping their heads, or stretched on chairs, wrapped in white protectors, a hand out to the manicurist, or chatted to the Russian assistants while their hair was being brushed with those new brushes just come on the market, made with rubber bristles widely spaced.

174

"I said to him: Hey what do you take me for? I'm not going out at *this* time of the night."

"And what do you think? The damm Chink overcharged me ten dollars so I had him take it all back and give me back the money."

"And I said to the doctor: Now you just wait. I'll start pushing, get ready to catch. And sure enough out it popped."

I pored over a magazine. Page after page of delectable cakes, bigger and more luscious than anything in the Greek Bakery of my friend Vera Thassounis, glamorous women with beautiful legs and hips, handsome smiling young men bent over them showing all their teeth . . . Mum, Odorono, Kotex, Camel, the so-important doctor, white-gowned, holding up the Listerine bottle: "Statistics prove . . ." Dread of halitosis, b.o., sweat, unpopularity, assailed me. Should I get Listerine for tonight? What if I had halitosis and offended? I stared at that wonderful world, the rich, the smooth, the happy, where wind did not blow sand into one's eyes, where beggars did not root into garbage, rot and die on the streets, where no corpses floated on rivers, where no one was shot or beheaded on calm Saturday afternoons for being a Communist, and where there were not five million people dying of hunger, to be rescued by musical evenings and theatricals. And here, glamorously curled, Cleopatra using Mum and Kotex, and some film star darting from a sofa with her hip out, and someone else getting divorced and remarried . . . It was feared that there would be typhus, in Manchuria there was bubonic plague, and in Shanghai the Japanese were bombing refugees . . . and in America, too, there were marchers, and hunger, and soup kitchens, and in England much talk of socialism and strikes . . .

"Your turn, Miss." A swivel chair, crescent-shaped leather-padded neck-rest. "Lean back and let your hair loose" into an enamel basin behind it. The first glamour is gone, everything reeks of ammonia and of woman. Woman, soap, disinfectant, ammonia, singed hair, woman. Miss Suzy pulls a comb through my hair, then rubs some jellied stuff into it, then her red nails dig in, kneading. "My you got lots of hair" – as if it was wrong to have so much hair. The red nails draw out grey frothy blobs. "My it's dirty." Tepid water pours down. "Put your head well back." Splash splash. Towels. Then under the drier which is too hot. In the mirror, a sallow face. "You should use our Cold Cream, our complexion softener." I am ugly, I am ugly, I shall never be beautiful. Mouth too large, eyes too small. "Side parting,

Miss?" Affably Miss Suzy holds up the curling-irons. A work of art. Woof woof. Brilliantine spray. Does one tip? How can one tip such an incredibly superior Miss Suzy? Do I have enough money to tip?

Mr. Vogel wants thirty-six dollars a months for his physics teaching, Henri Vetch of the French bookstore wants seven dollars for the last book bought yesterday. Tonight I must be attractive, almost pretty. Glacé kid high-heeled shoes at six dollars a little too big, silk stockings a little too pink against the new blue dress, but the curls will save the day. People will pause. Is this indeed Rosalie Chou, who types in the Comptroller's office at the Peking Union Medical College, this poised and beautiful person with Max Factor Pan-stik make-up and Tangee lipstick, gliding effortlessly about under all those lovely curls? They make my face twice as broad as usual, but perhaps that is as it ought to be, perhaps I shall be beautiful tonight; a big wave on the forehead wavering almost between my eyes; the nape of the neck with little curls, a miracle of art. "That's very nice thank you very much." "Six dollars." Six dollars and one for the tip, already the feeling that I am different, almost like the wax face in the window. Some of the curls are stiff to touch, and now in the clear cold there is a light aroma of burning coming to me from my own head. But Mama approves; Tiza pins two curls already uncurling themselves; when the dress is on, and the shoes and the stockings, Mother's face is smiling; "Don't come back too late," she says.

A rickshaw has been called, it is impossible to bicycle there, all dressed up. In the cold the rickshaw shambles on, coughing, panting, and the lamps are just coming out, along the Eastern Main Street, and already outside the German Club are some cars, and also some private rickshaws, with their fur blankets for the passengers and their gleaming lanterns. The German Club has a fair-sized hall with ferns, aspidistra, winter cherry. There is a black piano in one corner, at which a man in a black suit with a black tie and a stiff collar sits and plays, singing to himself, one of his feet goes on the pedals, the soft, the loud, to and fro. He is playing a march; two women walk about in long satin dresses with fur jackets on their shoulders, ordering the servants to put chairs here and there. In comes Mrs. Bürger in scarlet silk with fur stole, her hair is so short, it looks as if half of it were missing, she has rouge upon her cheeks and it makes her face longer, older. The ladies' room gossip is that she is two years older than her husband and two years seems an enormous long time, to me. Recently an American missionary lady has married a Chinese convert, her own student, who is now going to study in the U.S.A. on a missionary scholarship; she is twelve years older than he is and the secretaries pretend to be horrified. With Mrs. Bürger is her husband and Eugen, the brother of Fredi, and a tall corpulent man with a monocle and suit with tails who says: "Ja, ah ahhahahah ja" with great gusts of laughter in between his ahs. It is the German doctor in charge at the hospital who, Hilda has told me, offers to fit young girls who need it with contraceptive caps. "He is very modern-minded." Another couple, the man astonishingly bald, overwhelming pink baldness, a frieze of hair round the polished smooth glistening round cranium. I find my lower jaw hanging loose and snap my mouth shut; so absorbed looking at all those people coming in, short or tall, thin or fat, like a procession; I feel myself blush and turn and meet the blue eyes of the man at the piano; he has stopped the march and is drumming with one hand and smiles. His teeth are rather long and his face not unpleasant, his hair soft, hanging over his forehead, like pale yellow silk.

Mrs. Bürger comes up with a careful smile as if smiling too much might shatter something in her face.

"You are early, that is good, you did not wish to miss any fun. I think it is going to be a nice evening. Come and I will introduce . . . Herr Will, Herr Fruber, Miss Chou. Otto, good evening . . ." She waves to the man at the piano. "Come and talk. This is Otto Kurtens."

Some click heels, others shake hands, the man called Otto gets up and winks at me. I blush again.

Emilie Bürger moves on to the platform I feel unwanted and return to my chair and find the piano-playing man sitting on the next chair. "Let us talk. How old are you?" "Sixteen." He eyes me. His eyes are a little bloodshot. "You are only a little girl." That hurts. I pat my curls, "I earn my own living." "What do you do?" "I'm a secretary." "Oh," he bows with mock respect. "A secre-t-a-ary. My, my, how important." "And what do *you* do, if I may ask?" "I am . . . a flyer." He makes a gesture of wings. "You know . . . aeroplanes" I bend forward, inquisitive: "Do you know about the man who was shot down somewhere in Mongolia and put in jail and had to have his leg cut off?"

"Yes, I am that man."

I can't say anything, only look at him and feel the hot red

flow mounting and spreading. He bows mockingly, then stands and goes back to the piano, and again begins to play.

The curtain loops, the costumed singers begin singing and thumping their feet. The man at the piano plays on and on. I am still thinking of the terrible thing I have done. Because I read in the papers about this German pilot of the Eurasia airline, which is actually a German company, being shot down by Mongolian marauders, a few months ago. At the interval Emilie comes: "Have you enjoyed it?" I nod. Some people circulate with cakes, and sandwiches, and there is coffee to drink. Otto Kurtens is again there, a big cream cake on a plate, he hands it to me. "But I am already eating one." "Have two, all children like cakes." Then we sit and I tell him I have just finished reading Ibsen at the P.U.M.C. library, and he says: "You should read Goethe," and then teaches me a few words of German: "Auf Weidersehen, guten Morgen." When the last act is over everyone claps, Emilie says: " I am asking Otto to take you home." "I have a car, may I have the pleasure?" says Otto. He drives me back through the quiet night. From time to time, a rickshaw comes out of the darkness, the man's legs flash in the car lights, his body hurling forwards, then becomes a dark shadow behind us. We arrive home and Otto gets out of the car, stiffly, one leg does not bend. "Well, good night, sweet dreams, little girl." He kisses me lightly on the cheek. "Thus we do in Germany." He pronounces it Chermany. I stand looking at him. He says: "What is it?" I do not answer but shut the door on him, and now I go to bed, feeling grown up. I have been to a party, met a man who has lost his leg, who has taken me home in his car, and who has actually kissed me! Immense the great space traversed in one evening. He said "Little girl," but it is not true. I am growing up. And now all this world I covet, world where everything is knowledge and happiness and there is no torment, no worrying, will be mine – all that, and becoming a doctor, and doing something about the beggars. The next day at the office I ask Emilie about Otto. "Ah ja, such a pity, he does not like to speak about it. But after he had dropped you home he came back to the Club and played more and more piano, and got very drunk, he and Eugen and my husband; they broke glasses, but the servants picked up the pieces. And then they all sang songs. Fine marching songs. Ja, they have good spirit, these men. They love to sing. And Otto can play the piano and sing very good, they all like it when he plays, such spirit he puts in his playing." That evening, at the skating rink, I ask Fredi about

Otto. "Oh ja, he is a hero," Fredi says. And then laughs: "But with one leg what can he do? No girl will marry a man with one leg." And he slides forward, a magnificent sweep, the ice deep scored by his skates.

Many events seem to happen twice to me; even trifles, unimportant-seeming, recur, as if I were destined to live them again, time reconquered, but with added knowledge and a different outcome. I do not know whether this is because I purpose it, or because history at the moment repeats itself, and I am borne along, fated to travel again the what was.

Even the house where Otto lived, that year of 1932, even that house was to recur. In that same house, an Indian friend, a diplomat at the Indian Embassy in Peking, invited me to lunch in 1958. Nothing had changed, save the furniture. The high steps to the withdrawn gate with its knobs, its grinning lions upon their pedestals, the courtyard, the elevated veranda. I looked at the grey roof sweeping its serene and carnal curve overhead, and remembered Fredi and me, perched on that roof one Christmas night.

After that first meeting in February Otto took me out again; at least once a week we went out together, to a cinema, but more often driving to a park, or when the weather became warmer, outside Peking. Otto thought Peking most beautiful: "Such a pity, so beautiful a country and so badly spoilt by your own people," he said. Disorder and inefficiency he disliked. He did not laugh at me when I told him I wanted to be a doctor, but I don't think he quite believed it. Through him and his friends I learnt about Hitler, and the Nazis, some weeks, before Hitler came to power. "We are all Nazis, sure." Otto said. "And when Germany is strong again, we will revenge ourselves."

In that spring, and in the autumn, we went on Sunday picnics. Otto would take some friends, and we would go to the Jade Fountain, or the Western Hills. One afternoon he and Fredi and Anna and myself, and another German, a friend of Otto's called Hans Klein, drove in Otto's car to the countryside to see the famous German Sinologue, Dr. Hundhausen, who had done translations of Chinese novels. He was a large dignified man, his beautiful house full of Chinese bronzes, prcelain, jade, furniture. Reverently he handled all things, reverently read to us passages of his translations. I looked around wondering why it was that Europeans always had lovely things, but Chinese did not, why was it that Europeans prized those beautiful things, and most of us did not? They said Sung Ming, with such intense respect, with such glee showed what they had bought, dirt cheap, or found in their excursions, and here we were, with the Japanese shooting up our people as they pleased, taking Manchuria, bombing and killing at Shanghai, and apart from the 19th Route Army, no one did anything about it. But when I mentioned the 19th Route Army, Otto would look as sceptical as Olga: "No, you will see, they will soon stop fighting."

Driving back to the city through the late afternoon the sun came filtering across a curtain of willows by the canal, and the line: "In the city the willows make all the spring soft," which Teacher Wu had just written for me, was so beautiful, suddenly so real that I was going to tell the others about it when suddenly the Germans burst into song:

> *Die Fahne hach, die Reihe dicht geschlossen*
> *S.A. marschiert mit ruhig festem Schritt.*

"What is it, Otto?"

"Das ist the Horst Wessel Lied."

"It's our Nazi song. We are all Nazis, sure," another German said.

Otto was to elaborate on this.

"You see, Mädchen, we have been beaten, but now we are going to beat everybody else. That is why we are Nazis. We have to be. To make our country strong."

"I don't believe it."

"Jawohl, you will see. We will beat everybody. But I think the Chinese will never fight, the Chinese are cowards," he replied contemptuously.

And there was nothing I could say, for now it was May, and the 19th Route Army had given up fighting; we did not know that Chiang had cut off its supplies to force it to stop.

It was not till the autumn of 1932, when Teacher Wu had gone, and I had Mr. Wang to teach me, that my relationship with Otto began to change; and though he swore, knowing me untried, that he would not touch me, yet by October 1932 it was certain that he was deeply involved. "I don't want to because you are a virgin, but it is so difficult for me."

Propinquity made its usual stir, and curiosity, but I resisted. Otto did not cheat me. "I can never marry you, because I am a German."

180

Hilda was my counsellor that year; and she advised me to have nothing to do with Otto. She herself was in love with Leo Bielfeld, whom she was later to marry.

There was only one person that Otto objected to, and that was Leo Bielfeld. "Don't have anything to do with him, he is not a good man." I wondered why he was so upset about Leo. Was Leo a Jew? The antagonism was reciprocal. Hilda sneered at Otto. "My dear, you could do much better for yourself." "But I'm not going to marry him," I said, "I want to study. We are friends."

To my mother, marriage was the only thing to look forward to. I explained that I had no intention of marrying Otto. "But he loves you," said my ever-romantic mother.

Came a lazy Sunday, my only remembered lazy day in those many years. Autumn again, and so many unanswered questions, and I was going to Hilda's house. She had invited me. "Do come round, we'll just laze about, you're looking tired." I arrived that morning to find her, in slacks, in shirt, in the little outhouse in her garden which she had adapted for herself, as her bedroom, sunning herself on the steps; the garden round her quiet, a blue-grey magpie, enormous, browsing and brushing her feathers in the elegant acacias. Hilda no bigger than the magpie in my mind's eye (photographing the scene as uncomprehendingly as any camera), sang to herself, lighthearted. "I suppose you've never just done nothing – well now, relax . . ." Her dark hair, her one-sided smile, her teeth protruding slightly, all in her was charm. I remember the song she tried to hum, the whole general air of ease, of content, so deceptive, a deliberate casualness (save for the magpie), including my presence.

And now of course came Leo, as if by accident; and I watched and wondered what love was like. Hilda was suddenly so beautiful, so beautiful. Leo talked and talked, and made us laugh so much. I left in the afternoon, he stayed.

Hilda had painted bright red a large post supporting the roof in her bedroom. It was a large round one, like a tree trunk, growing from floor to ceiling. We sat round that post, she and I, the next week, for a while, and she was radiant, glowing. Yes, indeed, she was in love, and the earth seemed to hold no greater perfection. She told me that she and Leo were now engaged.

"Leo and I talked for hours . . . we won't have a baby just yet . . ." Her dark head against the red pillar, her throat, fragile loveliness; in my hand the "Pavilion of Iced Beverages," to read

181

before the next lesson. "With contraceptives, you don't have to worry about babies, it's not wrong to love, but it is wrong to have babies, when you don't want them." Hilda's voice, the red pillar behind her, all authority, dispensing knowledge.

All too soon the dirty old men about Peking who collected young girls were also trying their charms on me. These encounters happened chiefly in the church porch. There was old Mr. Cavier, a benevolent young-old gentleman with white hair, older than my father, who ran a newspaper. He heard me argue about the League of Nations; and offered me books; would I come to tea and see his library. I did go to tea. The books were there, but when his flabby small hand was laid experimentally on my chest, I removed it and left.

There was the German professor who jumped out of his rickshaw when he saw me walking along the marble bridge by the park one elusive morning in the pulpy shadow of the summer-bearing trees, and insisted that I go to lunch next Sunday with him and his wife, who was a teacher; he himself was a university professor. I, as a child polite to adults who ask: "What is your name?", had in the first minutes told him I was studying to be a doctor. Innocence or, rather, unsuspecting candour is also oil on duck's feathers; thinking he might help me, I went to lunch. A beautiful house; a European house as most Europeans in Peking could afford, furnished with Chinese rosewood furniture, silk and brocades; an embroidered table-cloth on the table, and many knives and forks, the use of which I ignored; his wife was a blonde woman with long earrings of jade who said to me: "I am never jealous of what my husband does with his girl friends." The professor tried to make me sit on his knee; I was off with my "Pavilion of Iced Beverages" (which I carried with me everywhere, simply because it confused me so much) under my arm.

Then there was Mr. Doriau, who sat in the library of the French Club, fingering the magazines which lay on the table, and since the previous year had tried to interest me in their contents, as he said: "To learn what is needed to be a woman." With the eagerness of the voyeur, he tried to introduce me to a young man in church, asking him on the church porch to come over to shake my hand, but the young man refused. Mr. Doriau became bolder and made a direct suggestion at the French Club, holding the page with suggestive picture of what he meant up at me. I became furious and shouted: "What do you think you are?" Some of his daughters had been my schoolmates.

I was also teaching to make more money. For about four months I taught a White Russian night-club dancer who wanted to learn French; twice a week I went to her small flat in Boat Beam Street, on Saturday and Sunday, at twelve, and taught her from twelve to one. She danced at the Alkazar night club every night. She had a sweet face, honest and serious, with sad brown eyes.

She was still in bed when I turned up at lesson time; she would sit up, propped on her pillow, pencil and copy book on her knees, the blanket round her, and a bed-jacket, crocheted, with lots of little fluffy balls of pink wool dangling from it, round her shoulders.

I had other pupils; Vera, my Greek friend, who used to pay me in cocoa and cake per coaching hour. Her mother now added six dollars a month to the income and also gave me two weeks at the seaside in their bungalow one summer.

Vera, like my sister Tiza, was more developed than I; well formed, as her mother remarked, with a mass of beautiful auburn curls, and the pure profile of the Greeks, a forehead-and-nose straightness which people admired. Vera was prudent and clever; woman enough not to worry about equations, quadratic or other; but she knew how to look after herself, and she had a mother she confided in.

"I told him nothing doing without a ring round the finger, Mama. And then he wanted to drive round but I said no."

Vera was not giving hostages to rumour or to perfidy. Her mother nodded, and placed another cake on my plate.

Today when I return to Peking I pass in front of the bakery once her mother's, and behind the glass door unchanged I can almost see the shrewd Greek face, vigorous and sane, the hand raised beckoning me, then opening the glass case over the cakes, and handing me one.

Another of my pupils was Fanya Maryanovskaya, a Jewish girl, three years younger than I. Her father was a tall, strong man, who traded in furs, her mother was short and fat; both adored their only daughter, Fanya.

I had seen Fanya once before I started to teach her; and that one encounter had ended my own musical education. I had neither ear nor affection for Western music, but a piano was bought, and I was put to it, because Mother said a young lady must either play the piano or paint. I played, Tiza painted. Every year at the convent occurred the feast of the Mother

183

Superior. On her feast day, the whole school put on a show: recitation of poems, a play of some kind or other, piano and violin playing. Mother Superior sat through it all with an encouraging smile.

I played a waltz and a rondo and was dutifully clapped. And then towards the end came a wiry little girl with a prominent nose, a falcon-like face, very thin, dead white. She had heavy-lashed eyes and dark bronze hair, an enormous stiff satin bow on top of her head. She advanced upon the piano, and began.

And suddenly I knew what music was. This life, talking and singing and praying, this emotion coming up, coming out, out of the black reticent box, this choking, this bursting inside, and these extraordinary spatulate-fingered hands upon the black-and-white toothy board, prancing, hitting, mastery, control, prayer, and all the girls were still, like the painted angels on the chapel walls. All the seas of the world were with us, white-foamed and tossing. I was holding my piece of music in my hand. I looked at it, tore it up. I knew then that music was part of Fanya, born in her; and also that this gift was not mine. It was hard to accept that there was something I could not attempt, not be successful at, not do – I always wanted so much to do *everything*, and I was constantly brought up short, faced with my own ignorance, limitations. I would have liked to be indefatigable, a genius, able to absorb, incorporate, engulf all knowledge, all activity, and sometimes I did not know that I was tired, excessively so, or making a spectacle of myself.

But music it could never be, never, never, though half-heartedly I put myself back to the piano in the following years, for an hour or two, hoping for the sudden miracle. And then in 1932 Fanya became my student.

She was practising the piano six hours a day and also had formal schooling to do, and she was a little late in her English studies. But she was a very bright girl, peremptory, infinitely self-confident, and both her parents nurtured that self-confidence, because they believed in Fanya's genius. Fanya's career was the aim of their existence, for this her father would have swept the streets, would have pulled carts with the meanest labourer.

One day Jascha Heifetz came to Peking, to give a concert. He played at the Grand Hotel de Peking, that awe-inspiring pile, lived in only by European dignitaries, American tourists, Japanese generals and a Chinese warlord or two (among them a

184

certain General Chang Eighty Dollars, so called because his dimensions were supposed to resemble a standing pile of eighty silver dollars.).

There, in the grand hall, Jascha Heifetz played. The price of tickets was high, but Fanya and her parents went. After the concert they begged for an audition. Heifetz granted it. Fanya played, he listened. And afterwards:

"He told me that if he could take me, he would, hands and feet and all," said Fanya, and her large wonderful hands, all fingers, came up, grabbing the air, exploding like enormous white flowers above her small beaked face, grabbing the future and its so many shining keyboards, "but I must have good teachers, good teachers, here it is impossible . . ."

The Maryanovskys were saving money to go to Europe, where Fanya might have good teachers . . . I have not seen her again since that time, which is more than thirty years. Her voice, with its self-confident flatness, rings in my ears today, and I scan the papers when a concert is to be given, for her name, sometimes afraid that a pogrom, somewhere in Europe, might have cancelled out those wonderful hands, that wonderful gift.

There were other students of mine, a Jewish doctor who wanted to study English; a Chinese girl who wanted to study typewriting. So that by the year 1933 I had saved three hundred dollars, and that in spite of paying Mr. Vogel and Teacher Wu. But Teacher Wang taught me for nothing, and though he throughly muddled me with the "Pavilion of Iced Beverages," I am also grateful to him.

Besides Fredi and Otto I met other men, and became friendly with them, though not in the accepted equivocal way. None of them made any advances, which is why I treasure their memory. There were two young Englishmen from the British Embassy; one of them, Roberts, took me to Chinese dinner at Ho Te Fu where the waiter was the brother of the ex-warlord Wu Peifu. Roberts was mad about Baudelaire, and recited the poet to me over our velvet soufflé of prawns. He was much in love with a beautiful Italian woman, the wife of some Italian diplomat.

The other was a jolly Scotsman named Smith; immensely fond of picnics. He was a student of Chinese and joined up with the Jungs and Otto and a very handsome if somewhat effete young Chinese official who was a fervent Catholic, named Henry Wang. Later Henry Wang was to become an important official in the

185

Nanking government. On these picnics, which were fun, Smith was an excellent and charming companion. He did not laugh at me and treated me as an intelligent equal. One day, looking at the peasants in the fields, he said: "You do know the Japanese are not very far?" At that moment the others were all shouting and laughing, the temples of the Western Hills echoed with German syllables. "I know. I often think of it, but what can I do?" "Nothing," he said, "nothing." Smith did not like Roberts, said he was a rather dull man, in spite of all the Baudelaire he recited. Otto used to drive all of us to the hills and back; and did his best to keep up with the walking; but often had to give up, for the stump of his leg hurt. He would then sit, smiling and wave us away. "You go on," he would say, "I shall catch up."

His amputation was above the knee, mid-thigh came his wooden leg, and he had difficulty keeping his weight down, because he had been much addicted to sport and now could no longer play games. At times, in the beautiful autumn, with the sunset saddening the slopes in the Western Hills and that slight whip of cold which says "go back," he would limp apart from us, face turned to the red walls that circled the old palaces. The mutilation stupidly acquired – for his captors had left him in prison, and the limb had become infected in those days when penicillin and other antibiotics were unknown – galled him. One day he said: "I shall kill myself, it is easy."

On the way home he drove to our houses, one by one dropped us home. Smith would always stay till the last, and we laughed a lot together. Otto would go back to his room, shut the door, weep over his lost leg.

One day Smith and I strolled round the walls of Peking and thus came to the Drum Tower and Clock Tower of Tartar times. And there saw the marble tablet of Tsien Lung with the inscription:

> We have seen this great city of Peking, a spirit city, turbulent and full of people; their minds would scatter and their hearts become confused, were there not a regulator of their days and hours; hence we have rebuilt these Drum and Clock towers whose use is manifold; their sound responds to the drops of water of the clock in our palace, one linking in harmony of answer to the other; the days and nights are not confused with each other, their beat is a heart which regulates all the affairs of men; they face each other in har-

186

mony; at all time, they protect the spiritual city from harm from the north; their sound is mellow and good to hear in the autumn, and they enunciate the seasons to come.

"The seasons to come," said Smith, "How I hate the thought the Japanese might be here next autumn."

"They won't," I said. "They won't. We must fight."

"Chiang Kaishek won't fight, m'dear. He's got enough on his hands."

"Then Feng Yuhsiang the Christian general will fight," I cried. "At least, someone will fight."

"D'you know, you're a dear," said Smith. "I wish we didn't have all these beastly politics. I hope you do become a doctor," and so he changed the subject. But I felt that of all the Europeans I had met, he was the only one who seemed truly concerned about the Japanese coming down, taking Manchuria, North China, Peking.

CHAPTER TEN

Joseph Hers. The name was important. In 1928, going with Father to a dinner of the Belgian and French Returned Students' Association, I had seen Hers for the first time.* Physically I remembered him well; very tall, gaunt, a bald head, piercing blue eyes, a big nose, a small moustache and beard, a loud voice and an air of command.

"He can help you with a scholarship, if you really want to study," Father said. "I have spoken to him about your wanting to study. Try to get him to listen to you."

That was a Saturday evening in the late spring of 1932. Hers, who lived in Shanghai, had come to Peking and was staying at the Grand Hotel de Peking. At that time it seemed natural that my father would call on Hers. Father paid visits to many people whom he never brought home, engineers, Chinese friends or acquaintances. My mother called it "those interminable conferences of your father's".

It now occurs to me that Father had sought out Hers precisely for the purpose of talking to him about my studies; in his uneffusive way, he did not tell me this; whereas my mother would

* See *The Crippled Tree*.

have said: "I've dragged myself on my knees to get Hers to listen to me, for your sake." But at that time I assumed that Father, like Mother, was either indifferent or hostile to my ambition; as a result I had stopped talking of study at home, shutting myself off from my parents.

And it was true that Jospeh Hers could help me, where no one else could. My father could not guarantee a prolonged education for me. Manchuria had been invaded by the Japanese in the autumn of 1931, Shanghai attacked by the Japanese in 1932; now it was May and there was a truce, but my father was constantly having to go "down the line" on inspection tours. "No one can tell what tomorrow will bring," he said.

In 1913, when my parents were newly back from Belgium, my father had seen Hers and through him obtained his first job, on the Belgian-built Lunghai railway. A feeling of gratitude dwelt in my father, and now in me, his daughter. Father had proved his worth on the Belgian-built railways; had served well, not sparing himself, never asked for a rise, never complained, done the hardest work, four of his children had died in the little towns along the railway . . . "Your father has never given us any trouble," Hers said of him to me.

Born in Belgium in 1884, two years older than my father, Joseph Hers arrived in China in June 1905, as an attaché to the Belgian Consulate. He was an excellent choice, with that vigour, meticulousness, and vitality which characterizes the explorer. Belgians are a sturdy, hard-working lot. Jospeh Hers learnt Chinese and much about China at a time when such pursuits were scorned. He became an assessor at the International mixed court in Shanghai. These mixed courts had begun during the Manchu dynasty. They had been set up in the foreign concessions to deal with cases involving Chinese and foreigners. Consuls representing the foreign plaintiff sat with a Chinese judge. But in the confusion of 1911 the foreign consuls took over the court, and acted in rotation, appointing their own judges. It thus became more an instrument of foreign extraterritoriality than an instrument of justice, Foreign assessors, Dutch, Russian, Swedish, Belgian, also took turns, as there was no jury system.

Like so many Europeans in China, Joseph Hers began to "love" China, a fierce, dominating, anxious, all-conquering possessiveness, characteristic of the warped, twisted, and alto-gether vicious relationship miscalled "love" between the dominating and the suppressed, the powerful and the weak; the spoiler and the cheated. Like many other foreigners he expressed this "love" in sexual imagery; to all of them, China was the WOMAN, the all-enveloping, soft, weak woman, who actually welcomed rape, welcomed being invaded. "Don't worry, China is feminine, she has always ended by absorbing all her conquerors," was their favourite explanation, and Hers said this too when I spoke about the Japanese. A great part of this love for China was their attraction to Chinese women; none of them, I think, realized how much this was resented by the Chinese. Though Hers knew the cruelties inflicted upon China, this sexual explanation, equating the violation of China to the defloration a woman undergoes in marriage, enhanced in them a feeling of superiority: The Great White Male seeding in the weak, moaning, submissive coloured female. And in this he was typical of nearly all the Europeans in China who declared the Chinese "forever unable to rule themselves, because they are weak, devious, volatile, timid."

In his capacity as assessor and as a consular attaché, he came in close contact with the gangsters and the kings of the Shanghai underworld. "I knew them all when they were petty thieves and procurers," he said, including in his gallery of rogues Dou Yuseng, the Benevolent Gangster who saved Shanghai for foreign business and Chiang Kaishek in 1927. His memories of prominent Kuomintang officials and their links with the Shanghai gangster world could not be written down. "I would have my throat cut." He knew and shook hands and occasionally dined with the Four Great Kings of Shanghai gangsterdom: Dou Yuseng, Chang Hsiaoling, Huang Chingyung (who became Chiang Kaishek's adopted grandfather), and Ku Tsuchuan, who shot the manager of Shanghai's great fun bazaar, The Happy World, for refusing to dine with him, and went free of punishment with a quiet bribe of twenty thousand dollars to the American and British police officials supposed to investigate the murder. Gangster Ku kept a pleasure barge on the river, decorated with sofas and tables for gambling and a special cook on board; he would generously lend this boat to eminent foreigners who wanted to entertain large parties; the only other comparable barge was that of the British firm of Jardine Mathesons.

In the Revolution of 1911 Hers, as representative of the Belgian financiers, was in charge of the assets of the Shanghai regional administration, which meant that all funds were withheld from

Sun Yatsen and his party, by order of Sir Robert Hart who had absolute control of China's customs, and delivered to the "strong man" approved of by the foreign powers, Yuan Shihkai.

But Hers was too full of energy to confine himself to the intrigues of Shanghai; he bestrode the land, colossal, his head covered by an enormous felt hat, Texan in dimensions; he derided those who remained in the ease and comfort of Shanghai, and walked every province of China. He became fond of archaeology and helped to excavate some old Chou dynasty tombs; I still have the photographs of one such, which he sent to me. He was also a good botanist, and collected specimens all over China. His contribution to this branch of science is very creditable, for he sent to the Arnold arboretum at Harvard thousands of specimens of plants from north Honan, then a botanically unexplored region. He went on safaris with a trail of porters, immune to fatigue, weather or insects. His appearance struck terror in village children, his height and voice made the timorous Chinese officials of thosedays cringe in fear. He acted like a master, as did all the white men in China then, and received in that age of compulsory servitude almost ingrained into the minds of Asians and Africans, the respect and deferential service due to a great man. From 1913 to 1944 he was secretary-general of the Lunghai railway, built with a Belgian loan from the Société Générale in Brussels.

Hers wrote to me about meeting my father in 1913. "We were looking for Chinese engineers, and needed them; your father was an excellent man. He never gave us any trouble." How patronizing the words were. But then not to give trouble was a compliment to the natives; I can still feel my lips coming together, biting these words into me; I would remember them.

In 1915, Hers founded, with Dr. Lu Tsentsiang, a Belgian returned student married to a Belgian woman, the Sino-Belgian Friendship Association, of which my father became, of course, a member. Dr. Lu was the frightened and pathetic delegate from China to the Versailles Peace Conference in 1919, later to become a monk in Belgium.

In 1918, at the end of the war, Hers was in charge of reactivating the railway negotiations between Belgium and China, in order to re-establish Belgium's markets. During the 1914–18 war the hold of the West on China's markets had greatly weakened; Japan had profited from this and almost, though not quite, succeeded in displacing England from her Chinese markets. Even the weak Chinese had begun some industries on their own; and for the first time since the 1860s China had actually been able to achieve a small surplus instead of a bad deficit in her balance of payments. But now the whites were back, and a realignment of their interests and markets was taking place. Belgian interests were in continuing the building of the Lunghai railway westwards, but this could not be done; soon enough all China was embroiled in civil and then the Japanese war, and it was only after 1949 that the Communist government accomplished on its own, in two years, what had been planned but not done, the westward extension of the Lunghai railway of which Hers spoke so often.

Hers was named president of the Belgian Chamber of Commerce in Shanghai in 1920 and was in Shanghai at the time of the massacre of the workers and the establishment of the military dictatorship by Chiang Kaishek at Nanking in April 1927. On these matters Hers, as a member of the judicial system as well as of the financial and business circles of the International Settlement, always remained monumentally silent.

From 1928 till 1938, Hers lived in Shanghai, but twice a year came north to visit Peking, Tientsin. In his capacity as president of the Sino-Belgian commission for education and philanthropy, one of his many activities was keeping in touch with the returned students from Belgium; after the Friendship Association he also set up the Sino-Belgian Inter-university Committee, to utilize the remainder of the Boxer indemnity funds of 1900. The Belgian Concession in Tientsin was formally returned in 1931, and Hers and many Belgians after him made quite a point about its being the first foreign concession voluntarily returned as a gesture of friendship and confidence to China. Actually the first to return concessions were the British. Their settlements at Wuhan and at Kiukiang lapsed in February 1927; they had been taken by the workers during the Northern Expedition and were not claimed back. The British Settlements near Nanking, at Weihaiwei, at Amoy were returned in 1929 and 1930, the Belgian settlement at Tientsin only on January 15th, 1931. The goodwill generated led to the creation of this Inter-university Committee, financed by Boxer funds. The Boxer indemnity, to be paid over something like forty years after 1900, had not been paid for some years because China's finances were getting so bad that by 1931 she was falling behind in all repayments. The Belgians decided that the indemnity money should be used to train Chinese students in Belgium. It was, therefore, with a view to getting a scholarship

191

for me out of this money that my father suggested that I approach Joseph Hers.

The next morning, Sunday, I put on my best dress, my best shoes, my only hat, and went to church to capture the attention of the great Mr. Hers. From that day in 1932 until today, Hers and I have been friends and enemies; quarrelled and argued, always about China, always about China. It is only a few months ago that it became suddenly impossible to reach him, for he was cloistered by old age, in that twilight which eludes contact, and as his last bitter letters to me revealed, he felt abandoned by those who had utilized his energies for so many years and who now found him too old. He was eighty-one years old, and still working, six months ago, in a very small office behind a large bank in Brussels. He read, collated and analysed news on China, the love, the rage, the bafflement of his whole life. For he was angered and scurrilous about the new China and incessantly sought bad news to publish about her, picking out the mistakes, leaving out the achievements. And in this strenuous, almost morbid preoccupation, he was not alone; so many, in America, were busy doing exactly the same thing. None of them could get over "their China," upon whose weakness they throve, becoming strong and independent; yet, at the same time, Hers was dying to go back, felt cut off from the best part of his life, which had been in China.

But it is due to Hers that today I am Han Suyin, for he did give me the money that I needed when I needed it; in the end, Chinese money, taken from the Chinese people; Boxer money, from that great peasant rising of 1900, which also catapulted my father into a new world.*

I remember well that Sunday morning, the quick stir of heat in the morning air, the hymn-singing of a choir of convent girls in the St. Michael's church, the dry squeak of the battery-operated hand fan of my neighbour, Mrs. Arnel, the Chinese wife of a Frenchman, kneeling with her daughter in the next pew, and the arrival of Hers, just after the sermon; in that way like my mother, who could not sit still during the twenty minutes of preaching. And by good luck he was in the opposite aisle. I turned my head and looked him full in the face, and he was looking round, and saw me. Then I knew that he would wait on the porch, after Mass, to speak to me. He would wait for me and speak to me. I knew it with every bone in my body.

* See *The Crippled Tree*.

When church was over he was one of the first to walk out, and my mother, I felt, unduly slow. Impatiently, I walked ahead of her. "If he has gone away without waiting for me . . ." But he was waiting, planted on the porch, his enormous hat on his head, talking to a respectful small crowd of simpering Belgian and French women and their daughters, all laughing that dutiful, ever-ready laugh, ear strained to catch the non-existent humour in his remarks; or just laughing because they did not know how to take his cutting, semi-insolent politness. He saw my mother, walked towards her, not looking at me, but I knew he wanted to talk to me.

"Ah, Madame Chou," he said, and shook her hand. "I saw Mr. Chou yesterday. How are you? And your family?"

Then of course he had to see me. He said something which I do not remember, to which I answered something I don't remember, but I know it was pitched to his own casual haughtiness. He began to laugh. I had won. I did not look round, knowing everyone watched. But I had won.

My mother said proudly: "My daughter works at the Rockefeller Hospital" – she always called the P.U.M.C. "the Rockefeller" with a reverent elongation of the name. I cut in: "I want to be a doctor, I am not going to type all my life."

Hers looked at me: "A woman doctor? You will be married, Mademoiselle Chou." "That's what I keep telling her," said my mother.

"But first I will be a doctor, and I want a scholarship from you."

He laughed again. "Ho, ho, ho, ho. Come to the hotel this afternoon at five o'clock. You and your parents, Madame?"

"I cannot leave my home, Monsieur," Mama said quickly, offended, "the housekeeping."

On our way home Mother said: "You made a good impression. I can see that. Now try not to destroy it," Her voice was chagrined.

"I know what I am doing."

I knew what I wanted. This man could give me a scholarship. And he was someone I could talk to. Olga, Hilda, Otto, Mrs. Bürger – they were all right, but Hers would understand this leaping fire in me, this want, want, want in me . . .

At five in the afternoon the hotel lobby seemed strangely grand. The only portion of it I knew well was the French bookstore, run by Henri Vetch, a lanky Frenchman with a great shock of hair, who sold disastrously expensive books. He had also a great sexual theory about China, which he expounded to me time and again, the last time in 1962 in Hongkong, but which I keep on forgetting. Vetch was sitting with Hers at a low tea-table in the large hotel lobby, and in armchairs were several other people, two Chinese in long robes who turned out to be eminent men, one of them being Dr. Weng Wenhao, the geologist, Director of the National Geology Survey, who had just become President of Tsinghua University. There was also a European couple, Belgians. Everyone spoke in French, and I remember someone Chinese saying: "That is the end. This is the end of China." And then sipping tea in small neat sips. Dr. Weng was a small man with a round head and a big dent on one side of his forehead.

Hers turned to him: "Dr. Weng, what do your students feel? All quiet?" "Well," said Dr. Weng, "it is difficult – difficult – " he sounded just like my father. "And what do you think, Miss Chou?" "I think we should kick the Japanese out," I replied. Hers said: "Hoho,hoho, hmmn." The Belgian couple looked at each other. From then on, in all the cities of China where white society made reputation, I was reputed to be Hers's Eurasian mistress. "She made straight for him, and never let him go." Of course I wanted a scholarship, but since our relationship, all these years, has remained non-sexual, perhaps it is time I should state it, although the noises society makes have never bothered me.

Then everyone started talking, leaving me out completely. Vetch was discoursing in that earnest, deaf-to-all-interruptions manner which never left him. Dr. Weng was patiently explaining geology to the Belgian lady. I drank tea, ate cakes, drank tea, ate sandwhiches, drank tea, went to the toilet and came back. I wanted to talk about me and what I wanted to do, I had not come to listen to a lot of grown-ups with their sentences I could not follow. It was mostly stories about people, this one and that one, how they squirmed and bribed and got on. "He has a million in it," and someone mentioned the League of Nations too, but "they will take a little excursion tour round, et voila, that will be all."

"This young girl here thinks it's nonsense," Hers, who had been stroking his beard, suddenly bawled. "Have you eaten enough? Or do you want more to eat?"

"I can always eat," I told him. "My mother says that I'm still growing."

And then everyone seemed to laugh except one of the two men in long robes, the Chinese, who had not quite caught up, and let drop: "Actually, I believe we should make peace with the Japanese. I believe it would be very much better for us, in the long run."

"But there is no war," said the male of the Belgian couple. "This Shanghai attack was a mistake, they will draw their horns in . . ."

And again there was nothing to do but to wait while they all talked, and finally someone said: "It all depends on America, what will America do?" Then they went away, taking time and making appointments with Hers, and Hers then looked at me blankly, and I saw he had forgotten why I was there.

"I want a scholarship to study, I told you so, this morning, at church." I said it rather impatiently. How dare he forget me?

"How old are you?"

"Sixteen, almost, and I have already been waiting three years."

"Fifteen, then. My God, you are a child! And Mademoiselle is typing! I don't give money to typists."

I stared at him, furious.

"You are too young," he said. "Come back in three years to ask me for a scholarship, and show me your certificates. What do you think we do with our money? Build kindergartens? Anyway you must have university training before we can consider you for a scholarship."

"That is what I am working for," I said.

"I will talk to your parents about it," he said. And then abruptly: "Come, let's have dinner upstairs on the roof garden."

We went upstairs, where I had never been; from the four-square roof garden one could see all the roofs, the yellow imperial roofs of the Forbidden City. "Ming, all Ming," said Hers, who collected Han bronzes and disdained anything after that. "All the Chinese have done since the Sung dynasty is copy, copy themselves." We ate soup and fish and beef and talked; I told him more of how I felt and what I read than I had anyone else. And he just hmmed, and then after dinner he said: "Well, child, go home or your mother will be worried," and I went home. "What did he say to you? Are you getting the money?" asked my mother. "Not yet, he says I'm too young."

A few days later my mother was told by someone that the

whole city was talking about my having gone to bed with Hers in the Peking Hotel, and she was much upset, though she quickly recovered, and took my defence. She told me that Hers being a bachelor had a reputation, of course, that he liked Chinese girls, and the Belgian mothers with eligible daughters could not forgive this. But Mother defended me and stood by me then, her fighting spirit up. I could not even be interested; wearily I thought: "He's older than Papa, how could I?" But even my friend Vera was shocked.

"You made eyes at him in church," said Vera to me, accusingly.

Vera had not been to church, but she had been told by someone.

"Of course I made eyes at him, I want a scholarship. How do you think I could have got his attention if I had not made eyes at him?"

"And then he took you to dinner."

"Of course he took me to dinner," I said. "He liked my conversation."

And Vera, being good, believed me: "It's true you talk very well."

The next week I received a note from Hers saying he had been away to Tientsin, but that if I wanted to, I could buy books from Henri Vetch at the French bookstore for the sum of twenty dollars a month, and put them on his account. That was the most thoughtful, most wonderful present anyone could have given me. I immediately rushed to the French bookstore, where I found Vetch, standing, reading (he always browsed in his own book-store), and showed him the letter. "Please help me select some books." So he made me buy Duhamel: *La Possession de Monde*. And from Shanghai, when Hers had returned, also came a book to read, by Count Keyserling.

I bought a bookcase, because the rattan one at home was old and sagging and there was no more space on its shelves. I went to the East Glory Gate furniture dealers and ordered a bookcase which cost me six dollars. It came within a few days, a bright shiny yellow bookcase. My father said the wood was not good, and would splinter. However, the books looked fine in it. I was to find the bookcase twenty-five years later in our house in Peking. It had not splintered, only the paint had gone.

In summer 1932 I had two weeks off, my annual holiday. Hers wrote to me that if I had nothing better to do, he would take me on an expedition to the Huangshan mountains which were

196

accessible from Shanghai, a distance of only about three hundred miles. Madame Thys and her husband, and a Mr. Vermer, from a Belgian company, would be going. "It will teach you something about China's peasantry," he wrote. We would return via Hangchow, the famous West Lake resort. I took the boat from Tientsin and arrived in Shanghai in July 1932 and Hers put me up at a small pension, tidy and very cheap, run by a Dutchwoman.

Sometimes alone, often with a friend, Hers every evening went from dance hall to dance hall, sitting at each one for an hour or two, and drank orange juice. At that time Hers had a Chinese dance-hall girl as his more or less permanent mistress, as was *de rigueur* for any European bachelor in China. She was from Soochow, where women are renowned for their beauty, short, dark-haired, vivacious, an admirable dancer. We went to a night club whose floor was all glass; with lighting below the glass; his girl friend, in a bright yellow dress, arrived and sat with us for a few minutes.

I watched the decorously gyrating couples, all vice subdued in surroundings which were Western – in China, ritualized, dignified, sinisized by Chinese self-control: "They have even civilized the brothels," Hers used to explain enthusiastically to the new arrivals from Belgium, businessmen, bankers, whom he took around. He would explain how it was never, never done to go to a high-class house and immediately go to bed with a selection. "That is barbaric, mon cher," he said to Vermer, a new arrival who was in a hurry. Here, one paid a formal call, full of etiquette, on one, two, or three houses, spent half an hour at each drinking tea, chatting with the madame, without even mentioning one's object. One did not even see the shadow of any girl, neither the first time, nor the second time. By the third visit the madame had gauged the visitor, studied his standing, received the information coming through the gangster service which was also indispensable to business. At the third or fourth visit, she might casually mention that a young girl might sing for the guests. The girl would not arrive for half an hour or more. When she did she would sit demure, eyes dropped, for a few minutes, sing a brief song, and withdraw. Perhaps another girl would be called. "Why, it might take months to sleep with anyone," said Hers, "Months," cried Vermer, "but what does one do if one is only here for six weeks?" "Ne jouez pas le goinfre," replied Hers.

In the dance halls the girls moved like clouds, distant, disdainful, their shawls (in fashion then) falling graceful as in the old

197

paintings. No drunkenness, no brutality. Respectable families with children sauntered in, to watch "Western dancing" as candidly as they would go to the cinema. They sipped tea or orange juice, and their innocence made the active search for young womanflesh which went on all the time somehow respectable. Hers admired Chinese women, their figures, their wit. I learnt much then of the habits of European males on the coast looking for a sleeping partner, of the Nanking officials and their mistresses, and their concubines, of the family relationships between the gangsters of Shanghai, their female protégées, regularly sent up, as "fresh material," for the high officials of the Nanking government to inspect. I also saw one evening, sitting and being admired, the then famous Chinese film star, Butterfly Wu. Chinese films were beginning to be made in studios in Shanghai. "The Chinese say her armpits smell," was Hers's comment on the famous beauty. She had a well-advertised dimple in one cheek. She was also an excellent business woman and later made money in many enterprises, such as a Thermos flask factory.

But all the brothels and dance halls were not as high class as Hers averred. In the back streets prostitution was at fifty cents apiece; there were fifty thousand licensed and one hundred thousand unlicensed prostitutes, and many of them were girls from the countryside enticed there by the gangsters. After the great famine of 1928, twenty-eight thousand corpses were picked up in Shanghai's streets, and in that year of 1932, thirty thousand.

After three days Hers announced that we were leaving the next morning at seven; I was to pack a small bag and come to his house at six thirty. I arrived at six thirty, but only four of us instead of the intended six departed at seven thirty. Hers, Vermer, myself and the chauffeur, a competent individual in black lacquered silk and a straw hat, who was a secret-society man and had been with Hers for a long time. He supervised the tying of the luggage at the back of the black Ford convertible. With the filming equipment, and Vermer's luggage, we only had room to sit. It was lucky that the couple who were supposed to come with us had given up. "Vermer will chaperone you," said Hers, uncovering long teeth and giving a baleful laugh. "I can look after myself," I replied. I had with me a few shorts and shirts, which I wore all the time. In all the villages, people asked whether I was a boy or a girl; my hair was cropped short and I strode about, and no one could make out.

We drove by the road for about two days, and arrived at the city of Hueichow, at the foot of the lovely Huangshan mountains, there to hire porters to carry food and luggage up the mountains with us.

We had passed through villages horrifying in their poverty. The stark horror, the filth, remain astringent in my eyes. It was worse, I thought, than in the north, because here besides drought and taxes was disease. "Hookworm, hookworm," cried Hers, waving his cane, "hookworm and liver fluke." Hookworm was endemic, the people were puffed of face, deathly pale, clad in stinking rags and dragged themselves about, the children were deformed and emaciated. There was a drought which got worse as we proceeded, every village loathsome, worse than the preceding one. We saw a rain-making ceremony. Decked with boughs of willow round their heads, the villagers had carried the tutelary deity out of its temple, and by the river bank (the river a gaunt trickle showing the white bones of its sand bed) were shaking him in his sedan chair, swinging him from side to side, meanwhile wailing and beating drums. Hers filmed the whole scene, uttering exclamations of joy at being able to see this – which the headman of the village did not like; he sent two men to stop the filming, but Hers waved his cane and went on. The procession then departed, drumming, and shaking the god, up the uneven, broken stone path to the village half perched on the slope of a hillock; famished skeletal dogs circled us at a safe distance. That evening a small cloud dropped five minutes of rain, no more.

We went on up the mountains, the lovely, the famous Huangshan, up old pathways hewn out of rock, immortalized in the poems of those who for centuries had climbed these, passing through some of the most beautiful landscape of China, which had inspired painters for a thousand years. The fifteen carriers with us put little sticks below projecting boulders, an offering to the spirits upholding the mountain-side; and since then I too, when climbing a mountain, place twigs under a surging rock face, not because I believe in mountain spirits, but it is a way of thanking the earth for its beauty, beauty of stone and sky and water, beauty all around us, loveliness abounding. The famous pines of Huangshan, growing between the rocks, outstaring the sun, tilted at impossible angles, were centuries old; in the heat haze we climbed slowly, Hers leading, his cane thumping firmly the rocky ground; I followed. Vermer remained behind; for after the second day he had lost interest in the expedition. There were mosquitoes at night, and they were merciless to him. Our three campbeds, legs planted in tins of water mixed with paraffin to discourage insects, were surmounted by clouds of fine mosquito nets. Vermer sweated uncommon quantities of liquid from morning to night; and also suffered from constipation. In the morning Hers brewed Instant Postum and we drank it; at first I disliked it but later found coffee strange to my palate. Everywhere he went Hers would know and name the trees and the plants; he stood like a giant tree himself, planted in front of an admirable expanding trunk sustaining a myriad leaves. "Look at this carefully, it is . . ." he would give the French, English, Latin, and Chinese names; later I found he had also brought two edible vegetables, one of them Belgian chicory, to China for cultivation.

All things Chinese – women, porcelain, customs, culture, vegetation, landscape – fascinated Hers. "No country in the world is as wonderful as China, it is a world on its own, a cosmic phenomenon, immortal," he would tell me. He also knew birds, would stop to name a pheasant, photograph a buzzard. And it is a pity that the Chinese people, for him, counted so little in their millions, and that he never connected the poverty and squalor of the villages with the necessity for what Teilhard de Chardin called "an end to white privilege," but that peculiar blindness is the distinguishing feature of most "Old China hands."

Nothing interested Vermer, he would obediently point his camera in the direction Hers indicated, but it was obvious he longed for the end of our safari. He would then show his photographs, in retrospect enjoy the trip.

As we climbed on, we came across mountain streams, bouncing their way over rocks, and I steeped into their cold clearness; we would stop under an arbour of trees for the afternoon rest, and in the delicious shadow look at the mountains, high, so high, swinging above us, clouds dreamily lingering over them, profiled in the river which now ran among the boulders; a landscape as lovely, upside down, walked with us. We crossed a bridge dating from the Sung dynasty, a thousand years old, its stones intact; Vermer clamoured that he had lost two handkerchiefs. At night we stopped in temples, and one afternoon reached the topmost peak and looked at all the plains below, and saw the sun shrink red behind further peaks, and night fall with the first glossy fireflies zigzagging the darkness. Also that night I fell ill with a high fever, and was brought down, ignominiously, on a stretcher the next day. Hers swore all the way: "I should have known better than to bring a girl . . ." Vermer, however, was pleased. He produced a thermometer and dramatically found my temperature 103.8°, thus making Hers descend the mountain a day earlier than planned; the next day, at half-level, weak but better, I started walking again. We reached Hangchow two days later, and by that time I was cured. But Hers never forgave me; thirty years later he was still making fun of me. "Mademoiselle finds it convenient to become ill . . . the whole expedition spoilt . . ." But during the journey he ranted even more at Vermer.

"Ah, mon vieux, if only your bottom was not so expansive, there would be more place in the car for us."

"Your bowels blocked? If only your tongue could stop wagging too."

Ferocious, Joseph Hers could be, and people quailed before him; I quailed too, but not outwardly. And though very susceptible to his opinions and judgments, I always bounced back, and in the end did what I wanted. When he teased me I pretended to be deaf, knowing he was trying to hurt, and this affected indifference kept him wondering. I knew he was a dominator; I must never be subdued. He would despise me. It was an odd relationship; a duel in certain ways. He realized that it would have been far too dangerous, not only for his own freedom, which he greatly prized, but because I would never have forgiven him had anything occurred between us. And I knew he would despise me then. "You want to dominate, you want to rule, you will never do anything but break men," he one day shouted at me. "And you can only buy women." I replied pat. Then he was silent.

When we returned he went straight to his Chinese mistress, but she was out; and I think he resented this very much, for he told me about it.

We lingered in Hangchow for two days, boating on the lake, visiting the temples before returning to Shanghai. In Shanghai, Vermer tried a pass at me, after giving me lunch one day, and later had tall tales to tell, but that is not uncommon among inferior men. He was only one of a long series of males, who for one reason or another, to boost their own ego, find it satisfying to boast of what they have not achieved. Every outstanding woman has to put up with this shallow malice. In the end it does no harm.

"Let him invent," said Hers, when I told him about it. "His imagination is probably the only satisfaction he has."

One hot morning in a place which was a club and to which Hers took me before lunch, I saw Dr. Hu Shih. The talk was all about Japan, the League of Nations, and what was happening. Hu Shih's hair stood quite upright in front, as if he had a rather soft black hairbrush growing on his head:

"China has had three revolutions on its hands at one and the same time, political, social, and intellectual . . .

"Our people are not ready, I don't think they are ready at all, they do not have the capabilities of a modern nation . . .

"We must do something, there must be reform, otherwise there will be disaster . . .

"What can you do without money? Actually Nanking is bankrupt . . . bankrupt . . ."

I gazed at him with awe, with intense respect. Teacher Wang had told me to read him. I wanted to say: "Dr. Hu, I am trying to read your essays," but my tongue stuck to my palate. And then he talked of Zen Buddhism. He was writing an essay on Zen. Meanwhile, outside the window, on the hot, clayey water which lapped the Bund, the Japanese warships went by. Dr. Hu Shih was too wise to notice them.

I returned to Peking by boat, sailing from Shanghai, and all the newspapers were full of the news of Chiang Kaishek's great victories. The Fourth Extermination Campaign had begun, and was to last nine months, till March of 1933. On the boat were many Japanese, travelling between Shanghai and Tientsin. I kept far from them. The Japanese women in third class spread clean sheets, each had her own territory on the floor, and neatly put their belongings round them. They then knelt, in front of a spittoon, and vomited carefully, steadily, into it, off and on, as long as our boat was at sea.

Christmas 1932. I was going to a real Christmas party, at the Grand Hotel de Peking, for the first time. Other Christmases had been at home, round a Bethlehem scene brought by my mother from Belgium; the cave in which the Holy Family had taken refuge, cohesive rock heap of brown cardboard, dried straw, white crystals sprayed by me, the Holy Child and its parents painted by my mother when she was a child in strong solid colours which still glowed after so many years in China, the same strong beautiful colours with which she had painted the Bible pictures in her Bible which I had inherited from her, solemnly on my tenth birthday. Angels hung among the cardboard rocks, small candles, pink, yellow, green, spiralled their flames. We sang; then came the gifts deposited by Father Christmas in our bedroom while we were singing. We were in bed by nine, instead of eight.

But now I was a grown-up, earning my living, and was going for the first time in my life to a Christmas party at the Hotel de Peking, in the grand ballroom.

"We will have a big party, with everyone," said Otto. But I was preoccupied, and it was, as usual, money. Money in the account was for studying, and though Mr. Harned had let me know that by January 1933 I might be promoted to seventy-five dollars, I wanted to save. My efforts to imitate the glamorous world of the whites, to which Eurasian secretaries like myself clung, were very costly, and I indulged in bursts of extravagence. For the Christmas party I asked Otto to help me to buy a dress. "Of course, I am glad to buy a dress for you." We went to the big silk shop called the Clock Store, a famous and great shop with an alleyway to the main hall. One heard the swish of silk in the alleyway before entering the hall. Attendants, all male (there were no women shop assistants, except White Russians in European shops), stood in front of large lacquered counters covered with fine felt, over which spread smooth white lawn. The hands of the salesmen unwinding the silk from their bolts, unfurling them with a great swoop, were also smooth and white. Everything to ravish the eye, silks and brocades and satins, all the loveliness and splendour of design, bamboo, coin, flowers, birds, came alive in these dazzling colours that glowed, upstairs and downstairs. Along the counters stood the customers, their buying eyes upon the rainbow profusion. The salesmen's nails were manicured not to damage the silks; they wore long blue cloth gowns, over the sleeves of the chief salesman were cuffs of white silk.

For Peking was also the city of silk as of all objects elegant, beautiful: jewel boxes, carved jade, books and furniture. There were other silk shops, sumptuous and elegant, and later my sister Tiza was to marry the heir to one of them at the wrong time; for it was after 1945, a few years before the Revolution finally shook off the debris of the old world. Tiza's husband, who also did some black marketing (as who did not, among the wealthy or those in contact with the American army then occupying Peking after the war), was accused by the very Americans with whom he had been dealing of black marketing. Yet it was they who sold him Army stores material, food tins, cigarettes, and miles and miles of wire, in that vast net of corruption and profiteering which accompanies the American armies everywhere they go.

The poor man disappeared, in the turmoil of Revolution. The silk shop, unclaimed, was confiscated after a year, notice having been put in the newspaper; but Tiza had gone, and did not want her property back. "Too much trouble," she said.

We entered the shop, Otto and I, and for me too were spread out the revels of satin and brocade; I finally chose a red silk with silver lilies woven into the fabric and had a long dress made out of it by the little tailor in Suchow Street, who charged me two dollars less than he charged his European customers. The tailor loved the silk and outdid himself, cutting a most subtle twist to the bodice, a one-sided dip to the neck, sighing with pleasure when he had done and saw me in it. Never again would I have such a sudden miracle; I kept the dress for many years, though I never wore it again. It was burnt by Pao, my first husband, in one of his moods of destructiveness, caused either by the vagaries of humour of his Chief, Chiang Kaishek, or his own inner torment when he joined the Blueshirts. Incineration is a common end to many things, but does not affect possessive memory.

It was a cold winter again, that winter of 1932–3, but I was not cold that evening, though I had on only a small lambswool jacket on top of my red silk dress. A carload of people, Fredi, Otto, others, came to the house to fetch us, my sister Tiza and myself. Tiza wore a blue dress, also of silk, her hair was long on her shoulders and curled; and both of us that night beautiful, though Tiza more so, and immediately someone fell in love with her, for though she was only thirteen, she looked grown-up. The car drove to the Grand Hotel de Peking, we entered, turned to the left, to the ballroom with its springing elastic floor, its square pillars with their looking-glasses on each face, to the dining-room, its tables set for dinner at twenty dollars a person that night. All the tables were decorated with crackers and flowers; there were great chains of coloured paper and balloons hanging from the ceiling amid the chandeliers; the yellow velvet curtains against the large windows shone like gold.

And since 1931 more Chinese came to the Grand Hotel de Peking. Officials on tour in the north, old-time warlords with titles in the government, their sons now officials of the Kuomintang; and ready to co-operate with the Japanese at any moment; Japanese, anxiously dressed, with ostentatious gloves, their wives at home, accompanied by Korean artistes, actually

204

Japanese courtesans in disguise. The whole of the North was being infiltrated by the Japanese secret service, over one hundred thousand of them, through the medium of drug traffickers and prostitutes, black marketeers, Korean and Manchu girls, still uncouth and lumpy in tight brocade Chinese dresses, trying hard to imitate the Shanghai style, their hair short and curly, smelling of pomade, trailing silver foxes over their shoulders, their stockings, not always seam-straight upon their legs. From the cut-glass chandeliers the light streamed upon the motley; and oh how impressive it was meant to be, with the foreign diplomatic staffs there. The diplomats still avoided Nanking, the new capital, because of the dearth of good houses and piped water; Peking was so much more comfortable to live in, with spacious, treeful gardens surrounding the houses, and the beautiful Western Hills, and the Summer Palace, Tientsin and the sea at Peitaiho, so near. Rather than follow the government to Nanking many diplomats remained here, and now in they came, the men in black, with black ties, the women in long shining dresses, their high heels tapping the sprung floor. There were tall Englishwomen with bent clavicles and bony elbows, their stride perceptible within the satin of their new ballroom gowns, men with red faces above high white collars followed them. In came the very beautiful Maria Cellini, the one Roberts the British Embassy man had told me about; groaning about love's sweet pain, and reading Baudelaire; only the other day he had said with deep content: "I had her you know, at last." Maria was in plain black velvet with a square neck, no ugly clavicle twist, so smooth her flesh, full her shoulders; round that superb throat a heavy necklace of real diamonds, her sixty-year-old husband's wedding anniversary gift. Both her husband and Roberts followed her, talking to each other. And there came Mr. Vogel, my professor of physics, with his wife, and little Miss Steiner, with her hard blue eyes and her sweet expression; Fredi and Eugen bet each other that Mr. Vogel would dance the first dance with her and also the last dance. In they came, so many of them, and someone at our table kept up a running commentary of their public secrets, some of which I had already heard in the ladies' room of the P.U.M.C. This was the way to live life, then, this was to be rich, important, powerful, and well regarded, this doubleness, one with the satin gown on, striding nobly, the other unmentionable and always mentioned, mirror image in a distorting mirror. This was the White Life, the Life Wonderful, Powerful, which earned thousands of dollars a month, places on the sunny beaches, cars, insolence, while Mr. Yeh the clerk and his six children survived on thirty-five dollars a month for the last ten years.

At a table for twenty, Germans, German Eurasians, I too sat, Rosalie Chou, Eurasian girl with small salary and big ambition. Next to me a Prince Lai, a Manchu prince, cousin (so they said) of Puyi, now soon to be re-enthroned Emperor of the new state of Manchuria. Prince Lai was always drunk, with a greenish skin and long moist hair. I watched, absorbing, as I ate, the life around me; fascinated, yet also repelled. This was society in the East; white society. I would walk out of it as easily as now I rose to walk into it, on to the resilient floor when Otto said: "Come, let us dance."

"I don't know how to dance." But Otto was dancing, stepping in time to music, dragging his wooden leg: "I hope he doesn't fall on the floor, as he did that time he told me about."

And Otto was sad, but pretending to be happy, humming to himself. I felt suffocated with self-consciousness. This was the life, fun, everybody seemed to enjoy it so much – this is IT!

There were many couples whirling on the floor, thickening the music with laughter, people left their tables, turned to each other, and immediately sprang into action; the long skirts skimmed, deployed and folded, there was haha hehe laughter, everyone showing their teeth at everyone else. What a spree. What fun. The Chinese woman who was the mistress of a Mongol prince, the Eurasian girl who was the mistress of a famous warlord were gyrating, the silver foxes of the Korean prostitutes whirlwinded. Fredi passed with Tiza in his arms; he called gaily, then attempted to leap up at a chandelier; bravely Otto pushed me round, taking little steps; and perhaps to encourage me, started kissing my cheek, which only made everything worse, so that I stumbled. Oh, how much I wanted to learn all there was to be learnt, and above all to learn why other people looked so happy, why they felt happy. This was the world, daring, bold, clever, wicked, doing all that was wrong in the catechism and yet successful, not afraid of hell. This was the thing to do in order to be rich and wear diamond necklaces; there was no hell for them, only fun and cars; how replete with food their bodies, while outside dried a million skeletons in the cold wind. What was this secret that made evil good and made good unfortunate? Bravely we danced on, although by now I had lost all sense of timing. Oh how clever,

how brilliant, everything, everyone . . . The waltz came to an end
and we sat down. "Champagne!" Eugen cried, and filled my
glass. Champagne, how nice. Is this champagne? The wonderful
drink that people whisper about? I thought it would be so much
nicer . . . There is Lily Hu, the Eurasian girl who went to Tientsin,
now she's back, they say she's got a baby, but she looks gorgeous,
all in gold lamé dress, skin-tight. And there is Anna, large mouth
painted, red hair with its dip in the middle of the forehead accen-
ted with black, in a green dress with black patent leather shoes.
She has large hips, but her face is so beautiful, so beautiful, lovely
mouth, strange light-brown eyes heavily circled with black,
Fredi, the good boy, good Fredi, with heavy good looks: "Let us
promise to keep ourselves pure . . . They expect us Eurasians to
sleep with everybody, they cheat us, but we are not going to be
cheated, we are going to be different . . ." Another cup of
champagne, and suddenly everything is truly wonderful, magic
success, enjoyment blown enormous. I feel like Clara Bow, or
was it some other star, holding a champagne glass and laughing,
laughing, pearls in her mouth, and pearls round her throat and
bubbles like pearls cascading about. But this champagne is sickly
stuff, surely something is wrong with me that I cannot, do not,
like champagne; I want some water now; not drunk, no, not
drunk of course, but there am I, dancing with someone else, and
then someone else, and it is very hot, and suddenly Hilda is there
pulling me by the arm: "Behave yourself . . ." I laugh groggily.
All through the evening I am asked to dance, not only by men at
my table, but men from other tables come to ask me; and one of
them is someone I have met once, with Roberts, he is from the
British Embassy, and he tells me his name again: "Hartley, I
don't suppose you remember." "No, I don't." After a few steps
he leads me off the dancing floor which now bounces to the
Charleston and we walk across the slippery cool marble of the
lobby to a small table in the quieter bar. "What will you have, a
crème de menthe?" "What is that?" It came: I sipped. Horribly
green, horribly sweet. "Oh, I've never drunk this before." "You
must let me come to see you, I'd like to see more of you." "Oh,
that's easy, you know where I work, come at any time to the
office." Elbows on table, I tell him my dream to be a doctor and
about the book on relativity which I have been reading, while he
stares at me out of funny-coloured flecked eyes; his lashes are
long and red, his hair thinning on his forehead in patches, he has
dandruff on his black suit. Suddenly in comes a woman in a

green gown, green like crème de menthe: "My dear John, I've been looking for you everywhere . . ." I say: "Do sit down and have a crème de menthe," and laugh, pushing my glass towards her. She has been waltzing with Smith, Scottish little Smith my friend, who tonight wears a kilt, waltzing away with him and blowing kisses all around her – it's meant to be funny. Smith had come prowling round us as we sat, and even bent to say something to Hartley, who replied: "Don't be funny, Smith," but I was talking about relativity, and the scene floated by me like cigarette smoke. Now I remember it. "Where is Smith?" "John, we must be going . . . the others are waiting." John Hartley stands reeling: "My dear, let me introduce to you . . ." "You dirty half-breed, leave my husband alone." John follows crème-de-menthe dress out of the bar. I shake my head to clear it. I feel like crying, but what is there to cry about? Did she really think I wanted her balding, old, dandruffy husband? It was he who took me away from the dance floor, to the bar . . . while she was dancing with Smith and throwing kisses about. But now Henry Wang comes into the bar, looking for me, and with him also Smith; in his sporran the silver coins click as he sits near me: "So Edna's got John back . . . what a pair they are, don't mind them, my dear, I'm much more fun," says Smith. Henry Wang orders brandy, which he thinks shows he understands what to ask for, and manfully gulps it all down, trying to pretend he is as good as any European at drinking, but suddenly turns pea-green, and has to run to the men's. "Green, green, everything's green tonight," I shout. "Come, let's dance," says Smith. "I can't dance, you know that." But Smith walks me round. "My dear, you're damned attractive, that's the whole trouble, take care of yourself." "Sure I can take care, I'm grown-up," and to prove it go back to the table and drink more champagne. And then there is the sudden bell, and a whistling, and sirens, and screams, and all the crackers exploding, and the balloons coming down, Christmas, Christmas . . . A Child is born.

Now everyone is kissing everyone else, and Smith, his glasses more owlish than ever, kisses my cheek. "Merry Christmas, my dear, and all the best." "Take me to dance quick," I say, "I hate kissing." Everyone is mouth-slavering everyone else, but Smith keeps a firm hold. He is an energetic, bouncy dancer, always as if performing a round-the-maypole bounce and hop, and he keeps his body away from mine, which I like. But we bump into many people, saying "oh sorry." And now everyone is singing:

"For he's a jolly good fellow," as it is also someone's birthday.

Now the dancers weave about in a long saraband, the tables are in disorder; the hothouse roses wilted, smoke stays in flat levels in the thick air; plates strewn with remains of cake lie about like ransacked bodies after a massacre. Fredi is very red in the face and shouting, Eugen links arms with Otto and other Germans, to sing the Horst Wessel song. "Are you Nazis?" someone shouts at them. "We are all Nazis now; Heil Hitler!" Otto replies.

There are whistles and crackers popping and someone tries to put a paper cap on my head but I refuse. He insists and I finally strike his hand very hard, and start screaming: "Don't touch me. Don't touch me." "Oh, you're not a good sport." "Leave her alone." says Otto, suddenly there. A dishevelled American tourist comes past, she is going from table to table, hanging her bright blonde hair over everyone and kissing them; she bends over me: "May I kiss you, my dear? Happy Christmas, I just love . . ." The saraband goes winding past me and Eugen pulls me by the hand into it, everyone hands on the hips of the person in front, stomping and singing; and the man behind me squeezes me hard and tries to put his hands round my chest so again I am striking hard, hard as I used to do at school, never looking where I hit, so he says: "Can't you take a joke?"; but something tight and strangling is growing in my chest and now I know I am going to cry, so I run out to the women's and it is full of people and I run out again, behind one of the yellow curtains and have a good cry; then I laugh and laugh and it is over. I am quite sober, quite clear again. I go back to sit down, feeling resurrected, calm, unearthly. There is Tiza, calm, beautiful, looking on in a detached and dreamy manner; with the Manchu prince staring at her and not getting even a look back, and other men all devouring her with their eyes, and getting nowhere. Such beautiful manners, so aloof, her perfect teeth showing just a little, I feel suddenly how terrible it is she should be here. She is only a little over thirteen. Someone has walked on the hem of my skirt, and there is a blackish stain upon it.

It is two in the morning and people are going home, my face has turned to wood, I cannot move my jaw, and this is fine, otherwise I might be saying out loud the words that rend me: "Holy Mother of God, have pity on me . . ." but the Virgin with the blue mantle does not drink champagne; not go to Merry Christmas parties for her Son, and the goddess Kwan Yin, the

209

All-Merciful, she does not hear my prayers, she is so far away from here . . . and only the face of Liu Mah,* Liu Mah the tiny-footed comes up from the years, with her comfortable smell of garlic and her burry voice, and the great welling tide of kindness, welling from her, as the spring-clear water wells from the Jade Fountain in the summer, limpid and clean-making, enough to wash away a world of filth, and now I can even hear the cool and nervous bubble of water, lithe and quick, and I long for the cold, stark night. I look at myself in the mirrored pillar, with my frizzy hair due to the beauty parlour, which is now half uncurled, and will be straight again tomorrow, though keeping a slight singe odour till the next wash. The Russian hairdresser has definitely burnt some of my hair at the back, I pull and the hair comes off in my hand. The lipstick that has cost so much and made my mouth so different, the bright beautiful dress . . . is this what I really want? Is this having a good time? Over there are Doctor Huber and Doctor Favre, both such important doctors, sarabanding away, and one of them is the one who squeezed me. Roberts has Maria Cellini cornered against a pillar, they hold champagne cups in their hands and look at each other.

"Come on, we go home." Out we are at last, in the night, the stars like frozen diamonds hung in the frozen sky; already dawn in the stone-cold air.

The leather upholstery at the back of the car is cold to touch. Tiza and Fredi and I pile in, awake with the sudden cold. We drive off and the gravel slushes under the tyres. Down Hatamen Street, bouncing on the pot-holes, the dust luminous, the early donkey and mule carts with their nailed wooden wheels grinding the darkness, the muffled men in ragged sheepskin coats with straw-bound feet shuffling by their pulling beasts, the crack of whips in air, the creak of wooden wheels and someone pinching Anna and Anna shouting: "Stop it," and I half wishing someone would pinch me too and perhaps I should be happy and not want to weep, and everyone singing, except Tiza and me. We arrive at Otto's house. Inside the drawing-room a fire sifts red-grey embers, Fredi throws some logs upon it. Someone puts on the gramophone: "Of thee I sing, Baby . . ."

The settee is covered with grey-green cloth, fairly rough, patches worn smooth with a fine hairy down of use; Anna sits next to me, her beautiful face turned upwards, smoking quietly.

* See *The Crippled Tree*.

210

How admirable the bone modelling; she bends towards me and her mouth smells of vodka; she kisses me on the cheek, a gesture of love and sadness, like a goodbye, then someone makes a coarse joke and turns the lights out. I go outside, into the courtyard; there stands Fredi in the cold, hands in his pockets: "Look at the stars, they are fading, like fountains in the sky being switched off; like people, all staring at us. Shall we climb on the roof to get nearer them?" "Oh yes, Fredi, let's." Already he vaults up on the veranda ledge, from there on to the low side wall, and pulls me up. We climb the herringbone tiled roof, sit on the grey, soft tiles, watch the stars fade, clean with cold. When we get back into the living-room the light is on again and no one is in the room but Otto, swaying gently, his hands in his pockets and his chin on his breast. He looks up. "Where are the others, where is Tiza?" "They have all gone to bed, some in beds together, and some alone, and some on the floor," says Otto. "Tiza is sleeping in a corner of the room, under a rug." "So will I do," says Fredi, and lies in another corner. "Hübsch" – he seizes two black satin cushions embroidered with golden dragons off the settee, flings them on the carpet, yawns and goes to sleep almost immediately. We go into Otto's room, and sit on the bed. There is no one else and Otto says: "Mädli, you are very beautiful." "Oh no, Otto." "Yes you are, all the men were looking at you. All of them wanted you tonight, you have so much life in you. You are beautiful, and your skin, it glows, and some day a man will take you and I would like to be that man, Mädli, but I have only one leg."

"But Otto, I do love you, even with only one leg, you are so kind to me, and you understand me."

"Mein Kind, you do not know at all what love is, Not at all. It is not fair to you. You are much too young."

Too young too young . . . I am exasperated, sick, and yet my heart is pounding, and looking at the stars has made me not afraid, not afraid of anything. "I am not a child, and I know, I do know what love is."

Fredi, snoring in the corner of the other room: "We must be pure, we must be pure . . . they expect us Eurasians to be available for sleeping with everybody . . . they cheat us, because no one protects us . . . but we are going to be different, to be different, to be different . . ." He snores.

Otto shakes his head. "Ach, Mädli, but if I don't start you, it will be someome else, someone who may not be careful, and it may be worse. It may be someone who will give you a child, and leave you with a child. I will be careful, always."

And by that time I too know that I want to have this strange business called making love over and done with. "Oh, for God's sake. Otto, don't make such a song and dance about it. After all, I've got to grow up, to grow up, I've got to know everything."

And so it is, and like so many millions of other women, the first time, such a little thing, without any feeling about it; only an astonishment, a disappointment, a feeling that truly, it is so little to make such a fuss about.

One goes to bed a child, one is expected to rise from it a woman. One expects to be changed. But there is nothing. I get up, and put on my jacket. "Now drive me home, Otto." "But what about Tiza?" Tiza still sleeps. We wake her, and put her in the car. She falls asleep again at the back.

"Will you forgive me, Mädli?"

"For what?" I was surprised. "For what? As you said, it had to come. And I suppose that you won't marry me?"

"No, I told you, I cannot marry you; I cannot marry a Eurasian; I am a German, an Aryan."

"Yes, I know." It does not make any difference since I don't want to marry him either. Soon the rutted tracks where the mule carts and the donkey carts tread their calvary is before us. Along it comes, slow pacing, a camel caravan. The car brakes, waiting for the camels to pass; they are already tawny from the sunrise; between their twin humps lie crosswise the sacks of coal from the coalmines beyond the Great Wall. Softly the camel bells sing; softly the cloven feet sink in the dust. Already the well winch is whirring, as the well-owner draws the day's first pail of water from the well.

CHAPTER ELEVEN

On the afternoon of January 4th, 1933, I went to my father's railway office at some minutes past five, to return with him to our house. It was a bitterly cold day, with large, thick flakes of snow, prelude to a snowstorm, drifting down.

I found my father with his friend Hua Namkwei, both in their overcoats, because of the cold; my father had mittens on his hands, leaving his fingers free. The two men crouched over the small, black stove with its long pipe going up and then at right angles horizontally out through the window, a windowpane having been taken out and replaced by a sheet of tinfoil with a hole cut in it for the pipe.

They looked so sad that I asked : "Papa, what is the matter?" Perhaps once again the railway line was cut. Another war . . .

"The Japanese took Shanhaikwan, yesterday," said Mr. Hua Namkwei. "This is the end."

And so it was. After Manchuria, now declared the independent state of Manchukuo by Japan, it was our turn in North China. The Japanese would take Peking . . .

Shanhaikwan was a small town which held the pass into the Northern plain, a pass between the mountains upon which the Great Wall had been built and the sea, hence its name: Shankaikwan, Mountain and Sea Pass.

Mr. Hua shivered in his overcoat. "We are never finished," he said wearily, " . . . never. What is going to happen now? Are we going to stand up and fight? Or no?"

My father did not reply. He put on his fur cap with the earpads, took his cane, the two men shook hands, and we went home. "Don't wait for me, I still have work to do," said Mr. Hua.

Hua Namkwei, I thought as we left, was now getting old, his hair suddenly snow-speckled, an uncommon thing in a Chinese, who do not whiten early. People made fun of Hua Namkwei for he was too honest. He refused to take home a sheet of paper, or a pencil, or even a clip. He never left the office earlier than the fixed time, nor did he arrive late, although no one could check what he did as he was the Chief Engineer. "It is dishonest," he said, "this is state property, state time, I cannot abuse it." Once when his son Simon Hua had tried to take a pencil home his father stopped him. "If everyone did like you, there would be no hope of China ever becoming great again:"

My father was just as honest, except in the matter of pencils; he allowed me, at times, one blue and red half-worn stump. As we went home, walking against the biting wind, my father bought a newspaper. At home, my mother took the *Peking Leader*, the English newspaper. The news of the latest Japanese feat was in it, very cautiously reported, and without comment.

In the next few days, Banker T. V. Soong, Chiang Kaishek's brother-in-law, arrived by plane in Peking. There was a great commotion; pictures of him appeared in the newspapers; seldom

213

did anyone as elevated as T. V. Soong come to our forsaken city, now that the capital was Nanking. The papers said that this showed "the government's determination to resist this latest encroachment," but ended up by saying that "Nanking must remember that a peaceful solution exists in any situation."

The only thing that happened was that all the imperial palace treasures which were in the Forbidden City were packed, crated, and taken to Nanking.

These treasures, which had belonged to many dynasties, were national property; the former palaces, open to the public, had become a museum; I had wandered through enormous Ming halls, looking at the paintings, the jades, the porcelains; a large crystal ball about two feet in diameter, of intense blue with icelike sparks embedded in it, on a stand, was my especial wonder. My mother had lingered over the ex-emperor's bed, and removed a small bit of the hanging; I remember it was rough, camelhair type of cloth, yellow with crude markings, and surely a fraud, the original probably stolen by a eunuch.

Despoiled of the old treasures, the Imperial City emptied, only the icy desert wind filled its courtyards with angry dust. Peking was more abandoned than ever, its people more silently angry. "Is that all? Is this how we shall be protected from attack by the Japanese?"

"They will sell these things to the Americans for dollars," people said bitterly, warming their hands over their teacups, in the small shops.

"Carpetbaggers," repeated Uncle Liu. He wore his fur-lined robe, and had come to wish us happy New Year in February, the Lunar New Year time; with him was my cousin, his first daughter. She giggled and whispered to herself, for she was quite out of her mind, encephalitis had damaged her brain in 1928.

More than ever China was in pieces, Nanking's foreign policy causing increasing anger. The Northern military commanders asked Nanking for help, but Chiang Kaishek sent neither troops nor planes; the weak northern forces retreated before the onslaught of the still advancing Japanese, and then suddenly, out of obscurity, leapt again a defender, a name, none other than Feng Yuhsiang, our Christian general.

"I told you so," I cried happily to Otto, "I told you Feng Yusiang would stand up and fight."

That 1927 meeting when Feng and Chiang had met and sworn brotherhood in a railway carriage was now remote; since then, most bitterly Feng had regretted being cheated by a smooth-faced small man, as he put it. Chiang called him in retaliation a northern ruffian. In 1929, Feng had gone to war against Chiang, and once more straddled the railways, and my father had taken hurried trips down the line, which had led to his becoming ill, and therefore a Catholic for a short while. Chiang skilfully played off one warlord against another. The nimble militarist melée had lasted till 1930, but when Chiang was in peril for a short while, foreign gunboats had appeared on the Great River to sustain him. After all, he was their most useful man, their elect, with the support and backing of America, of England. They had put their money on him . . . Now again, in 1933, Feng rose, denouncing Chiang Kaishek, and became for us a rallying point, a patriot, a hero.

In February 1933 Feng, together with other generals, Sung Cheyuan, Fang Chengwu, Chin Hungchang, made a stand against Japan. At Hsifengkow, and later at Kupeikow, these gave the Japanese the only fight they had in their conquest of Jehol province and north Hopei. In March 1933 the Japanese were eighty miles from Peking, and curfew was proclaimed in the city.

Once more Chiang sabotaged his own people; he sent a telegram urging that the defences be abandoned; threatening to court-martial the offending generals. General Chih Hungchang in November was captured by Chiang's secret police and assassinated; General Fang Chengwu had to flee to Hongkong.

And that spring, from the Red bases in the south, came yet another offer: United Front against Japan, co-operation of all the people to resist the aggression of Japan.

This proclamation infuriated Chiang Kaishek. He cut off all money and supplies of food to the troops fighting the Japanese as he had done the year before to the 19th Route Army defending Shanghai; the Japanese, flushed with victory, advanced to take yet another province, that of Chahar; in May 1933 Feng Yuhsiang fought them in Chahar, and organized "The People's Anti-Japanese Army."

In July this army, which had the backing of all the people in North China, and for which comforts and funds amounting to one hundred thousand dollars had been collected in many provinces, actually cleared the Japanese out of Chahar.

This victory of Feng Yuhsiang greatly angered Chiang Kaishek, who cabled Feng, upbraiding him for his disobedience, and accused him of being "surrounded by Communists and taking their advice." Meanwhile the incredibly pro-Japanese Ho Yingchin, Minister of Defence, signed a truce with Japan, called the Tangku Truce, which was, once again, a capitulation. It gave Japan control of Jehol province and withdrew all Chinese troops from it and also from northern Hopei province. And Hopie province was the province where Peking was situated. "It won't be long now before the Japanese dwarfs are here," said Uncle Liu.

The wounded sent by train to Peking filled the small hospitals. Chiang, who denied there had been a battle, could no longer deny it when the soldiers were laid in rows on the pavements. Not allowed into the good quarters, they rested in the dust, in the suburbs and along the country roads; millions of flies fed on their suffering flesh.

From other parts of China, protests rose, out of their own pockets some warlords sent money to Feng Yuhsiang.

The *Shanghai Daily News*, an English-language newspaper, for the first time began to denounce Chiang Kaishek's fascist organization, the Blueshirts, now very active in North China, arresting and murdering all those who disobeyed Chiang's orders of non-resistance to Japan.

Feng in disgust dissolved his army in August 1933, and retired to the sacred mountain of Taishan, while the Japanese reoccupied without a struggle all the territory which he and his subordinates had cleared. There was nothing Feng could do; Chiang Kaishek not only refused money and ammunition, but cut the food convoys to Feng's army.

Feng climbed the sacred Mount Taishan, one of his favourite retreats, and there meditated, Chiang sent him one hundred thousand dollars. but he returned the envelope untouched though he was hard up. Lord Lytton of the Lytton Commission, sent by the League of Nations, asked to see him, but Feng refused. He went into obscurity, but was not forgotten.

In 1941 I saw Feng Yuhsiang again, in Chengtu. In September of that year Feng Yusiang, all six foot four and two hundred and forty pounds of him, gave us a talk on the campus of the University in Chengtu, Szechuan. Hitler had just invaded Russia; and Feng spoke to us, predicting his defeat: "for no one can vanquish a people defending its own homeland." That was the last time I saw him. Next, I heard of his death, on a boat in the Black Sea (he was on a visit to Russia).

Today his body rests on Mount Taishan, which he loved,

painted, and wrote about. His memory is honoured. For he was a patriot, though a warlord; he came in at the end of one era and the beginning of another; were he alive, he would be today in Peking, along with many another ex-warlord, with many another patriot.

In the spring of 1933 the fighting between Feng Yuhsiang's army and the Japanese was only eighty miles from Peking, and one could hear at times the gunfire. The Japanese might take the city, any day, and many were frightened. The news of the Chinese victory elated us, and there was collecting of money for Feng's soldiers, although outwardly one was not allowed to show any joy; soon afterwards, Chiang Kaishek was to nullify that manifestation of resistance. Everywhere went government spokesmen, to tell us that we must "co-operate with a friendly neighbour."

Throughout the years my mother had preserved her jewels, brought with her, part of her dowry. In memory's sight, they become enormous. Rings with sapphires and rubies, a profound drowning enhanced by diamonds; heavy soft-honey gold, twenty-four carats; pendants the size of eggs, brooches like half a hand encrusted with emeralds. They were her grandmother's inheritance, kept in a lacquered box locked with a key. She stirred them in front of us, a conflagration in both her hands. I coveted a jet necklet, for I loved the sheen of black, and once, briefly, had owned a black kitten, a kitten so small and dainty but which was given away one afternoon when I was not there by my mother, a loss which hurt for years. The jet necklace was kitten memory.

That spring, my mother placed her jewel box in the safe care of the Scheut mission. During the 1920s, when the warlords came and went, she had stored them with the French priests, who grew large strawberries and made goat cheese in an area outside Peking, now part of a commune growing fifty times as much fruit and vineyards as before. In 1933 Mother placed her jewels with the Scheut missionaries, who had a mission house in the West Quarter of Peking. And within six weeks they were stolen.

That desolate afternoon when the letter came, Mother almost fainted. She who was always so verbally undaunted, now became wordless, wept long, very long. The next Sunday we went in a family group to the Scheuts, alighting from our rickshaws between an alleyway of young trees planted from the outer gate to the grey brick buildings smelling of must and sombreness. The

217

Superior stood there, in black robes smelt of dye in the young heat. He and a priest, with a beard, took us to the safe, its door wide open. "You see, Madame. We have left everything as it was . . . everything was taken out of the safe."

"The police . . ." said Mama.

My father peered inside the safe, his hand picking at his chin. I too looked at the smooth black inner walls of the empty safe. Looking, looking, conjuring jewels where no jewels were – the black jet necklet; my little black kitten.

"We have told the police, Madame, but surely you know they are always in league with the robbers."

"Perhaps offering a reward . . . ?"

We went home. Mother's voice veiled with grief, her body bowed with grief, unusually quiet. Then my grandmother died, of neurasthenia, which she had had for some years, and which was at that time a fashionable disease for the elderly. Mother became ill with phlebitis in her leg, and dragged herself about.

"I have lost everything, everything . . . Oh God, what have I done? Why is it that life has cheated me of everything?"

The Scheut fathers felt they owed us something. Two younger priests, a sallow man with a beard and a round and jolly one, the latter a typical Flemish peasant with curls, and cheek veins already bursting under his fine skin, his blue eyes a little haggard but merry and boisterous and his robe damp with constant sweat, called at our house to remit to Mother a hundred and fifty dollars. She thanked them, and when they were gone burst out: "Only one hundred and fifty dollars! What do they think? My jewels were worth thousands, thousands . . ."

But the sobbing had to stop. A few months later the jolly round priest was back, drinking coffee and telling his adventures; his blue eyes more haggard, his face blotched and puffy, his black robe more sweat-clogged than ever. He had been sent to Inner Mongolia, and there some Mongol soldiers fighting in guerrilla war had kidnapped him one Sunday afternoon as he was taking his siesta after the morning church service. They had tied him to a little donkey, and made the beast trot away with him. He raised still trembling hands, showing thick downy wrists, as if ropes were still about them. For three days they had held him, and then let him go. And now he was back at the Scheut mission headquarters, but had a nervous breakdown. He could not understand what had happened. "It is terrible in Mongolia, I have seen so many skeletons on the road. I can no

218

longer sleep at night." He came several times before his repatriation. His hands shook and his eyes began to pop, and he repeated the same story. "But what about my jewels?" said my mother. "They were real, Father, real diamonds and rubies and emeralds." "Oh Madame," he would reply, raising his quivering hands: "had you seen those skeletons walking . . ."

Part Two (1933-1938)

CHAPTER TWELVE

In 1963 Tan Leeton, a former classmate of mine at Yenching University, asked me whether I would go with him and his wife to the Yenching University Alumni annual gathering in Hongkong. Once again time's card deck was shuffled; in the present rose the carboard ghosts of the past.

These traditional Old Student gatherings of the Yenching Alumni are held in a cement-floored hall belonging to some Protestant church in Hongkong. Many others there, like myself now middle-aged, faced again their own youth, recollected as moon in water. A yesterday under the beautiful willows of Yenching University campus was resurrected as we became transported from this cold grey ugly hall, with its redolence of pious discomfort, its ill-fitting curtains and its badly lit stage, upon which an amateur troupe of Yenchingites would perform some amateur scenes of the good old days in Yenching. Soon the audience would sing the old old Alma Mater song. Tan Leeton, who recites poetry to himself in buses, while walking, and perhaps in his sleep, murmured:

> "In the west city the willows
> Make all the spring soft,
> Move old sorrow afresh.
> Remember that day in spring
> When the willows' green trailing arms could not
> Hold back your boat.
> Suddenly no one was there,
> Empty, on went the river."

Hail, O hail, Yenching . . . into the past, among the gracious buildings, in the enormous garden with its nameless lake and rocks and artificial mountains and running track and twenty-two tennis courts and marble bridges and pavilions, with its painted ceilings and red pillars, which was Yenching University in 1933 . . . and now the whitewashed walls of the Methodist Hall of Hongkong heard the college song:

> "Drawn from ev'ry part of China
> Here to old Peking

223

Loud in praise of Alma Mater
Hail, oh hail, Yenching."

Tan Leeton had kept the face, the attentive expression which he wore when in German language class, across the two desks between our seats, he stared at me, astonished, for I was laughing uncontrollably. He then wore a long blue gown; was good at French and English. Looking round, he now remarked that he could recognize several classmates, now playfully shouting nicknames to each other. When Yenching alumni foregathered, the Yenching spirit that we had been urged to cultivate by the American President of our University, John Leighton Stuart, took hold; an effusive demonstrativeness, which was only a measure of our nostalgia, asserted itself. "It is as if there has been no Revolution, no change . . . Yenching alumni still do amateur theatricals, and always someone plays a guitar, as if we were still under the willows of the lake on the campus, and always someone else sings a Hawaiian song; it is almost frightening, this clinging to what is real only in our minds . . ."

Sorrow long-winded, mirth narrow-bound, we evoked old friends, retold old jokes. In the gathering that year there were some classmates of mine. But so many of those who had been in Yenching during the 1933 to 1936 period, when Leeton and I were freshmen there, were not here in Hongkong in 1963. We spoke briefly of the absent ones. Of Liang Szeyi, the daughter of the famous reformist Liang Tsichao, upon whose "Pavilion of Iced Beverages" I had toiled so uncomprehendingly. She had been with Leeton and myself, in the same freshman class in medicine. She is now an executive in the Women's Federation, married to a doctor, an overseas Chinese, also our classmate, also in China. There were Chang Shuyi and Lee Yuehlien, Han Kangling, and others, all in China today; and among them the prestigious Kung Peng, now Assistant Minister of Foreign Affairs, the most brilliant of us all, who had gone over the hills to the guerrillas of the Red Army, and never looked back.

Others were in the United States, or in Formosa: Lien Hsinyue, who had been my best friend in Chungking, and who reported to the Kuomintang Secret Police on us; Robert Pang, who had nearly destroyed me, at least destroyed for me whatever identification I could have achieved with the student body; others . . .

At the entrance to the hall, three middle-aged men, recovering the boisterous gestures of their youth, hawked a magazine:

Yenching University Alumni Bulletin: Special issue in Memory of Dr. John Leighton Stuart, late Chancellor of Yenching University.

We were issued with cards upon which we wrote our names before pinning them to our coats. "That's also an American habit, wearing one's name written on one's chest. Come to think of it, Yenching was so American, and yet so many Yenching students went over to Mao Tsetung." The hall, the jokes, the amateur theatricals all reminded us how American, missionarily Christian, our Yenching University had been, and yet this had not prevented the students walking over the hills to join the Red Army and to fight for the Revolution of 1949.

I opened the Special Issue Bulletin; old photographs of Yenching stared out of the pages, on the cover was a painting of the Yenching pagoda which was really a water tower. Inside were more photographs: of the willows of the three-arched marble bridge, of the pine trees on the artificial hillocks, of the lake and its vistas twisting as if in wooden agony, all this carefully constructed prettiness which gave the campus a fairy garden aspect. There were snaps of skaters on the lake, in the cold winter; of girl students playing basketball and volleyball in the gymnasium with its beautiful parquet floor, specially imported from America; of Chinese-style buildings under snow with their curved eaves and painted pillars; photographs of Leighton Stuart, President and Chancellor of the University, later to become American Ambassador to China in the years of Chiang Kaishek's debacle . . .

Nostalgia, guitar-plucked, bizarre thumping echoes of a melody non-Chinese in China . . . Many of those present lived with this constant nag. Yenching, youth, the old days. They had not been back since the Great Change, and some would never go go back. "Why don't they go back and look at Yenching campus today?" I asked. "I don't know, perhaps they cannot make up their minds," replied Tan Leeton. "Perhaps most of them are on the side of Chiang Kaishek?" "No, I don't think they are on any side, except on the side of self-interest, making money, rearing families and especially avoiding insecurity, avoiding poverty. Some hope to go to the United States on a quota, there to be comfortable and secure and happy, away from all the troubles of Asia and the revolutions to come. Others are longing to go back, to reidentify, but they are afraid of changing. Others are just lazy, or don't care, preferring to clutch the substance of memories become unreal rather than face today's realities." Yet Hongkong is only a chuggy forty-minute train trip to the frontier with China. Every day, hundreds of Cantonese go back and forth across the ephemeral Bamboo Curtain, where a small bridge spans a childish stream, and Hongkong policemen and Chinese policemen, as like as brothers, face each other with calm demeanour across a wooden traffic block. It is still the practice, to thrill the American tourists, for travel agencies to take parties to the border and point dramatically to the bridge, the river, the uniforms at the other end: "There, over there, Red China . . . real live Red Chinese," yet at the Lunar New Year one hundred and thirty thousand Chinese from Hongkong visit their families across the border. I had also been part of that back-and-forth motion which so many propagandists say is impossible. I knew that the grass-cutters on the Hongkong side return every night to the Chinese side, and no one worries about it; that nearly all of Hongkong's food, and one-third of its water, come from China; that half the shops of Hongkong trade with China, that every week dozens of businessmen from Britain, France, West Germany, Sweden, Belgium go into China and back again . . . and yet the hoax is kept up, for the benefit of credulous American tourists . . .

I had returned to Yenching, revisited the Nameless Lake, the tall nine-storied pagoda, viewed the chimney which I had once climbed and which still spurted the same sparse smoke. I had felt the willows once again blow their long strands about my face in May when an eternal morning is woven in the day all day, and the last petals of the cherry blossoms go drifting by. I had trod the paths of my youth and laid low many memories. After a while, a few of those now middle-aged, congregating in the cold hall to seek the warmth of comradeship made young again, came to speak to me: "You have been back to Peking; we read about it in the newspapers. Tell me, what is Yenching like today?"

"It's all right, it's all there, only it seems to have shrunk, there are so many new buildings . . . Yenching is now part of a very large Peking University and Tsinghua, its sister university, is now an institute of technology . . ."

"How I wish I could go back."

They wished. Sometimes they moved, more often they were frightened, afraid the American Consulate might pick out their names, and in Hongkong, British Colony, blacklist them. They might lose their jobs, or find things difficult, should they want their children to go to America for university training . . . some of these fears were well founded, others were conjured up by their own timidity.

It is so in Hongkong, an accepted part of our lives. Classmates, schoolmates, bonded by Old School ties, so potent in China, eat in the same restaurants, pass each other in the street, shake hands, exchange remarks, but the lines are still drawn. It is always so in a civil turmoil; many of us have relatives on both sides; even the great ones. The sister of Madame Chiang Kaishek in Formosa is Madame Sun Yatsen, vice-chairman of the People's Republic in Peking; Chou Enlai's cousin is in Formosa . . . and so the cleavage goes, all the way through the intellectual class of China. In Hongkong we carefully compartment our knowledge, making clear distinctions between principles and friendships, and trying to maintain both. Here we know which restaurants, which newspapers, which old schoolmates are with Peking, or not yet with Peking, or with Formosa. There is no drama, no tragedy, no hatred, no bitterness; for all this has to be lived with and endured, eaten and worked with. Only the tourists can still be fooled; but nobody minds that.

In the winter of 1932, while still working as a secretary at the Peking Union Medical College, I had obtained an interview with Dr. Mei Yipao, then Dean of Students of Yenching University, and now a professor in the United States.

Dr. Mei was a thin, bespectacled Chinese scholar, of so distinguished and cultured an aspect that he represented, physically, the epitome of Chinese classical scholarship. His voice was gentle, his face harmonious; his gestures forbearing and courteous. However much, in later years, we were to disagree, without Mei Yipao, and his understanding of my difficulties, I might not have been admitted to Yenching University. True, I had about me a ferocious intensity which impressed people; not only Mei Yipao, but also his brother, Mei Yiling, whom I met walking about the curio shops of Liu Lichang market (for he was a collector), was kind and helpful to me. Mei Yiling was fat, Mei Yipao was thin. Mei Yiling was the more courageous, Mei Yipao the more didactic. Of the two I preferred Mei Yiling; but I must also record my debt to Mei Yipao.

In his quiet sitting-room, with tasteful grey settee, two scrolls of calligraphy on the wall, delicate porcelain, tea and cakes (such good cakes too), Dean Mei Yipao interviewed me briefly, gave

227

me some pages of Chinese to read, asked me to comment on them; nodding his head imperturbably as I stumbled along, making the most terrible mistakes. By now the "Pavilion of Iced Beverages" had overthrown my grasp of the language. Dr. Mei did not discourage me. He said he would do his best. He did. I received a letter and application forms, which I filled in.

That is how I gathered enough courage to take the entrance examination to Yenching University in June 1933. I asked Mr. Harned for a week's leave, and he gave it to me.

The entrance examinations for Yenching University were held at a middle school, in Peking. In the early morning I rode to it on my bicycle, and still remember the thrust of my front wheel when I pushed it in a row with others already there and the gatekeeper telling me I had put it in the wrong row. For there were two rows, male bicycles and female bicycles, sternly divided by the width of the courtyard, and I had put mine with the male. The courtyard was a spacious squareness paved with that grey brick which in the heat becomes almost powdery and turns a wonderful grey-blue in the autumn; acacia trees in leaf were about, a honeysuckle wafted above the wall.

The courtyard was half full of candidates, many young men, some in long blue cotton robes, others in jackets and trousers. A good many girls with sweaters on top of their blue cotton dresses long to the ankle. Blue was always the favourite colour in China, everyone wore blue cotton, and constant washing gave it a powdered look. Later I was to have many blue cotton dresses made, but that day I was the only girl in European dress. I stood in a corner and lit a cigarette. I was alone. No one else stood alone; everyone went about in groups of twos or threes. Suddenly I saw myself, appallingly different, and I wanted to get on my bicycle and ride away, but this could not be done, so I lit another cigarette and puffed furiously. I must have looked so arrogant, puffing because I was so frightened, and fear makes one put on a face, obstinate and defensive.

It was a Camel I was smoking; I had been smoking almost a year, seeing Hilda do it so well. Smoking, and wearing the brown amber necklace given to me for my birthday by Otto, trying to look as Hilda did, alluring, calm, in command of the situation . . . whereas I was never in command, every gesture a fight against shyness, clumsiness. And now, all this which was right at the office was unbelievably wrong. Either too young, or too old, too Chinese or too European, too much or too little, I was never right, I never could look right. In that pebbled courtyard, waiting for the examination to begin, my out-of-place cigarette confirmed the terrifying fact. I was too different . . .

So I smoked, and was conscious even while doing it that the gesture cut me off even more from the others, though the hubbub round me was polite, for I was simply ignored. No group gathered to stare; no one sniggered, no one in fact did anything; they were too busy talking to each other, walking up and down, reading, or laughing at each other's talk. Perhaps they were as puzzled by me as I was frightened of being there, but too well-mannered to show it. Certainly had I approached one of them for help, I might have had help, but I approached no one. As the bell rang and we filed into our numbered seats I considered running away, going back to my job at the P.U.M.C. There, after all, I had my place, work, salary, friends . . .

The examination lasted four days, and except for the paper in Chinese I did very well. I realized now how badly I had been taught Chinese, or rather not taught at all. Mr. Wang had not acquainted himself with the necessary syllabus or required reading. Even had I done three more years of Chinese, studied with pertinacity, with attention, six hours a day, I would barely have been able to do the paper that was set. How could I, between 1931 and 1933, working at a job, coaching students for money, studying physics, and all the rest besides, how could I have had enough time to study as I ought to have studied?

The examination was over, and I was back at my office, typing for Mr. Harned, waiting for the outcome . . . and the outcome was that I had passed in all subjects but Chinese. When the results were published in the papers, my number was not among the successful ones; for Chinese and science and mathematics were the three most important subjects, which every science candidate must pass. Mrs. Bürger said that it did not matter. "Why should you want to go to university anyway, it is not for a woman. You do your job and marry a good man, and that is for a woman."

The flat matter-of-fact voice, emitting flat sensible words meant for consolation. lumped like indigestible pudding in my stomach. I went to the ladies' toilet to weep. A small drowning, until Olga, called by another secretary while I sobbed, walked in and shook me. She took me to her office and gave me an aspirin and a cup of coffee. "Of course I don't care," I told her and started sobbing again. Olga had the kindness not to say a word.

229

She sat looking out of the window, and let me cry. Then she went to Mr. Harned and told him I was unwell, and came back to tell me I could have the rest of the morning off. I went home and I could not say a word to my mother. I bicycled out to Otto's house and again I wept. I had lost eight pounds in the last three weeks. Otto ordered his cook to make me some potato cakes, but I could not eat them.

The next morning a letter came from Dr. Mei Yipao, telling me that the Board had considered my case, and they would allow me to enter the University because I had done so well in the other sections, and they realized my difficulties. Since Yenching admitted overseas Chinese students, whose Chinese was not up to standard, they would now stretch the requirements to include me.

I do not remember whether I wrote to thank him, I was so happy. I immediately told Mrs. Bürger. Then in came R. S. Greene, the Director of the P.U.M.C. who had been American Consul in Hankow. I was always too shy to speak to him but now I did, and told him I was going to the University. And he said: "Well I am very glad, you fully deserve it, you have worked so hard." "I lost eight pounds," I told him. I had also used up half my annual fortnight's vacation, taking the examination, and now I should have to go on working till the last day and anyway I wanted to make more money. But Mr. Harned said that for a long time now they had considered raising my salary, and they would make it retro-active to March, at a hundred and twenty dollars a month. A waterfall of money, all at once! When I left the P.U.M.C. everyone was very kind to me, and I promised to come and see them often, and I was sorry to leave, for it is always difficult to break a habit. But I had to get used to breaking habits and I was going on, going to another world, and it was not too early to begin this apprenticeship.

John Leighton Stuart, founder of Yenching University, and its President, died in 1962 in the United States.

Today, his name is not honoured by his ex-students in Peking; not because of what he did for Yenching University but because of his tenure as Ambassador of his country from 1946 to 1949.

That a missionary and educator should become a politician and a diplomat is not uncommon in America, but it is certain, even from his autobiography, that his influence, at a moment of crisis, was not towards more understanding between America and China, but towards the hard-line policies pursued by the United States and stigmatized by more thoughtful Americans since.

John Leighton Stuart was born in 1876, of a missionary family already two generations in China; of such families as Peggy Armstrong, Henry Luce, and others. It is in these families that one finds, occasionally, individuals who, by virtue of their birth and early years in China, are assumed to have, or arrogate to themselves, the distinction of knowing the Chinese better than the latter know themselves. Endless, edifying, and given ponderous significance, their arbitrary pronouncements on the character, inclinations, virtues and defects of the Chinese! They are, in fact, sentimentally attached experts, like the French colons of Algeria, who "know" their Africans, or the British Old Shanghai hand, who also "knew" all about China. Now a good many feel bereft of *their* land, *their* roots, *their* mission, China. There are brilliant exceptions such as Pearl Buck, who has recognized her place in China's past but not in China's present, has accepted it, and does not suffer the paranoia of frustration which leads some of the others to hate and hurt China in her present because they want to bring back the past.

Already in the 1870s America's chief assets and investments in China were in the field of missionary endeavour and education and not, as England's, in the field of commerce, railways, and other tangible inroads into China's economic life. America spoke of this policy as "long-term missionary investment." These cost less, and irritated the Chinese less than the direct export of capital, manufactures, and personnel of other Powers, and they earned America a great repute for being different and doing good, although the Open-Door policy of 1898 had been evidence that a different motivation existed. "It is by no means certain [says Putnam Weale] that a race of American historians will not arise who will find that the avowed altruistic character of American policy has been one of the main factors in disturbing the Far East." The story of America's search for Asian frontiers would not be complete without beginning at the beginning, and that is the missionary investment in China. In 1930 American *business* investment was 196 million dollars, 6 per cent of the total foreign investment, while British business investment was 1,190 million, and Japanese 1,140 million (36.7 and 35.1 per cent respectively). The influence of America in China, however, bore no relation to these business investments; it far outstripped the British or the

231

Japanese. In fact, a French diplomat was to remark that goodwill was in inverse proportion to material investment, and that "spiritual investment pays greater dividends than any other form."

Leighton Stuart was at once the product of such an investment in the Christianization of China, and an instrument for its accomplishment. Through education and missionary work, ineluctably linked, the promotion of a policy which had begun in the 1850s was pursued with far-sighted tenacity. Leighton Stuart realized that this Americanization could be achieved through the co-operation of nuclei of Christian Chinese intellectuals, who would continue, of their own volition, the process of turning China into a client state of America.

The outcome of this idea was Yenching University. It was as the founder of Yenching University that Leighton Stuart emerged from the level of the average missionary, deep sunk in theological squabbles. In 1918 he began to campaign for a *Christian* Chinese University whose academic standards would be as good as anywhere else in the world and which would rival the atheistic, left-wing, and brilliant focus of intellectuals represented by Peking University, In other words, it was in the field of the mind that the battle for America and Christ would be waged in China.

Peking University, started in 1903, was entirely Chinese, the product of the Reform period which had planted New Learning in China at the turn of the century, and by 1919 it had become the chief centre of learning, scholarship, and also of militant student movements in the emergent nationalism in China. It attracted a galaxy of brilliant scholars, progressive and patriotic. It was there, as a humble assistant librarian, fetching books and newspapers for the intellectuals, that Mao Tsetung started on his fabulous career. The University was the centre of the famous May 4th, 1919, student movement against the Peace Treaty of Versailles. It had pioneered student unions, co-education; it was the bane of all the warlords, and became the bane of Chiang Kaishek and his reactionary Fascist Blueshirts.

The idea of founding another such furnace of intellectual fervour and debate, but an Amercanized one, was Leighton Stuart's. He believed in creating an elite, which would stand up against "dangerous and extreme" currents. It took him almost ten years before he could collect the cash necessary for the University.

Most of the foundation money came from American private

individuals, none from the American government. The grounds of Yenching University and some of the buildings, altogether five hundred acres, were donated by a Chinese ex-governor of the province.

Thus, due to the generosity of the American people, and also to many contributions from Chinese, the most beautiful university campus in the world, Yenching, was created.

By 1937 Yenching University endowment had reached the sum of $2,500,000 in American currency. Two other Americans whose efforts in this respect must be recorded are Harry Luce and his son Henry W. Luce, now owner of *Time* and *Life*. A pavilion erected to the memory of Mr. Luce Senior stood in Yenching campus, and was a picnicking spot for the students.

Yenching's name came from the ancient name, some 2,500 years ago, of a state of which today's Peking was the chief city. "Yen" means swallow, the city thus named because of the millions of swallows winging over it in autumn. "Freedom through Truth for Service" was the motto of Yenching.

Writing about the students of Yenching in his autobiography, Leighton Stuart interjects a sad note: "Some of them have been disappointing – most of them perhaps in some respects." The present government of China counts among some of its younger leaders, its diplomats abroad, its professionals at home, students of Yenching University. Perhaps this is what Dr. Stuart found disappointing.

The face of Leighton Stuart, on the cover of the Yenching Alumni Bulletin I was given at that Old Student gathering, showed his bushy eyebrows, deep ensconced eyes, priestly mouth. A man who did what he thought was right, and felt disappointed and betrayed because the results of his actions were not those he had sought.

Important historical work, analysing the effect of the personal emotion of such missionaries upon American foreign policy, must one day be done. The anguish of those from whom the spiritual guidance of millions is wrested, the soulful paternalism which made their life worth living scorned and rejected, this too has its place in our current dilemmas.

Leighton Stuart felt that an educated, American-Christian Chinese elite, self-propelled and self-supporting, would play a role of great benefit. That it would primarily be shaped to preserve America's best interests and markets in China may not have occurred to him. Perhaps he really believed that such an "enlightened" elite would bring prosperity to China's millions without a revolution, and especially without getting rid of the financial thraldom imposed upon China by the West – including America. This was an illusion; no such elite is going to serve *any* interests but those of its own class, and its interests are irremediably tied to the interests of its mentors and financial backers, and *not* to those of its own people. And since these backers would be foreign rulers, intent on returns for their investments, this elite would become an ideal servant one, keeping its own countrymen in tutelage, turning its own country into a state, dependent upon America's bounty . . . Never in a thousand years could such an elite accomplish, in spite of the most pious expressions and flamboyant announcements, the reforms that it would proclaim itself ready to accomplish. It would be pie-in-the-sky for ever. Many in the world are still fooling themselves today, as perhaps Leighton Stuart fooled himself then.

"I have observed," wrote Stuart, "an unpleasant phenomenon of Chinese student life . . . organized outbreaks of patriotic demonstrations . . ." He was aware that even the most Christian of educational trees, Yenching University, might one day bear strange fruit.

Yet who knows but that one day, with pride, with love, the people of America, who gave money for Yenching University, will also recognize the Revolution of China, and other revolutions to come, as authentic a cry for Liberty, for Equality, for the Brotherhood of Man, as their own Revolution two centuries ago?

At the most beautiful campus in the world, Yenching University, I arrived one day in September 1933, a freshman, to enter the three-year pre-medical course. This was to be followed by five years of medical study, at the same Peking Union Medical College where I had worked as a secretary.

The Yenching student bus operated at regular intervals, leaving Peking in the morning at seven in time for the eight o'clock lecture. It also had week-end services for the convenience of the students. The bus fare was forty cents. But all students were required to live in the dormitories in Yenching, and most of those with families in the city returned home at week-ends.

The front gate of Yenching University was an imposing red, with beautifully carved stone lions on either side. I crossed a small marble bridge over a rivulet, two Imperial marble columns drew the eye over to a vista of curved roofs, beds of peonies, hill slopes, pavilions. I had a paper in my hand telling me where to register; and which of the four women's dormitories was to be mine: Dormitory 3. I walked to the dormitory, up the stairs to the room number, opened the door, walked in. There were three girls sitting on chairs, a fourth shoving a suitcase under a bed. One of the girls said: "Christ" when she saw me.

I had been assigned to a room with three overseas Chinese from Hawaii. They were sophomores and juniors.* Emma, Irma, Pinkie were their names. Pinkie was the one who said "Christ".

The fourth girl was a Chinese, very myopic, very Christian, who could not get on with the Hawaiian Chinese and two weeks later left to room with someone else who had been a friend of hers in middle school. She was radiant when she left us. She disliked us all.

The difference between myself and the three Hawaiian Chinese was as great as between them and the China-Chinese students, such as this girl. The Hawaiians called them *pakehas* (*pakeha* being a Hawaiian word for "stranger"), and found them gauche and puritan. The Chinese found the Hawaiian overseas disconcerting. This was as useful a lesson in what environment does as any could wish. Never would I, in future years, commit the mistake of thinking that all Chinese are the same. The overseas Chinese had a good many adaptation problems, as many as a Eurasian like myself. The thoughtfulness of the authorities, rooming me with three overseas, was actually a mistake. I was to find out that my preoccupations, though not my behaviour, were closer to the China Chinese than to a great many overseas Chinese. But as a result of this first assignment, and also as a result of my strangeness, I became from the start isolated in a minority group, the Americanized overseas Chinese from Hawaii. And this was not what I wanted.

At first we did not get on well at all; Pinkie, Emma and I were hostile to each other. Irma was much easier to get on with, and she had a great sense of humour. But they were very nice girls, and I became much fonder of them when I no longer roomed with them.

The room was also bad for me from the point of view of my studying Chinese. The three spoke mainly American, interspersed with Hawaiian words. They sang songs about Hawaii, the ukulele was their favourite hobby, and Pinkie danced the hula-hula with

* Freshmen: 1st year; sophomores: 2nd year; juniors: 3rd year; and seniors: 4th year.

235

great charm. They had been sent by their parents to study in China, and found the ways of the Northern Chinese difficult. Although most of the Yenching students were from wealthy families, and therefore Westernized, adaptation is a strenuous process. The overseas who came from Indonesia, from Malaya, from other Asian countries found it very easy to adapt to the China-Chinese ways because their home backgrounds had remained Chinese in all essentials: food, language, dress, and especially preoccupation with Chinese political and social events. Even among those from Hawaii or from San Franciso, who turned up at Yenching, some did adapt uncommonly well, and became thoroughly included among the China-Chinese students because they became involved in student movements and demonstrations against Japan. This was more marked among men students who were scattered and not rooming together. I think in particular of one, Arthur Chang, now prominent in medical work in Peking, a hard-working, honest young man, with great courage and simplicity, who put himself to the study of his mother tongue (he, like many overseas, had then little knowledge of it) with great assiduity. Placing three or four overseas Chinese together in one room lessened their adaptive capacity; they fell back into their home ways, and learnt far less than if each of them had had to adapt on his own.

Of the three with me, Irma was trying hardest to study Chinese, and to make friends with Chinese girls. All three are now back in Hawaii, and making no effort to go back to China. I was happy to see them again, my three Yenching room mates, in January 1965, in Honolulu. Time had mellowed us all, smudged away the sharp retorts which Pinkie and I had zestfully exchanged. In a way I had grown much more Asian, much more concerned and involved with Asian problems and the Revolution in China, so much more than they would ever be. They had become much more American. But time had taught us tolerance of each other.

Pinkie, a dominant character, having made me welcome by saying "Christ," showed me my bed, the last in the row of five, and cracked a joke about there being plenty of space for more. To which I replied something rude. We thus started most uncordially. Pinkie was used to having her own way, and Emma, greatly influenced by Pinkie, sharper than Pinkie in an under-stated manner, one day took away, and distributed to the Hawaiian Chinese male students, some Babe Ruths which had been given to me by Tiza's current financé.

Having shoved my suitcase under the bed, I strolled out, first walking to the registrar, trying to change rooms. But it could not be done. I circumambulated the lake with its little island on which a pavilion housed a large bell that struck at the hour and half hour; scanned the many-roofed pagoda, circled the chimney, the auditorium, other buildings, all done in the Chinese style, set about with peonies and roses, and pines, willows, acacias, plum and cherry trees. I saw artificial rocks and hillocks, a lotus pool. Pleasaunce beyond compare, small paradise enclosed, Eden renewed to live in, with the red and blue and gold of painted ceilings, twenty-two tennis courts and two sports stadiums, one open one, enclosed, and outside the back gate the small village of Haitien, which had once lodged Manchu bannermen and now catered to the University with its small restaurants where students tired of the canteen food went for delicious meals in the evenings.

Dr. Leighton Stuart gave a party to welcome the freshmen. There I met the teaching staff, mostly American missionaries and their wives. I was to get used to their heartiness, their attentive exudation of good cheer, their careful jokes, their prolonged laughter. As a Catholic I found it difficult to get a adjusted to married missionarism. Catholic priests were firmly celibate, one smelt them celibate. But here I became confused with these men and women of God genteelly drinking Coco-cola, dancing with unction, their children and their wives about, the minds kept assiduously clean and the mild jokes putting us at ease. The baking of cookies and the buying of Chinese curios and carpets and the work of the Lord. Leighton Stuart spoke kindly to all of us, kindly, and we laughed or smiled. He put his hand on a shoulder or two. We were his flock. I was seized by a fit of hysterical laughter, which I could not explain. All through my stay in Yenching, I was to be nervously afflicted by spasms of uncontrolled laughter at unpredictable times.

After two or three weeks I found I liked Miss Hancock, a bright, chirpy Scot, precise and unplatitudinous, who taught mathematics. To her I voiced my doubts about God; she sat grieving a little. She was a small woman, tense as a trigonometrical formula, with a silver purity of voice and manner, and great teaching enthusiasm. She taught with a fierceness of love which made her face red and her eyes sparkle like blue diamonds. She listened to me, and then, hands folded, told me that all her life she had believed in God, and now that she was old more than ever. Her voice was contained and low, quite unlike her lecture

237

voice, and all the more impressive. She gave me wonderful tea with marvellous cakes and scones made by herself.

Mr. Band, the physics teacher, was English; he and his wife were to go in 1938, with a group of students, to Mao Tsetung's Red base in Yenan, and teach there for a while. The students liked him because he did not treat them as if they were children. There was Dr. Sailer, the Mental Hygiene teacher, tall, lean, tensely relaxed. I tried to get him preoccupied with my personal problems and wrote down half my life for him, but not the other half. After a course in Mental Hygiene my inner life was as unhygienic as before. There was Miss Boring, who taught us biology. She had brown hair smoothly drawn back in a bun, framing a rectangular face with a very firm jaw and large chin, and she had square glasses atop a firm, straight nose. She bubbled with enthusiasm, but it was the kind of jolly cheer which I could not get used to. Dr. Sailer told me that one of the difficulties of teaching Asian students was that they were indrawn, they never came out with a spontaneous thought, they were always afraid of losing face and saying something funny and being laughed at. There was a Christian Fellowship group, which went about converting students. Nearly twenty per cent of the Chinese students of Yenching were Christians, connected with the Y.M.C.A. or Y.W.C.A. They sang hymns, and seemed to derive great satisfaction from this activity. I did not join; Christian Fellowship had a vague, indecisive touch, and my Christianity was the authoritarian kind, which invited rebellion. This soft, inchoate, feather-quilt Christianity I did not understand. Its sweetness and light touch did not touch me.

Ragging was also a feature of freshman life. The majority of students resented it but it was carried on, by a minority, to inculcate the team spirit and to turn us all into good sports. The "freshies" had to put up with wearing paper hats, being made fun of. Some of the overseas students organized a ducking and endeavoured to throw a couple of girl students in the small river; but as all the Chinese refused to be thrown, an American girl (there were three American girls from missionary families, and also several American language students, later attached to the consular service, studying Chinese at Yenching) volunteered to give a good example and to be ducked; which proved absolutely nothing to anyone, except that the Chinese were not good sports, I suppose. I refused to be touched with such fury that I was left alone, and accounted a particularly bad sport.

Then there was sports day; I distinguished myself by dropping the stick in the relay race. I could skate and swim but had never played games. Since sport was a required subject, worth two credits out of the eighteen I had to take in the first semester, I had to learn games. This filled me with indignant astonishment, the same anger as when I had found "drawing" a required subject for the School Certificate, but non-sport was simply impossible, unless one was a cripple.

A thin, pleasant-faced American woman, voice low-pitched, demeanour unalterably patient, asked me what games I would like to play. I said none. She endeavoured to explain to me the team spirit, told me how important it was for my future and the "community" to acquire "team spirit." I said that I had always done things alone. She said sports was a good way of making friends. I said I could not visualize the process of comradeship at that level. For me, friendship consisted in long walks, argument-filled talks, chiefly on controversial subjects; batting balls at each other did not create friendship. But I was willing to try, and I tried. Volleyball. Basketball. Softball (women's baseball). Desperately I hurled myself at balls which eluded me, was immediately seized with overwhelming self-consciousness, for everyone else seemed able to catch or throw, except me.

I admired a stout, round-faced, ever smiling girl, with short cropped hair, Lee Yuehlien, also in the pre-medical course. Yuelien put herself to tennis, which she had not played; played steadily, every day, her progress emphatically visible. I stood, looked, envied, but it was only in my second year, through knowing Herbert Lee, a Hawaiian Chinese, who was an excellent tennis player, that I tried to play tennis, an endeavour which greatly tried Herbert's patience, but which in no way informed me on the intricacies of tennis. Very soon I degenerated to croquet, which was a kind of punishment at Yenching for those who failed at sports, but even then I only hit my ankles with the mallet. I transferred to gynmastics class, and tried tap dancing. A Scandinavian nature dancer came along, and Irma went to nature dancing. I tried; standing rigidly and looking fiercely down my nose at the floor. Actually the trouble was that I had other tastes beyond my age, acquired when I was living as a grown-up, earning my living. A taste for smoking; a disastrous taste for clothes both expensive and unpractical, a taste for books. I also had had a lover, Otto, though I had given him up when I had

239

passed the entrance examination. And now he had gone, was living in Shanghai, but I was left completely out of gear with normal adolescent wants, too grown up in some ways, in others still a child. Perhaps I was a great deal less crafty than some of the girls at Yenching, who under a languid and haughty exterior concealed far more guile than I would ever acquire, but only a cause outside myself, an impersonal preoccupation, like the one soon to engulf the student body not only of Yenching but of every university, that of resistance to Japan, would have captured my volatile, unfixed, inchoate soul. But this did not happen; for it was forbidden, under pain of capital punishment, to manifest patriotism.

Soon the aloneness which I masked, the solitude I suffered, were to worsen. Three weeks after my becoming a freshman at Yenching something occurred which today still hurts me, brings me back to the hermit cavern within me in which I live and will die.

In that first term I went home on Friday afternoons as I had no Saturday lecture; the new leisureliness, compared to the previous hectic two years, improved my temper ravelled by constant tiredness. Relations at home with my mother improved. I did not volley at her mouthfuls of insolent, hurting words on sight; she mollified enough to ask me whether I had a good light to study by. I continued giving two lessons over the week-end; it brought me some extra money.

I have already mentioned the beauty of my sister Tiza; its effect upon men, who visited our house to pay court to her. One of these suitors was a high and important Chinese official and so important that he went everywhere with a meal-taster, who used to nibble first at his food, in case it was poisoned. He also had a special dish in which he poured a little of his drink, and watched for a turn of colour. I never quite found out what he actually did, but he had smart Western suits as well as Chinese silk robes and was fervently in love with Tiza. His car, with a bodyguard and a plainsclothesman or two to keep a lookout for would-be assassins, was stationed at our door many times. He brought gifts, various and fairly costly, necklaces, silk in bolts, flowered velvet, stockings, a large ring for Tiza; these she stored in her treasure chest.

Tiza had a grace and beauty uncommon among so many beautiful Eurasians in Peking; bone structure, features, poise, gestures, the sureness of a feminine personality, good taste in

240

dresses, and my mother's approval and love. I remained a frowning urchin, with a young colt stance. but Tiza smiled with that particular turn of her round amber eyes, and men would be subjugated. Tiza was born a woman, I would always remain a juvenile. Long and heated arguments, relativity, the Japanese, animals denied Paradise, and an unprepossessing capacity for insulting the male ego through opinionated contention, have continued in me through my two marriages. For the woman who is also creator, artist, the professional woman, equality of spirit means a forgetfulness of the sexual relationship, and this the male does not forgive.

Mother told Tiza that she was beautiful, which she was. Mother told Tiza that beauty was enough, a woman needed nothing else to make her way, and her end was the marriage bed. Tiza knew that she could pick and choose, from among the many who came to sit in our stiff chairs, to make conversation with Mother.

But Tiza, and later Marianne, like my mother in her time, in spite of admonitions to get married, to provide for themselves the happy security of that most ubiquitous and legal of all insurance benefits, a husband, would never be able to put finance before passion, reason before heart. We were not crafty or cold-blooded enough. After a while the important official with his bodyguards, his caskets of jades, his motor car and the enormous banquets he gave us, was told by Mama (who complained that she always had to do the dirty jobs while Papa went into his vine contemplation) that Tiza would not marry him. He bowed and departed; we never saw him again. I remember that he never ate anything at restaurants, not even at his own banquets, even after his meal-taster had approved. He merely chewed and spat the food out again. Papa for a while was worried, the man was powerful and might take away Papa's job in reprisal. But Mama pointed out that Tiza had said no, and this to Mama was more important than anything else. "My daughter must listen to her heart," declared Mama, transported back to her own romantic youth and the tempestuous love that had landed her in China. Always she would stand by Tiza, whatever happened.

Soon after that Tiza was in love for the first time; a candid, innocent love, with an American marine.

Shawn was a quiet, well-mannered, likable young American of Irish descent, whose parents had a farm somewhere in Iowa. He had met Tiza at the skating rink. He wanted to marry her and since in 1933 she was not fifteen he promised to wait for her. Meanwhile they went out together to the Y.M.C.A. Club, to eat hot dogs and drink Coca-Cola, then to a movie, and then home to sit in Mother's stiff armchairs and talk while Shawn held Tiza's hand. Shawn went to church and waited for Tiza on the porch. It was decent and honourable, quite unlike my relation with Otto, born out of his despair and my disorientation. Tiza was not a nomad unable to communicate with her own parents. She was the well-beloved and always devoted daughter. Her women's magazine romance enchanted everyone. Shawn called me Sis. "Say, you could come to the States and stay with us." When I returned home, one Friday, about a month after entering Yenching, Shawn suggested that he should bring a buddy, and that we all go together the next day (Saturday) to see a movie, then to the Club for hamburgers.

A brown-eyed, brown-haired young man, very shy, appeared the next afternoon, both Shawn and he in civilian suits. Sedately we walked to the movies, Tiza wore an engagement ring, Shawn bought some popcorn. It was a Ramon Novarro film, and Ramon Novarro was Tiza's favourite, his picture was in her picture album. Walking down Hatamen Street on our return, I learnt that Ted (so was the name of my date) was lonely; sitting and eating hamburgers, the three of them drinking Coca-Cola, and I coffee, Ted showed the pictures of his sister, his brother, his house, his Pa and Mom and their dog. And suddenly I knew I was bored, bored with Shawn and Ted and their conversation, which was an iteration of remarks on things around us; on games, on the film we had seen, some mild jokes which I could not grasp; felt as if someone was digging a big hole in soft earth and I was disappearing in it. We returned home walking, for the weather was still fine. Shawn did not dance, and wore a little gold cross round his neck, and we passed the Alcazar, the night club on Hatamen. The yellow glare from the windows shone at us briefly, and I thought of my ex-pupil, the Russian dancing girl, and wondered whether she was working.

We came home and drank Mother's coffee, and promised to meet again next afternoon. Mother said Ted reminded her of her own Irish trip when, a young girl, she had gone there as a governess and contracted typhoid fever. The next morning, delivered by hand, a letter came from Ted for me, saying he was *pleasured* to meet me, and I must *beleive* him when he said that I made a big impression on him. I stared at the writing, unformed, childish,

242

at the spelling mistake, and suddenly I was a snob, a proper intellectual snob. The man could not even spell properly! The childish handwriting, the spelling mistakes, provided me with the excuse I needed: "I'm not going out with Ted. I have to go back to the University. Tell him I'm sorry." Back I went to Yenching, bicycling all the way; and it was lovely, the air turning October cold; I had on a blue cotton Chinese dress, quite new, and a sweater and tennis shoes. The swallows were flying, flying high, bevelled crests of deep blue. Finely, finely, the fallen leaves swirled in a little wind; even the dust was friendly.

I went back to the dormitory room and wrote out a "programme of study" for myself. I kept that programme a long time, pinned inside the drawer of my study table, where I could see it as soon as I opened the drawer. My programme of life, good resolutions, a soul made new, a new life . . . I will conquer them, I thought, meaning the Chinese, the other students, I will make them respect me and accept me. I will make friends . . . I will be like them. I will work, and work . . . I will take up calligraphy again . . . every morning, I shall train my hand, with the brush; I shall move away from these Hawaiian Chinese. I can't study with ukuleles around, anyway. I shall . . .

Four days later, in the morning as I was going to the first lecture, Liang Szeyi, my classmate, pulled me aside on the pathway among the willows leading to the lecture hall.

Liang Szeyi, the daughter of Liang Tsichao, was a sturdy beetle-browed girl of great character. She sat next to me in class. She was very straightforward. She said to me: "There is an attack on you in the Students' Weekly, have you seen it?" "An attack on me," I said, surprised. "Why?" "You had better read it yourself." She left me.

I got a copy of the weekly, printed by the students and circulated in the university. Yes there was something about me: three paragraphs. I stared, at first unbelieving; then I folded the weekly and carried it with me to the lecture. And to another lecture. It was only in the afternoon, when I had carried it about with me for a few hours, that the sense of the three paragraphs hit me.

"Chou . . ." it said (giving my full name), "a female freshman in the pre-medical course, whose Chinese is deficient, because she *prefers* European languages and speaks French, English and German perfectly, was seen walking with two American soldiers, to the movie theatre. Afterwards the group went to a night club on Hatamen Street, and later they entered a private hotel on the same street. Such conduct is unbecoming to a student of our honoured university . . ."

It was no use re-reading it, hoping the words might be stared out of print; hoping it was a nightmare. By four o'clock in the afternoon I was getting a little dazed as the words kept at me, like stones thrown at my head and I could not avoid them, I was being stoned by these relentless hitting words. Of course, Chinese girls did not go out with foreigners; not respectable Chinese girls going to university with homes to return to. That was quite true. Only Eurasian girls went out with foreigners; in fact all the girls in the office at the P.U.M.C. did so. And some of the French Eurasians at school with me had married men in the French army. And of course there were foreign troops stationed in Peking; French and British, and American, and the Chinese resented them, and quite rightly. I had read enough history to disintoxicate myself of the French and English versions of history. Of course, I should have known. But I had not thought about the way in which this simple action, going out with Tiza and her fiancé and his friend, would be built up, into this version.

"But this is very bad, you must do something about it," said Irma, shocked when I showed her the paragraph.

The next morning, on her advice, I went to see the Dean of Women to complain.

The Dean was a bespectacled, thin, Christian Chinese woman; I laid the paper on her desk, explained to her that Shawn was my sister's fiancé, that he was in the U.S. Marines, true; that we had gone to a movie, then to eat hot dogs, and that the rest was untrue.

"I do not see," I said, "why this slander has been printed about me."

"Well," said the Dean, "of course your background is a little different . . ."

"I know that. My life has been different so far. I have been a secretary, and tried to earn a living and saved money to come here to study. I understand that this university is an American university; the Chancellor, Dr. Leighton Stuart, is an American. Supposing that one of these Marines had been Dr. Stuart's son, and had taken me out; would that still be wrong?"

"Oh," said the Dean quickly, "it's not your going out with a *foreigner*, it's, it's . . ." her voice trailed and her spectacles became opaque. "We shall investigate," said the Dean, "I promise you."

244

I went back to the dormitory. I did not cut the lectures, but I avoided everyone; and because I avoided the others, they avoided me. And because they avoided me, I imagined that they had all read this murderous notice, and looked down upon me and condemned me. And my homeless heart drew round itself great walls of bitterness, wrapped itself in bitterness stronger than steel, ramparts of rancour, and I stared stonily in front of me, more arrogant than ever, and silent, refusing to explain, disdaining to explain. Let them condemn me. Let them judge, these wonderful Christians singing their hymns! I would not talk any more. I stared at my lecture notes, and could not read a word. I was dreadfully, dreadfully afraid that I might break down and weep . . .

Three days later, in the evening, the dormitory servant came to call me and said that a young man, a student, wanted to speak to me.

I came down the stairs, to the gate of the dormitory. Male students could come to the gate of the dormitories, where they waited for the girl they courted to come out to walk with them. At half past ten the gates were locked, and everyone had to be inside the dormitories.

I saw a tall, heavily built student, in the long lined gown and the scarf, almost like a uniform, which male students wore those years; underneath they had Western style trousers and shirts, but the long gown kept them warm in the winter. "My name is Pang," he said, "Robert Pang; I would like to speak to you. Shall we go for a walk?"

We talked in the grey early night, relieved by lampposts. No part of the campus was left in darkness; all the paths lit, and he talked, walking swiftly, so that I could scarcely keep up.

". . . you remember, we met on that sports day, we talked together . . . I've come to tell you that I'm in terrible trouble, and only you can help me. I'm going to be kicked out. Only you can help me."

"Why," I said, "what have you done?" I did not remember him.

He gulped for air. "I wrote this thing about you in the paper."

"You," I said. "But why? Why did you do this to me?"

"Oh how can I explain? I'm sorry, I'm a fool . . . you see, you don't know, but I hate Eurasians, hate them, hate them . . . because in my family too, we've got mixed blood, and I can't stand it . . ."

245

"But why to me, why to me?" I could only repeat this, so stupidly.

"Oh, I don't know . . . I was crazy, crazy . . . you know once I was in love with a girl, and she was Eurasian, and she did something, and I guess I just wanted to revenge myself . . . but now they are going to kick me out. Only you can save me, if you go to the Dean, and say it's all right, you won't press any charges, you must save me, please, please . . . my mother's got heart trouble, this will kill her . . ."

He was sobbing, and I promised. We loitered a while, while he rambled on; and I did not hear him, for I was stupefied. "Why do it to me? Why to me?" I pitied him now. His round face, in the lamplight, was shiny with tears. Real or fake, I shall never know. But he truly pitied himself, even if he had had no compassion for me.

So I went to the Dean the next morning, and said that I would consider the incident closed if a rectification was put in the paper. And it was, a lame thing: "We understand," it said, "that Miss Chou was merely taking a walk with some relatives." The insolence escaped me. Afterwards I occasionally met Robert Pang on the campus, but he eyed me from afar, with something supercilious in his eyebrows, and I never spoke to him.

Robert Pang is now running a restaurant somewhere in America; he who objected to my walking with American Marines is now serving them food and drink. Perhaps one day, since it seems to be my luck that everything should occur twice, I shall run into him. Perhaps enter his restaurant, to have a meal, for chance is so facetious, and when the old shadow falls across our mutual recognition, I wonder what new story he will have thought up?

Were all humans able to circumvent or surmount by cold reasoning the gashes of circumstance, the conflicts that oppose nations, that break individuals, might be handled differently, comprehended out of existence. But our life is a striving to see through dark glass. Each of us echoing grove, where the clash of past voices dulls and confuses the present crystal, goes on reverberating their mistimed clangour long after the primal sound has died away.

And so the incident, Robert Pang and his malice, though no more referred to, ate its acid corrosive way in me; biting deeper and deeper, a wound that I did not recover from; for even today, writing it out, my heart becomes a hollow thudding chamber,

246

dome of dead clamour, dazing me with a rage I no longer want, I never recovered from it. It became my lost leg. It certainly crippled me for the rest of my time in Yenching.

Had I been able to mention it at home; had I had a friend to confide in, a friend whom I looked up to, for guidance and re-assurance, things might have been slightly different. But there was no one.

No one but Otto; and he was gone now, transferred to Shang-hai. He had gone that summer. I could not tell Hers, dreading his sarcasm.

When I returned home that Friday, my mother met me with a tale of woe: Ted had come, with Shawn, at the appointed time. "He was prostrate, when he knew you were gone. That boy has a *heart*," said my mother, looking at wicked me, guilty of having broken that heart. "He was serious, I could see that," she added, and it was obvious that the vision inhabiting my mother was of her two daughters marrying two Americans; never for a moment did she believe my studying could lead to anything. Only marriage counted. Finally Tiza had taken Marianne with her, "but Marianne is just a child," said my deadly innocent mother. Thus another victim, Marianne, was being prepared for the future. And this too was my fault. But worse was to happen.

For Shawn now turned up; and in the talk that followed I must have somehow let fall something of my bitterness; said that students of Yenching University did not go out with U.S. Marines; and that evening there was a terrible scene, with Tiza weeping and screaming, prostrate on the bed, and my mother bathing her forehead with eau de cologne. After the usual movie Shawn had told Tiza, at the Club, over hot dogs and a milk shake, that he knew he was unwelcome, that he would not have "Sis" look down on him, that it was better he should go away, stop seeing Tiza, and that perhaps they should think of the diffi-culties for children of a mixed marriage . . .

And Tiza cried and cried, and of course it was my fault; my mother accused me of trying to break my sister's heart and romance and happy future marriage, out of jealousy. "You can't get anyone for yourself but a one-legged cripple, and he has *abandoned* you now and you are jealous of your sister, you who run around with mud up to your knees . . ."

Then it was my turn to run out of the house crying my heart out. But not for long. The homeless heart retreats, wrung dry of misery, and learns to laugh at itself, but it is not a nice laugh.

247

From that time Mother and I became more estranged than ever; and Tiza and Marianne started on that way of life, which was to end with their marrying Americans and going to live in America, but not in the way they expected.

CHAPTER THIRTEEN

It was my fault. My fault that I was not wiser, less fragmented, less tormented. But I was not quite seventeen, my adolescence not exactly the accepted normal. I was a reprobate, felt one, and now stuck my chin out, groggy as a boxer after a heavy blow. I was actually having a nervous breakdown without knowing it. "I'll show them, I'll show them. They talk about me. They look down on me. I'll give them plenty to talk about. I'll do my worst." And thus headed straight for semi-delinquency. These problems of behaviour are now better understood, but at that time, in that social context, they were not.

In the weeks that followed, I did my best to confirm the gossip about me, with overt schismatic behaviour. I had already climbed the Yenching chimney, precisely because I was afraid of heights, because it had never been done, because I liked climbing. Now I deliberately broke every rule. I bicycled about in shorts, I laughed in classes, I was rude to everyone. Nothing could eradicate from me the sense of resentment, the feeling that all was spoilt, everyone already against me, so why should I care?

My parents now removed themselves to Tientsin. My father was transferred there by the railway administration in November 1933. Very suddenly, Mother, Tiza and Marianne followed a little before Christmas. The house, however, was not closed, as they hoped to come back to Peking in a few months. A servant, Hsueh Mah, was left behind to keep the house in order, and my father and mother occasionally returned, for a week, as Father also had to report to the railway administration Central Office in Peking.

Hsueh Mah, our servant, whom I was to find again when I returned to Peking in 1956, was a countrywoman from near Chengchow; my father had brought her back after a trip down the line in 1931 or 1932. She was a dwarfish woman with bound feet, and two enormous teeth protruding from her mouth. She never spoke, but always screamed, in the manner of peasants who shout across the fields to each other; and also in the manner of peasants, when she spoke, she put a hand behind her ear, to cup it as a shell strives to catch its own sound; this the pedlars who shouted their goods on the street also did; and Hsueh Mah, when I saw her again in 1956, had not lost the habit. She had been married at sixteen to a man she had never seen, as was customary; and her husband had beaten her on the wedding night, to instil fear and meekness into her, as was also customary. Hsueh Mah did not like being beaten and ran away. On her bound feet she could not run very far, so that she was caught, beaten again, starved for a few days, and again beaten. She bore a son, then again ran away, with the same result. Her unhappiness was well known to all in the village, and when she was thirty, again she ran away, this time to Chengchow, and hired herself as a servant. My father found her cleaning the railway offices, and brought her to Peking. Hsueh Mah was radiant, and worked like a slave, standing in the garden on clear mornings and shouting her happiness to be delivered from her husband. But she could not divorce him until the Revolution came in 1949. Then the first thing she did, when our street committee was set up, was to divorce her husband. By then she had not seen him for twenty-five years.

When my parents went to Tientsin with Tiza and Marianne, Hsueh Mah remained. She was to remain and look after my father when my mother and Tiza left him in 1948. During that winter of 1933 to 1934, she was the only one to greet me when I went home, to a very cold and empty house.

I did not know where to spend my Christmas holidays; the University campus was almost deserted; I sent a cable to Otto in Shanghai, and took the train. The only place, the only friend. Animal warmth. Refuge. And thus I was not lonely. But everything was different. This stay with Otto for two weeks did not renew, but definitely broke, our relation. I now began to realize how different, how mutually incompatible were the various worlds I had entered and lived in. Even one term in Yenching had changed me; Otto was already dropped, and even though I was immersed in hostility against the whole student body, imagining all of them Robert Pang's accomplices, yet I could not retrace my steps, return where I had come from. I did not tell Otto about Pang. I prattled of everything, bought two very expensive dresses, stockings, shoes, a coat; I ate enormously, gorging on rich food which gave me pimples, then I asked him to give me two hundred dollars and returned by train to Peking. When I said goodbye to Otto, standing on the platform, that was the last time I was to see him.

As a wounded beast goes to its lair, burrows deeper, out of sight, out of reach, and from the darkness imagines yet greater enemies lurking, interprets each movement outside as danger, so I became unreachable.

I wrote again to Otto, breaking definitely. Otto wrote back: "You are right. But please don't do anything foolish; don't run after men and make yourself cheap, be careful." He added as p.s. "And especially be careful about Leo Bielfeld." I tore up the letter, Otto receding, destroyed as the shredded letter in the waste-paper backet was destroyed. Why did Otto always pick on Leo Bielfeld? He was Hilda's future husband. I had no intention of seeing Leo. Perversely I went to visit Hilda, precisely because of Otto's injunction. She was still at the P.U.M.C., still a secretary. Olga and Hilda and I sat in the Palaeontology Department and talked as in the past – six months ago; for me already another world ago. That was in January 1934, and the glass cases contained new pots from Choukoutien, and Olga was full of stories about Davidson Black and Teilhard de Chardin.

I never saw Otto again, nor did I write; it was twenty-five years before I heard of him again.

Suddenly, as my taxi in Hongkong stops at a traffic light, someone bends, puts his face in at the taxi window; Alex Klein, Otto's good friend, sharing his flat in Shanghai, winter of 1933–4.

I left the taxi, and we talked, drinking coffee at a near-by restaurant. "What has happened to you, what has happened to Otto?"

"I am all right, but Otto has vanished."

"Vanished?"

It was 1945; Germany had been defeated; Alex was captured by the Allied troops; spent eighteen months in a prison camp where he was denazified, certified clean. "I do good, I make good money. But Otto he is not like me, in active combat, he is connected with some industry or other, I am not quite sure which . . . and when the news comes of the surrender of the Fatherland, he gets into a plane, and he flies off, into the sky. So we think he is most surely vanished."

Alex Klein was making his life anew, a salesman now, selling spare parts for planes, for some German firm; for Germany was getting up again, getting up again, and once again, all over Asia, her smiling, blue-eyed, indefatigable salesmen with their bulging briefcases, behaving well, selling well, respectful, correct and punctilious, selling good German things . . .

I do not ask Alex Klein whether he sings to himself, occasionally, the Horst Wessel song that I heard that spring of long ago, when he, and Otto, and others, sang in the car, driving in the blood-red sunset of China.

"It was a good death then, clean, in the limpid azure."

"Ach, always the poet," Alex remarks. "But a clean death, in the strong sky, yes. I think the city where he was born, his father's house, all, all had been razed clean . . . psssssht . . . with the bombs. He could not bear it, he always took things hard, like his leg, though he didn't say much about it, and so he vanished. Ach, ja, that's how it is."

At the University the first term examination results were published. Surprisingly, I had done quite well, getting three A's out of six subjects (my worst, of course, being sport). I had not done as well as Lee Yuehien, the fat girl who played tennis so steadily, who was brilliant and got all A's, nor as Han Kangling, so good at skating, but well enough. Once more several classmates tried to befriend me. "You did well, you are clever," said Liang Szeyi; two other girls also came to speak to me, and Yuehlien came to present me with a lovely box, with an embroidered cover, a jewellery box. Han Kangling also talked to me, and Chang Shuyi, a lovable, sweet person in third year, who wanted to be a social welfare worker, and was engaged in many student activities, also tried to interest me in something other than myself. Chang Suyi offered to teach me Chinese. "Your Chinese is better than the overseas', though not perfect, but with application and in time you can be as good as any of us." For a brief while, I thought "I'll try again," but confidence had gone out of me. Like a young horse beaten about the head too early I stampeded at the slightest thing, sometimes wept behind the gymnasium, more often had fits of laughter, and became incredibly suspicious. Even compliments, friendship proffered, became in my mind attempts to lure me into trust, and then to hurt me. I now gave up extra teaching at week-ends went to parties, with the only set I knew, the old set, the Jungs, the German Eurasians, the secretaries at the P.U.M.C. Drinking, dancing, wasting the hours and smoking until the air was streaked with horizontal layers of blue haze. And then to confirm my downfall, some three weeks after the first term examination results, Donald Heyward killed himself in Yenching University.

Donald, the son of Mrs. Heyward, who had suggested to my mother the American nuns' college where I had learnt typing and Gregg shorthand, had also entered Yenching University. I had not seen him at the entrance examination, perhaps because he came in straight from the American school he attended. I met him occasionally, walking to or from lectures. He was not in the pre-medical course which was part of the Science college, he was in the Arts college. He had failed the preliminary test in mathematics, which occurred at the very beginning of term, and which decided whether or not one would be allowed to enter the Science college. This test has made me appreciate the high level of mathematics of the Chinese middle-school scholars. One was required to have a passing grade of 65 per cent. I made 68, only scraping through; most of the other students made 72, and a mathematical genius, a young boy of sixteen, incredibly brilliant, made 98 per cent. Donald had gone to Arts, though it was said his mother had intended him to pursue pre-medical studies.

The pre-medical course was supposed to be one of the stiffest in Yenching. It was only when I got to Belgium that I realized the level was low compared to what was expected of one in Europe. Nevertheless the failure rate, in the first year, was of the order of 35 per cent; out of seventy students in the freshman year only fifty were left by the second year, and by the third year there would be only thirty-five to forty to enter the Peking Union Medical College. Later I was to find out that this attrition was not due to the students so much as to the limited number of places available for medical training at the P.U.M.C. That in a China so terribly in need of all technical and professional knowledge, where there was not one doctor per 100,000 head of population, such a limitation occurred, was nothing short of criminal; but it did not occur to us then; we were all told that this was done to maintain a high standard, an American standard.

After graduation from the P.U.M.C. a fellowship for post-graduate work in America was possible. In spite of U.S. marines, in spite of the American gunboats upon the rivers, in spite of America's "neutrality", tantamount to acquiescence, in the Japanese aggression, in spite of her enormous military sales to Japan, American influence in education made these scholarships much sought after. Yenching was the epitome, the crowning flower of American educational effort in China, and to go to the P.U.M.C. was reckoned the greatest achievement of all. Hence Donald's failure to get into the pre-medical course was already a humiliation.

And then Donald failed again, failed the first term examination. He was found dead in the men's dormitory where he had a room, two or three weeks after the results were published.

Why did Donald kill himself? Why? Thirty years later, at the Yenching Alumni gathering in Hongkong, while upon the dusty stage the amateur theatricals proceeded, a silly, sad aping of a cremated past, and spectral obedient laughter rose among the ex-students of Yenching now turning old, I was again to ask the question that I had asked myself thirty years ago.

"Why did Donald kill himself?"

"I don't know," replied my friend Tan Leeton. "Donald was a funny fellow; always keeping to himself, and a little arrogant. He wouldn't have anything to do with us. He was always sure that he was cleverer than all the others. I suppose he couldn't stand failing. I know he told someone that his mother would be terribly disappointed . . ."

I remembered my own arrogance, which went much deeper than Donald's, my own silent, unknown nervous breakdown.

"Perhaps he was just unsure of himself . . . unsureness, fear, makes one appear arrogant."

"We couldn't get him to join anything; so after a while we left him alone."

It was nobody's fault, nobody's fault but circumstance. Donald's suicide precipitated me into further alienation; into withdrawal, the only way I knew to solace my terrified heart; hardening my exterior, going out of my way to shock, show that I did not care, I did not care.

And so all the kindness, the held-out friendships, of Liang Szeyi and Chang Shuyi and Lee Yuehien broke on this acrid foolishness I built for myself against being hurt.

A week later, I met one of the three American students who were studying Chinese language on the campus. "My God, it's a bad thing to happen . . . that guy couldn't stand being teased, he wasn't able to take a joke, maybe someone tried to tease him . . . it wasn't a pretty sight . . . I was one of those who found him, you know . . ."

253

"I won't kill myself," I replied, laughing, and ran away, laughing, laughing.

Donald was a Eurasian, like myself, a Eurasian who had killed himself; how easy now, now that I have surmounted all this, how easy to say: "Nonsense, it was not because he was a Eurasian. It was because he was unsure, his mother had pampered him. Other young people in many places in the world have killed themselves; for love, for many other reasons." But at that time it was easy to think: "I am a Eurasian, every hand is against me, everyone despises me, I have no way out . . ." How easy to despair, to give in, to go through life ascribing every defeat to that one single thing, being Eurasian.

"And they didn't even write nasty things about him in the paper, as they did about me," I thought contemptuously. "The mollycoddle, to kill himself for failing an examination, or being teased, or both . . . I'm going to show them . . . I'm going to show them . . ."

What was I going to show? And whom was I going to show? I was not going to commit suicide, that I knew. My appetite for life is much too strong. But I did all I could to hurt myself, thinking I was showing how little I cared for the others, and only, in the end, hurting myself.

What could I do, but hurt myself? And if this was not enough, who should turn up, a little after Easter, in April 1934, but Hers himself, on one of his inspection tours. I went into the city to see him. He stayed, as usual, at the Hotel de Peking. We met, as usual, in the lobby, where he fed me, as usual, with cakes and tea. He was distrait, not interested in my studies, though I showed him my good report. "Women cannot study, what the hell do you want to be a doctor for? All the women students in the universities get married and then give up everything and stay at home. They never move a finger, except to play mahjong. It's a waste of time and money." I always dreaded a sudden caprice of Hers, stroking his small goatee and saying: "We have decided not to give you a scholarship." The "We" he used was a screen, actually Hers himself decided, I knew that. Now he made fun, fiercely, devastatingly, of my blue cotton Chinese dress, my socks and tennis shoes. "Last time I saw you, you were trying to dress like a young lady, now you look as if you were ready at any moment to post slogans on walls and shout with all those young hotheads who went to Nanking last year. They wanted to fight Japan and take back Manchuria, when the Young Marshal, who after all is the master in Manchuria, has run away with a hundred and eighty thousand troops. Ha.' His scorn was intense.

In March that year, 1934, the Japanese had just made Puyi "Emperor" in Manchukuo, and still Chiang stuck to non-resistance, still America did not budge from neutrality, and still another campaign, the Fifth Extermination Campaign against the Communists, was to be launched . . .

That April evening Hers gave a cocktail party to some Belgians; one of them began talking to me, saying the Chinese were primitive, like animals. As if I was not half Chinese . . .

After the cocktail party (at which I drank vodka laced with orange juice) I found myself left in the care of a young Belgian, probably a bank clerk. Hers was going to a Chinese dinner and had ordered this young man to bring me. It was held at a famous restaurant near Chienmen. In the middle of dinner I noticed that I was the only girl there, the rest were men, both Belgians and Chinese. In came the singsong girls, eight of them; they sat on stools behind the men. They did not all come together; first four arrived, then another three, and then after a long interval the last one, heralded by a stir, a hubbub of admiration. Hers was the guest of honour and she sat next to him. Her smallness and beauty, her pert and lovely face are still alive for me. After a little interval, and a small cup of hot wine, she began to sing, not a twittering soprano, but high and clear and strong, the notes slapping clean into the room.

The young man said to me with an effort: "Now I had better take you home."

The last thing I saw was Hers, sitting, looking at the singsong girl. She had, between her hands, a rubber hot-water bottle, as all the singsong girls had in those days, to keep their hands warm. Her dress and shoes were silver. She kept her eyes downcast. Her hair was smooth, blue-black.

I went home, thanking the young man (he probably hurried back), and told Tiza about the nice party and the food. But I could not speak about the girls; for a long time the picture of the girl in silver was in front of my eyes, and her movements, the delicacy of her hands turning the hot-water bottle over, adjusting the cape upon her shoulders, the way her voice rose, suddenly, throwing the melody at the room, then suddenly stopped. She was very young, no more than sixteen or seventeen.

There was nothing I could tell Hers about myself. He went back to Shanghai; I said I would come in the summer. "I will try to find some Chinese intellectuals for you to talk to," he said to me.

I got through the second term; and though not doing so well as in the first term, it was still creditable. I made friends, now, with an overseas Chinese, Herbert Lee, who was attending Chinese classes with me. He was never to know what prompted me to cling to him through that spring, nor to know what Donald's death had meant to me, but he took me out on long bicycle rides; I fell off my bicycle more than usual; always in a semi-daze, born of the strong turmoil within me, and part of these fits of abstraction, the waking trance, which I had had since I was twelve, but which I did not recognize and was much ashamed of. In that short hot season Herbert and I were young and in love except that the capacity for love had gone out of me and I only knew need, not affection . . . Sometimes he would say to me: "You poor kid, you poor kid," sometimes he called me "Unconscious". In the end he was hurt, for he was sincere, and I was on my way, going, going, never looking back. But it was Herbert Lee who staunched the raw wound of my spirit, and perhaps it is not too late to tell him so.

In July 1934 I again went to Shanghai. Where else during the summer holidays could I go?

It was not possible to travel by train, the stations were in no way secure because the Japanese and Kuomintang secret agents were swarming over the trains, looking for suspected intellectuals and revolutionaries. I went to Tientsin, boarded an English boat and arrived by sea. I found my way to Hers's office in the French Concession and sat in the waiting-room. He was out to lunch. He returned at three thirty and said: "Oh, oh." He stared into space and pulled his beard.

"I must find you a decent house to live in or everyone will be saying that I have abused your youth. Come." We strode away, the sun was hot, the tarmac melted under my shoes; I had to run to keep up with him. He put me in a small hostel for women, run by Catholic nuns. One had to be back at eleven at night.

I do not know what I thought I would accomplish by going to Shanghai. "Come, baby," Hers would say, and take me out to lunch, business lunches held on the top floor of the Cathay Hotel which was air-conditioned. In the evening again he would take me after dinner to the dance halls. There he would sit watching and I would sit drinking orange juice. He never danced. I stared and envied the beautiful girls dancing so gracefully; visioning myself, light, sylph-like, stepping with flower-in-wind effect as did these girls. I searched in the newspaper advertisements and discovered a dancing school. Hers said: "Okay, if you wish to learn here is ten dollars." I took the ten dollars and I had my first lesson. A White Russian instructor, a wheezy gramophone. Half an hour cost six dollars; but five lessons cost twenty-five dollars. I had five lessons and I was inept as before.

Hers did not repeat his April imprecations against women studying. Trotting at his heels, I learnt a good deal about what was going on in Shanghai at the time. Every day people came to see Hers, to eat with him and talk with him. The Fifth Campaign against the Red bases, begun in October 1933, was still going on . . . Here in Shanghai in the International Settlement and French Concession the censorship was less rigorous and the foreign newspapers gave more news than in Peking. And everyone said: "This time, the Reds are done for."

Hers also would talk about these pacifications, for so they were called. In 1933 Chiang Kaishek had read the book of a historian named Hsiao on the Taiping peasant revolt of the 1850s, and studied the campaigns undertaken by Tseng Kuofan, the general-in-charge of the Imperial armies, to suppress the Taiping, which he did after fourteen years and with fearful ravage. It was reported that Chiang Kaishek asked his German advisers to read this book; and to spare nothing to root out the Communists. The Fifth Campaign proceeding with its six hundred thousand men in that summer of 1934 followed a combination of Tseng Kuofan's strategy and that of General Hans von Seeckt.

In 1933 General Hans von Seeckt had come to China to survey the Kuomintang military establishment and to advise on the methods to be employed against the Communists.

In 1934, von Seeckt, with Hitler's full approval, had taken over as head of Chiang's military advisory group. The Fifth Campaign against the Communists was directed by von Seeckt.

Later, in 1936, Chiang's second son, Weikuo, was sent to Germany, to be trained there. My first husband, Pao, who was his great friend, also spent some weeks in Germany in 1936. Chiang Ching-kuo, Chiang Kaishek's elder son, was still in Russia, where his father had sent him in the 1920s.

The use of Germans in the army was not new. Since 1927 Chiang had sought the services of Germans, to replace the Russians; Max Bauer, associate of Ludendorff, had arrived that year and built a staff of fifty Germans, instructors at the Whang-poo Military Academy, now become Chiang's private training outfit for young officers loyal to him alone.

In March 1935 von Seeckt was replaced by General von Falken-hausen, whom I met in 1939 in Chungking at a great feast given to him by General Ho Yingchin, Chiang's Minister of Defence. There the young officers, including my husband, toasted victory to Hitler and death to England in the coming war . . . and yet my husband, Pao, had been trained at Sandhurst from 1935 to 1938 . . .

An entire ring of blockhouses, only five hundred yards apart, had been built around the Red bases; more were being erected in smaller concentric rings. A total economic blockade was en-enforced against the armies of Mao Tsetung and Chu Teh.

Chiang's troops razed entire villages, creating a no-man's-land between the non-communist and the Red territories, and thus the trade which had been going on between villages, whether Red or not, was stopped. The smuggling of salt by Hakka pedlars, almost traditional (my own ancestors had dealt in salt for centuries, first as pedlars, probably smugglers, then as officials in charge of salt control), almost ceased. Rice, cooking oil, cotton for clothes, every necessity, became very scarce in the Red areas. For many weeks on end the troops of Mao Tsetung had only sweet potato to eat, no salt; and the lack of salt caused serious morbidity and death among the men, especially in the hot summer.

Many of Hers's friends talked about the impending annihila-tion of the Communists. "It will all be over in a few months, this time, their goose is cooked." By now even Hers was beginning to get worried about the Japanese; was it their intention to take over the whole of North China? What would happen if Chiang, free from the Communists, allied himself with Japan and threw the whites out?

"The Japs are going to poison one hundred million Chinese with heroin," said a stocky Belgian priest who came to see Hers one day. "I have just been to Kalgan. They have factories making the stuff; agents all over the north selling it . . . you should see the Japanese Concession in Tientsin these days . . . all the warehouses full of opium."

"When will they take Peking?"

Of the Chinese intellectuals Hers said I would meet I remember one who spoke French well, discoursing fervently one morning at the Sino-French Club:

"What is eating the heart of the Kuomintang? Not ideology,

258

surely. And not nationalism . . . especially when it means giving in to the Japanese. Corruption is worse than ever, only the Kuomintang party members get jobs . . ."

"We are finished, we are finished . . ." another voice said.

"Perhaps when the Fifth Extermination Campaign is over, we shall then turn against Japan."

They talked and talked in the darkened room, with the revolving fans displacing the humid heat about us. Outside was the famous Bund, the broad, broad and yellow river mouth and the gunboats moored there. "It does no good to rush things . . ." "One can only grovel before the bureaucracy of the Kuomintang."

"The British have always been on the side of Japan."

"They have always been afraid of Russia entering India and now with that man Gandhi, India is very restless though it will take at least another century for the Indians to attain a minimum of self-government . . . the Indians are incapable of discipline . . ."

"The British do not believe that the Japanese really want to kick them out of Asia; they think they can manoeuvre them. It's a misconception."

"Our only hope is America, but she will not move." "Too much money selling scrap iron to Japan."

"China has always absorbed her conquerors, this won't be the first."

Back and forth, on and on during those hot hours, talking and arguing; and meanwhile the Japanese moved in, one by one the provinces fell.

Despondency, despair. Hers hohoed and hmhmed and stroked his beard; and at lunch he said to me:

"The Chinese intellectuals of today really don't know where to turn. Communism is finished, *foutu*, disembowelled; and there is nothing else to take its place. So one turns to opium and the other to women and the third to Zen Buddhism and none of them can do anything at all. And now there is also this New Life movement going on, another absurdity. And Madame H. H. Kung, the wife of the Finance Minister, has just bought herself another half-million dollars of real estate in America."

The New Life movement made everyone laugh; but not openly. In its essence it was an attempt to return China to a neo-Confucian past, rigid, moralistic, feudal and unreal.

Its proponents were Chiang Kaishek and his wife. Chiang's

259

policy of non-resistance to Japan was more and more unpopular; and like many another ruler who has lost support, he had to become increasingly authoritarian. One way to reinforce his authority was to choose those elements of our past invoking a gallery of moralities long dead, which would bolster his inflexibility and lend it the colour of righteousness.

My grandmother, the Lady Hung, would have approved of the New Life movement, except that she practised it, whereas no one practised it in China of 1934. So, too, would her father, the Lord Hung who had been such a good friend of Tseng Kuofan. And Tseng Kuofan, who had suppressed the Taiping peasant uprising, was Chiang Kaishek's favourite reading material and greatest hero. Chiang read Tseng every day, saw himself like Tseng, "mowing the grass" of peasant revolt. And now we were all to be saved by a resuscitation of the old virtues; it was quite ridiculous.

Loyalty to the Leader, filial piety, the chastity of women, esprit de corps among the young officers, righteousness, honour . . .

To make the New Life movement more palatable a dose of Christian missionary social uplift was added by Madame Chiang: brush your teeth, button up your collar, don't spit, and don't take bribes. The latter, added in, made everyone laugh even harder.

Inaugurated that spring of 1934, the New Life movement had immediately gone into effect, with banners everywhere. I was stopped on the street by a nice policeman because I wore a sleeveless dress.

Rickshaw coolies in the heat of summer, with a temperature of 101, were enjoined to run fully clothed, or to tie a towel round their shoulders in the pretence that they had a jacket on. But many could not afford a towel and were jailed for indecorousness . . .

All brothels were to be closed; but since foreigners were protected by extraterritoriality, many houses of prostitution registered as "foreign companies limited".

The Japanese and Korean houses of pleasure in North China flourished. One hundred thousand women were now under Japanese control in the prostitution and narcotics trade. Seven thousand Korean and Japanese drug pedlars circulated freely in the northern provinces and in Peking. As for Shanghai, its one hundred and forty-eight thousand prostitutes probably increased rather than decreased. They now dressed as schoolgirls, and advertised themselves as female returned students, to give English lessons.

Corruption, bribery, nepotism, which were so current in the Nanking government, increased with an influx of American money for "reconstruction" in 1934 and 1935. Many new villas grew in Nanking, owned by the officials of the government.

The money collected for the five million flood refugees also never reached them; from time to time someone inquired about it, but neither loud nor persistently. It disappeared in the new villas.

A few opium smokers (again unfortunate rickshaw coolies) were arrested and paraded each with a rope round his neck and then shot, as an example of the New Life, and to show that the poor cannot afford the vices of the wealthy.

Safely seated in the small clubs in the International Settlement, Westernized intellectuals inveighed bitterly against the humbug. Many other writers who dared to denounce Chiang were in hiding or in jail.

This moral leap back into the past was not a phenomenon peculiar to China or to Chiang. Pétain at the crumbling of France in 1940 returned to virtue, family, piety, a paraphernalia of long-dead hypocrisies, absconded virtues, to keep the face of control over despair.

Madame Ngo Din Nhu of Saigon tried boosting Confucian virtues to buttress her formidable family's rule. No padded brassieres, no swimsuits, no dancing, no birth control . . . which did not prevent her brother-in-law, President Ngo Din Diem, from being liquidated by the C.I.A.

In that summer of 1934, with slogans of the New Life pasted all over the cities of China, I walked the Chinese section of Shanghai, Yangtsepoo, oozy with ruins and filthy with misery, saw the policemen openly accepting bribes from the pimps in the squalor of back streets. Broken-down prostitutes looked at me; hideous women, crackling with laughter as I looked away. I walked in a trance, sweating, but not understanding.

"Go and see a bit of life," said Hers. "Stuck in your university, you think everything can be done by slogans. You will see that the Chinese are worse to their own people than Europeans."

A small rat-like man with glasses took me to a silk filature, in Chapei or Yangtsepoo, quite a way from the International Settlement. It was an area impossibly squalid, a slum of sagging huts, stinking unpaved alleyways. A barn-like structure, with a small courtyard in front, was the filature. Inside, great vats of boiling water, furnaces, and children looking about six but who the rat-faced man told me were all of fourteen, standing round the vats. It was hardly possible to see what they were doing with the steam rising from the vats, and it was suffocatingly hot; but they were plunging silk cocoons in bundles wrapped in fine webs of gauze in the vats. The children's eyes were peculiar, bright red with trachoma, their arms were covered with scalds, and they worked almost naked; the temperature outside was ninety-eight degrees inside it was one hundred and three or perhaps more. The smell was bad, and I could not stand it and no one wanted me to stay very long. "These are refugees . . . we give them work, otherwise they would die of hunger . . ." The rat-like man told me how kind his manager was to give employment to these children, one hundred and twenty of them. Quickly we went out again. The car of the manager who had arranged this instructive trip for me because Hers had asked him to do so, was waiting beyond the mud lanes, as these were impassable; it whisked me away, back to civilization, in the French Concession . . . "Now you have seen the problem," said Hers. "Too many poor people in China." Later I found out the silk filature belonged to a Japanese concern.

Years later only did I meet Rewi Alley who had been an inspector of factories in Shanghai. A New Zealander who had come to China for three months in 1927, someone had spat at him as he landed. "Funny way of greeting people they have here," thought Rewi, and stayed in China forty years. From 1927 to 1938 Rewi worked in Shanghai, fighting against the factory owners, against the callous indifference of the foreign administration, against the appalling conditions, which reproduced those of nineteenth century England. He toured the flood and famine areas in north and south and middle China; and knew the hideous use made of the refugees. For ten years he urged and pushed and got nowhere.

From the famines, the floods, the civil wars, wave after wave of children would arrive at the city with their parents. And they were sold by their parents, or hired out to work, as was done in England. The factories refused to employ men, they would only take women and children. From the refugee camps and the orphanages children would be bought. In crowded lofts, in rickety barns such as this, they were put to work; twelve, fourteen hours a day, no Sundays off; they made flashlight bulbs for the five and ten cent stores; they slept underneath the punch press machines; twice a day they ate gruel, and they died of beri beri, swollen with festering sores, within four months.

"I shall never forget the irrepressible gaiety of dying children, in the lead battery factories . . . as I went to take their urine . . . the word child applied to the under twelve. Over twelve they became apprentices till they were eighteen. Apprentices were paid like children."

"The foreigners always said: It's up to the Chinese administration." And the Chinese could not do anything even if they wanted to (which they did not) because over seventy per cent of the factories were owned by Japan and Britain.

The foremen in the textile mills were armed with guns and whips. The girls, mostly from the countryside, were brought into the city in batches of thirty, worked fourteen hours a day and slept in lofts on floorboards. The prettiest were sold to the brothels. Rewi saw many a girl working with a child strapped to her back, another child tied to her leg, for there was no place where the children could be left while the mother worked.

The silk filatures of Shanghai had long lines of children, many not more than eight years old, standing twelve hours a day over boiling vats of cocoons with swollen red fingers, many crying from the beating of the foreman who passed up and down behind them with a number eight gauge wire as a whip; their arms were scalded in punishment if they passed a thread incorrectly.

"But we've also been through this, you know, we had it in England during the nineteenth century," an Englishman loftily said to me when I told him of my gruesome visit. "And look at the British worker now! Always on strike, the Bolshies, if it hadn't been for Ramsay MacDonald they'd have cut our throats!" "These people would starve if we didn't give them employment." This was philanthropy.

"The thing that made me sick was when the manager of the Shensing cotton mill built latrines in the exit doors, of which there were only two; there were about two hundred girls in the structure and a fire on some straw matting caused a panic, many of the girls were crushed to death trying to get out; the manager had only a very small fine to pay and all Shanghai society was indignant, because he had to pay a fine. After all, it was the girls' fault for panicking . . . Four hundred women were blasted to death in a rubber factory, ninety women and children burned to death in a celluloid factory explosion . . . there was always money for fine buildings and roads in the International Settlement, but no money to have even the most elementary safest devices in any factory . . . nothing else counted but PROFIT." Thuy Rewi Alley, reminiscing, twenty years later.

Of the textile mills of Shanghai, 77.2 per cent were foreign-owned, 22.8 per cent Chinese. Woman and child labour was near 85 per cent of the total; the monthly earnings were fifteen (silver) dollars for a male, thirteen for a female, eight for a child (under twelve) working twelve to fourteen hours a day for seven days a week. Though the government had passed labour laws in 1931 they were never put into effect. *And all this went on till 1949.*

In these conditions invested capital was regained in profits within two years, and after that all was pure profit. The average life-expectancy in China in 1935 was twenty-eight years; in the mills in Shanghai it was far less. No New Life here, and no chastity possible. The mill girls had to please the foremen, and the pimps were always there.

"You see, the Chinese don't care, you can't expect Europeans to do everything for them . . . We are trying to alleviate the refugee problem by giving the children some work . . ." At lunch, the well-fed men in the air-conditioned dining-room "explained" these horrors as if they were charity.

And I too began to feel that perhaps they were right. Perhaps this was the human condition, the law of Nature. After all, why should I bother or care? Why should I care about what was happening here?

Perhaps it was true that this was fate, destiny, that the Chinese were degenerate, their brain capacity lower; true that they did not feel pain and died like flies because so it was and so it would always be. "They are happy that way, see my boy, he is happy with his fifteen dollars a month, he gambles it all . . . he would be *incapable* of handling more money . . ."

And every evening Hers would go out, sit at some dance hall or another, eyeing the gracefully gliding singsong girls while I drank orange juice. And intellectuals came, and sat with him, and talked about "the real China".

"The real China". What was the real China? They talked about the mysterious, inscrutable mystery of China, not only Europeans, but the Chinese themselves, these Westernized intellectuals in their long Chinese robes and impeccable accents from Paris or

New York; talking of something impalpable and eternal, and sometimes complaining (because they were safe in the International Settlement) that Chiang Kaishek did not allow freedom of debate. But soon they returned to the awesome question: "What was the True Soul of China?" Many and varied the answers, so profoundly shallow, a wide stream of murky idiocy, a gargle of myths . . .

A fortnight passed and my ear began to hurt. One day at lunch Hers told me: "I have an escort for you. Simon Hua. His father is in the railways with your father."

"Of course I know him," I said. "Simon and Leila his sister, they've been in France studying. I even typed for Mrs. Hua. Not very long, though."

"Oh oh. Well Simon Hua and Max Ouang, whose father is also in the railways, and whose mother is French, are now both in Shanghai. They came to see me this morning. They will come to dinner with me this evening. Two handsome young men to take you out instead of one old one."

I looked forward to meeting Simon again. Then I might tell him about the misunderstanding with his mother. Mrs. Hua had always wanted to write novels; she had written one, which was published, and she was writing another when, in 1931, for a brief week, I did some typing for her. This was a novel which she never finished, I believe; or perhaps she did finish it and it was never published. Today, aged eighty, she still writes, and starves herself in Paris to have her books printed privately.

I remember that afternoon, sitting in the drawing-room of Mrs. Hua's house, in the Street of the Immeasurably Tall Gentleman; at the table, pencil poised (I would take dictation first), and Mrs. Hua, hair piled on top of her head, walking up and down on the blue-and-fawn carpet.

"We shall make revolution, we shall make it . . ." and then went on to describe the coffee house, upstairs, a meeting of young men, the founding of the Communist Party, in France . . .

It was interesting stuff, but not the way she dictated it; every time she described the young men, she said they were handsome as the day, spiritual, pale . . . When she had one of them clench his fist and at the same time throw back his head with its fine curls I protested:

"Chinese don't have curly hair."

When I typed it down, I corrected one or two sentences. I

thought Mrs Hua would not notice, because she had redictated the same episode four times. But she did notice. My work came to an end.

We had dinner together, Simon Hua, Max Ouang, Hers and myself. I could scarcely recognize in the tall, handsome young man who discoursed in such perfect French and with such authority the young boy Simon who had stood on Peking streets in 1925 placing pamphlets in the hands of the passers-by. He was certainly brilliant, and talked marvellously. I listened, enchanted, as he rearranged the world. Max Ouang was equally handsome, equally brilliant and was a most successful architect in Shanghai. Simon was studying architecture in France, and he and Max spoke of Le Corbusier, Jeanneret and Alvar Aalto, mentioned other prestigious names, criticized everything round them, demolished the Bund, trenchantly dismissed the palaces of Peking, linear perspective and aesthetic planes, fluid and square . . . A new world, how much more was there for me to learn? I listened, but I had a bad ear-ache. Gallantly, the next two days, Simon and Max took me out, together and separately; valiantly they made conversation with me; but chiefly they spoke to each other and forgot me, or arranged as soon as I had been fed (either by both or singly) to drop me back at my hotel while they went out together. Max had a car, a sporting model. All three of us drove out of Shanghai one day along a road the Kuomintang had built. Both sides were planted with maple trees imported from America. "What a lamentable performance," exploded Simon Hua. "Roads that lead nowhere; a lot of foreign exchange in foreign trees when China has the best trees in the world."

"Well, I've just had a big contract from the Nanking government to build some private houses," said Max in a satisfied tone, "so I am not complaining." Afterwards Simon told me that Max was a dreadful capitalist, very selfish. "He must be a millionaire by now, or pretty soon. Of course his father is almost an official of Nanking."

I preferred Simon Hua to Max Ouang; the latter was so obviously preoccupied chiefly with his own advancement. When I told Simon about his mother's novel he laughed. "My mother is always writing or doing something. She now has another cause. She wants to bring peace on earth and an end to the persecution of the Jews."

Max took Simon and me to his flat and showed us the interior decoration he had done. There was a large settee and some tiny chairs with rather twisty legs; striped cushions and curtains matched. "It's very vieux jeu, but Max does not know it," said Simon, in a superior manner. Max Ouang's conception of architecture was quite different from his. Otherwise Max would not have been so popular with the Nanking bigwigs.

Simon and I had a share of common childhood memories. "Do you remember Tiza and me holding hands while you performed on the violin, and all of us were required to clap when you bowed?" Simon also laughed at himself now.

"I must, have been a funny little boy."

"You were."

Simon had memories of the railway where his father worked, as my father did. Stretched on Max's settee and I sitting on Max's chair (much less comfortable) we reminisced. "Do you remember hopping from sleeper to sleeper and did your father also take you with him on the line?" "My father had a special bogie which was always hooked on at the end of the train and every year he went for a tour on the railway; there was a platform at the end of the bogie from which he could inspect the track."

For all Simon's long stay in France his heart was still in China. At twelve he had been at school in Peking, participated in the anti-imperialist manifestations of 1925, and that was when I had seen him handing pamphlets to passers-by. A few days later the Peking warlord government had fired on the students, killing ten of them, and Simon's parents had become frightened lest he should get too involved in the student movements, the patriotic demonstrations.

Simon's father was the most profound influence of his life. "My father is the most honest man I know; also the most systematic; do you know that he has compiled a summary of the history of China? But I suppose no one will publish it. He always wants people to *understand* things. What enraged him most are those sinecure holders in the railway office who only turn up on pay day."

"My father is like that too."

"You both have extraordinary parents," said Max Ouang acidly. "Extraordinary for China, I mean. But I'm afraid that all this ancient virtue leads one nowhere these days." That night he took us to a most expensive restaurant, in his most expensive sports car.

Simon remembered a servant, a cook they had had for twenty years. He was very bald and Simon had one day thrown gravel at his bald head. Hua Namkwei his father had shut him up for a whole day without food to punish him; the cook secretly had brought him food. "I could never get over this." The cook's kindness and forgiveness overwhelmed Simon.

"That is why I am a Communist," he said gravely.

I sat, stunned. Suddenly everything became incomprehensible again. Only at dinner, the other night, Hers had said: "And if ever the Communists had come to power, everything would have been much worse. China would have been *finished!*" I believed Hers. Our newspapers in China were full of the atrocities committed in the Red bases; especially of "the free love" practised in the Red bases. Now Simon said this, quite calmly, quite matter-of-factly. I put my hand to my ear. It did hurt badly.

Simon left the next day for Peking, then he would return by Trans-Siberian to Europe. Before he left he persuaded me to go to Europe too. "You must go, it will widen your horizon; my sister is studying architecture in Belgium at the moment. If you ever come to Europe let me know."

Max returned to his real-estate building of villas; he had obtained an order for some Shanghai residential villas from H. H. Kung, the Minister of Finance, and he was also building for the Catholic Church which owned a vast amount of land round the city of Shanghai. "I'll probably make a hundred thousand on the deal."

I went to an ear specialist as my ear had got immensely painful; the drum was full of pus and had to be lanced. I could not stay on in Shanghai, and so I decided to go back to Peking. The last evening Hers had a dinner engagement with other people; as usual, he took me along, in the casual manner which was his, and I as usual sat and ate and listened. After the dinner Hers went to a dance hall and I began to ask about my scholarship again. Would he, would he not, let me know definitely whether I would get one? And suddenly he shouted: "You have a terrible reputation, do you know that, terrible . . ." Apparently some official from Nanking, whose son or daughter was in Yenching, had made derogatory remarks about me. I looked at Hers; I said, my voice hollow even to myself: "I study, I try my best . . ." I felt the floor was dropping away from me. But he turned benign again, just as suddenly. "You are not a major. According to Chinese law you become a major at eighteen which is next year, then we shall see."

I never told Hers about Donald Heyward or about Robert Pang. Explaining is difficult for most teenagers. Inability or

268

unwillingness to tell an adult what one really feels, to clear one-self. Pride, adolescent resentment, a conviction that one cannot be understood. I did not explain anything to Hers, nor did I point out that if I had a bad reputation, it was something which had started the first time I had had dinner with him. But it added to my sensation of failure and defeat. Everyone was talking malice, I would never be able to make good, never, no one understood me or even tried to. I was condemned without a hearing. I decided that I would go away. I would go to Europe, leave all this misery and squalor behind me. "What do I care? Why should I break myself here?"

I returned to Yenching more alienated than ever from the only community that could in the end provide me with the intellectual aspiration, the dedication I needed.

And yet once again the students made overtures of friendship to me; Edith Bien, Nancy Chow, invited me for a picnic. They held it at the Lang Jun Yuen, the old beautiful, desolate garden adjoining Yenching, part of the property acquired from a Manchu prince at the foundation of the University. The trees were old, decayed, exquisite. Wild tangles of reeds and grasses circled a small lake of deep emerald. Infinite sadness exhaled from its desolate unmoving face. Scattered about, a tumbled pillar, a broken-down pediment, retold the defacement and destruction which had come with the foreign soldiers in the sack of Peking in 1860. Some lecturers from Tsinghua University, neighbour to Yenching, and a professor there, Professor Ching, also invited me. We would eat, drink coffee, argue the evenings through, four or five of us. The practical necessity of illusion was one of the themes we discussed. I remember getting very heated one day on the necessity of fighting, but there was an unreality, a non-solid touch to all that was said or done. And one day I overheard whisper of a raid that had been carried out by the police on Peking University one week-end, and of the torture of some students who were kidnapped. One of them, a girl, had red pepper poured down her nose to make her confess she was a Com-munist. All this happened, and yet we went on behaving as if it did not happen. We went on talking philosophy and literature – I would come back from a pleasant, exhilarating meeting, and like sudden frost suspicion would clasp me. I would rehearse the conversations, the gestures, for hidden meanings, sneers . . . had I said too much, too little, would they use this against me? They were not really friendly; they were laughing at me behind my back . . . when they seemed to listen, they were really out to catch me . . . Deep and biting ever deeper, doubt gouged, destroying trust, friendship. I walked a labyrinth of my own making, groped in the dark miasma of fantastic distrust until I could no longer feel that anyone or anything was real, and least of all myself.

And yet, something of world import was taking place. Simon Hua, met again twenty years later, remembering that brief summer in Shanghai of 1934, would say it first.

"There was I, Simon Hua, so progressive because it was the chic thing, the done thing, to be a member of the French Communist Party in 1934. I was on a trip to China to visit my parents; staying in the International Settlement of Shanghai, not even going to see a factory, talking of architecture, never visiting one of those terrible hovels, and all the time the most important thing in the world was happening. The Long March."

The Long March. The Fifth Extermination Campaign had almost succeeded, by sheer massiveness.

By July 1934, when Simon and I were in Shanghai, seventy per cent of the districts controlled by the Chinese Communists had been destroyed.

The Red armies would have been annihilated had they not broken through the encirclement in actions involving heavy losses.

From October 1934 to October 1935 the epic of the Long March was to unfold itself; an epic whose narrative needs its own volumes, and which in the history of mankind will stand for ever, a monument to man's courage, endurance and daring. All we knew was that the Communists were on the run.

It was twenty-two years later, interviewing a veteran of the Long March, now a tall, stooped and scholarly man of fifty whose passion for music was at last fulfilled as he directed a choir, that a small personal note of that great Odyssey came to me. "Well, we ourselves did not know, at the beginning, that we were actually on the Long March and that it was going to be such a big thing. All we knew was that we were getting out of the bases; we were surrounded and being choked; a million men against us, tanks, aeroplanes . . . defeat after defeat . . . In that September of 1934 when we began to get away we broke through one cordon of encirclement, then a second, then a third, and we marched through the late autumn and early winter, westward, always

270

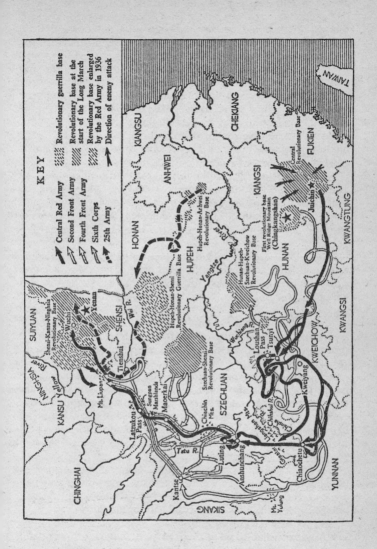

westward, with the rain soaking us to the skin, and the wind in our faces, and we headed towards Szechuan province. We thought if we could get to Szechuan all would be well; for Szechuan was not letting Chiang Kaishek come in; the warlords of Szechuan did not want Chiang there.

"But we had so much equipment with us; trains of stores, and even bedding and furniture, all sorts of things; and this slowed us down. We were about a hundred thousand in number and very visible, a long, slow caravan. Every day we were attacked; front and back and both sides by Kuomintang armies and by local warlords' armies; we fought them and defeated them, and went on, but every time many of us died, and then we got to Tsunyi, and it was January of 1935.

"There we held a big conference, to study our further moves, to assess our losses; by that time most of us wanted Mao Tsetung to lead us, and no one else; when we listened to him we were successful; when we did not we were defeated. So a great clamour went all through the Red armies: 'Listen to Comrade Mao Tsetung.'

"And after the conference the armies heard that the wrong line was repudiated, there was a new leadership, and Mao Tsetung was at the head. I shouted for joy, for happiness, and so did all of us, the soldiers shouting and hugging each other for joy.

"The first thing that Comrade Mao made us do was to throw away all the useless things we carried with us; all of them we threw away and travelled light and swift and clean. Thus we survived the hard, long journey, climbing so many mountains, crossing so many rivers, fighting all the way, every day until we reached our base in the north-west, Pao An, and later at Yenan. One hundred thousand of us had left the bases in October 1934, only twenty thousand reached Pao An in October 1935. But we had survived; and we were not disheartened. And we trusted Mao Tsetung. So we began all over again."

Not only did I know nothing of the Long March then; neither did Simon Hua, nor did a young American, who with his wife had come to Yenching in that year, and settled in a house in the small village of Haitien, behind the back gate of the university.

And yet within eighteen months this young man was to be the first newspaperman to go to the Red base, in the north-west, and to see Mao Tsetung, and Chou Enlai, and many others, and to

272

interview Mao Tsetung. He was the first to write the wonderful epic of the Long March in that immortal classic: *Red Star over China.* *

His name is Edgar Snow. In those days, it did not occur to an American that to seek the truth about China was dangerous; and perhaps it is fitting than an American, living near Yenching University, attending courses in Chinese there, should have been the first to write about the Long March and about Mao Tsetung . . .

Meanwhile the Japanese pressed on, taking more and more of North China. By the end of 1934 they were gathering for another series of "friendly" encroachments.

Another almost unnoticed event took place. The Young Marshal Chang Hsuehliang, once governor of Manchuria, who had lost it to the Japanese without a battle, and had gone away on a rest and study trip to Europe, now returned. But he returned a different man.

Chang Hsuehliang had been a dope addict; easily swayed, easily cowed. He returned restless, nationalistic, and cured of his dope addiction. He began to demand of Chiang Kaishek some positive action against the Japanese. His Manchurian troops, he said, were homesick and getting out of hand. To take the mind of his soldiers off their homeland Chiang sent him and his Manchurian soldiers to Central China first; later, in January 1936, to the north-west, to fight against Mao Tsetung, who with his exhausted remnants had just reached Yenan.

Chang Hsuehliang made his headquarters at Sian. The close proximity of his disgruntled troops, of his own discontented self, to the Red Army base produced a strange result. Within two months, a tentative liaison between the Communist executive committee and the headquarters of Chang Hsuehliang had been established; within four, his Manchurian troops were listening to the slogans and attending lectures. In the Sian colleges were many students from Manchuria who had fled from the Japanese when they invaded Manchuria. These now joined Mao Tsetung's trained cadres, returned to teach the soldiers of the Young Marshal. "Chinese must not fight Chinese! Resist Japan, fight our way back, reconquer Manchuria." And this was precisely what the one hundred and eighty thousand Manchurian soldiers of the Young Marshal wanted; what they sang about, at night, in their camps:

* Random House, 1938.

My home is on the Sungari river,
There are the most beautiful flowers and trees . . .
The loveliest fields of golden wheat.
There is my home . . .

Time waited, crouched in its corner, the future was being prepared. The Long March, seeding machine of the days to come. We knew it not.

CHAPTER FOURTEEN

In the spring of 1935 Hers wrote to my parents for their permission to send me to continue my studies in Belgium, since these were the terms of the Belgian Boxer indemnity fund scholarship. He had no authority to finance my studies at Yenching, nor at the Peking Union Medical College. My marks had fallen off in the second year; I was too sick in mind to study properly and much too unhappy. I wanted to leave, to go away.

My mother now objected to my leaving home, as she put it. She and my father jointly wrote a letter to Hers rejecting the scholarship for me, saying that my unstable character did not give them the feeling that they could burden themselves with the *repayment* of the money, should I fail in my studies.

This matter of repayment of scholarships was a wayward affair. A good many recipients such as myself never seem to have returned a cent. On the other hand, the brother of Max Ouang the architect, Carlos Ouang, told me that in those years, 1934, 1935, he was harassed by demands from Hers to return the money that he owed for his own studies in Belgium. Since the Ouang family was well off I never understood why he had needed a scholarship in the first place. But that was another of the vagaries of scholarships; many were given to the sons of wealthy families, instead of being given to bright but needy applicants.

Hers wrote to tell me of my parents' decision and then arrived on his annual spring visit to Peking and Tientsin. The time was May. I took the train to Tientsin one week-end and we met there.

I arrived in Tientsin to a regular family scene; my parents had rented a house in the French Concession, a tall, narrow house, smaller than our Peking one. There was only a very small front garden with a dusty bush, and some shaggy grass patches with dry bald spaces between. I wept and shouted; my mother was hostile but quiet. Tiza, always kind, made me wash my face and took me out. She met one of her beaux, an Italian. The three of us went to watch a Basque team play Jai Alai, a very fast ball game, at the Canidrome. Dog races were now very popular in Tientsin and many gambled on the dogs. At the Canidrome I met an old schoolmate of mine; she had married a Corsican sergeant in the French army, her sister had married a Swedish junior clerk in a business concern. Everyone was getting married, everyone looked sedate, happy. There sat the couples, by twos and fours, sipping drinks, laughing. For them life was urbane, a small-hemmed handkerchief. They had what they wanted and so long as they could eat and sleep and watch the Jai Alai and bet on dogs they wanted nothing more.

Tiza was also getting married; she was engaged again. We did not speak of Shawn. He had returned to America and stopped writing. There was an Italian orchestra; Tiza and her beau danced. She was learning painting and Italian, preparing to go to Italy after her marriage. I do not know why I picked this time to quarrel with her fiancé and two other Italian friends who had sauntered by and sat with us. It was about Mussolini and the bullying of Abyssinia; prelude to the war later that year. Fiercely I denounced the Japanese too, and though they were Italians, and the Axis was being formed, they had no illusions about Japan. "They want to kick all of us whites out of China," one said soothingly. They were charming, made jokes and laughed and did not want to quarrel with a woman. "Women are for beauty, they should not try to understand all these men's things," they said. Later Tiza told me: "If you always argue no one will marry you."

That evening in bed Tiza and Marianne and I were like children again, laughing and pillow-fighting and forgetting everything that had been between us; I felt generous and gave Tiza a necklace I had, and she thanked me. I forgot then, for a little while, what had rankled so much: that my mother used the money that I gave her to buy dresses for Tiza.

"But I too need clothes!" I had shouted at my mother.

"Your sister needs them more, she is growing out of everything," my mother had replied.

It was not so much Tiza's growing out of clothes, but her good looks, and her sweetness, which made Mother want to buy her pretty things; and as usual the drawers bulged with her dresses, her handkerchiefs and her underwear. But she never liked to open the drawers to show me all this, and as long as I did not see them, I forgot she had so much.

Marianne never came into this jealousy; she was the little one, the youngest, a vigorous child six years younger than I, and much lighter in colour, her skin very fair, her eyes greenish grey. I had always treated her when she was ill; a boil on her face, a disfiguring one between nose and forehead, I had lanced and squeezed for her. No one worried about her. She was very strong, a beautiful swimmer, tennis player, and dancer. She was happy, always laughing, even when she cried she laughed at the same time, and we paid no attention to her except to tell her to be quiet.

That night, too, we paid no attention to Marianne, we only told her to go to sleep, while we talked, and she obediently turned round and went to sleep. I did not give her anything, it did not seem necessary, she was such a child.

The next day my parents and I had a meeting with Hers in his hotel, the Astor, opposite Gordon Hall in the British Concession. "Alors," said Hers to my mother, "have you decided, Madame, about your daughter's studies?" My mother twisted her hands on her lap. We hated each other, but at that moment I could not hate her, only watch her with wearied repulsion. Did it matter what she said? I was nearly eighteen and at eighteen a person is an adult in China; even Hers had to acknowledge that at eighteen I could decide for myself. Asking my mother was only a formality. I looked at my father. He was not looking at me but plucking his hairless chin, and waiting, waiting for my mother to speak. I felt so tired, so tired . . . "If I don't get the scholarship I will become a prostitute in Tientsin. I swear to God," I said. The words fell dully, ridiculous in the silence because they shocked no one. Hers said: "I think your daughter had better have her chance, Madame, she has proved her determination to study."

"But it is not a career for a woman, it is not a life for a woman to be a doctor," said my mother feebly. "A woman must marry and be happy."

"Madame," said Hers with devastating irony, "not all women are destined by God to be a happy wife and mother as you are."

I rose first, knowing it was over, and the others rose after me. I said: "I shall leave in September. Now I am going to the sea for a

276

month. I need a rest." And thus went home with my parents for the last time.

I had ten days by the sea in Peitaiho with Vera Thassounis and her family. Vera had invited me; Vera, her mother, her elder sister with her baby, made a feminine, chatty, fuzzy background which soothed me, Greek liveliness, Greek food, Greek humour, the sauna bath of sun and heat. I slept and slept.

The deep affection between Vera and her mother fascinated me. Vera talked to her mother, referring everything and everyone to her. Mrs. Thassounis nodded, looked at the daughter with a deep, reflective stare, and nodded again. "I shall always remember your cakes, Mrs. Thassounis," I said to her.

Then I spent a week in Tsingtao, another seaside resort with a marvellous beach; and climbed Laoshan, the near-by mountain which has springs with medicinal water. I then decided to spend three days with my brother and his wife in Tientsin, in their house in the former German Concession. Thus I dawdled, going round saying goodbye, and lingered the summer through.

After the spring of 1929 spent with my brother in Tientsin, our quarrel, and my mother fetching me back, we had become friends again when he went to France to conquer yet another degree, and wrote regularly to us. His success at the Sorbonne University mollified his grievances; for a short while a common emotion of pride at his triumph united us; my mother could boast of the position her son had acquired, for he returned a full professor to teach at the Jesuit College of Hautes Études in Tientsin. Moreover, he returned married. Hélène, a Belgian girl, was actually my grandfather's choice; my brother loved his wife deeply, for he was capable of love as Tiza was, as my mother and father were, sacrificing both world and time to a single person. When Hélène became insane, from 1938 to 1963, my brother exiled himself for her, spent his money on clinics, hospitals and pilgrimages to miraculous Lourdes to make her well again.

In 1932, when I was working at the P.U.M.C., the couple paid a visit to my parents in Peking.

Hélène was much addicted to kissing, being a Walloon. My brother and she appeared together at church. On the way back my brother wanted to show his wife some of the city streets. We strolled, the three of us, down Hatamen Street and I pointed out to my brother the lane where the Russian dance-hall girl lived and told him I was teaching her French. I also pointed out the

Alcazar nightclub where my pupil worked. I thought that this would interest Hélène. She wore high heels, pink stockings, a lacy semi-transparent blouse with a dark skirt. I could see the straps of her slip and the straps of her camisole and the straps of her bra, three straps, on each shoulder; she had a cloche hat and a big bag and the skirt was a little tight. I thought she had large hips and rather thin legs; her hair was brown, she brought it forward in a loop on the forehead and over the ears. As I spoke and she walked, lifting those unsteady high heels on the pot-holed and scarred pavement, she suddenly emitted something like a squawk, and started walking away from us. My brother ran after her and seized her arm. I could hear her say: "No, no oh no."

Then my brother was angry with me and asked me not to tell dirty stories: "You understand, my wife is a very proper woman, she has not seen much of life." I stared at him. What had I said that was wrong? "You told about teaching a dance-hall girl, that's terrible," said my brother.

By the afternoon Hélène seemed to have forgotten this episode, she did not refer to it again, and two days later she and my brother returned to Tientsin. Only one short note came from my brother asking me never to upset his wife again. "You must understand, she is respectable."

Now I was going to stay with them for three days. Their house had a small garden round it; it was Catholic property. Elder Brother was pleased to see me and took some photographs in the garden. "You've grown quite beautiful," he kept on saying, pummelling me playfully; I was tanned by the sea, strong and lithe. "She has a skin like silk," shouted my brother to his wife. Hélène was expecting a child; in flowery voile (three straps showing through) she looked enormous. It was obvious that my brother's horizon was narrowing. He never read the newspapers, they never went anywhere. Hélène insisted on doing everything herself, she had no servants. "They are all thieves." They had no friends. My parents were staying in Tientsin not far from their son and daughter-in-law, but relations were again broken off and they did not visit each other. My brother told me the reason; it was a long long story, querulous, pathetic, so long that I forgot it. He had begun to verbalize his hatred of our mother and had the habit of cataloguing, making numbered lists, one, two, three, four, five, all the good reasons he had to hate her. He showed me letters he had written to my parents, letters they had written to

278

him. It was pitiful, abominable and yet all too real. It became a fixation with him, and Hélène encouraged it. I knew how unfair Mother had been, not only to him but also to me; in the end my brother and I always agreed. "She only loves Tiza. No one else exists for her. No one else." And even then, because she was so much younger than all of us, we clean forgot about Marianne.

We spent three tolerably happy days. I carefully avoided all controversial topics; I let my brother talk. He and I again went for long walks. "My how muscled you are, everything is hard, hard," he said; my stomach was flat and hard and he and I boxed like two young boys. In the afternoon we went to Kiessling's. "If you weren't here Hélène would not go." Hélène nodded. "It's three weeks since I last put my nose outside my own door."

Hélène was flabby and my brother was getting fat, the two of them consumed many cakes. "Eat, eat, my darling," my brother kept on saying, "it is for the baby. It will do you both good." She ate and he looked at her eating. At night she went early to bed, we sat and talked for hours.

They had their small universe; close and shuttered against all comers; outside it were terrors and evils, his own mother, the Chinese among whom they lived. My brother had now given up trying to be Chinese; he told me that, for the sake of the child that was coming, he was going to change his name. Hélène did not want the child to have a Chinese name. We did not realize that this was the beginning of Hélène's insanity. But these years between 1932 and 1938 were the only happiness that my brother had and it was real happiness. He clung to it, and twenty-three years later when all had gone to pieces and he was alone to look after the mad woman who did not recognize him, he sat with me on the hard bench of a station café in France and spoke of those years with Hélène and of the happiness she had given him . . . "Yes, I've been happy. Yes, I had my share of happiness on earth . . . yes, she has been the only woman in my life."

In August our house in Peking was cooler than the street, except at night when the day's heat oozed out of the walls. Hsueh Mah looked after me; she screamed and her teeth were like a rabbit's. There was water and food. I wandered about the city, insatiable, looking, looking. The summer rains had come and gone; the quartered red melons were like great raw wounds pitted with black gangrene, spread out on the stalls and covered with white muslin against flies. On the denuded glacis, the plain round the Legation quarters, a team of English officers played polo; their voices sounded like a distant call to arms. In the newspapers there were reports of the famine in Middle China, which had started in the spring . . . Twelve million people were dying of hunger; an appeal had been made for money and food; there followed a small list of donations gratefully received by the Famine Relief Commission. The starving people had been eating mercy earth, a kind of clay; it made their bellies swell and they died in a coma.

A certain foreign company was paying out a 45 per cent dividend twice in the year . . . "labour is plentiful, and since the advent of the Nanking government, there has been no danger of strikes . . ."

Upon the gates of Paotingfu City had been nailed cages containing the severed heads of five Communists, workers on the railway, suspect of trying to organize a union. One of them was twelve years old.

Bandits were infesting the roads, even the Western Hills were not safe.

Everywhere the Japanese were coming in; Teilhard de Chardin described them: "khaki uniforms, hobnailed boots and narcotics . . . it is impossible to imagine such serenely immoral brutality." They came, there were always more of them, swarming everywhere. They were already in Peking in August 1935. "The Japanese Concession in Tientsin is the nerve centre of heroin manufacture with nearly a thousand 'foreign companies' openly selling heroin and cocain." Thus the *Report on Narcotics* of the League of Nations, that year.

In the small hutungs – grey entrail coiled unpaved and dusty, twisty lanes of Peking, with such names as: Lamb's Tail, Little Dumb Lane, Vinegar and Wine Alley, Little Stone Tiger – on the grey walls enclosing the houses were scribbled at dawn, wiped off by the police at noon, many slogans:

"Resist Japanese Aggression!"
"Chinese Must Not Fight Chinese!"
"Return to Us Our Own Mountains and Rivers!"
"People of China Unite!"

In a dilapidated wooden cart, tied by the neck with a rope, three men were drawn to execution. Were they Communists, were they opium smokers? No one knew. Dull-eyed they jolted in

280

the cart. Dull-eyed we looked. All we knew: that they were the poor, the unprotected who could not pay, while the Japanese army officers and the Chinese officials were making money out of the narcotics trade in North China.

Twice in the August of that year 1935, the Communist Red Army, while on the Long March, had issued appeals for a United Front for national resistance to Japan. Perhaps that is why there was a recrudescence of "searching for Communists" through the heat-sodden city of Peking.

Just two months before, in June, the Japanese had taken some more of our province of Hopei. The Nanking War Minister, General Ho Yingchin, came to Peking. Everyone now said, "He is more a Japanese than a Chinese, so eager is he to give China away!" "He has not only agreed to evacuate Chinese soldiers from the whole province but also to abolish his own office in Peking, the Military Council!" Daily more Japanese military police and agents came in, to keep peace and order.

I walk by the Grand Hotel de Peking. The courtyard is full of big black cars. In the colour-swallowing dusk, many policemen hover, and there is an air of sinister importance about; one can smell it at a distance; it makes the common people of Peking stand far away, lest their shadow fall upon a Great One, and wrath in return fall upon them. Out from a car, with a clank of metal, comes a Japanese general in khaki; he holds a long, curved sword, longer than he is from waist to boot heels, in a white-gloved hand.

There is also a fat Chinese general with a few officers behind him; they all stand to attention while the Japanese alights from the car. There is a bark of command, soldiers present arms, the officers salute, the crowd watches while the Chinese and the Japanese generals shake hands, and then laugh together, pulling off their similar too-white gloves, white rabbit paws, ghouls in the advancing night.

The cicadas end their summer shrieking, by the crumbling palace walls I stare at the tinfoil canal water. The cypresses and sycamores are a thousand years old, so they say; the stark crumble of a corner tower is only from yesterday; its yellow tiles awash, amid an offshoot of roof glass and tottering shrubs that have eaten into it and brought its fall.

All is going to pieces, unkempt, uncared for. I am offered the glazed head of a small Buddha gouged out of some blue and gold tiled shrine.

Children scribble and chisel their names on the carved marble pillars of the great Ming palaces, on the pillars and commemorative stone tablets reared by emperors, supported by turtles of longevity.

Disfigure, destroy, stone the yellow-tiled animals at the end of upturned roof eaves. Destroy, despoil. What does it matter? All is dirt, indifference, corruption, despair.

The people cry to heaven in their hearts but heaven is deaf, heaven is blind, the sky is wide open but nothing pours out of it, nought but despair . . .

I return to our first house, the house in the Manchu quarter of Peking, where in the spring the courtyard burst with Judas tree magenta and the lilac was mauve and white. My father had tended the laburnum already there and planted the vine. The vine was the only plant, apart from carnation pots, which my father transferred to the other houses; the lilac and the Judas tree were left behind. Also left behind was a pomegranate tree and a jasmine called seven-mile perfume, and of all the courtyard gardens this one had been the best.

I walk to the dead end of the lane and touch at the street door the two small stone Pekingese-lions, and sit on the two large cubic stones outside the house, blue and polished with sitting. Often the large amah of a house farther down the street came to sit with me on these stones, and we used to talk. She looked so much like Liu Mah, the Liu Mah of my childhood. Hawkers came to the door, ambulant barbers, cake sellers. They cooked the cakes in front of us, steaming them. They shaved their clients' heads and cleaned their ears as we watched, and there I saw the last queue cut, in 1926. There were also makers of coloured paste figurines, heroes and theatre characters, beautiful ladies and swirling fierce generals, created so deftly in front of us. Oh it was lovely to live in that house, and I was angry when we left it. Now I look and look at it, for I am going away. I am going to Europe, and I want to fill my eyes before I go. It was also in that house that my best kite flew away to perch in a tree, sailing the cold winter sky till night fell, and it was gone the next morning.

The dragonflies are drowsy in the August heat but not Leo Biefeld, not Hilda. Round the swimming pool Leo prances, happy, happy; a tall, gangling man all legs and arms and gesticulation and funny jokes and laughter, exuberant all the time. He has just returned from Tientsin; he and Hilda have taken me for a swim in the natural swimming pool here in the Western Hills, at the temple of the Black Dragon Pool. Leo's screams sound like a distraught flock of crows. I wonder why Otto has never liked him.

Thirty years later I have the answer.

For Eugen Jung turns up, brother of Fredi, brother of Anna. Eugen turns up in Hongkong, bringing himself almost unchanged, tall muscled spare as when he played ice hockey, and bringing the story of everyone I knew in that desultory casual conglomerate of people reared between a war and a war.

"Leo Bielfeld . . . yes, I think I can understand why Otto told you not to have anything to do with him; because he was so involved in the narcotics trade with the Japanese."

"Did Hilda know?"

"His wife, you mean? No, I don't think so. Very few people knew, only a few of us men, Germans, and of course we kept quiet about it."

Leo Bielfeld was never a nice boy; early on his family in Tientsin disowned him; they were Germans solidly established there but they wanted nothing to do with him because at a young age, besides his small import-export business which was a camouflage, he was really carrying on a narcotics business.

"As you know, the narcotics business, peddling of drugs, heroin, opium, was really very very big business in North China after the Japanese came into Manchuria. They made vast profits out of it; the Japanese heroin manufacturers were spread in all the big cities; the ostensible managers and owners employed were actually Koreans, the Japs did not appear, but the money and equipment came from them and the profits went to them. The drug traffic was on so enormous a scale that several international organizations protested, but it was no use. In every big city in North China after the Japanese occupation there were large plants for manufacturing drugs; a big heroin factory at Nan Chihtze, right in the middle of Peking, blew up one day when I was still in Peking," said Eugen.

Already in the early 1930s Leo Biefeld was in touch with drug pedlars, and under cover of business smuggled for them from Tientsin into Peking and from Peking into other cities of North China. He owned a fast car and would go driving, carrying packets of heroin and opium; since he was a white, none dared to search his car, and in that time no papers were needed to travel in China. He made a good deal of money that way and all through the Japanese occupation of North China he got on very well.

"Leo married my best friend," I said. "She was certainly much in love with him. She told me how he went on business trips, and one day she went to the railway station to meet him, and she wore a white dress with a big black hat, and Leo was bowled over. Then he proposed to her and they were married. That is how it happened. Hilda told me so. She was my best friend."

"I don't think she knew what kind of 'business' he was in at the time," replied Eugen. "During the 1930s and afterwards, when the Japanese came, I saw them in Peking, in Tientsin; they had plenty of money, and since Leo was German, they were free to go where they liked, since the Germans and the Japanese were Axis partners. Perhaps his wife did come to know what her husband was doing, but accepted it as 'normal'. In wartime people change so much that what is rotten seems normal then. And it was such a time, of corruption, of vileness and squalor, we all did black marketing, we all did bad things, and it appeared normal – people don't realize how they change in a war. And afterwards, they forget the terrible things they have done.

"And then things went wrong. The Japanese began to lose the war; and though they held the cities of North China by order of the Americans, who were afraid that if the Japanese left too soon, the Red Army of Mao Tsetung and his guerrillas, who were very strong in the countryside in the North, might come into the cities, yet they could not hold them. The Communists captured the city of Kalgan, either in 1945 or in 1946, I don't remember. Kalgan was the great production and distribution centre for drugs, and it is situated at the pass in the Great Wall, about seventy miles from Peking. The whole area was covered by Korean drug pedlars, who went into Mongolia where the opium was grown, and brought it down to Peking, and from there on to Central China. The Japanese were also smuggling the opium to the Nationalist officers and generals, of course, who used to do a regular trade in it, selling their guns and ammunition in return to the Japanese. So it was a many-way traffic. And Leo Biefeld was in the middle of it. Anyway, he and Hilda were in Kalgan, on this opium business, when Kalgan was taken by the Communists. And they were caught.

"I got the details from another German, a young German who was with Leo Bielfeld and his wife in jail. Along with them was also a young Chinese Kuomintang officer, who was also taken prisoner. Whether the two of them were also in the drug traffic, I don't know. The Communists made Leo and everyone else write their life history. You know the way they do it; make you write your life story, your own autobiography, and then check it. Once, twice, three times, Leo wrote his, and always the Communists came up with some discrepancy, something left out ... so it showed that they suspected him. Of course, Leo lied about his drug peddling; he said he was a merchant for such and such a company or concern, and the Communists found out that the company had closed years ago, so that he was telling lies ... that is the way they do it, catch you in your own lies.

"So they had them in jail, Leo and his wife. And then there was fighting for Kalgan; the Kuomintang were flown in by the Americans, to take it from the Communists. The young German and the Kuomintang officer escaped from the jail during the fighting. They walked and walked across the hills, and the Kuomintang officer died on the way. So the German who escaped told me, but no one knows what exactly happened, maybe he was killed by the German, who knows? But Leo and Hilda did not get away. For Leo died. He died in jail of dysentery. Of course nothing could be done, there were no medicines, and fighting everywhere, and shooting, as the siege of the city was fierce. His wife and other prisoners were taken away, walking tied to one another, with chains on their feet, taken away across the hills by the retreating army. Afterwards I understand that some relatives came and tried through the British Red Cross to find Leo's wife, tried and tried but she was never found.

"Yes," said Eugen, "there were so many like Leo then, in cahoots with the Kuomintang authorities and with the Japanese, peddling narcotics. Then the Communists came, and they made a big shake-up, in Tientsin, in Peking, in all the cities. During 1952 and 1953 they cleaned up all the trade, and they shot many, many drug dealers and gangsters, and they closed all the heroin and opium factories, and everything else they cleaned up, just like that."

From autumn to autumn goes the caravan of time. Thirty years later, in September 1965, I went back to Peking to enjoy the autumn, its best season, to remember. Six hundred students from Japan, on friendship bent, were promenading round the parks, arm in arm with Chinese students, swearing that this time they

285

would not go to war, brother against brother. The sidewalks of the main streets were thick with trees; a winter premonitory breeze whipped their leaves and made one remember the tasselled horsetail whisks which Mongol horsemen once bore in their hands; now the remaining ones hung for sale in a new shop on Long Peace Street. Below the whisks, in the same glass case, were embroidered theatre slippers with their pompoms of floss silk, blue and pink and lavender and prim pale pistachio, two by two; exactly like those Anna Jung had worn when she sang in the East Market theatre. In the Summer Palace the wind soughed in white pines like lanky ghosts caught by day, and the sun sparkled off their white and motley barks. So clear the air the Jade Fountain seemed but a hand away, and from its foot surged the eternal water nourishing a hundred thousand lotuses in its flowing. The dragonflies, gossamer gold and orange, with among them the occasional black and magenta one, a kind more common in South China, hovered more airy than air. About the streets were mounds of fruits, in the shops the mooncakes thin, white, flaky, sold by the tens of thousands. Even the Hotel de Peking had lost its terrors for the child Rosalie of the past; the smooth and springy dance floor was still there; now covered with a long carpet; the mirrored pillars reflected tourists trooping across its length to the new building. The new Peking Hotel, placed next to the old one, incorporated it so that the once magnificent ball-room had become a corridor, leading from the old to the new.

The slanting sun touched the blue and grey pebbled pathways, made them lustrous. The Western Hills were early autumn crimsoned; the temples where Hilda and I had wandered, the swimming pool where Leo had filled the echoing air with German jokes, all, all was there, replete with memories, and beautiful with new care. In the courtyard of my friend Yeh and his Manchu wife the peaches on the peach tree were ripening. On the evening of the Moon Festival there would be a party round it, the ripe fruit would be plucked from the tree, and eaten beneath the moon.

CHAPTER FIFTEEN

"Go to Europe by the Trans-Siberian," Simon Hua had urged.

And I decided to follow his advice. The ocean voyage was more expensive, slower.

On board the Japanese ship to Dairen, from whence I would start the railway journey across Manchuria (become Manchukuo), a small Japanese man in a blue suit, with a blue tie, came up to me. He asked me where I was going, and I told him I was a student going to Belgium. He went away, returned with a piece of paper. He wanted me to draw the map of Europe and show him where Belgium was. He said he had not found "Belgium" on his map. I drew a map and wrote the word Belgium in Chinese, in English, in French. He took the paper and went away.

When the boat moored at Dairen, and the passengers were being processed through the dining-room to show their passports for landing I found myself sandwiched between two policemen. The blue-suited man led the way to the Immigration officers. He handed them the paper I had drawn.

The man in the blue suit was obviously a security officer on the lookout for spies. Spy-mania was a disease of the Japanese at the time. They were especially suspicious of students. After some questioning, the Immigration authorities appeared to believe me; I was allowed to land in Dairen. I went down the gangplank. A young man was waiting for me on the quay. He was taller than I, which was very tall for a Japanese in those days. He had a milky skin, and the wavy hair which many Japanese have from their Melanesian mixture. He introduced himself as a newspaper reporter, and announced that he was accompanying me to my hotel. I was spending the night in a hotel in Dairen, as my train was only leaving the next morning at nine.

"I don't know where to stay."

"I will take you to a good hotel," the young man replied.

A taxi waited; my suitcase was stowed in it. My trunk was travelling by itself, consigned all the way to Harbin.

The Yamato Hotel room was spotless, all white, almost like a hospital room. There was a wash-basin behind a screen. The young man installed himself in the pale cream armchair; I wondered when he would leave. I told him: "I must wash my face," hoping he would disappear, but he did not.

So I drew the screen round me and washed my face and hands, and then opened my suitcase. "I want to change my clothes."

Again he showed no sign of budging. I went behind the screen, and changed. He was obviously not going to let me out of sight, but neither was he on rape intent. When I had changed, I sat on a straight-backed chair, and he asked me all over again my name, my mother's and father's names, my grandfather's, where I had studied. I answered as best as I could and told him that I was catching the nine a.m. train to Harbin.

"Now tonight I take you to Japanese dinner. What would you like to eat?"

The only Japanese food I knew was *sukiyaki*. In Peking many a Japanese restaurant had opened in the past three years; they had *tatami*-lined rooms where one sat on cushions. I had been once with the Germans, glimpsed two Japanese soldiers raucously singing, four geishas kneeling round them.

The young man said: "*Sukiyaki* only for festivals. I will take you to real Japanese eating."

Outside the hotel the taxi was waiting, the same one which had conveyed us from the quay. That pleased me. I felt almost important. How convenient; no foot trudging, no cheap hotel and nothing to pay! I thanked the young man. "I think you are looking after me very well. I am grateful to you."

He nodded. I think he was very pleased, for now his tongue loosened, and we conversed of Dairen, "the premier port" as he insisted on calling it. He asked me whether I was going to Vladivostok; I replied: "Not if it is not on the railroad." He asked me this three times during the meal. I told him finally that I did not even know where Vladivostok was.

The restaurant he chose was in a park, the Nishi-koen park. It was large and there was an open-air veranda where we sat watching the light stippling a dark canvas stage which was the city of Dairen. Everything was clean, I felt drowsy and hungry. My escort (police or not police he was my escort) ordered noodles with ice, and other Japanese dishes; he ate sparingly, I ate copiously. He was reproving: "We Japanese have much discipline, we always eat little." "I always eat like an Eskimo or an express train," I told him. He did not understand and I explained. He wrote down what I said in a notebook. I went on eating long after he had done; I filled my stomach, for I had learnt to gorge when whale was available, that would save buying breakfast, and perhaps lunch, the next day. I was worried that my money might not last me for the whole journey by Trans-Siberian, where meals were extra. But I did not explain this to the young man, who disapproved of my appetite.

"You are very different from Japanese women," he said.

Mellowed with food, we returned to the taxi and now he took me to Hoshigaura, the Star Beach, forty minutes out of Dairen. The night was cool and dark, we walked about, and he began the more delicate job of trying to find out what my thoughts were on political matters. What did I think of Italy? What did I think of Mussolini? What did I think of Italy in Abyssinia? That summer Mussolini had already laid claim to Abyssinia and a beat of war drums was distinct in the West. I told him no country had a right to invade another country and he was silent for a good while. Then he switched to America. What did I think of America? I said I did not think anything of America, I did not know it, but so far as I knew the Americans were rich and powerful. Did I not think that America had a destiny, he said. I was very puzzled. "I don't understand politics, what do you mean by destiny?"

"We in Japan have a great destiny. It is our noble duty to lead the Asian peoples and to liberate them from the yoke of the white people, and especially from America."

I kept silent. There was no point in arguing for or against this view. I had heard it expressed, read it in the newspapers. I had seen the Japanese generals entering the Grand Hotel de Peking that summer. "I don't think you can ever conquer China," I said.

"We are friends with China," he replied. "You know, I am really a socialist. Are you a socialist?"

I said: "What is that?"

He gave up politics and started talking about himself.

By that time I knew the limitations of his English, and he knew the limitations of my thoughts on politics. He told me that he was in love, and asked me whether I was. I said no, I had thought myself in love, but I wanted to study, and I had gone away, even though sometimes people thought themselves in love with me and I with them. "I have to study first."

"Oh, you are wise," he said, and appeared delighted at my seriousness and for the first time since leaving Tientsin my heart smote me at the thought of the friends I had left behind; for such is our contradictory heart, that the moment we abjure an emotion, it comes over us like a strong wave, washing us down again. But in no time I was up for air, and listening as he told me his own tragedy.

"My fiancée, she is a leper."

"A leper? You mean, leprosy?"

"Yes, she has leprosy. So I cannot marry her."

"But what will happen to her?"

"I do not know."

"Oh."

The same taxi conveyed us back to the Yamato Hotel. He said good night, and I went back to my room. All my clothes had been hung neatly, my suitcase put away. Again I was grateful, though I suppose everything had been looked at, in case I was a spy. I slept soundly.

I had an idea that the young newspaperman would be back for breakfast, and was half expecting him, but he did not turn up. I left a note at the desk to thank him for his kindness to me and then realized I did not know his name. I addressed the letter: To the newspaperman who took me out last night. Thinking it over I expect the Japanese police – if they were the police, and if the young man was a detective – must have realized they were wasting their time, and given me up. There was the train at the station and I caught it for Harbin. I do not know whether someone tailed me to the train or not. It did not worry me.

In Harbin the Belgian Consul-General Mr. Dobry and his wife stood on the railway station and took me to their house, where I spent the next two days waiting for the twice-a-week train across Siberia. Hers had sent them a letter, telling them of my arrival, and I had sent a cable from Dairen the previous afternoon.

Harbin was a Russian city, outpost and garrison on the Trans-Siberian railway. After 1917 many White Russian refugees had settled there; there were about one hundred thousand of them in the city.

The Consul's flat had high ceilings, dusty windows, green curtains with fringes, and an enormous sofa in the middle of the living-room (its springs were poor, and when one sank into it, it was extremely difficult to get up again). I slept on the sofa, as there was no spare bedroom.

Monsieur Dobry's wife was a lively person, younger than her husband but with the effect of keeping him young. He sang: "Walls have ears, la didah waaalls have eeears . . ." several times a day, and she shushed him affectionately. They took me to a night club, with Russian dancing girls. I insisted on dancing with one, a rather fat and oily middle-aged matron with black dyed hair, and a black dress. Her hair seemed to have sweated into her dress. She appeared so tragic to me. Monsieur Dobry had danced with me once, then given up; he was good, but not prepared to coach me. In China no one minded when girls danced together, or boys danced together. There was no impropriety. In Shanghai the taxi girls often danced together to relax instead of sitting stiffly in their chairs waiting for customers. Effortless, nonchalant, beautiful, never watching each other yet in step, no one could tell who led, who followed, so perfect their movements. I had watched with envy, and Hers who did not dance used to make me even more envious.

"Et voilà . . . that is what you ought to learn . . . to charm your swains . . . I wonder what they see in you?" (He was always furious with the young men whom I brought along.) "They're shorter than you" – it was not always true – "you seem to be carrying them along as you dance."

Well, here and from now on, I decided, began Europe for me. That Europe where all these dances came from, that glamorous Europe, streets of gold, where everything was wonderful. Every European city had people dancing happily at any time of day; I had seen it in a film.

Why should I not dance with one of them and thus practise dancing? No sooner thought than I rose, and the woman (she must have been about forty) said: "Oh," in a kind of happy voice, and we danced a foxtrot (I think). I said: "Thank you," she said: "Dofvidaniya." It was friendly and nice.

I returned to the table to find Mr. Dobry pale with rage, his wife staring at the tablecloth. We left soon after. Driving back they maintained a terrible silence. At home he said: "Mademoiselle, women don't dance together. At least, women comme il faut [respectable] don't. My wife is rather unhappy about what you've done."

I noticed then (I was sleepy) that indeed his wife had left the living-room without saying good night.

"It is not done to dance with these girls, they are . . . they are women of loose morals, one does not frequent them."

"Then why do we sit all together in the same night club?" They were earning their living by dancing. We went there to dance. Where was the difference?

The next morning, the good-natured Dobrys had forgiven me, and teased me about my naïvety.

"You are too innocent, you must be careful, or you will be like a small plucked chicken in Belgium, men will take advantage of you," said the Consul, roguish.

We drove to the banks of the pleasant Sungari river. It was a warm, sunny day, though a hidden blade of cold concealed in the warmth, like a sunken knife. There must have been thousands of people on the shores of the river, sunning and bathing, and they were all Russian. As far as eye could stretch the river wound banks like chocolate ribbon, speckled with people. A brown and sunny feel was about; and yet there was a hidden terror, a never-let-go emotion clutching one, and I was to have it again later when I met Jews refugeed in Belgium, gone away from the death-in-life ghettoes and death traps of Germany and Poland, where in the next few years things were going to be more hideous than they had ever been in China. "Walls have e-a-ars," sang the Consul, as we returned from the Sungari river.

On the third day, telling me how nice it had been to put me up, the Consul and Madame Dobry saw me on the train.

"Be good, and behave yourself, and don't trust *anybody* in Europe, or you'll get hurt," was Madame's last admonition to me.

Of that train journey, the flashback postcard effects recur, and first of all Lake Baikal in the morning; the train conductor, a splendid Siberian, overpowering the seams of his stiff uniform, flinging a great laugh into my compartment with a "Lake Baikal", so that I do not miss it.

A rose-pink wilderness, the taiga, trees all whistlered, a smoky frieze of trunks clasped in pink mist and in each other's arms, a foggy line of roseate water, silent forks of birds, arrowing darkly the luminous pearl that is sky. This is Lake Baikal; the train stomps on, it makes a powerful steady sound, breaking the undulating forest that nestles it. The carriage sways. All through breakfast (for me only tea with jam, Russian style, for I cannot afford a full breakfast, I am counting the days and the money) Lake Baikal, through the window, stretches its pink palate yawn at a sky gradually blue, and then itself turns turquoise, and shuttered behind a forest suddenly overwhelming, dark pillars, swirl of bronze strewn leaves. Lake Baikal, rose of water among the trees, silent birds without a name winging soundless above it; the taste and smell of the bread and the jam-in-tea that morning.

I remember the stations, long hours of train between them. At one a barefoot boy, slyly, secretively, for one U.S. dollar sold me two beautiful ikons of wood; one, of the Madonna, with a copper crown beaten into the wood, a dark child in her arms; and the other a bearded Christ with the usual out-of-chest heart which always made Tiza cry: "How it must hurt, how it must hurt."

In the same soft-class carriage there were two Englishmen and one Frenchman. The Frenchman was in a compartment two away from mine, the Englishmen shared another compartment, I had one to myself all the way to Moscow. The Frenchman was a man with sad brown eyes and stomach ulcers; he was being repatriated for his health, and spent most of the time talking to me about his ulcers and his wife. We sat together for lunch and dinner in the restaurant car, and sometimes walked the station platforms together, when he showed me pictures of his wife and children. The two Englishmen also sat at our table, they joked, drank Scotch, a case of which they carried with them. Their jokes were incomprehensible. The Frenchman and myself were blank while they both guffawed at their own wit; "those Russkys", "the bolshies", calling each other loudly "comrade" after three days became boring.

The stations were much alike, generally deserted. Only occasionally were there people about, people no more poorly dressed than the White Russians in the cities of China, and certainly fatter. The Englishmen, walking up and down in their shorts, said loudly: "Look, the children haven't got shoes on." But I was not conscious of stark poverty, on the contrary. It wasn't as poor as China was by far, and China was my yardstick. As we proceeded westward there were more people in the stations, selling eggs or fruit, women with dark red cheeks, bright like polished apples, women like the Mongols, burnished and coppery, embroidered aprons tying in their bellies, embroidered kerchiefs round their heads.

At Chelyabinsk another family came into the soft-class carriage, an American engineer, his wife and son aged five. The man was tall, thin, and I never saw him smile.

Soon it was obvious that his wife and child were terrified of him, especially the child. Meals were ugly, the man staring at his son with hate-filled blue eyes. One day, as the child dawdled over his milk glass, the man held the glass and made the child drink the milk quickly, in great gulps. I shall never forget the boy's eyes over the glass rim; blue with black lashes, very much like his father's. Afterwards the child vomited the milk on the table, and his mother took him away. The Frenchman again took out his photographs, his wife was quite fat, her skirt hung badly; he gazed at her picture with mouth half open: "When we get to Moscow, I shall send her a cable."

We were a day and a night in Moscow. We were given rooms at the Hotel Metropole by Intourist. It was a magnificent palace with lofty pillars, vaulted ceilings, red carpets. I had a large room with red velvet curtains and a high, large bed with a canopy; there was a marble angel playing a lyre in one corner. I wanted a bath. I went downstairs, and asked for a bath, and forty minutes later a large strong woman attired in black, like a French soubrette, with a white lace cap, came into my room and dropped a curtsy. She then led me to the bathroom, which had a marble floor, mirrors, a gilt chair, an enormous tub filled with almost boiling water. Another curtsy as she left me. I plunged into the bath when the water became less hot. Through the window one could see many roofs with flat tiles, so unlike our curved Chinese tiles. New tall buildings, some new houses with bright glass windows. I liked the towel the maid gave me, it was as large as a bed sheet. I draped myself in it and washed my underwear in the bath water, and hung it in my room to dry. The bath cost me one valuda, about one U.S. dollar, and I gave a tip of forty cents, upon which another curtsy was dropped at me.

When I was dressed, I sought out my Frenchman, who was downstairs in the lunch room. There was an enormous table heaped with things to eat, a gargantuan spread. Boulders of beef, hills of cavair, mountains of piroushkys, avalanches of potato salad. After lunch Intourist gave us a guide, the Frenchman and I agreed to share costs. The lady guide, brisk in a black tailored suit and blouse, spoke excellent French and took us to see the Kremlin from outside, the St. Basilius Church, Lenin's tomb, some new workers' apartments, and the park. I liked the park best; there was a large swimming pool and any amount of young people, girls and boys, swimming and laughing and playing ball and diving in and out of the pool. Though it was cold, the sun shone brightly. I thought how wrong everything we heard in China about Soviet Russia was. In fact, people were nicer here than the Europeans in China. I saw women sweeping the park alleys, all in black, with boots on, and they smiled at me. On the street people also smiled. There were children about, fat and red. Something kept surprising me, it was to see white people working, waiting on me in the restaurant, thanking me, tidying rooms, sweeping, carrying my things, curtsying at me . . . In China, White Russians worked, but not as servants; White Russians were not really Europeans, they were refugees. Europeans sat in offices, drove in cars, grasped telephones masterfully, played tennis and polo, and always gave orders. Never had I really seen a white man do manual labour, except Otto, fiddling with engines, but that was a technical thing, and we all thought engines wonderful things which only white men could make. As I proceeded westwards, I saw more and more Europeans work, and soon it did not astonish me any more.

In Berlin I did not get down, the train only stopping for forty minutes, and it was early morning. A boy on the platform was pushing a trolley with buns and sandwiches. I was hungry and bought one. I gave him American money, and he said: "Not enough," and thus cheated me of a dollar when his bun probably cost only twenty cents. Then a man in uniform came in and said: "Heil Hitler!" and examined my passport. The train was being hosed down, and there was a loudspeaker somewhere bawling marching songs.

On again, through the European landscape, everything so diminutive, so neat, doll land, as if the world had shrunk, become tighter and smaller after the great empty wilderness of Siberia and the bigness of China.

And then Brussels, grey grey, small small, on an October day, and the taxi asking me fifteen francs to go from the station to the Metropole Hotel where the Cook's agent in Peking had told me to go. I said: "Too expensive," and he started shouting at me with that frightening coarseness which had already begun to startle me in Berlin. And then, on the platform, among the grim unsmiling hurrying people I saw someone looking round with that peculiar lift of the nose I recognized, my mother's nose.

"Grandfather," I called, "Bonpapa . . ." The nose turned in my direction, and the resemblance was striking. I was to get used to the Denis profile, the Denis mouth and eyes and their way of looking at one. I waved my hand. He came towards me slowly, very erect.

"Is it you?" he said.

"Yes, it is me."

"Have you had a good trip?"

"Yes."

The taxi man looked at me, then at the old man.

"It is my grandfather," I said.

"Ah yes, well, you owe me two francs, mademoiselle."

My grandfather majestically extracted two francs from a small leather purse he carried, meanwhile hooking his umbrella on his arm.

"There, two francs, and for nothing, monsieur," he said.

"Thank you, monsieur," said the taxi man.

"Of nothing," said my grandfather. "Another time, do not try to cheat innocent young girls, monsieur." Then he turned to me. "Let me look at you. "Yes . . ." He took me in. Then he said: "Well, I hope you won't be like your mother, and run away with a Chinese."

"No," I said, laughing, "I've just come from China, come to study here, grandfather. I certainly won't run away."

CHAPTER SIXTEEN

The Université Libre of Brussels, which I attended from October 1935 to July 1938, was one of the most progressive universities in Europe. It was committed to *le libre examen*, the free examination of any problem, untrammelled by previous beliefs or religious pressures. How such a free-thinking university could exist in deeply Catholic Belgium was one of the paradoxes of the liberal, enlighted 1930s, before the Second World War. In today's narrowing horizons, with its increasing intolerance, its almost perpetual witch hunts, covert if not expressed, I look back with nostalgia to those years in Brussels, where going to the University meant not only to study, but also ardent discussion, fervent, word-fiery debate on all topics, interminable argument about anything and everything. It also meant, most definitely, having opinions on everything, from abstract art to music to politics, and anyone who professed no opinion was apt to be crushingly regarded as colourless. There was a pantechnicon of student societies, from the Catholic through the liberals and socialists to the Trotskyists, the Communists, the Belgian Fascists, called Rexists. There were societies to safeguard the rights of the bald and others demanding votes for women in the Congo. There were fist fights, and once a year, in a grand spree, the students took over the city, paraded floats, broke some beer glasses and some windows, shocked the respectable, drew the curses of the clergy; it was a wonderful university, and I had a wonderful time.

Only a few days after I enrolled a Communist student tackled me about my politics; I told him: "None." He replied: "I am told you are a Trotskyist." "Never heard of him. Is he a Belgian?" He did not believe me. Yet it was true that in my large but patchy reading I had not come across the name of Trotsky. Later I was told who he was, but never mustered enough interest to read his books.

The atmosphere of the University was shot through with discussion; and I attended almost every debate. Here, here, at last, was the robust aliveness, the hot dispute that I had craved. When I had been there a week there were posters about lectures and protest meetings for the Abyssinian war. Twice every week, and sometimes every day of the week, meetings, lectures, concerts, forums at which lecturers, professors, visiting academicians, Ministers of State, participated, were held at the University. I wrote to Hilda: "Now I begin to understand what democracy means." I marvelled. Was it really true that one could say anything one wished, and not get tortured or beheaded? I could scarcely believe it. But here it was so. No secret police, pouring red pepper down one's nose . . .

The Scholarship Board was run by a charming nobleman, the Baron of Y —, who sat in an office at an enormous desk with a newspaper and a picture of his wife upon its glazed expanse. All the Baron Y — wanted was that we, his students, should give him no trouble and pass our examinations. I received fifteen thousand Belgian francs a year, which paid for books, tuition, food, lodging, everything. It was more money than I had ever had, not only enough to live on, to study, to buy books and clothes, but also to travel. Student travel was cheap in those years. I went to England, to France, to Italy, to Switzerland. My grandfather was indulgent. "It is good for the young to travel, to see the world, but don't run away too far." I kept up a stream of postcards to him, wherever I went, and it made him feel happy. I spent one-half of my holidays with him, in his old man's retreat for gentlemen and ladies, in Flanders, not far from Brussels. The slow, slow pace of the old man was sometimes irksome to me, but he was so kind that I put up with it. I learnt not to worry him, to walk slowly with him, to say yes and no while he talked and I thought of other things; he looked at me with pride, and never scolded me. I gave him the affection I had not given to my own mother; and I think he was happy during those three years, less lonely, able to boast about his granddaughter. It made my going away later all the more grievous to his spirit's spring. In a way it was very wicked of me, to make him love me, to look so pliant, obedient, placid, and then to leave him suddenly. For he was old, and could not understand why I never came back. He never understood. Before he died he wrote me an angry, Denis letter, breaking off his affection to me – and it was not possible for me to explain.

My grandfather took me to call on Aunt Lucy and her husband, General Henri Denis, who lived just off the Avenue Louise in Brussels. Henri Denis soon became Minister of Defence, and gave imposingly official dinners. As "the little cousin from China" I was often invited as a filler-in. Aunt Lucy, a kind, Spanish-looking, soft-hearted woman, took to me and with great kindness fed me as often as I wished. Because my Chinese dresses (I had had three silk ones made in the last year in China) evoked much admiration and made a conversation topic, I was a welcome guest. The Prime Minister, Paul Henri Spaak, whose cherubic round face has not changed in thirty years, was often the guest of honour. He already showed skilful mutability, a subtle confidence in himself, which made him the long-lived and able statesman he has remained. He was a socialist, or reputed so; and the diehards in the Belgian upper class, to which Henri and Lucy Denis belonged, prophesied disaster. To hear them one would have thought Spaak was some Chinese warlord or even a Red, ready to cut their throats while they were asleep ... Henri Denis said: "How imbecile they are." And anyway, the *haute bourgeoisie*, Baron so-and-so, Count so-and-so, came to dinner, and after a time all Henri Denis guests said that Spaak was "socialist but reasonable". I sat with them, listened to their comments, and never had an opinion except on China.

Aunt Lucy's only son, Jean, was a very popular young man, who belonged to the smart young set. He took me out several times, to dances and night clubs with young couples who talked about horses and winter vacations in Egypt, and the great merits of Hitler. For quite unlike the University, where Hitler was abhorred, the smart set was fanatic in its admiration of Hitler. Hitler may have his methods, they argued, and these methods, may not always have been savoury, but he knew how to deal with "the Reds", and Germany was getting on splendidly, and he also kept the Jews in their place, and because of those talents he could be forgiven small peccadilloes. "Between a very fascist country and a very communist one I would always choose fascism," said Jean and his smart set, with the air of enunciating some Confucian wisdom.

Meanwhile at the University during that year and the next two a good few Jewish students began to filter in, refugees from persecution in Germany; in whispers they would tell of the things that had been done to them, in the ghettoes of the German cities; of the things that were now being done to those still in the ghettoes. But only in stifled whispers, half-apologizing for being such a nuisance, for being the persecuted. They were in Belgium on sufferance, they must not give trouble, not make too loud a clamour . . . I became friends with several of these Jewish students and their families. They were so quick of mind, supple of understanding, always discussing ideas rather than things or people, and at the end of our talks they exploded in that clear, cleansing Yiddish laughter, flippant, self-derisive, with its undertone of desperate cheerfulness. They lived on the run, knew it, and every moment, with every cell of their body, made life precious, extravagant, for this was life before death. They studied with ferocious application; heard and made wonderful music with savage fervour, argued with all their intellect, poured themselves out into a cascade of living because they were so near to extinction, ignominious and sudden.

Their passion for knowledge swung me away from the smug, the self-satisfied, the mediocre; I got away from the upper class with its neighing laughter and its talk of horses and women; and the condescending small talk about China with the cousin from China, and the agreeableness of the glazed politeness overlaying the fetid cruelty; and the good time if one only remembered *not* to discuss Ideas; for any talk of the wrongs done, of national independence, or anything like that, and click click one heard the machine-guns clicking in their insolent clipped: "Tiens, tiens, intéressant," and soon they were ignoring the little cousin from China who had been so insolent talking about *their* cruelties; they were back to horses and races and the form of a cabaret dancer with marvellous legs; and the singular merits of Hitler and Mussolini "giving a lesson to those coloured bastards in Ethiopia . . ."

There were hours when I felt giddy as if somersaulting down a cobbled street, round and round, sometimes on my head, sometimes on my feet; on and on, turning cartwheels. My life had not changed, always I seemed condemned to these wide splits, plunging alternately in hot and cold, fascist and victim of fascism, upper class and refugee. I had had some training in the art of alternance, but had not thought that it would continue here in Belgium, that here too force of circumstance would keep me dissonant, fragmented, belonging to no one world; or if the Denis, now accepting me, made me feel of theirs, my heart was yet on the other side; in spite of me, in spite of my yearning to be respectable, successful, approved of at last, I would never really *become* respectable, approved . . . perhaps my mother was right, I had a "nostalgia for mud", a desire to be among the underdogs.

In the most expensive and exclusive of night clubs, with the usual ghostlike chandeliers and a lithe acrobatic woman doing terrific splits in a sexy act with two men, cruelty like a tiger slithered among us, and I choked, hearing the talk : "Me, I'm all for kicking these Yids in the teeth . . ." "Have you heard the joke about the circumcision ceremony?" "They're apes anyway, just climbed down from the trees . . ." At that time Italy was dropping bombs on Abyssinia and claiming that this was part of the civilizing mission in Africa, and a lecture by a certain professor had been given in a hall in Brussels proving that the cranium contents of Ethiopians was underdeveloped. I remember one day taking exception to a specially revolting story, supposed to be amusing, in which sex and sadism towards the "niggers" had been tastefully mixed for the amusement of the smart set which included three beautiful aristocratic young women, whose mothers had been brought up at the same convent as my mother. The raconteur was a young man of the Walloon nobility with long names dating back to the kingdom of Burgundy and owning castles along the river Meuse. This particular young man was deemed irresistible because whenever he was asked what he had done that day, "Eh bien, qu'as-tu fait aujourd'hui?" he would reply: "I've been on horseback," with a broad beautiful smile which set everyone roaring with laughter. They laughed and laughed, the women, heads thrown back, showing the cleft between their satin-stroked breasts. When he asked me to come riding with him I replied so rudely that the company froze. I went on making things worse by saying that I did not like jokes about Jews, niggers or Chinese, or any other human being, and I remember the astonished contempt with which the stupid and beautiful eyes of one of the women stared at me, as she then opened her lovely mouth to burst into more throaty, provoking laughter, at the end of which: "But how amusing she is, the little Chinese!" she cried.

This smart set was not particular to Belgium; it was found everywhere in Europe; later I was to meet some of its specimens in England. I became acquainted with it only because of the accident of my mother's birth in what is called a good bourgeois family, and the fact that Henri Denis was now a Minister of State. Henri and his wife Lucy were not like that. Henri was a liberal of the older tradition. "Negroes are people," was Henri Denis's favourite remark. "One day they will have machines, industries like us." He was a man of intelligence, logic and exactness; he called Hitler a madman, and the Belgian version of Hitler, a man called Degrelle (who had organized the Rexists, something like the Nazi Brownshirts in Germany and Chiang Kaishek's Blueshirts in China, and who marched his cohorts up and down the streets of Brussels as Oswald Mosley paraded his adherents in London), "a first-class imbecile".

The students of the University were mostly anti-fascist. This was 1935, 1936, the years of the Front Populaire, of socialism, of Arthur Koestler, of demonstrations, for Abyssinia and for Spain. The young were fervently bent on peace, heroic in their faith that the will to peace would guarantee peace, while their world was being set on the course to war. How invincible youth looked at that moment, how convincing the slogans of "No more war", and how pitiful it all was, as day by day one watched the heart of peace corrupted from within, eaten away from the inside, and the apparatus of war and the appetite for savagery condemned the young who clamoured for Peace into the khaki liveries of slaughter. There was Abyssinia, and the League of Nations doing its usual verbal acrobatics and nothing else about it, as was the case for Japan in China. Sir John Simon kept running about, the French Foreign Minister ran about, many speeches were being made, the newspapers affirmed that sanctions would bring Mussolini to heel, and slow sanctions were recommended which were meant to be ineffective, devised to be ineffective, as today in the case of Rhodesia.

The young still believed that legalism would eliminate war, that the League of Nations could do something. They were not aware of the realities of power, of the military industrial complexes, the alliance between Army and Money, the monopolies, everywhere pushing to carnage. They denounced Krupp, the arms monopolies, but felt their own desire for Peace a Citadel strong enough to stop war. A young Jewish lawyer named Bachrach, a gentle idealist, lectured to us telling us how useful the League of Nations had been in preventing this or that conflict, and all the time all the time Abyssinia was going on and Spain was beginning, and all the time Japan was continuing its invasion of China. Bachrach, as a Jew, had been ill treated in Germany and run away, but when someone said to him: "Will it happen here, in Belgium or in France?" he would reply: "Never, never. Here there is democracy. We must defend it, we shall." But still he deluded himself and us with hope where hope had gone, or rather, had never existed.

Today, I am reminded of Bachrach, of his faith in the League of Nations, that abortion; for since then we have had the United Nations – it too murdered by secret treaties, which negated all the fine pious hypocrisies baptizing its birth. Bachrach's candid eyes, his soft fluid Talmudic speech so grammatically precise, pouring the soothing murmur of his faith in Humanity, in Legality . . . so many were like him then, in our University of Brussels. Because they hated violence, they thought their hatred was enough to guarantee non-violence, because they had a will to peace, they were convinced this will to peace was enough to guarantee peace – oh tremendous illusion! oh error of errors! They all went to war in the end and many died, and today I wonder, my companions of those years, my friends of those years, all the wise guys and all the silly ones, the Communists and Fascists, those that sang "À bas la calotte" and the Internationale then got married in church and became businessmen; and those who shouted "Heil Hitler" and today are suave, prosperous businessmen talking of democracy and indignant because Germany is up again and wanting to rearm . . . I wonder now, whether you remember yourself when young?

One thing that stood out clearly to me in those days was the arrogance of some of the young Communists, or would-be Communists, at the University: an arrogance which I have never found among the Communists of China, but which, today, I still find among those disdainful intellectuals who proclaim themselves Communists in France, in other Western countries, yet have long forsaken by compromise the issues they claim to uphold. This does not apply to all; I met others who said little, were modest, laconic, and self-sacrificing, and most of these died in the torture chambers of Hitler, or were shot when the Gestapo took over Belgium, or went to the terrible death camps. But those who were arrogant, sure of their own superiority I have watched them, clever at survival, turn and turn about, turn coat and save themselves. In those years at the University of Brussels, I entered no organization, gave adherence to no party, refused to be convinced into any set programme of ideas. "This is very feminine of you, you are entirely non-intellectual," some said to me. This was true. I listened, I read, I argued, but more to find out what the reply would be than out of passionate conviction. Chiefly I listened; it would take me a long, long time, many years, before I could profess any belief in anything, before I would make up my mind.

In the winter of 1935 and the spring of 1936 the invasion of Abyssinia was proceeding at a gallop. In Brussels there was an exhibition of Abyssinian art, lectures by eminent experts, for and against the Ethiopians, student debates and resolutions passed by the student organizations against Fascist Italy. It did not require a political education to sympathize with the persecuted against barbarism, even when it disguises itself as a "civilizing mission". And then the war in Spain began, and overshadowed the Abyssinian war, and engaged the total attention of the student body. I remember trying, at one debate on Spain, to mention China, and the Japanese invasion in China. But my interruption was brushed aside. It was obvious that the "Far East", by its very name, was beyond the rim of emotional involvement. The International Brigade was formed, to fight against Franco, and some young writers from England went, and also some students from Brussels University went off to fight in Spain. Later in Paris, as one of many students in a delegation to a great Peace Meeting which took place there, I was to watch La Passionaria, and an ex-president of the Popular Front of Spain, making speeches. Wonderful, vibrant their voices; and oh the deafening clamour of applause, the multitudes parading with banners against war! But it could not shake the very system by which war was wrought. For the great armament combines were doing very well, very well indeed, and they would soon do even better. I thought the best thing I could do was to volunteer to look after the refugee Basque children. The Basques had been dreadfully bombed; it was after Guernica; whole populations had been slaughtered by German and Italian planes, who were trying out their equipment in Spain, and all the speeches of the League did nothing to stop them. There were two hundred Basque orphans at the rest centre where I worked for a short while, boys and girls under twelve. Dishing out their meals in metal plates, taking them for walks, was all one could do. As they walked they sang, marvellous songs, keeping time easily, marching to the song's beat. "They sing revolutionary songs they learnt when their parents were alive," someone told me. They were handsome, swift, thin, with bright eyes and naked brown legs. The Belgian women brought clothes for them, we sorted these out by sizes. The Belgians were overwhelmed by the Basque children's vivacity, some complained the children were rude and uncivilized and relieved themselves on the road. But other Belgian women wanted to adopt them. There was a committee to provide money for them; the Red Cross was active. The bland face of charity was enacted for them; I wonder what became of them later.

On the other hand the reports of Stalin's purges and the Siberian camps were splashed in the newspapers. As Simone de Beauvoir wrote in her book, *Les Mandarins*,* these reports shook the left wing, induced that climate of doubt and confusion which was to bedevil political action in the European Left for many decades. Here were the horrors perpetrated by the fascist powers upon the Ethiopians, the Jews, the Spaniards. From there came the ominous rumours of what was happening to the Communist Old Guard in Russia; the confessions of some of them were openly debated at the University. Uncommitted, except at the point where everyone becomes committed, which is the boiling point of indignation and revolt at injustice, I escaped the mental traumas of that period, but some of my friends went through great agony of mind. I remember a grey-bearded professor who stood up to say: "Bukharin was my friend, my great friend. I cannot believe that he was a traitor, a hidden spy and saboteur. I cannot believe this." I listened, I listened, all ear and no voice. Yet it seemed to me more truthful to say: "I don't know, I can't make up my mind," than to be peremptory on a handful of words. "But you must have an opinion, everyone *must*," someone cried at me. "I have, I think it's wrong of Italy to invade Ethiopia, wrong of Japan to invade China, wrong of the League of Nations not to do anything about Spain, but don't ask me more, not yet."

I was not sure of my own thinking; I wanted to be sure, absolutely sure. The apparatus of opinion-forming by demon-

* Gallimard, 1954. English translation, *The Mandarins* (Collins, 1957).

strations did not appear to me as foolproof as all that. I could see that although in the University the opinion was overwhelmingly anti-Franco, yet the "good bourgeois", the people outside the University, the smart set and many of the government's socialist members, thought highly of Franco. I also realized that a lot of energy and fervour could be exhausted in mere talk and that action must follow resolution. In China, where talk was not free as it was here, people *had* to resort to action, and perhaps this was a good thing. But I did not voice these heretic opinions for I would have been called all sorts of names. My brilliant fervent friends at Brussels University would never have understood that I was trained in a hard, warlord school, and therefore naturally understood Power and the mailed fist, but not democratic legalism . . .

Yet I knew that *words* are never enough to operate change, that the parliamentary and legal processes of debate and opposition, so headily believed in by so many at that time, and which I also discovered with such pleasure (but which never convinced me of their omnipotence), were actually a small delusion, True, I loved that sensation of freedom, but I was not convinced, as Bachrach was, that it would really bring about the eviction of Mussolini from Ethiopia, Japan from China, nor that it would turn the tide of war in Spain. For Power remained in the hands of those for whom profit was all, and human lives and suffering nothing, and after the verbiage, they would move in for the kill, and they had the apparatus of slaughter in their hands. And in that strange, horrific, dichotomy of word and deed even the word "peace" became a sinister farce.

Some of the newspapers told us, right down to 1938, that there would not be another war, because the "desire for peace" of the people was so strong. Henri Denis lamented that the young conscripts in the Belgian army and the officers lacked stamina and the will to fight. Youth, the Catholic papers deplored, was on pleasure bent. Of course they discounted the young who went off to join the International Brigade and to die in Spain. Picasso painted Guernica, the factory workers struck for Spain; they truly felt they would save the world from fascism. Meanwhile the newspapers went on praising Japan for its "firm stand against communism", the Rexists paraded in Brussels, and Hitler's shadow grew greater by the day, engulfing Europe. Abyssinia was taken by Italy and the farce of the sanctions which were never meant to function was played ad nauseam to a world rapidly growing in cynicism and moral degradation. Haile Selassie fled to England and was entertained at a literary luncheon given by Foyle's. But nothing *real* was done, nothing really *was* done. And even then, in 1936, after a few months in Belgium my warlord-trained instinct knew there was going to be war. "There will be a world war," I said, "I can smell it coming." I was immediately accused of *wanting* war, and of being a Fascist!

But so are the silly constituted, that when unpleasant facts are stated to them, they stone the person who states them. So I shut up. And then I decided that perhaps I was wrong, all wrong. "You are not an intellectual," they said to me. And it was true. I was now pulverized; I sat back, docile, and accepted, accepted vagueness, inchoateness.

And now I think that it was better so, a growth delayed. For a long time, I would be seeking Verity, like Lao Tze, and finding its fragments scattered, until one day wholeness would be restored. But until then: to know all truths approximate, dependent on a sum of knowledge in constant flux; to accept all situations as unstable, and nothing constant but change; to practise trust and honesty, but demand from others no corresponding or similar virtue; to balance prudent suspicion with trust, to see hope in destructive despair – to pluck good fortune from calamity, and know but one thing surely: that the main stem of the tree of life has always climbed towards the sun of greater awareness, and that no matter how great the persecution is, the blessed verity of life itself will triumph in the end – this, which is the Chinese wisdom of living, inherent in me though I knew if not, was now, in Europe, to grow; by contrast and opposition, to strengthen in me quietly, unknown to myself. And so, though at times, like Teilhard de Chardin, I could exclaim: "Lo, where truth was, the likeness of her, and where day was, the likeness of the night," yet fortitude knew also the reverse, and was content to wait, demanding of the earth but one thing: to live each day its sum of added knowledge, and reach whatever wisdom it was in me to attain.

While I was thus engaged in this external and internal and far-ranging and raging debate, I met again Leila Hua, whose brother, Simon Hua, I had last seen in Shanghai in the summer of 1934. Leila was beautiful. The Belgian students raved about her flawless skin, enormous eyes, raven blue-black hair. She had a Jumpy figure, but this did not disconcert in a land where stockiness was prevalent. My first impression was of her conceit, and as

I never accepted meekly being pushed around it made friendship impossible. Leila had become a member of the Communist Party, and within twenty minutes launched into a diatribe about my lack of political sense, then categorically pronounced on art, literature, science, politics and architecture. Since I was ignorant of art, literature, politics, and architecture, I listened, but not happily. Soon we were rivalling in intransigence. She talked categorically of Marx, Lenin, and it made me averse to reading Marx, Lenin, or indeed anything connected with superior young people like Leila who snubbed me so hard. I would see how they turned out, I promised myself. Neither was I more attracted by the active recruiting of the Rexists and other fascist groups; they awoke only disgust in me, they were so vile, so filthy in their abuse of anyone who did not think as they did, and so obviously sadistic.

I shall always remember a Rexist meeting, to which some right-thinking Belgian friends took me. It was in a large hall in the centre of Brussels. The hall was crowded. A platoon of middle-aged women marched in; they had on hunting skirts and felt hats, their chins were up, their right hands raised in the Hitler salute; Léon Degrelle, the Belgian fascist leader, climbed the rostrum. He made a speech, each paragraph ended with the words: "and so Rex . . ." and the large packed audience, particularly the women grouped round him, screamed the final, apotheotic word: "Vaincra!" (shall triumph!)

"Young fools," said Henri Denis. But among his son's friends were a good many who said: "He isn't bad, this Léon Degrelle, at least he will help us give the Reds one of those kicks in the —" "Between a fascist or a communist country, I would prefer a fascist one, any day," they repeated.

What preocuppied Aunt Lucy most, however, was not Stalin, Spain, Abyssinia, or even the perpetual language dispute between Flemish and Walloons which still goes on today, but the romance between Wallis Simpson and the King of England. This actually took more space in the Belgian newspapers than anything else. Aunt Lucy asked me to lunch, especially to hear the announcement on her radio set of the King of England's abdication. We listened as the well-bred voice read the prepared speech. Then Aunt Lucy cried softly. Another heart-searing event was the death of the Belgian King's beautiful wife, Queen Astrid, for which Aunt Lucy, being the wife of the Minister of Defence, wore black for a long tine. Henri Denis in 1937 became suddenly very preoccupied with the defence of Belgium; all the talk was now of the Maginot Line, which was being extended to Belgium; and there was outcry because someone said Belgium must have fortifications to resist attack, either from Germany or France. This made the Walloon separatists, who wanted friendship, or reunion with France, very angry. They roared that France would never attack Belgium, any aggression would come from Hitler. But the Flemish extremists, the Rexists, and the Catholics were pro-Hitler and anti-France, and it was said that many people at the king's court were also, secretly, pro-Nazi. "And they have the support of influential people in England," said Aunt Lucy. "So-and-so, so-and-so, they are all for Hitler. Because, at least, he will protect us from the Reds." Henri Denis, as Minister of Defence, had a hard time, being insulted by both sides.

Aunt Lucy made me physically comfortable. Not only was excellent food in vast quantities served at her table, but she asked me to her country house in the Ardennes. I spent a week-end there, in the dank forest, fawn-haunted, and wondered that trees were so enormous, and flowers could grow so large. Another holiday at Le Zoute, the then fashionable seaside resort, was also contrived by Aunt Lucy. She found me too thin; wanted to fatten me up; her dinners had fourteen courses including the most wonderful pâté de foie, and I ate as much as anyone.

One evening Aunt Lucy and Uncle Denis met me with a young man, Louis. Louis was a University student who for the three years I was there was my steady friend, and who wanted to marry me. We had gone together to the concert hall, to hear some symphony orchestra. "Are you going to marry him? He is very handsome, your young Walloon solicitor," said Aunt Lucy. "I don't know." "If he's rich, you'll have a happy life." "He is not rich." "Ah," said Aunt Lucy. And then gushingly: "But a solicitor, if he's good, can become very well off, especially if he's got a good family background." She would have been shocked had she known that marriage was not what I worried about.

My grandfather was more abrupt. "You have not ended your studies. When you are a doctor . . . oh then, you can pick and choose. But marriage and a profession do not go together. If I were you, I would not think of marriage for at least ten years . . ." "I am not thinking of marriage, bonpapa." And it was true, though I toyed with the idea, as I played with other ideas, as I visited museums. Louis was handsome and young, and much in love with me. We were both at the University . . . what more could a young girl want? Especially when I passed my examinations so well, and both the first and the second year achieved a Great Distinction. The Baron of Y — was highly pleased. "You are the best student we have had so far; your record alone justifies the merit of what we try to achieve," he ended, pontifical.

Louis was in his third year in the Law Faculty when I met him, which happened within the first three months of my attending the University. A Walloon, he was a member of the Walloon separatist movement, which asserted that Wallonie was part of France, and wanted a reunion with France. Since my Belgian relatives were Flemish Catholic, made a point of speaking Flemish and disliked the Walloons, calling them freemason and anti-clerical, I found it amusing that Louis should be so different. This relationship, which lasted the whole time I was in Belgium, and soon took the form of an unofficial engagement, was exactly what I wanted. I wanted calm, order, steadiness. I did not want adventure, promiscuity, flitting about. Passion in me is prosaic; perhaps because I have never looked upon a man as an ideal human being, or an acquisition. Perhaps because I could not really begin to love until very much later.

When the end of my relation with Louis came it had nothing to do with love, but with an issue far removed from our personal lives.

But if I was clear in what I wanted, what I needed, and how far I was prepared to go, it was not the same with Louis. In the beginning, I think he was pleased and happy at the feeling of being noticed by someone different; someone with an "oriental" appeal. Then came the second phase: he felt emotionally involved; and as so many European men do, revolted against "being caught". I learnt then that men in the West are profoundly afraid of emotion, hating to accept the bond it creates and its responsibilities, afraid to the very marrow of being hurt. The moment Louis felt himself in love, he wanted to break away brutally because he said he did not want to be dominated, to be "burdened". He told me so. He told me I had won. Won what? I stored the information in my mind, and never really forgave him, for I had felt greatly hurt in my pride. "Never, never," I swore, "will I allow myself to be let down. I'll always break first."

Louis treated me with a surface courtesy and deference which does not exist in Asia. But what was the use of opening doors for me or pulling out a chair, if in another way he did not respect my ideas? Why should I be ready to leave my study and do what he

309

wanted to do, when I wanted to read, or talk with someone else? He could accept feminine caprice, but he could not accept intellectual absorption in something other than himself. When he could regard me as a weaker being, subject to vacillations, not knowing my own mind, wayward, and possibly treacherous, he was all indulgence to me. That I was none of these things, but that I could forget his existence for a debate, a book, was to him a continued and irritable astonishment.

I announced to him that I would be going to England for a fortnight, to visit some friends who had invited me. It was the truth; he did not believe it. "You might be going on some adventure, or with someone . . ." "But I would tell you if I did," I replied. The idea that I might have to lie had not occurred to me. Later, I realized that this suspicion of a woman's motive is common, is even expected in the Latin male context. But it hurt me.

When Louis insisted on coming with me to the railway station it annoyed me more. And then he insisted on kissing me when putting me on the train, which was so silly. Then he walked by the train side for a while. All this exhibition, quite natural to a Latin, annoyed me intensely. All this simply because I was going to England, which was across a little bit of sea, nothing at all. "Why," I said, "in China I travel three days in a train and don't think anything about it; and I've come all the way from Peking here, nearly sixteen days in a train, and that's nothing . . . and you make a fuss about my crossing the Channel, which is just a small canal to me."

"But why should you want to go to England merely to see friends, if you are not deeply attached to them?"

"But I like friends; and besides I'm curious, I want to see a new country."

When I returned, Louis sulked, and left me at dinner to continue my meal alone. I was upset, but two days later he was back repentant. Some months later, again he suddenly decided that he was too much in love with me, that this strangled him, that he had to do something about it, and leave me. This time it did not worry me. I knew he would get over it. He did; my very indifference made him more attached and suddenly he began to accept me just as I was.

CHAPTER SEVENTEEN

I had met Dr. Barbour at the Peking Union Medical College. He was a geologist, a friend of Davidson Black and Père Teilhard de Chardin. He had needed a secretary to type his reports; Olga had asked me to do it: "That will earn you some extra money!" Dr. Barbour was a quiet, gentle-voiced man, with timid brown eyes, who did not frighten me. He was very pleased with my typing; I was fast and could take dictation direct on the typewriter. He paused frequently, pulling on his pipe. I worked for him for about two weeks; he paid me handsomely and invited me to dinner. When I was in Belgium, he wrote to me: would I come for a few days to stay with him and his family in England?

To England I went, autumn of 1936. It was difficult to obtain a visa; s udents from Brussels University, especially Chinese students, were not welcome in England. That was because of the demonstrations against the war in Spain, the socialist trend among students in both France and Belgium, the fact that in May 1936, in China, a League of National Salvation had been organized, and the Chinese students in London had sponsored such a meeting. There had also been some large meetings for peace in London, and all that was for peace was considered Red, communist. When I went to apply for a visa at the British Consulate in Brussels, a bland, clean-shaven, insolent young man, of the same breed that continues till the present day to combine ignorance with superciliousness, seemed convinced that my aim was to blow up Buckingham Palace, or attend peace meetings, and he refused to give me a visa. However, Dr. Barbour wrote a letter, and then I received a visa. I vomited my way across the Channel, and the first thing that struck me on landing in England was the extreme cold for which I was unprepared. On the map, England was in the same latitude as Belgium; and I had heard about the Gulf Stream, and how brisk and mild the climate of England was, but England was quite different from its reputation. It was raw and dank, the air held a million clammy fingers of cold insinuating under my dress, my feet were perpetually damp in the thin shoes I wore, and though Hyde Park was green, it was also very wet. It neither rained, nor did not rain, it was just wet all the time.

The Barbours lit a fire for me (they were quite warm in woollies, it was September), and I began well, eating copiously. I found myself perpetually hungry and could understand my mother much better, when she told of being so hungry in England. Mrs. Barbour was a very nice woman, motherly, comfortable, who wanted me to be happy. In the next few days I was taken by the Barbours to the countryside, and marvelled at the grass, so green, so green, at the modulated, prim, controlled, man-fashioned landscape, where nothing was gigantic but everything tame, wizened, modest, almost to parsimony, even the mountains were hills. I did the sights of London, found the Thames too narrow, would not believe it to be the Thames until twice assured it was, was astonished that this small and rather dirty leaden water rolling its murk could be the Thames, and never got tired of strolling by it, to catch its elusive fascination. I found the Tower of London much too low, Windsor Castle baffling, Buckingham Palace odd and the changing of the Guard neither amusing nor impressive.

Was this really England, whose mighty name had shaken our hearts in Asia, with terror and fear at her power? Thi narrow, grey, cold little island with rather dirty houses and gentle, kind people, hurried intent people, harassed by the greyness and the wetness of their island? Polite people, shy people, and so many poor, so many poor, when I had thought the streets of London paved with gold . . . I could scarcely believe it when salesgirls thanked me for purchasing some extra handkerchiefs (I had a cold). I had come prepared to find a nation of supermen and superwomen, something like a perpetual viceregal pageant; and I found a country of ordinary men and women, far less well nourished than the Belgians, with children pale and scrawny. The paucity and inferior quality of the cooking depressed me. I lost my fear, wondered that so many Asians should remain in the habit of subjection to the West; why, if we in China were well organized, I thought, we could do much better. And so I lost my fear of England, and fell in love with it, precisely because it was such a sham, so poor and grey and wet and dirty . . . and yet its people put up with all these discomforts. And it was in England that I knew myself just as good as anyone else, liking and dis-liking individuals on their own. Even more quickly did I fall in love with the English language, that rich and inexhaustible treasure of moods and music, feeling and thought, endless ambrosia, a firm enchantment, lifelong.

I found the intellectual content of conversation in England far less logical and precise than in Belgium. The equivocation, the hints and indirections, were baffling and designed to create a perpetual mind fog, in which one lived, and somehow it made one comfortable, thus to proceed by fumble. Very quickly I found out that the best way to deal with arrogance when and if met with in England (and of course it existed) was a return insolence, a jab so swift but accompanied by such an amiable smile that the other person was bereft of any cause of complaint. "Never hesitate, punch them, and they will respect you." They did have a sporting spirit in England, I felt, perhaps because they did not flap about non-essentials, and though cheating was part of the game, they were phlegmatic about being cheated. Whereas a Frenchman or a Belgian would carrry a grudge loudly, an Englishman would wait to catch you out. It was simple, once one knew them, knew when to trust and when not to trust their ingenious machiavellian English minds, as rich a treasure trove of deviousness as their language is of metaphor. A gifted and creative people, and I mourn that history, and inept politicians, have brought this nation to the ineptitude and moral lowness of today.

My weeks in England with the Barbour family were extremely happy, in spite of the cold, the damp, the drizzle, the food, and the furious postcards which Louis addressed to me. Mrs. Barbour was so motherly that I broke down, and confided to her my pain over my own mother, the enormous, separating impossibility between us; Mr. Barbour took me to the British Museum; I went to the National Gallery and started to understand Western painting. The only thing that eluded me, and still does, is Greek sculpture. The eye of beauty in me had dwelt upon Chinese artistic production, and later was to take perfectly to Indian sculpture. I had already been to the Louvre, there to contemplate, arduously, the fig-leafed or draped bodies along the ample halls, in the sieved light of a long afternoon. A stance in front of Venus de Milo had produced in me only this one reflection: "the head is an afterthought." On the glorious body, the torso's abandon, all care had been expended; and as a result bellies were far more expressive than faces; buttocks more intelligent than cheeks. But the head, the face was always the same, with blind stupid eyes, unyielding straight nose, perfect imbecile mouth. The neck was always not quite rightly set upon the body, and these vapid curls . . . after thirty years, and more museums than I can remember, I still remain on this my first impression; in so

313

many of these statues the head means nothing. When I came upon the Victory of Samothrace, I was happy, stupefied with its power and grace . . . for she was headless, otherwise who knows but the sight of the perfect movement might have been obfuscated for me by the sightless stare of a bland face?

The most interesting encounter during those weeks was with the Oxford Group. The Barbours belonged to it. I attended a session, and it was very unlike anything Catholic, somewhat like a Christian Fellowship meeting in Yenching University, with tea and eatables too, but without the singsong. There were many velvet-covered chairs, in which people, mostly adults, sat calmly. It was in someone's house, and a man named Peters made a short speech on absolute honesty, absolute purity, absolute faith, absolute love. Then a duchess (perhaps my memory is at fault, but she was a Lady somebody, possessed unshatterable English upper-class diction) told us about her sins. In the Duchess's catalogue of sins there were no concrete, factual details; she merely kept repeating that she'd done "all sorts of naughty things" without specifying which kind of naughty things. And now God's message came to her, she listened, all was well. Somehow I gathered that the Oxford Group was pacifist; the next morning, before breakfast, I too, with the Barbours, tried "listening" to God. Alas, He did not say anything in the silence to me, and gradually one persistent demand welled up from me during that ruminative hour: "When are we going to eat I am hungry." But since I could not get up and confess that the only message I received was about breakfast, I had to keep quiet.

Some days later Mr. Peters came to tea, a tall, handsomely ascetic young man with great powers of persuasion. We started talking about China and Japan, but soon it was obvious that we were not really talking of the same thing at all. I tried to tell him about Japan and China and the worry that Japan might take all China, and he said that China could give an example to the whole world by *not* fighting at all, laying down arms, letting Japan do her worst, and reciprocating with "absolute love". I felt more worried than ever when he had said that, and when, somehow, I gathered this was what was meant by pacifism. Because that was not what I meant. I had rather idly called myself a pacifist, thinking this meant someone who loves peace, but I was not prepared for peace at all costs. Then, as now, people, students not excepted, have a mania for pigeon-holing someone – a most tiresome inclination, since it neither explains the contradictory

314

in a person, nor allows for the growth of a concerned human being. I had decided to call myself, for the sake of not having to explain my lack of opinion and tire the muscles of my tongue, a pacifist, which sounded to me the least compromising of all labels, and which had the beautiful advantage of not being an *Organization*. One did not have to attend meetings, or even emit opinions, one merely had to say, when people became irksome and boring: "I am a pacifist," and this was enough. The word conveyed to me the flavour of non-cruelty to animals, and refusal to kill man. It was a label against all labels. But now I was being confronted by real pacifism in the shape of Peters asking me to let the Japanese trample all over China in the name of Peace. This was too much. The previous evening I had been to see some other friends, the Turners. They were actually a mixed couple, the husband a Welshman, the wife a Cantonese from Hongkong. We had met in Brussels at the World Fair, and while I was with the Barbours I rang them up. They had invited several Chinese students who were at that time studying in England and we had all eaten some food cooked by Mrs. Turner. Among the Chinese students was my future husband Pao, whose full name was Tang Paohuang.

After the excellent Chinese food we had talked of war and peace, naturally. Mr. Turner said that there was a systematic over-optimimism among the Left, which contributed to fascist temerity, and vastly encouraged it. The communist parties, he said, were repeating that the "workers" of Germany would never follow Hitler in a war. Yet already Hitler's armies had re-occupied the Rhineland in March of that year. In England, too, the mood was one of peace, and war was declared inconceivable. "You're just like Churchill," said someone. "He can't get over the First World War, and he's dying to get another one going." "But there is a war in Asia," I interjected, and was met with that vague, opaque look of the sleep-walker, I felt almost guilty saying such a thing. I was not in favour of "peace", therefore I was pro-Hitler. And then Pao said something to a lady next to him who was talking of the Gospel, and how one must learn to love the Germans. "We may love our enemies, but we must fight them first," he said. And this made me look at him and smile. Pao was handsome, with a nice smile, beautiful hands. The muddle-headedness which equates victim and aggressor, exploited and exploiter, good and evil, and talks of "peace" which is only surrender, appeasement, was in the air, in Europe, in England.

Anyone who talked of a possible conflict was called a warmonger, as Churchill was. In China, too, whoever talked of resisting Japan was dubbed a Communist and liable to jail or shooting.

And this confusion in Europe was due to a natural revulsion from the horrors of the First World War. "We must avoid even believing that there could be a war," said many well-meaning people.

Yet in October 1935, there had been the bombing of Ethiopia and the "slow sanctions" of the League asked for by Laval of France had in no way diminished the Italian onslaught; in February 1936, Italian armies had entered Addis Abbaba, and nothing had been done.

In August 1936 war had started in Spain. And in France, the socialist Prime Minister Léon Blum had acquiesced in non-intervention in Spanish affairs, which meant stopping arms and weapons to the Spanish Government from the democracies, but *not* stopping Hitler and Mussolini from sending arms to Franco! And in October 1936 the King of the Belgiums, realizing that war was coming, wanted to end the alliance with France and England, for he said this alliance did not protect him from the mechanized forces of Hitler. "We are alone, though protected in theory," said Henri Denis. He was to become more gloomy as the months brought war even closer.

Step by step war was being prepared. I saw Léon Blum at a great rally for peace in Paris, his droopy moustache and elegant diction filled me with astonishment. Could one really trust this man, with his tortuous phraseology? What was really his view of the world? But for the first time the working class of France were receiving paid holidays; the forty-hour week was proclaimed and this appeared an apotheosis of working-class triumph. If they could achieve this, of course there would be no war. Lulled by these concessions to the workers, that summer had seen a wonderful exodus; for the first time workmen and their families going to the beaches to have a holiday. But actually it was a hollow panoply of triumph, it weakened still further the will to resist fascism; it made it appear that it was sufficient to stand on a platform and denounce the employers, the bourgeois, fascism, for them to cave in . . . It was a bribe and it worked. Meanwhile fascism was marching on to real triumphs in Italy, in Germany, in Spain, spreading its phalanxes in every country. And still, and persistently, whenever someone like myself said: "But there will be war, and in Europe too" (and I was only talking from instinct,

316

because I could smell the wind of war, smell the fetor of future death, trained as I was to smell the mind of power, unblinded by the shining deceptions of parliamentary legalism), one was denounced as a fascist, or a reactionary, and told that even to talk of war was to bring it on. "How can you doubt of the mighty power of Soviet Russia and her will to peace? To doubt Russia is to aid fascism." That was what the left wing said.

And now here in England I was being told that real will to peace was to let Japan do what she wanted . . . "Yes, we must fight them first," I thought. And that ended pacifism for me.

On my return to Belgium, there was a recrudescence of meetings as the University opened. There were impressive demonstrations, films showing Léon Blum, the French Prime Minister, with his drooping moustache. The forces of peace did look massive, invincible . . . they shall not pass, *no pasaràn*, La Passionaria, the crowds, the paid holidays . . . and even then at the core of it all, a thorough muddle-headedness; for the will to peace is not the same thing as enforcing peace; to clamour "they shall not pass", when at the same time Léon Blum, the socialist, allowed the German and Italian planes to bomb the cities of Spain, while he refused under the principle of non-intervention to supply arms to the Spaniards fighting against Franco, was not to work for peace. To assemble the League of Nations and call for sanctions which everyone knows very well will not be applied, while announcing at the same time that one does not intend to fight aggression, is not the way to peace. All this happened in 1936; and all the time America, having declared her "neutralism", was actively supplying seventy-five per cent of Japan's military needs in her aggression in China; and England, that parliamentary democracy, was dangerously near to making a deal with Hitler, and Chiang Kaishek was imprisoning anyone who demanded resistance against Japan.

How hoaxed we were, how deceived! All those who marched to say there would be no war had war thrust upon them. Today it looks as if the lesson had still not been learnt; for once more the world is going towards another war, and once more the peoples are lulled by a dreadful lullaby of "peace" which is capitulation, which is surrender, and those who, like Winston Churchill then, call for a facing of realities, are called warmongers, as he was . . .

Simone de Beauvoir, that honest woman, expresses it best, when she relates in her autobiography how: "No one then felt how all the parts of the world held together . . . the Sino-

Japanese war, the Gandhi campaign in India – only moderately touched us . . ." She too greeted the "appeasement" of Munich with ease of heart; with happiness; really believing that this meant *Peace*; and failing to see that to sacrifice and jettison principles and human beings whether far away or near is a crime against humanity, against peace . . . she relates how, talking to the Intellectual Herbaud (whom years later, in 1958, I found as limited as Simone de Beauvoir did in 1938, a goldfish in a goldfish bowl, loth to comprehend anything outside the narrow hobble of the Left Bank in Paris), he said to her: "Any sacrifice is worthy if it maintains the type of democracy that one finds, for instance, in England" . . . This Europocentrism, the universe of man reduced to a small Europe, that is still the vileness, selfishness, disease which consumes and will destroy Europe one day. I felt this arid vice at the core of all that was said and done during those years 1935–8, hence nothing surprises me in what happens today, a dreadful repetition of the past.

When I had been two weeks in Brussels my grandfather took me to Antwerp to see his brother Eugène Denis. For the visit my grandfather dressed with special care. "You understand, it is not my brother, but his wife; she is very comme il faut, she would not like my cap." Habitually Grandfather wore a tweed cap as most railway engineers do, as my father did. He had worn the cap even when taking me the first time to call on General Henri Denis and his wife Lucy; but when he went to Antwerp he wore a homburg, and held himself more than usually erect, in a stiff starched collar and a tie with a pearl pin. He then looked like the photograph of him which my mother had at home, sitting in pinstripe trousers and cutaway, a carnation in his buttonhole. The pearl tiepin was the same as in his photo at home, his umbrella was furled as impeccably as a Englishman's.

I put on my hat; it was blue, purchased at the Uniprix off the Porte de Namur, at a sale, and a pink ribbon wound its brim. There was no way of making my hair, which was thick and long, look nice under it. My navy-blue gloves satisfied Grandfather: "Like this you look tidy." We boarded the train in Brussels; my grandfather cheerfully saying good day to the ticket clerk, whom he knew, and introducing me: "My granddaughter from China." It had taken him only four days to like me and now whenever we were together, he gave me his quiet loving care. How piercing the memory of his voice, his little gestures of love, when he insisted in giving me the better seat in the railway carriage: "in this way you will see the landscape." And the careful extraction from his pocket, wrapped in tissue paper, of a ham sandwich – "the young are always hungry" – and the way he watched me eat it. He resembled so much my mother but with a tenderness which had never been mine and was now running over, now all mine, so that I always wanted to weep and say "bonpapa", and throw my arms around him. But he would have called this "hysterical" and been fearfully embarrassed, and so I never did it.

Within an hour we were in Antwerp, but with the sensation of having voyaged, almost; the meticulous beautiful grey lace of the city of Malines had hoisted itself above the orderly meadow squares with their fat cows, glazed with ease, placed like toys in a toy garden on both sides of the diminutive railway. "The Belfry," said Grandfather, proudly pointing. But all was to remain diminutive, like a toy to be wearied of, compared to the largeness of China, the intensity and the vigour and the unendingness of China. For my grandfather the square belfry of Malines was a great monument; its climb comparable, possibly, to Mount Everest. "Do you have such things in China?" At first with him and his acquaintances I tried to talk of China, of the bigness, the vast plains, the mountains and rivers, but it was obvious they did not believe me, a river a mile across was simply exaggeration; for them China was a land of camels, rice, pagodas, slit-eyed bandits, stump-footed women, beggars relieved by the grace of God and the Flemish Scheut missionaries who went about doing good, temple bells, opium pipes, cut-throats, Fu Manchus and babies for sale. I employed the evasive non-committal reply, "Yes we do have towers, Bonpapa." On a trip to Namur, Louis and I had passed some ridiculous little stream and he had said: "You see that is the river Meuse," and I said: "Is that a river?" and Louis had been angry. Grandfather, too, became angry if I told him how big China was.

The house of my great-uncle Eugène Denis was narrow and straight with an extensive (by Belgian standards) garden at the back. It was neither showy nor overstuffed. My great-uncle was extremely tall and thin; he had always been told he looked like King Leopold II and he did; his long beard, well combed, glistened, his gestures were slow and noble. My childhood had been nourished with tales of terror about Uncle Eugène by my mother, who resented the Antwerp relatives whom she accused of snobbishness, but as Uncle Eugène stooped to shake my hand

and his beard flowed gracefully down, very much like the beard of a Chinese stage actor and the same colour, I lost all fear. His wife, my great-aunt, the beautiful and vivacious Anne van de Boegarde, all in rustling black silk with jet beads and her hair as in the days of Queen Victoria, allowed me to peck her cheek, and neither frightened nor worried me. I took off my hat and gloves and sat on the sofa and immediately was at ease. There was an atmosphere of restrained judicious comfort; these people would not be fooled, were not sentimental; but were fair, they would give me justice. I set out to obtain it. I was myself, without need to think ahead of each sentence or gesture. And by the end of the afternoon, we were happy with each other. My cousin, Armand Denis, came in, with his wife, an American, of the Roosevelt family. They had completed a photographic safari in Africa; Armand, from childhood, had cherished animals and hated cruelty; he could not conceive of civilized man finding pleasure in the wanton massacre of animals, and he had started on the career which would make him famous: photographing, later televising animals in their own setting, at play, in search of food, as much as possible without disturbing them. And since a horror of cruelty done to the "soulless" animal had always been mine we got on well. Armand had brought a cat, a very ordinary cat, on his shoulder, and many photographs of African tribes in his album. Their various types of nakedness included one which incited shocked giggling in his mother; a single seashell upon the head of the male organ for all clothing. Armand was keen to return to Africa. "Africa is magnificent, so big, so empty, breathlessly large – you can go for hours and never see a human being. Here one is so cramped, everything is so small." His words conveyed the majesty and emptiness and magnificence of Africa and his hunger for its wideness. Later he was to establish himself in Kenya.

Many years later Armand was to tell me how there had been debate as to whether I could be received or not, but all had gone well. Eugène Denis was to write and to say: "What tact she has, a rare intelligence," which coming from a person so reserved was like a kingly accolade and made all well between the Denis family and myself during the three years I was in Belgium.

There were less than twenty Chinese students in Belgium, about twelve of them were in Brussels; most studied engineering, for Belgium's reputation as a technically advanced country persisted.

320

About one-third of the students abroad spent ten, twenty years away and succeeded in never passing any examination but getting funds and having a comfortable if not very productive life. Wild horses would not have dragged them back to endure the discomforts of China, nor would they ever do any real work; they were part of a lot which the Germans when they invaded Belgium in 1940 put on a train and forcibly sent back through France to China. But the other two-thirds worked hard and well, especially the scholarship students.

I had not come to confine myself to the small circle of Chinese students (all of them men) in Brussels, and this was the origin of a grievance some nurtured against me. My arrival, my presence was causing some of them an emotional turmoil. They were even more upset when they realized that I was not limited by their ideas of whom I should see or what I should do. However, this did not prevent a few of the worse ones, when they were in debt or needed help, from coming to me for financial assistance, although the rest of the time they would be unpleasant when possible. After a while, however, they learnt to leave me alone, and with some I made good friends. Among them was a Dr. Yu, a nice small man, very ugly, who had been in Belgium fourteen years; after graduating he had accepted a job in a Belgian hospital. He often told me of his desire to go back to China, but so far he had not done so. He was in some ways a perpetual adolescent; frequenting the student café, arguing interminably with the students there. Another young student whose cheerfulness I appreciated was Wang Kiding. His father and grandfather had been hereditary officials at the Manchu court; his father ambassador abroad for many years. Wang Kiding had not known much of China. He was quarrelsome and would take on any number of large Belgians and challenge them to fight. He fell in love with a Belgian girl but knew he could not marry her, his family would object. He went back to China and it was twenty-nine years before I saw him again, briefly, in Hongkong. He was now an ambassador too, but in the Chiang Kaishek regime in Formosa. We did not talk politics, and confined ourselves to memories of our student days in Belgium. There were other students, some very worthwhile, others the typical wastrels, sons of well-to-do families. Some of them, like Dr. Yu, received the Chinese newspapers, all of them, even the least studious, followed the news from China. And that is how we read, through the papers, but also through letters from friends, and chiefly through the Chinese Students' Union in Paris, which was affiliated to the Federation of Students' Unions in China, of the great student movement of December 1935.

CHAPTER EIGHTEEN

In September 1935, when I had left China, the suppression of protests and of demonstrations against Japan by Chiang Kaishek was almost complete. Yet by December 1935, the students rose to protest in a way which reminded China of the May 4th movement of 1919, when in two hundred and twenty cities there were demonstrations against the Peace Treaty of Versailles.

And among those who rose to demonstrate in Peking, the students of Yenching, many of them my classmates, played a prominent role. Tan Leeton, Liang Szeyi, Harry Chang, Wang Jeumei, Kung Peng . . . so many others . . .

On August 1st, 1935, while on the Long March, the Communist Party issued an appeal, calling for an end to civil war, united effort against the common foe, resistance to Japan. At that moment the Red Army had dwindled to about thirty thousand men; it was still on the Long March, and it seemed the height of folly to issue, at that time, a challenge to Japan. The statement was of course suppressed, news of it only filtered through to Peking by the end of October; but it was carried in the Chinese students' newspaper in Paris. Tan Leeton, who personally took part in the student demonstrations of December in that year, later told me his own story:

"You know, Suyin, that Ho Yingchin, the Defence Minister of the Nanking government had signed yet another truce with the Japanese that summer; what you saw in the courtyard of the Peking Hotel, the Japanese and Chinese generals shaking hands, was possibly to celebrate this truce. Not only did Ho withdraw all Chinese troops, but also promised to withdraw the Kuomintang government civil organs and local offices from the cities of Peking and Tientsin; he also agreed to set up a buffer autonomous region in North China, and guaranteed to suppress all anti-Japanese movements among the Chinese people, as 'disturbing our relations with a friendly state'. He reiterated Chiang Kaishek's edict, making it a capital offence, punishable by death, to maintain that resistance to Japan should precede the total extermination of the Communists.

"You know yourself, Suyin, how Yenching University was, so meek, so mild, so Americanized. One week, we were singing hymns and having hot-dog parties; the next, we were carrying banners and marching and shouting. Even some of our overseas Chinese, apparently so Americanized, so completely non-political, suddenly became roaring revolutionaries, and marched and endured everything just as we did, the beatings, the hosings by the police, everything. Some said we were communist-inspired; others have written that it was not so, since our own American teachers, American friends, such as Edgar Snow, also persuaded us to demonstrate that December. The truth is that like secret blood, among us, ran the whisper : about the call from the Communist Party for a united front against Japan. That was the call given in August, and it had seeped in, it corresponded so much to what we desired. We were not all Communists, only two among the whole Students' Union of Yenching were actual Communists, but we were patriots; the call was what we had been waiting for, and from then on all of us began to look towards Yenan, towards Mao Tsetung. Though many of us never became Communists, yet we now realized that our only hope to save our country lay in Yenan, not in Nanking; in Mao Tsetung, not in Chiang Kaishek.

"On December 6th, 1935, we learnt from a student, whose brother was a secretary at the Military Headquarters, that the independence of North China from the South would be announced on December 10th; the Japanese wanted this done. Imagine anything so abject, the Defence Minister of a "National" government ordering the dismemberment of his own country, so that the Japanese would control North China through a puppet regime!

"Some of our Christian Fellowship of Yenching went to see Edgar Snow, and his wife, Nym Wales. The Snows also thought we ought to demonstrate, urged us to manifest. "The Kuomintang has become a symbol of pessimism, stagnation and repression," Edgar Snow said. I was a member of the Christian Fellowship, looking to God for China's salvation, and finding God deaf. Like scores of Yenching's Christian students. I ended by turning to the Red Army, and it did what God had not done. After that I was still a Christian, but I felt that God only helps those who help themselves.

323

"There had been so much systematic suppression of students and intellectuals after the 1932 aggressions in Manchuria and at Shanghai (with shooting and killing of students at Nanking, when they went to demonstrate) that in the next years, 1933 to 1935, the student movement appeared quite dormant. It was even claimed nothing would make the Chinese students move again. Out of almost forty-five thousand university and high school and middle-school students in Peking, there were only three genuine card-carrying members of the Communist Party, the rest had been killed, jailed or had surrendered; but communism does not depend on card-carrying. There were many more secretly studying, in secret cells.

"You, Suyin, left in September; Yenching University reopened after the summer holidays in October. There was tenseness among us. Though we sat at our desks, and the lecturers droned on, none of us could really study. We felt things were happening outside, which would decide our lives. This feeling was well put in the long petition we issued when finally we took our grievances out in the open: 'Even though our plains of the North are so wide and spacious, yet we feel shrunk, as if there were no place for us to put our student desks, no earth, no ground under our feet left to us . . .' We felt shrivelled in spirit, and we began to get together in groups, to discuss what was happening. But the right of assembly was forbidden, and the only way we could assemble was in Bible study groups, in singsongs. Some of the professors were very good and arranged these occasions for us. Leighton Stuart was on leave at that time, he had left Professor Lu Chihwei, the Head of the Psychology School, in charge. Lu was not at all happy about demonstrations. He kept on saying: 'Students must study, not meddle in politics.' So did Dr. Hu Shih, who had now become Chancellor of Peking University.

"At that time in all the universities there were students from Manchuria, refugees from the Japanese. They had their own Tungpei University, moved from Manchuria, established in the west sector of Peking; a good many had also gone to Sian, where they had demonstrated against Tai Chitao (Tai Traditional Wisdom, Chiang Kaishek's old friend), when he had told them to 'study and leave politics alone'. They had tried to beat him, and stoned his car.

"When we heard that a North China political council, which was to make North China 'independent' from South China, was to be established by the Japanese, with the agreement of the Nanking government, on December 9th, in Peking, our Students' Union decided to act.

"Students from other universities – Tsinghua, Tungpei, Peking University – came to Yenching to a meeting. The reason why Yenching, although so Westernized, so American, so Christian and a private university, became the meeting place, focus, and breeding ground for these meetings and demonstrations was precisely its select character. The students attending Yenching came chiefly from well-to-do upper-class families; it had therefore been subject to much less police surveillance than other universities, and there were fewer spies planted among the students, or loitering about the precincts. That is why Yenching became a kind of headquarters for the student movement in December 1935. Of course the situation changed very quickly in 1936.

"On that day, December 9th, six hundred of the eight hundred students of Yenching came out to march; we walked all the way from Yenching, along the Summer Palace road, to the west gate of Peking, a distance of about eight kilometres. The police had closed the West City gate; we stood outside it the whole day, and manifested there. Towards noon Huang Hua, who is now Chinese Ambassador in Africa, and whose name then was Wang Jou Mei went back to Yenching to get some food for us, for none of us had had any food since early morning. The canteen cook made dumplings for us. He wanted to use the university bus to take the food to us, but Professor Lu Chihwei as acting Chancellor refused permission. Huang Hua, however, persuaded the bus drivers, who sympathized with us, to bring the food out to us, and each of us ate a dumpling that day, and the small shops outside the gate gave us hot water to drink. There were also eight hundred students from Tsinghua University manifesting with us, altogether about one thousand and five hundred, standing outside the gate, making speeches, singing songs. Inside the city the students from Peking University, Tungpei University and other institutions were demonstrating, but we were kept locked out of the city, we could not get through the gates.

"The whole of the Peking police was alerted; in their black uniforms with rolled grey leg bands, twirling their batons, or armed with Japanese rifles, they were fierce to look at, but not too happy about arresting students. But the military police of Ho Yingchin, helmeted and rifled, were quite different; they were known for their German-trained brutality. By eleven o'clock there were five thousand students assembled inside the city, but they were prevented from moving to the Defence Minister's office, so they sent a delegation there, but Ho refused to receive their petition. The foreign diplomats in the Legation quarters had alerted their troops and considered barricading themselves in; the Japanese had erected barbed wire round their Legation and also called their troops to be at the ready. Ho Yingchin became scared, and postponed the inauguration of the spurious independence council for a week. On December 10th, the next day, we had a large meeting in the Yenching auditorium, and we declared a strike, for all the university campuses. Someone, delegated by the staff, shouted that this session of the Students' Union would not be recognized by the administration of the universities, but we pushed the fellow out of the auditorium and went on with the business on hand. We then organized study groups, teach-ins, refused to attend classes, and on December 16th, on the day the spurious 'independence council' was to assemble for one more try at setting up, we decided to hold another demonstration.

"This time we were more clever. Two days before our student leaders sent into the city a contingent of students with the Yenching flag. The students went in on the bus, as if they were going to the cinema, or visiting their families. Tsinghua students did the same. And so the flag of Yenching and the flag of Tsinghua were also represented in the demonstration within the city. Meanwhile, that morning, the bulk of the students marched to the West Gate, and again it was closed. We then walked on to another gate, further south along the city wall, called the West Side Gate. This had already been breached to let the railway through; but did not lead inside the city, it led only to the outside suburbs. We walked on, following the wall, until we reached Chienmen, the South Front Gate. Chienmen was not closed, because of its proximity to the European Legation quarters; the administration wanted to keep face. We assembled in the street leading up to the South Front Gate. This street is called the Heavenly Bridge, because its southern end leads to the Temple of Heaven, its northern end, inside the city, leads towards the Central Square, the Square of Heavenly Peace. We reassembled and formed ourselves in squads to enter the city, but the police and armed guards from the wall fired a volley in the air. This disconcerted us, and we stopped. The police had erected a barrier of sandbags, we could not get into the city. They also began to beat up those of us who were in front of the procession. They surrounded us, tried to catch us from behind, and to beat us. Some of the students were frightened and began to disperse, but one hoisted the Yenching flag, and shouted: 'Forward, forward', and we re-formed our ranks. Back we marched, to yet another gate, the Hsuan Wumen (now known as Peace Gate); it was a very old gate, very dilapidated, and we might breach it. From where we were we could hear the shouts of the students inside the city, a mighty clamour, as they assembled on Heavenly Peace Square; but we could not get to them; Peking, boxed within its walls, seemed impregnable to our student squads. Again we had to demonstrate in front of Peace Gate; and again we did so, all day, singing patriotic songs, distributing leaflets. Finally, night came and we returned to Yenching.

"Meanwhile, inside the city the student marchers had been attacked by the police. From the big police station on Wang Fuching, once called Morrison Street, policemen erupted, and with them came the fire department, which went to work with hoses, turning the water jets full on the paraders. It was freezing weather and the students were soaked. Then the political police went to work; they arrived on their motor-cycles with machine-guns, and began to club the boys and girls. All this sounds so stale, so jejune; when you read of the dogs and the cattle prods, and the tear gas, being used on Civil Rights demonstrators in America today, we were humanely treated by comparison. But the crowds were indignant, even the rickshaw coolies began to shout: 'Leave the students alone. Why don't you fight the Japanese instead!' About sixty students were arrested. The others walked home, and by now even the police were joining in the shouting: 'Down with the Japanese imperialists. Down with their lackeys, down with traitors who sell our land to the imperialists.' Altogether eight thousand students demonstrated on December 16th. It was a great success.

"It delayed the setting up of a so-called 'Independent North China'. Within a few days there were similar demonstrations in Tientsin, in Shanghai, in Wuhan, in Canton, in Sian, even in Nanking itself; in about forty cities, big and small.

"That winter our Federation of Students' Unions organized groups to go down to the countryside; and from that time on, small groups of students began to go to Yenan. We saw pamphlets advertising Kang Ta, the Resist Japan University, established in Yenan. And many aspired to go; quite a few did go.

327

"In January 1936 our students went to the villages, to the countryside, some for the first time in our lives. I was one of them. We found the peasants asking: 'Will the foreigners come again to Peking, as in the Boxer times? Why does not Chiang Kaishek fight the Japanese?' Visiting the villages round Paoting, I saw for the first time in my life the horrifying conditions of misery under which my own people lived; I stayed with them, and one night in a peasant's hovel was worth ten years of study. The peasants had not forgotten the Boxers, they still sang the songs of 1900. They had Monkey God shrines, for the Boxers had invoked the Monkey God who had the power to call armies out of the whirl-wind, out of dust; so the peasants called on Sun, the Wise Great Monkey, fighter against Evil. I learnt so much in two weeks among the peasants. It was a turning point in my life.

"Later I was sent to the south to organize links with the students in Shanghai and Nanking. An association called the Vanguard for China's National Liberation was formed in Peking and Tientsin, and then everywhere else, including at Sian, where the Young Marshal, Chang Hsuehliang, was quartered with his Manchurian troops. There were also a good many Manchurian students there, and they were in contact with Yenan.

"Chiang Kaishek ordered the Students' Unions to send dele-gates to Nanking to be admonished by him, but this time we were not caught. Some of us had gone in 1932, because we still believed in him; now we knew we could not trust him.

"But during 1936 the Kuomintang government was able to split the students in two camps; so that there was a lot of conflict within the Students' Unions. In most universities it took the form of clashes between students on the Right and on the Left. The student leadership in Yenching passed into the hands of a Kuomintang agent, who is now Minister in Formosa. At that time he seemed a very patriotic student, always ready to make speeches denouncing the Japanese, demanding resistance; in a very short time he had become the head of the Students' Federa-tion; later he was found out as agent provocateur and expelled. In Yenching, Leighton Stuart did not allow these clashes to get out of control, but in other universities the right-wing students denounced the left-wing students to the Kuomintang police, or beat them up. In Yenching there were denunciations, but no raids by the police."

"Whatever happened to so-and-so?" I asked Tan Leeton, picking names out from those I knew. "Oh, she was really a secret agent and she went and talked to Miss X———, you know, the one who lectured in Physiology, and I was not allowed to go on studying. She denounced me."

"Where is she now?"

"In Peking, a doctor, nothing has happened to her. She did it out of Christian conviction, it was well meant."

"And so-and-so?"

"Oh, he was very brave, spent two years in jail, with chains on his feet."

"I always thought he looked such a playboy."

"That was a façade he put on; most useful, he did a lot of good work, playing the playboy.

"The famous Dr. Hu Shih, now Chancellor of Peking University, tried to talk to us that winter; he was now thoroughly converted to Chiang Kaishek's policy; he told us we were much too weak to fight Japan, that to fight would be foolish, and we must 'listen to the government, and to wiser people' such as himself, no doubt. He told us that the only way to save our country was for us to bend our heads over our books and to study . . . At this we all shouted at him, shouted loud and long, and he got off the platform and went away. From that time on Hu Shih no longer counted for us, we despised him completely.

"In February 1936, three universities in Tientsin and Peking were surrounded and scores of students arrested. Night raids, with heavily armed police; trucks to take the students away, clubbing of recalcitrant students. Altogether twenty thousand policemen and troops were mobilized; two hundred students and teachers were thrown in jail; others were compelled to end their studies, many professors and lecturers had their services terminated. All the schools were now heavily guarded, and student identity cards were checked at the gates.

"In March occurred the Kuo Ch'ing affair. Kuo Ch'ing was a student arrested by the police, who died in prison from torture at the hands of the police. The Students' Union organized a great funeral demonstration. We paraded a coffin through the streets, shouting slogans and waving banners; and we wore black armbands. Kung Peng was one of the students who carried the coffin, and she and Huang Hua and some others were held by the police and got a few blows; they were nearly arrested but got away in time. For we had also our secret sympathizers, even among the officials.

"We then organized summer camps to provide a way out of the interdiction of assembly.

"The Western Hills became a favourite spot for 'picnics' of student groups. There, among the pines and oaks, in the shadow of temples with their vermilion statues, by secluded rocks and pools, the first student militia base was founded, which functioned all through the Sino-Japanese war; it became the first outpost on the road out across the hills for students and young people wishing to join the Red University at Yenan.

"By the end of 1936 we planned another demonstration. It was held at the Drum Tower on December 12th, and six thousand people were there. By now it was evident that the whole population was in sympathy with us; but the secret police was very active, and things were difficult.

"The next day, December 13th, all of us, the people of Peking, were awakened by newsboys shouting: 'Extra. Extra.' For on December 12th, the previous day, while we were holding our demonstration, Chiang Kaishek had been kidnapped at Sian. And Sian was the headquarters of the Young Marshal, posted expressly there by Chiang Kaishek to fight the Red base at Yenan. Chiang Kaishek had gone to Sian to upbraid the Young Marshal for slackness, and to organize a Sixth anti-communist Extermination Campaign; Chiang's kidnappers were none other than the Young Marshal himself, together with the Kuomintang garrison commander, Yang Hucheng. For the last ten months as 'pacificator', in charge of annihilating the Communists, the Young Marshal had had a Communist liaison officer functioning in his headquarters. For he, and all his troops, and all of our people were heartsick and tired of civil war, heartsick and tired of mismanagement and shame. All of us wanted to fight Japan. And by now it was absolutely clear to us that it was not Chiang Kaishek's Nanking government, not the Kuomintang party, miscalled Nationalist, but the Communist Party, and the Red Army under Mao Tsetung, which represented the aspirations of those who loved their country and did not want to become slaves to Japan."

CHAPTER NINETEEN

The kidnapping of Chiang Kaishek at Sian at first bewildered the Chinese students in Europe; we did not understand its significance for some weeks. To this day, certain details remain obscure, and there are as usual two main and several subsidiary versions. The official Kuomintang story, given by Chiang and his wife, remained available in publications for some years. The Communist one has never been made official.

Already in the previous year, a change of tactics in the Communist Party approach to the problems of their own survival, and of fighting the Japanese, was obvious. From fighting both Chiang Kaishek and the Japanese, Mao Tsetung, in December 1935, had defined the basic task of the Party as the formation of a broad revolutionary national united front. "The united front, and not closed doorism . . . is right." Mao Tsetung was aware of the mounting tide in China itself against Japanese imperialism, and of the growing disquiet in Great Britain and also, in some quarters in the United States at Japan's overweening ambitions in China. Although Japan had promised to uphold the Open Door policy, and Great Britain, thinking she would share the spoils, had tacitly agreed to her invasion of Manchuria, it was evident that Japan was actually intent on expelling all other influence from China.

In 1932 and 1933 Japan seized the Chinese customs receipts in Manchuria and refused to remit them to the British- and American-controlled customs in Shanghai. Japan expelled the foreign staff of the customs; publicly humiliated Englishmen in Tientsin; encouraged widespread smuggling of her own goods, and chiefly of narcotics; imposed limitations on foreign imports, and favoured Japanese paraffin by a camouflaged discrimination, until Standard Oil was sold at twenty-nine cents a gallon and the Japanese product at five cents a gallon. In 1935 and 1936 Japan closed the English company of Jardine Mathieson, the German Siemens, and the American firm of Andersen Meyer and Company, both in Manchukuo and in North China. The Western Powers, so understanding of Japan's needs when it was only a question of cutting up China, now found themselves hoist with their own petard.

Around Chiang Kaishek, in the Nanking government, two cliques manœuvred. One was the pro-Japanese, with the notorious Ho Yingchin, Minister of Defence, at its head. I was to become acquainted with Ho Yingchin in later years and found him an acutely xenophobic man. All through the ensuing Sino-Japanese war he was to sigh, shaking his head: "We should not fight each other; it is America, Britain, we should fight." The other clique was the pro-American one, with Dr. H. H. Kung the Finance Minister, and Dr. T. V. Soong, brother of Madame Chiang Kaishek. They were beginning to reflect the unease of Britain and America at Japan's insolence.

In May 1936 the Red Army appealed again to the Nanking government for united resistance to Japan; in August, from Yenan, the Chinese Communist Party addressed a letter to the Kuomintang in Nanking, calling for a united front against Japan. Chiang Kaishek not only rejected both these proposals but in October flew to Sian to plan his sixth Communist annihilation campaign.

There he saw the Young Marshal Chang Hsuehliang and scolded him for his lack of vigour in suppressing Mao Tsetung's Red Armies. Chang Hsuehliang replied that his Manchurians only wanted to return to Manchuria and did not want to fight communism "with all their heart". Irascibly, brooking no "indiscipline", Chiang nevertheless set up plans for the Sixth Extermination Campaign against the Communists. The Fifth had taken a million men; this one would take two millions; the rest of China would be denuded of soldiers, left wide open to the Japanese to take, while Chiang marshalled forces against the Red Army which at that time consisted of not more than thirty thousand men.

To show that he meant business, on his return to Nanking Chiang jailed seven scholars and intellectuals, members of the National Salvation League, who had demanded resistance to Japan. His indomitable sister-in-law, Madame Sun Yatsen, joined in the protests. On December 7th, Chiang returned to Sian, to direct the Sixth campaign against Mao Tsetung.

Chiang's entry into Sian was not a triumph; there were student demonstrations against him, and against his aides. These were set off by the Manchurian students, some from the Tungpei University in Peking, who had travelled to Sian especially for this purpose; others had been studying in Sian, and had been in touch with the Communist Party at Yenan, only two hundred miles away by road from Sian.

Chiang ordered Chang Hsuehliang and also General Yang Hucheng (Yang Tiger City), the garrison commander of the area, to suppress these trouble-making students. But Chang did not do so. Instead, seeing the demonstrations, he promised them "satisfaction". Very distressed, he tried to expostulate with Chiang, who told him to keep silent.

An ex-police officer at Sian, who was actually a Communist agent masquerading as a police officer, told me his story: "The whole of Sian was well penetrated by us. We could have killed Chiang at any time, everyone hated him. But the Party told us to keep him alive. We had to protect him against his own Kuomintang armies, the Manchurian troops who wanted to murder him. During those December days Chiang was staying outside Sian, in the ancient pavilions and gardens where the famous beauty of the Tang dynasty, Yang Kueifei, and her lover the Tang Emperor spent many delightful seasons; a hot spring gushed there, where she bathed, and where Chiang also bathed during that cold December."

The room where Chiang slept, near the hot spring, is preserved as it was when, suddenly roused by a shot outside, which killed one of his bodyguards, he crept out through the window, and climbed the hillside upon which the pavilions were built. He scrambled up the dusty, rocky hillface, hid at the end of a long, narrow gully, between two boulders. There he was found, two hours later, shivering with cold, having lost a shoe and limping. He had also forgotten his teeth, left in a glass on his bedside table. He was placed in a car by Chang Hsuehliang's aide, who had come to rescue him: "Kill me, why don't you kill me?" mumbled Chiang, covering his mouth with his hand. "We don't want to kill you, we merely wish to have a talk with you," his captor, a young officer of the Manchurian troops, is said to have replied.

Chiang was driven to the governor's mansion, part of the Young Marshal's headquarters at Sian. He refused to eat, but had a bath and change of clothes; later it was discovered that his false teeth were still in his bedroom, and they were restored to him. He then ate some gruel. Meanwhile his other advisers and staff had been captured; they were imprisoned separately, and after two days were easily brought to sign a statement saying they wanted to fight the Japanese and stop fighting their fellow Chinese. The Young Marshal sent a circular telegram to the nation, explaining that Chiang was well and safe, that he had hitherto been advised by "small men" who had not counselled him properly, that he was remaining in Sian for a while "to confer on national questions". The circular detailed an eight-point programme for coalition government, cessation of civil war, armed resistance to Japan . . . in short, the United Front.

On December 15th Chou Enlai, who had been jailed by Chiang Kaishek in Canton and narrowly escaped death in Shanghai in 1927, turned up. "Mr. Chiang, I am glad to see you in good health." The episode and the conversations form the subject of somewhat fanciful but highly diverting reports. Unfortunately no exact transcript of what was said has been published, and I doubt whether any such will ever be.

Back in Nanking there was uproar; Ho Yingchin wanted to send bombers to "bomb the Communists and rescue our beloved Leader". But actually this course would have brought about Chaing Kaishek's murder. Either the people, enraged, would have mobbed the residence, or the soldiers would have killed him. Perchance a well planted bomb would finish off Chiang himself. It was an open secret that Ho aspired to the succession . . .

Madame Chiang Kaishek prevented this. "Are you stark staring mad?" she shouted at Ho Yingchin. And with great difficulty, for already the orders were given, the fleet of bomber planes was recalled, though a few, it is said, did jettison some bombs in the outskirts of Sian. Then Madame Chiang and her brother T. V. Soong flew to Sian. With them was Donald, an Australian adviser, who had at one time been in the Young Marshal's employ, and was now employed by the Chiangs. Madame Chiang cabled Chiang Kaishek: "I have come to live or die with you." On the way their plane had to make quite sure not to be shot down, by order of Ho Yingchin.

An ironical touch was that the aeroplanes sent on this bombing mission were the very ones raised, by taxation and voluntary donations, as a birthday present for Chiang Kaishek that year.

If Chiang had died, the whole country would have disintegrated into civil war, and the Japanese would have annexed China with great ease, with the help of Ho Yingchin and Wang Chingwei. Ho Yingchin was looking forward to that "Together, Japan and China can dominate Asia."

Madame Chiang, who greatly to her credit kept a cool head,

Donald her adviser, and T. V. Soong, now joined in the talks with Chou Enlai.

On December 24th the stubborn Chiang Kaishek accepted the conditions laid down: cessation of the anti-communist campaign, resistance to Japan. There was an explosion of joy all over China. Almost at once, he became the most popular leader, to all appearances, the country had ever had . . . but he knew well that this popularity was due to his change of policy, forced upon him, in the final analysis, by the people's will, expressed through Mao Tsetung.

And now the business of face-saving was to be attended to. Official accounts of the Sian incident were published. Chiang wrote that the Communists had read his diary, that this had made them repent, and release him. It must be concluded that in the end it was the Communists who had what they wanted: a united front. There would never be a Sixth Extermination Campaign.

In ostensible triumph Chiang flew back to Nanking on December 26th; all over China there was great rejoicing; "Our Beloved Leader is back," the newspapers proclaimed. There were parades in all the cities. There was no mention of Chou Enlai, of Mao Tsetung, of the talks held in Sian. "The rebels repent, Chang Hsuehliang begs for punishment." Thus the editorials, saving the face of Chiang Kaishek. But those who knew were not duped.

Chiang Kaishek *had* lost face; and possibly that explains what happened to the most vulnerable person at hand, the architect of his enforced change of policy, the impetuous, but not sagacious, Young Marshal Chang Hsuehliang. Meanwhile Mao Tsetung issued on December 28th a statement: "Chiang should remember that he owes his safe departure from Sian to the mediation of the Communist Party, *as well as* to the efforts of Generals Chang Hsuehliang and Yang Huchen." This was a warning to the Young Marshal that he should beware of reprisals against him.

No one can tell us exactly why Chang Hsuehliang was so foolish as to accept to return with Chiang Kaishek to Nanking; why, knowing the vindictiveness of political leaders, and Chiang's propensity for playing off his opponents one against the other, he put himself in his hands.

The explanation is comprehensible only in a society where feudal concepts of chivalry and allegiance still prevail. The Young Marshal was sworn brother to Chiang Kaishek, they had exchanged oaths and blood, a sacred bond. He was so elated at having brought his "elder brother" to see reason, to behave patriotically, that he does not seem to have reckoned with Chiang's well-known traits. He was persuaded that in six weeks or so he would be sentenced, as apparent punishment for his insubordination, to battle against the Japanese; and this was exactly what the Young Marshal craved. His reputation had suffered in the loss of Manchuria; he dreamed of becoming a popular hero; and fighting Japan would make him one. It never occurred to him that as soon as he was in Nanking, no longer protected by his own troops, and by the occult presence of the Red Army at Yenan, Chiang would go back on his brotherhood oath. The Young Marshal was kept in custody not for six weeks, but for thirty long years. From 1936 to this day, Chiang Hsuehliang has been a prisoner. When Chiang Kaishek fled to Formosa, he took the Young Marshal with him. At first General Yang Hucheng, Tiger City, was also a prisoner. He was executed, by Chiang's orders, twelve years later.

A hard destiny for the generous, impulsive Young Marshal, just when he had cured himself of the drug habit, had begun to show promise, and nobility of character. But he could not be forgiven for having been the instrument of change. Chang Hsuehliang has paid all these thirty years for this turn of fate, for this wound to an ambitious man's self-love; but sometimes, in spite of this, I think he must be laughing to himself, even in Formosa.

There was little the Chinese students could do or say in Brussels, for the Chinese Embassy actively discouraged us from even noticing events in China. "Students must study, leave politics to us." The Ambassador, once a year, would harangue us, rather fiercely, on our duty not to meddle. After the Sian incident the Chinese students in Belgium, allied with those in France and Germany, sent two delegates to the Embassy asking for their approval for a National Salvation League branch in Belgium. The Embassy refused; and we were all told to beware of communist infiltration. Our scholarships depended on it; and being so few, it was easy for the Chinese Embassy to keep track of us. Nevertheless, a National Salvation League was formed, despite official coldness, or rather, it came out in the open at last, and most of us joined it. Something new was in the air; and changed it, as it soon would change us.

In July 1937 I went to Italy for the summer holidays with Louis and two other students. In the same train was Minette, also studying medicine in my year. She confided between two stations that she was in love with one of her professors and that her parents were opposed to it. They were sending her to some relatives in France for the summer. But she would get off the train and join her beloved one at the frontier. They would be together for a few days.

I bought a newspaper at the station, and on opening it read that the previous day, July 7th, the Japanese had been attacked by Chinese troops at the Marco Polo bridge in North China. Gunfire had been exchanged. A picturesque description of this latest incident was to come into my hands later. "Shortly before midnight, the manœuvres developed towards realism, and live ammunition was used on both sides." This careful description, due to the prevailing censorship, was the beginning of the undeclared Sino-Japanese War, to merge into the Second World War two years later.

At first the news did not have much impact; had I not seen the Japanese in Peking in August 1935? Had not live ammunition been used for the last six years? It was merely another incident ... At another station another newspaper told us that the Chinese had violently attacked a Japanese patrol maintaining peace and order and ensuring the running of the railway in North China.

"How absurd," I said. "The Marco Polo bridge is in China. I've often gone over it. It's just six miles from Peking. The Japanese merely want to take some more of our country, so they fabricate another incident."

"Marco Polo bridge? What a funny name for a bridge in China," said Minette.

"It was there at the time of Marco Polo, that is why." Next to the tenth-century marble bridge with its four hundred stone lions, each one different, was the railway bridge, which I had crossed with Herbert Lee on an excursion in the countryside. I had managed to fall between two sleepers, and Herbert had pulled me out, sighing "unconscious" and wondering why I was so clumsy.

"Do you think it will be a serious incident?" asked Louis.

From a childhood composed of such alarums and excursions by night, I could only reply: "We shall see."

Three days later, as we rode the train towards Venice, an Italian sitting in the same compartment, and who had recognized me as a Chinese without being told, showed me the banner headlines in the Italian newspaper: "The Chinese employ bacteriological war in their attack against the Japanese." I

337

shrugged. "What an imbecility. It's the Japanese who are attacking China, invading China, not the Chinese." Louis, in bad Italian, explained this to the Italian, who nodded and offered me a cigarette politely. "Do you think there will be war?" asked Louis. "I don't know," I said.

I finished the Italian tour (it took four weeks), and every day the Italian papers gave the news. Shanghai fell, Peking fell – the Chinese were committing atrocities, the Japanese were rescuing babies, doing good. "Lies, all lies," I said. Venice, Rome, Naples . . . Pompeii; the Italian Fascists with their extraordinary boots and cockfeathered helmets, their black shirts, the monuments, the trumpets, pictures of Mussolini everywhere. I went about like an automaton, rigid, alienated from my surroundings. Louis began to worry: "Your temper . . . what is the matter, what have I done?" We joined up with other students in Naples; Vesuvius had not blown its top, it smouldered, still a majestic cone. We walked its slopes eating grapes; a pailful of *lachryma Christi* for two lire; I wondered what was happening to my father. Shanghai was being defended from the Chinese "by Japan's heroic, chivalrous troops." "It was attacked in 1932 by the Japanese, Shanghai is in China," I said. The journey home through France was unreal, I was cut in two, completely. One me went to see the cathedrals, the museums, Arles, Avignon, Rheims; the other was elsewhere . . . I was getting very nervous, I could not eat, I could not sleep. We returned to Brussels; Louis had many photographs. He was now launched in his career as a young, promising solicitor; and he was also a commissioned officer in the Belgian Air Force.

I returned to my lodgings, a sunfilled room, very comfortable, and having put my things away, met Louis again to go to dinner, and then for a walk in the Bois; a warm, comfortable cat-cosy night wrapped itself around the avenues and trees, the pond which was called a lake had a small boat asleep on its stillness; in the pavilion, where an orchestra cackled brassily, the good people of Brussels sat drinking coffee and eating ice-cream and cakes under festoons of coloured paper flags. They seemed contented, immobile, in a world where nothing could happen. "How peaceful," murmured Louis happily. And all of a sudden I exploded. All this placidity, this happiness, if this was happiness, I did not want. I did not want this deadly sleep. Almost I had become a sleepwalker, like those around me; almost closed in on my own life; my own pettiness, growing round me that shell of small contents and mean comforts, my room so comfortable, my books, my friends, my Louis, a good husband-prospect, my grandfather . . . A world that narrowed me down, narrowed me down, although I had had the impression, until now, that it had broadened me because I saw plays, read books, discussed ideas; I had thought, therefore, that I was growing more enlightened, more intelligent, when actually it was exactly the opposite; now I knew it, with lightning conviction. I dealt in the amusement of a shadow-intellectualism; not here, but there, was reality, outside this Europe-bound circle, the immense reality I had not even begun to know about, the reality of China, China my very bones, breath of my spirit, life of me . . . I could talk about authors with as much assurance as Leila or Simon Hua; I could listen to music without boredom; discuss the cinema; appreciate painting; I had seen museums and become "travelled" in the Western sense. And now all this had become worthless trash, despicable vomit. I almost cried out, with nervous pain. "You are tired, you must rest." Louis was worried, solicitous. He could not understand what was happening, why so abruptly I changed, rose, walked away. He too was faced with change, the change in me. An enormous strain had interposed itself between us, even while we travelled; I had become altogether frigid, completely uninterested in any approach; vacant, bad-tempered, moody, saying: "Leave me alone" as I plunged into formless silence. Louis had known me long enough to realize that he must not use the coercion that might bring another woman round; he must not accuse me of having lost interest in him; accuse me of being interested in another man, sulk, use jealousy or personal distrust to get out of me reassurance of love. He tried, however, compelled by convention, though half-heartedly: "Have you stopped feeling for me? Is there anything that has changed?" "No." In the next week, finding me still hermetic, he tried again. Minette was back, calling her professor a dirty old man; there was a blonde student with her, and also an African girl from the Congo, very beautiful. We all had coffee together at the students' coffee house, and Louis took the African girl home. He rang my bell two hours later. "I want an explanation of your conduct, otherwise I shall not return, I promise you." I did not reply and made coffee. What could I say? That what was eating my heart out was something with no face, no name, that I myself did not know what it was? Louis said: "Are you ill?" "Yes." "What is it?" "I am homesick." His brow cleared. "Is that all? Of course, the war . . . it is hard, but worrying won't make it any better." "No." "You know," he said, "I really love you, I would do anything . . . I think of you all the time, I will do all you want." If anyone had told me that all one's feeling, all one's emotions, passion, could be changed so swiftly because of this thing which had nothing to do with me, a shooting at a bridge thousands of miles away; because of this war which was my concern and yet was not my concern; if anyone had told me that I would give up what I had worked for, for this which can never be owned or acquired, but only served, and served with no reward, I would have roared with laughter . . .

But it happened to me. Suddenly friends, and all that I thought I cared for, became flabby ghosts demanding an attention I could no longer give. Things smelt different, felt different, were alien where they had been familiar. Before my mind could dissect, analyse, my body told me already by its refusal to accommodate, by its hostility to the environment it had been lapped in, that I was a stranger, as untameable as an alien from Mars. Insomnia, irritability, fits of weeping. The tranquil years in Belgium were at an end for me, I had to go back to China; to go back against all reason, against all logic. And in China, all this, which was now my life, would become a butterfly dream.

It was in my power to choose. I could choose There or Here, two ways of life, two selves, two destinies . . .

Oh not immediately; not right away. I must not do things rashly . . . there was my grandfather; perhaps peace would come, my third university year was only beginning, and I had done so well . . . I decided I would finish the third year, then go back to China, unless of course peace was made, a truce, as so many times had happened. Because going back meant giving up medicine, at least for a while, and I so much wanted to be a doctor; but I could not imagine staying six more years away from China. "I shall die here of homesickness."

On October 10th, the annual Anniversary Day, the Chinese Ambassador, for the first time, made a semi-patriotic speech, but ended up by telling us to study.

Until then all student activities for China against Japan had been very strictly repressed, but now it was no longer so. The United Front was on, it was now all right to do something. I was now enrolled to deliver lectures on China; to travel all over Belgium, in towns and villages, and later in France, to speak for China.

The Committee for Aid to China was formed. It was the name

340

of an organization sponsoring lectures, meetings, film shows, to inform and to rally public opinion in Belgium for China. This Committee was organized by the Belgians, in liaison with the members of the National Salvation League. In the same Committee were liberals, right-wing businessmen, socialists and Belgian Communists. The latter were far more busy about Spain and Hitler and often specified that, on a platform where China was mentioned, there also should be speakers for Spain.

Of that period between October 1937 and July 1938, when I passed the final Bachelor of Science examination with the highest distinction, only a tornado picture remains in my mind, a whirlwind of scattered images, sudden stills like relay posts, landmarks on a galloping road, jumbled faces, sentences, trains, slow, dirty, cold hours of trains as I toured the coalmining districts in Wallonie, northern France and its industrial cities; frostbite, cold lecture halls, platforms with one electric bulb, sagging beds in cheap hotels, platforms draughty and forbidding; half-filled dingy theatres in provincial townlets, plaudits, dinners, demonstrations, teas, talk, talk, talk, holding a newspaper and going to sleep, holding it. Talking of China, re-coining in appropriate words the tragic horrors happening in China for people who had no conception of China, for whom it was the furthermost point of earth, for whom all Chinese were sinister opium-smokers, slithering slit-eyed bandits, and not human beings. If even Simone de Beauvoir, that intelligent French intellectual, found China incomprehensible, and was sincere enough to write it,* how much more so my audiences, uninvested with knowledge, riddled with tormented pictures of bound feet, tortures, opium, Belgian missionaries martyred by the Boxers, schoolchildren making silver balls out of their chocolate wrappings to "buy little Chinese babies" out of misery? Who could blame them for believing the fiction of the newspapers, that Japan, a noble, heroic country, was out to "preserve China from communism?" Today the same fiction holds in thrall much of the Western world, as America uses the same old stale clichés as Japan did, in a renewed attempt at the conquest of Asia, and the fiction still works, is still believed.

In those seven months I did one hundred and twenty-eight lectures, conferences, meetings; I also wrote twenty-five articles on China. I lost a stone in weight; my clothes began to fall off me.

* See *La Force des Choses* (Gallimard, 1964); English translation, *Force of Circumstances* (Weidenfeld & Nicolson, 1965).

What can I pick out of this whirlwind? Faces. Georgette Acker, now dead. Georgette was a Communist, a courageous, kind woman, forgetful of herself, sincere. She cooked, she cleaned, she attended meetings of the Aid China Committee and she was immensely honest, believing in the shining glory of a new society; she had been to Russia, returned elated. She was the kind who sat up all night addressing envelopes, stamping pamphlets; nothing was too small for her to do, nothing too discouraging to attempt. She cooked for the students who demonstrated in the Place du Nord, or at the Porte de Namur; she was always ready with hot bouillon for those who had colds, cold compresses for the headaches of the more important and temperamental speakers. I saw Georgette again, many years later, in 1946, when I went for a brief holiday back to Belgium. She was as kind as ever, but no longer a Communist. She told me how she had left the Party, or rather drifted away. She and Acker, her husband, had been in the underground resistance movement against the Nazis throughout the Second World War. "And also our dog, Poubelle, till she died," said Georgette. They had lived in hiding, passed messages, operated a clandestine radio. Then had come the radiant hour, war's end; the Nazis beaten, Brussels a feast of flowers, the tanks of the Americans grinding the cobbled streets, the carillon bells on the Grande Place pealing, pealing, Georgette had hurried to the headquarters of the Communist Party in Brussels. There were three or four teenagers sitting behind desks: "Who are you?" She was surprised, surely they must know of her . . . "I am so-and-so, a comrade . . ." "Never heard of you." "But I've been in the Resistance . . ." "Leave your name and address. If we need you, we'll call you." She had left her name and address, and never been called. "They dropped me." She had attended one or two public meetings "but my heart had gone out of it." She settled down to a job her husband became a businessman, and she acquired a second Poubelle. "The future is in Asia, here in Europe we are all corrupt, even the Communists, they are corrupt, they have become dividend-receiving bourgeois."

Acker her husband was a born organizer, with the vivid forceful, almost American personality of an executive. He was heavily built with dark eyes and a great sense of humour. Someone like him was needed to manage the extraordinary Committee for Aid to China with its Catholic priests, politicians of all shades, socialists and Communists, surely the most diverse, heterogeneous assemblage.

A prominent member of the Committee was the Abbé Bolland, a priest who had known Teilhard de Chardin well, and who founded a society of Catholic laymen and laywomen to work in Catholic social services; something like a liberal movement in the Catholic Church.

Abbé Bolland, like Teilhard de Chardin, was an unconventional Catholic priest, a humanist. He was shortish, portly, with a purplish face, a resonant voice, enormous energy, a great sense of rabelaisian humour which exploded in jokes unfit for even the unclerical, after which he would sign himself, wink and say: "Jesus Christ must have heard worse ones." He had a small quarrel going on with his bishop; at that time priests who protested convincingly against Hitler or Mussolini or, like Bolland, denounced Japanese aggression in China, were liable to trouble, suspension from holy duties, as today when American Catholic priests, obeying their conscience, protest against the war in Vietnam. Abbé Bolland and I often took the train together to lecture at small towns. "We should be ashamed of ourselves – we sent them Christ in a crate of opium," Bolland would thunder on the platform, and the great cross on his chest would catch the light. "Call ourselves Christians? We behave worse than any pagans have ever done . . ." He smoked many cigars, teased Georgette Acker: "My daughter, you may believe this or that, but I'll see you in Paradise yet. In my Father's house are many mansions, for those with a heart like yours." After a Georgette meal he would rumble, "For cooking like this I'll give you absolution any time." He liked being billed on the same platform as I was: "Such a contrast, an ugly priest like me, a beautiful girl like you. I hope it's shocks my bishop." It was forbidden to him to talk of Spain, so he confined himself to the problem of China, and occasionally to Hitler: "I've got to pretend the poor wretches in Spain are not Catholics . . . oh misery."

One or two of the more leftist members were hostile to me, because I was not a left-winger. "What can you expect from the niece of a General, Minister of Defence of a capitalistic state?" They asked me what I thought of the Belgian king, of royalty in general, and I replied that I had never thought about it since we had no king in China. This struck them as disingenuous, although it was true; I do not feel that I should have opinions on everything. But the partly educated always insist on having opinions, and the less they know about a topic, the more violently tenacious they become in their beliefs founded on nothing but hearsay. The

343

label of a reactionary bourgeois was duly hung about my neck; however, I was useful, and they put up with me. To begin with, I was good-looking and this is always an asset at lectures. It draws the audience, which would stay at home otherwise. When I mounted a platform the audience paid attention; my Chinese dress was a great attraction. It did not matter what I said, they sat through the talk, staring at the high-collared, form-fitting garment. As Father Bolland said: "They like your legs, and we collect." A stampede of men would contribute money, after the speech, for the pleasure of shaking my hand (I stood by the collection stand). Their wives would push them forward when they lingered to ask questions about China; but would stand in their turn, to ask if this was a real Chinese dress and what did I do to keep so slim.

Twice I had the opportunity of lecturing on the same platform as Isabelle Blum, at that time an important member of the Belgian Communist Party. Madame Blum is built to last; a forceful woman, active and vital. We disliked each other. Admittedly I was a student, and certainly my activities for China were emotional, not political. I simply had to do something against the injustice, the cruelties practised upon the Chinese people; I was happy that Chiang Kaishek had decided to fight Japan, and now, like so many of the petty bourgeoisie, I forgot the past, and looked upon him as a national hero, since he had now decided to fight Japan (or so we thought). One afternoon, at a Committee meeting, sitting informally, talking and having coffee and cakes in the living-room of a newspaperman who was one of the members, Isabelle Blum descended upon me, and in peremptory fashion began to tell me what I should say at the next lecture. As I have never taken kindly to being ordered about, I told her I disliked being interrupted when I was eating. She was furious, and half a dozen of the Committee members rose to cajole her back into good temper. "But, comrades, did you hear what that chit said, did you hear the way she spoke to me?" she cried. It was represented to her that I was a child, impertinent but useful, without a notion of Marxism, a reactionary, an insolent bourgeoise, but with audience-drawing power. We duly travelled together a few days later, to an industrial district in Wallonie where Isabelle Blum spoke for Spain and I after her for China. In the train she opened a briefcase and consulted papers, throughout the two hours or more it took to get back to Brussels. Later, she did forgive me, for she was a large-hearted person and not vindictive, and even spoke to me agreeably, and hugged me once to show that she did not bear a grudge. Acker was more angry at me than she was. He told me that she was "a very important" woman, who could "make rain or sun" for many people, because she had close friends in the Ministry, and that I was wrong to antagonize her. But I was not courting patronage, what was important to me was talking about China, not reward; was denouncing injustice, and the war to come which I could see so clearly now, coming forward with great steps. And the massacres of Nanking, the horrors at Shanghai, were eating out my heart; I could not eat, I slept badly, woke up in nightmares.

The third year had a very heavy programme; we were in anatomy dissection rooms five mornings a week; we also had a course in philosophy, laboratories in histology, physiology and biochemistry. I often had to cut lectures, especially afternoon ones, because of conferences or meetings; and now I relied on other students' notes. In the first two years I had done my own notes, typed them, later sold them at a good price to other students. They were much in demand, since I made excellent grades the others felt my notes must be valuable. There is always a feeling that luck can be transmitted through objects and my notes had acquired this repution for thoroughness. But now I was relying on other students' labours, a comedown for me, but I could not do otherwise. I found one excellent student, Émile, who used to write down everything that was said at a lecture, and I borrowed his notes; he was a very nice boy, obviously smitten, and he did some of my dissections for me when I was not there, so that I would not get bad marks. When I came to the anatomy laboratory one morning in three, I galloped through the dissection and one day in my haste committed the most reprehensible crime of all: I removed a large portion of the median nerve in the arm. As every medical student will know, one has to do a clean dissection, paring off unwanted fat and enveloping tissue, exposing the vital structures: nerves, arteries, veins, muscles, devoid of fibrous tissue or fat wrappings. Rigid and smelly, exhaling the acrid fetor of disinfectant, the corpses lay on their cement slabs. The one I shared with five other students was a very fat man who steadily dribbled oil throughout the weeks we spent on his body. He gave us uncommon trouble with his basket-weave tangle of yellow semi-solid fat which enveloped everything: nerves, arteries, veins, muscles, intestines, heart, liver; even his brain oozed fat. When I ripped off his most important arm nerve, a "structure" to be preserved at all costs, a thrill of horror ran through the anatomy class. Our professor had threatened anyone who removed "an important structure" with failure, for "Gentlemen" (he never spoke of ladies, though there were twelve women students), "he who wields the anatomical scalpel with such undexterous barbarity is *unworthy* of the noble art of surgery . . . he deserves to fail."

Now the atrocity had been committed, and by me, one of the two "great distinctions" of our year. (The other one had been won by a young Jew, Lipshitz; in fact for two years he and I competed neck and neck). There was the arm of the fat man, palm up, and no median running to his armpit. The other students at the slab were four men and a girl, a Jewess who had had a terrible time with the Nazis. Her boy friend had been mutilated with a red-hot iron, and this had made her extremely nervous. It was Émile who rescued me. He produced with the air of a magician some thick white string from his pocket. "I always get from Maman a bit of thread for such accidents." On the spot we constructed a most magnificient median, running in all the right places; we also tied together several other tendons and blood vessels which I had nicked. We dipped the thread in the serious liquid which exuded drearily and constantly from the corpse, to give it the right colour. When our professor came round, he said admiringly: "Now that is what I like, a *clean* dissection. Congratulations." Our table held its breath; the surrounding tables, who might have reported on us, also kept quiet. This was exceedingly noble of them, though afterwards they said a lot to us in private. But the students were very good to me. They knew I scoured the countryside, and that I had even attempted the Flemish part of Belgium, much harder to propagandize. For the Flemish were one hundred per cent dour Catholics; the Rexists were strong among them and to speak against Hitler or for China was equivalent to communism for them. There were Sunday prayers in some parish churches for Hitler and Franco, and a strong Catholic influence at Court too, I was told, because the king was Flemish . . .

The newspapers, especially the Catholic ones, were not in sympathy with China. A particularly prejudiced series of articles appeared in *La Libre Belgique*, the most prominent and respectable Catholic newspaper in Belgium.

These articles, by a French correspondent travelling with the Japanese troops in China, extolled their successes, lauded their humanity, the wonderful "civilizing work" Japan was doing in China. "The Nippon knights, with the courage and loyalty of noble aristocrats, enter China as a knife goes into butter," wrote the correspondent, who omitted to observe the raping, butchering and looting which had cost fifty thousand non-military citizens' lives in Nanking. "They will put some order in the chaos of this indolent, vapid, geographical expression . . . China will be saved from COMMUNISM," he wrote. This theme of anti-communism, justification for any kind of monstrosity, was as effective then as it is now with the uninformed and the uncurious; transforming the most apparently well-intentioned man into a drooling, ferocious moron, who no longer reasoned but beatifically acquiesced in utterly degrading crimes because they were "anti-communist". And in that year, and for those people, Japan was the white angelic champion of democracy, safe-guarding China from falling into the hands of communism; few knew, or remembered, that Chiang Kaishek had wasted China's substance and a long and bloodstained decade in massive anti-communist expeditions.

According to this French correspondent the Chinese people were hailing the Japanese as deliverers from communism. The *Libre Belgique* ran these special dispatches, bountifully illustrated with photographs of Japanese soldiers smilingly giving candy to children, and shooting roped "Communists".

One day I could not stand the sight of these articles any longer. I dressed more carefully than usual, put on my hat (bought at a cheap sale and readorned with pheasant's tail feathers given to me by my landlady when she had had pheasant for lunch). Thus attired I went to the office of the *Libre Belgique* and asked to see the Editor-in-Chief. I used the name of General Denis, said I was his cousin. My lofty manner worked. I was ushered with all speed to see Monsieur Huysmans the Editor. Monsieur Huysmans was a middle-aged, middle-sized man, with a kind, studious face, concealed behind glasses. He stared at my hat. I told him I did not like the articles in his newspaper. They were not true. "But the Japanese are protecting the Chinese from communism," he said. "That is a lie, Monsieur. How would *you* like it, Monsieur, if tomorrow Hitler were to come into Belgium, to protect *you* from communism? And that may happen, Monsieur, that may happen . . ." Monsieur Huysmans looked at me, wordless. I continued: "Can you not understand patriotism? Have the Chinese, then, not the right to fight back against an aggressor in China?

What God-given right have the Japanese to come into China to fight so-called communism?" "Yes," he said, "I see. I see your point . . . well, I cannot stop the series, but I can do something, I promise you."

And he did. For he was an honourable man. Right in the middle of the second page, facing yet another eulogistic article on Japan, Mr. Huysmans put an article describing my coming to see him and relating our talk. "I feel that this young lady has a point. Obviously, is there any justification for any country to invade another? . . . This question must be answered; and perhaps it behoves us to reflect whether to see the conflict in terms of a crusade against communism is altogether fair . . ."

The League of Nations was again being convened; there were Chinese delegations coming and going for various purposes including a financial one; Dr. H. H. Kung, China's Finance Minister, visited London for a loan. Then another delegation came to Brussels and I was asked to do some translating work for it, translating verbatim into French the speeches that were being made. I came to know Dr. Chang Penchen, the head of the delegation, and a Dr. Yang, an American graduate, who was in charge of the Press side. I did some translations into French and he took me to dinner. Distance had effaced the defects of the Kuomintang, patriotism had enhanced their appeal. Was there not unity, an end to civil war? I was now sublimely unconscious of any defect; would not listen to any criticism; thought Chiang Kaishek a hero, saw every delegate, even Dr. H. H. Kung with his paunch and his ever-restless glance behind very thick glasses, as a heroic defender bravely resisting the Japanese. I asked Dr. Yang how things were in China. "Oh, it's not so bad, but of course one can't get to Shanghai, and where the government is now, in Wuhan, is a beastly place, and of course no one is allowed to dance or go to the night clubs," was the reply I got. I then asked, would not the democracies help China, and Dr. Yang took off his glasses and polished them: "America is selling to Japan seventy-five per cent of her military equipment. That's gone on since 1932. Twenty million tons of scrap iron a year has gone to Japan from the U.S.A. They're making money – we're not blaming them. After all they're businessmen. But they'll have to help us too!" he added ambiguously. And then: "Say, isn't there a decent night club here?" At that time I knew nothing of the economics of warfare; the things which appeared incomprehensible to me I put down to my own ignorance. That was the way it was, and it did no good to puzzle too much over it. Another time, going to lunch with Dr. Yang and some other delegates, quite a fracas occurred, because two of the delegates wanted American steak rare, as done in the U.S.A., and there was no such thing in the restaurant where I took them. I thought that since China needed money for arms and equipment one ought to be thrifty, and tactfully I had taken them to an ordinary Belgian restaurant. The ghastly error was soon repaired. Someone from the Embassy arrived and led us all, in the usual fleet of cars, to the most expensive restaurant in Brussels. Dr. Yang and his friends smiled again.

Out of the jumble emerges another face: Ai Yiken, a student known as a left-winger, who worked very hard on the Committee. Ai Yiken was a tall man from Manchuria, and he was obviously disliked by the Chinese Embassy. He had founded the National Salvation League, Brussels branch. I only began to know him well after October 1937, and he turned out to be a far nicer person than the students I had met previously. He was also immensely reliable, and very quiet. The Chinese Embassy had denounced him and the founding of the Anti-Japanese Salvation League. There was an unpleasant scene at the Embassy when the Ambassador (who now had to back the Committee activities, though with obvious reluctance) called up Ai Yiken and several other students, including myself, and enjoined us "not to exaggerate" and to "stick to our studies", to put "first things first", and also asked Ai Yiken when he proposed to begin studying. Since Ai had lost his scholarship, taken away because he was a left-winger, he found it very difficult to attend the university full time.

Wang Mansung, a short-statured, pugnacious student, also lectured under the auspices of the Committee. Few of the Chinese students actually had volunteered to do anything, except Ai, myself and Wang, and later Dr. Yu, who also took part in lecturing. Ai was not a good lecturer, he had to read his speeches, but he had a sincere straightforward way. He took me to lunch one day with friends of his, who turned out to be small Cantonese tradesmen long established in Brussels, and who were also feuding with the Embassy. They were very patriotic, simple people; quite different from the official delegates. They gave money to the Committee, came to lectures, clapped loudly, and even if their French was very poor they got up and shouted at hecklers in Cantonese. They always did the leg work, nothing was too low for them to do to help. The Ambassador called me and warned me against them. "They are Communists," he said. "But don't we want to save China?" I asked the Ambassador. I could not understand the political partitions; surely patriotism came first.

One day Wang Mansung asked me whether I would like to have dinner with him. There was an evening lecture, but after that we would eat together. He turned up at my lodgings, and we went by taxi to a private house in the best part of Brussels. It was a large, elegant house in Boisfort, the best residential quarter. At the door of the sitting-room stood the host, Mr. Chen, and another man, whose name was given to me as Mr. Hsu. Mr. Chen was tall, handsome, manicured, beautifully dressed. He spoke with the nonchalance of authority, had studied in America and was on the Embassy staff, newly arrived. Hsu and Wang said yes, yes, quite right, every time Chen made a remark. Chen mentioned the Ambassador casually and said he had come to straighten things out in the Embassy. "We must be forward-looking, we must tighten up the organization in this time of emergency. Loyalty is most important." He offered me a cigarette from a silver box. The goblets into which he poured a liqueur which I did not drink (for it was that dreadful green crème de menthe), were solid crystal from Saint Gobain. The whole room as I looked around seemed replete with expensiveness, though not with the integrated comfort of my relatives, Uncle Eugène Denis of Antwerp, or Henri Denis and Aunt Lucy. "I've come to have a look around, to pull things up a little," Chen explained to me. "And you can help me, Miss Chou. There are a lot of students who are quite troublesome, quite disloyal." I concurred heartily. I felt that the Chinese students, who could do something to help the Committee, had not been exactly enthusiastic. One of them, now a minor Embassy official, was especially nasty. He never did anything but gossip, making up terrible stories; he could never pass any examinations and hated me because I passed so easily. Finally his family had sent him a Chinese girl from China, he married her in Brussels, and told everyone that she snored while he tried to make love to her. I felt that such people as he should do more to help. Chen led us to the supper table in the dining-room, a round table with a revolving central desk on which the dishes were placed. Every item of food had been sent from Paris. "The delegation of old Kung brought it in for me," said Chen, speaking thus of H. H. Kung, the Finance Minister. Such Chinese food I had not had for years. Chen questioned me and I replied: my studies, my ambitions . . . yes I wanted to be a doctor. He complimented me. I had kept up my Chinese: "You are patriotic. We must always remember that we are Chinese . . . have you read Our Leader's speeches?" I hadn't. He gave me some books. What did I think of the Committee, didn't I think it was too left-wing? I said: "No, on the contrary, more students should work in it." "Yes, yes, quite right, quite right, we also think we should not leave it all to the Communists. You just keep in with them, but if you notice anything you can always tell me," he said blandly. "Tell you what?" I asked. "All that you notice, about all the people you meet." I was uncomprehending; what was there to notice? Perhaps he meant people who took money for Spain instead of China? For that was a recurrent worry in the Committee, the allocation of funds. However, I did not dare to ask precisely what I should notice, for fear of seeming too stupid.

The next morning, early, Wang Mansung was at my door. He said Hsu wanted to talk with me. I was to meet them both at such and such a house, such and such a street, at about eleven thirty that morning. I went there and Hsu opened the door. It was a small flat; Wang was not there. Hsu was a man with a very pale round face, looking more like a Korean or a Japanese than a Chinese. He always wore a mackintosh and a felt hat, and he never smiled. He made me sit down at the table, sat opposite to me, took out from the drawer a framed picture and set it up. He also unrolled a sheet of paper on which were printed words. I stared at the picture. It was that of the Generalissimo Chiang Kaishek. Hsu then said to me: "We have decided, Mr. Chen, Mr. Wang and I, that you are a patriotic and upright spirit, and that you can be of great use to your Motherland. In these days are many traitors. As you know, Generalissimo Chiang Kaishek is Our Leader, and to him we owe our complete loyalty. We must actively combat any foreign ideology, only thus will our country remain strong. This is the Loyalty oath to Our Leader and the Motherland which every upright young student must take." He then read it, sentence by sentence and made me repeat it. I don't remember all the words but I remember that I asked him: "Do all the students have to do this?" "Yes," he said, "all good loyal Chinese students are now in our group, but this is a secret, you must not discuss it, some may be treacherous." Then he made me put up my hand, took my thumb, briskly placed it on an ink slab, then on the sheet of paper in front of me, at the end of the oath. Then he made me sign. "Henceforth you are enrolled a member of our Resurrection Association, the Fu Hsing Society. Your name in the society will henceforth be Chang so-and-so . . . I congratulate you, Comrade Chang." We shook hands. Then Hsu and I went out. Just before leaving the house he said to me: "By the way the enrolment fee is twenty francs." I had twenty francs on me and I gave them to him.

I had just been enrolled in the fascist, anti-communist Fu Hsing Society, which was the widespread outer periphery of the Nazi-type organization around Chiang Kaishek. Into this outer circle, students, teachers, intellectuals were recruited, but the inner control was by a nucleus of military trained officers, the Blueshirts, directly under the Secret Service of Chiang Kaishek. It was true that many students were recruited, always in a one-by-one way, in Europe. In China, they were simply taken by the lorry load to a meeting place; the doors were shut, and they were forcibly enrolled.

We walked to a small restaurant and had something to eat; I was thinking, slowly realizing that I had been trapped. The next month came a bill for twenty francs, and the next. I never paid the bills. After four months came a letter saying that I was no longer a member; thus I was expelled from the Resurrection Society almost as fast as I came in. I think they realized that I would never be a reliable or trustworthy member; and since I was always unable to supply any information on any other student, probably worthless.

During the three months I was supposed to be a member, Wang Mansung was specially nice to me; and I realized that he too was a member; and pretty soon afterwards Dr. Yu also got recruited. He whispered it to me at the coffee house for the students. Wang asked me what Ai Yiken or others were doing and saying; but as Ai Yiken was not doing or saying anything that I could find treacherous (and to my mind the only treachery was collusion with Japan), I would invariably answer: "I don't know." "Ai Yiken is a Communist," Wang told me. "Well, he is a very quiet one," I would reply. One day I lost my temper: "I thought we were fighting a war, and I am so busy giving lectures on China and I don't like snooping for anyone." A few days later came the crisp letter throwing me out.

Later I learnt that in Germany two students had been badly beaten by the Blueshirts, and one man had actually died. The murder was passed off as accidental death.

During those three months I went two or three times to lunch or dinner with Mr. Chen and his wife, a very lovely woman. She had

352

the most beautiful voice; the most lovely skin, the most perfect figure. All the Belgians admired Mrs. Chen's delicate, fragile beauty, and I was much afraid of her, for there was also a dazzling cruelty in her enchanting smile. It was from her lovely lips, in that bell-toned voice, clear as the sparkling water of the Jade Fountain slipping its perfect crystal from stone to stone, that I heard what I was to hear so often later from the lips of Ho Yingchin and other generals of the Kuomintang: "We must not fight Japan, America will do that for us – we must reserve our strength to fight the Communists, later . . ."

When the dykes of the Yellow River had been broken and millions of people were dying in the floods, a Belgian friend drew my attention to a statement, made by a Chinese general: "There are so many poor people in China, the more of them die, the better . . ." "This is fascism," he said, indignant. But I had heard the same remark, at the house of Mr. Chen, the day before.

Not all the students in the University were pro-China. We made an appeal, when bombs fell most cruelly on the Chinese cities, trying to collect signatures for a protest. I was told rudely by a young student: "I couldn't care less if bombs fall on *you* out there, so long as they don't fall upon *us* here." Many times the same sentiment was expressed to me: relief, actual relief that bombs (which have to fall, once manufactured) were being used far away in the East, upon "the yellows" and "not us . . ." because it spared "us", meaning the Europeans. "The more of you die, the better we live," cried at me one day a doctor (oh shameful the word). Others said: "Oh, you know it's too far, it has nothing to do with us, we can't understand it," and refused to sign. Sometimes I replied: "The bombs will be falling on you next year, just wait and see . . ." They would laugh, and some would insult me.

And today in 1965, I hear the same words as in 1938: "Oh, this does not concern us . . ." "But the war in Vietnam is to protect *us* from communism . . ." "Well, so long as it isn't *us*." I marvel that thirty years later, the same monstrous selfishness, the same refusal to think, the same cowardice and inhumanity should once again be helping those who make war to advance to a wholesale slaughter.

Paris was the centre of peace demonstrations in those years, chiefly because of the Front Populaire and the socialist denomination of the French government. In 1938 a great meeting was held there; it was in a theatre, and this was the first time I met Jawaharlal Nehru.

As a delegate of the Brussels Chinese students, I sat in a row with other delegates, and next to me was this quiet Indian, introduced to me as Mr. Nehru. The man who introduced him, also an Indian, told me that Nehru was the representative of the Independence movement for India; Nehru had just come from Switzerland, and he was going to speak in Paris. He went on the stage afterwards, and spoke about India's demand for independence. That evening he was with many other delegates and students in a small restaurant, and sat in a corner, with a hand frequently to his chin. He was thin, and appeared frail and sad, possibly because his wife had died only recently and he was in grief over her death. We talked a little about India, which I did not know at all. "You must come to India," he said; I think he said that to a number of students like myself. "I am going back to China," I replied, "but I don't know whether I shall have time to go through India, maybe next time." Later that year he went to jail again. I was to see him many years later, but he did not remember that first meeting in Paris.

During that spring we had another visitor, and that was Mrs. Yang Hucheng, the wife of General Yang Tiger City, who had helped to kidnap Chiang Kaishek at Sian. She was a young woman with a round face, who told me she had done some soldiering too. She had with her General Yang's son, and she only stayed a few days. Ai Yiken and the left-wing students arranged a hotel for her. Ai asked me whether I would like to meet her, and I did, going to her hotel and having tea with her. She also gave a Press conference, but it was not very well reported. I was too ignorant at that time to know exactly what had happened, and everyone was reticent. It was certain that Mrs. Yang was not welcome at the Embassy, and later Ai told me that her husband, General Yang, was in jail. "But why?" I cried. "Because he is supposed to be a Communist," said Ai, with that careful, colourless voice he always put on when he spoke about such topics.

On July 29th, 1937, Peking had fallen officially to the Japanese; I stopped writing to my parents in Tientsin. In November and December Shanghai and Nanking fell. In March 1938 a Japanese-controlled government under Wang Chingwei, the former Leftist, was installed in Nanking. Chiang Kaishek and his government were installed in Wuhan.

354

In April 1938 I told Abbé Bolland: "I am now stopping the lecturing and the conferences, examinations are in two and a half months; I must pass them."

Acker, now secretary of our Aid to China Committee, was angry when he heard this: "How can you do this to us? We were counting on you."

"You can find other people. I've only got two and a half months to do a year's work. I must pass my examination."

Others pleaded, then taunted: "We thought you were eager to do something. For China."

"I am."

"You know we must bend every effort to help China. China is doing badly in this war. Only we in the West can save her."

"I don't think lecturing here will save China."

"But that is really denying the masses . . . how can you judge? Surely you are not going to say you don't believe the masses can save the peace?"

"I am not denying anything. But there are many lecturers now. I must pass my examinations. And anyway what's the use . . . there's going to be war all over the world pretty soon."

At this Acker and other members of the Committee became rather peeved. I had hurt their feelings.

"Don't you think we are doing enough? Have you seen the last demonstration? We had two thousand students parading . . ."

"Yes, it's fine, it's wonderful. I think it's wonderful. But I have other things to do."

"We always knew you were always just a dirty little bourgeoise uniquely preoccupied with your own interests."

Others called me a renegade. I could not explain to them my involved decisions. Could not tell them what I was doing and why. I have a thick skin, I told myself, even though I felt very miserable. But I had to do what my self told me to do, and I would never listen to anyone else . . .

For two months I worked like a machine, like an automaton, catching up on my studies. I had seldom opened a book, scarcely read a word of physiology or anatomy . . . I disciplined myself, drinking black coffee, eating bread and cheese, working from eight at night to three in the morning. A walk every afternoon. Regular as clockwork. I saw no one, went nowhere, except twice to see my grandfather. He knew little of my platform performances, nothing of the long weary hours by train to so many

355

small hamlets, to the coalmining district, in the depressed areas of Belgium. . . He only knew what I wanted him to know, that I was working flat out. Once he came to see me, bringing ham, fresh lettuce, some pears. He smoked a pipe and watched me work, his eyes brimming with pride. "Oh, if you get a great distinction again, I'll buy you a watch."

Already my grandfather had given me half of his savings bonds. He wanted to, insisted, had brought them to me at Christmas when I went to spend some of the Christmas holiday with him. He told me how much money they represented, a sizeable sum. "It is half of what I have saved. I give it to you. I have enough with my pension to live on . . . put this money away for you." We had rented a small safe-deposit box at the bank, it had a code to work it open. I gave the name of Aunt Lucy to work the opening and shutting of the safe box. This pleased my grandfather and Aunt Lucy. "You see, she has a heart," said grandfather, gloriously vindicated. Alas! Alas! I was to repay his affection so badly.

May came, the chestnut trees wore huge white chandeliers; the may blossom was out, foam on the bushes. Then came the roses; I did not see them. June passed and Louis, now an up-and-coming solicitor, took me for walks. He gave me dinner and wore his Belgian Air Force uniform, very smart.

Came the examinations. I passed them with the highest distinction of all; there were only two that year in the whole university. My class gave me an ovation. "What are you doing for the summer holidays?" I said: "I am going back to China."

Now I had to announce it; to my grandfather, to the scholarship Board, and also to Hers who turned up in Brussels in July. For Shanghai had now been taken, and Nanking, and his house, furniture, accumulated curios and collections had been left behind. He had returned to report to the Bank, perhaps to live in Belgium for a while. Baron Y——, at the Board, was dumbfounded at my decision: "But we have guaranteed your scholarship for five years, we have made special provision for you. You are our most brilliant student." Since he could not stand any emotion, and I had given him two at once (passing so well, then turning down the scholarship), he rang up Hers and said he was "washing his hands of me." He was an unending source of clichés, and after a time all the students knew what he was going to say before he opened his mouth. Hers took me to lunch at the Metropole, we walked all the summer afternoon, across the forest

356

of Soignes and back; arguing, shouting, screaming at each other. He was to remember this walk for many years. In the end he said: "Baby, you are mad."

What would I be doing in China at war at this time? This wasn't a young ladies' picnic; it was war. God knew whether I would be able to get in once I went. And what would I do? Where would I live? And he thought that I was serious, that I wanted to do medicine.

"I don't know why I'm doing this but I have to go back."

"You are mad, stark staring mad." Hers strode furiously: "No, absolutely not, you will not go back, I have to look after you. Your parents are in Tientsin under Japanese occupation ... I am responsible for you."

"I am going back."

"Do you think you are going to save China? You don't know China. Living in Peking is not China. What will you do? Why don't you read history? China has always absorbed all her conquerors, the Chinese should not fight; China is feminine – a feminine country is always conquered – ends up by *devouring* those who rule her – as women do, as women do," he smashed his cane with something like fury across the May bushes. He turned sarcastic: "What will you do if some drunken Japanese soldiers get hold of you?" then dramatic: "You think the Kuomintang is a noble affair? I tell you more soldiers die of cholera and starvation and epidemics than of war wounds, millions are dying, while the officers are making money. The Chinese Kuomintang is more cruel to its own troops even than the Japanese," swish, swish went his cane.

"I am going back."

"And your boy friend, that mooncalf, Louis?" (Hers never liked any of my men friends.) "And your grandfather? And your career?" Then he turned again. "It is not Chinese of you, this extravagant patriotism. Look at the other Chinese students. They are not thinking of going back. They will stay here, quite happily. And when you do go back you will find yourself a stranger. A stranger. You are Eurasian, not Chinese. Like all émigrés, you want to be more Chinese than the Chinese themselves. God knows whether the Japanese won't have taken all China by the time you get there."

The next day Hers, with two of his nieces, took me to the seaside, Le Zoute. We lunched with a very wealthy family, the Schroeders. Mr. Schroeder was an armaments manufacturer. Mrs.

Schroeder was a very sweet woman, she owned the vaguest of blue eyes, the pupils diffused in the speckled irises. One never knew whether she was or was not looking at one. She was a spiritualist, and spoke at length about the superiority of Spirit-over-Matter, and how Evil had its role in the Ultimate Bliss. She believed in planchette, calling the dead, and said I had a lovely aura round my head. The Schroeders had a magnificent villa near the sea, a chef who cooked the most delicious fish I ever tasted in Europe. I have subsequently met a few armaments manufacturers and their wives. It may be pure coincidence, but in each case the wives were interested in supernatural phenomena, Life Beyond Death and Transcendental Good. One was deeply involved in Moral Rearmament while her husband kept her in supreme comfort by supplying this world with lethal weapons.

I wrote to a shipping company and obtained a second-class one-way berth from Marseilles to Hongkong, leaving late August or early September. I now told my grandfather that I was returning to China, and he nearly had a heart attack. He was eighty years old, and one had to be gentle with him. I gave him back the bonds he had given me, and he received them with hands that shook. It hurt me to hurt him, but I explained that I had to go otherwise I did not feel happy. "Are you going back to see your parents?" "Yes," I lied. I also had to tell another lie, that it was only a matter of a few months, then I would be back. In fact, I also half persuaded myself that I would return in a few months. "Are you sure you will be safe?" "Of course I will be safe," I said. I told him there would be no war where I was going, and that the newspapers always exaggerated things. "But one is better off here, here all is peace," said my poor grandfather, "I can't help feeling it's dangerous out there." I did not tell him that I thought it would not be peaceful in Europe either. Hitler, on March 11th, 1938, had marched into Austria and the Anschluss had been accomplished so easily, so easily, and "Why die for Schussnigg?" said the Europeans. "Why die for Austria? Hitler now will have enough." And now Hitler was going to take Czechoslovakia, and still Grandfather did not feel worried about Europe: "Of course there won't be a war. The last one was horrible enough. I know, because I was on the *Lusitania* going to England. Our ship was torpedoed and I hung for thirteen hours on some floating beam in the sea. I was saved. But this won't happen again, no one wants war again." The Belgian king had now dissociated himself from the French and British alliance. "No one will attack us now. We are *completely* neutral," said my grandfather.

The syndrome of cowardice, of appeasement, was in full blossoming; even left-wing intellectuals would later say: "Why fight for Czechoslovakia?" And acclaim the Munich agreement and Chamberlain's "peace in our time". With all this, I felt I was estranged, for to me the war was coming, later perhaps, but it was, and I felt increasingly more disgusted but could not explain my disgust since I was not intellectual, and so many intellectuals were explaining that "democracy" must be preserved and "peace" must be preserved at all costs, and for this they were cheerfully selling other people's lives to Hitler. And I daresay that in the end they would have sold themselves too, had it not been for a few patriotic, courageous men, sick of dishonour and cowardice . . . men like Winston Churchill.

As for Louis, he was more concerned with the protection of France than with any other subject. He thought the Maginot Line impregnable, as did millions of Frenchmen then, except General de Gaulle and my cousin Henri Denis and in England Liddell Hart and General Fuller. Why worry, if France was safe behind her fortresses?

"I thought we would go to see Greece . . . you must see the Acropolis, you will then realize what Greek art is – it will change your ideas about statues," said Louis, attempting to divert me from China. He arrived one night at midnight, stood in the street asking me what I really meant by "running away". It would have been funny if it had not been pathetic. "Can't you see," I said, "that I cannot LIVE like this in Europe while China is attacked?" And then he too saw it as I did but still refused the conclusion. I told him that I would return. I would be gone three months, four at the most to see what was happening in China, then I would return . . .

"At least let me accompany you to Marseilles."

I set off, saying goodbye to my grandfather, who waved and waved on the train platform. The image of the old man with his English tweed cap waving at me still fills me with grief, with a bitter, hopeless sourness, an after-the-event sorrow all the harder to bear because nothing can change it; it is fixed for all time in one's mind. At the next station Louis and his family were there. His two sisters, his mother, all were very friendly to me; they were hoping a wedding would occur "after you have seen your parents." Louis climbed on the train. He had brought his Air

Force uniform with him, because he looked handsome in its blue-grey smartness.

We reached Paris. Two days looking at the Louvre (again Venus, and again I shook my head, I could not vibrate in front of that all too sumptuous marble). Notre Dame. Île de France. Civilization. Culture. Art. Music. *Douceur de vivre*. Balm the sun, honey the air. Comfort. "Why not stay? Life must be horrible at the moment in China with the war." "That is why I have to go." "None of the other Chinese students have left." "Some will. You will see. Some will be going back."

Rheims, to see the cathedral. Standing in the light of the great immortal flower of colour and all the world made gorgeous in its light. And then to Vichy to say goodbye to Hers, there to do a cure for his liver. Hers in a large hotel with much glass, itself like a cathedral, the glass streaming red blue yellow upon our faces. "Here you are, Baby, here are sixty pounds, money for your steamship ticket." "Thank you." I take the money. "I will pay you back." I had already got my steamship ticket with the money saved on my scholarship, but I had none to spare so I took the sixty pounds. Hers gave us dinner. As usual he showed all too plainly that he resented Louis, but apart from saying: "H'm, h'm" and gazing right through him, could not do much about it. Anyway I was leaving.

Now that only a few days remained before sailing I was beginning to feel acutely uncertain. Was I right to go? Was I wrong? Would I retrace my steps? . . . suddenly I was frightened. After all, I was giving up everything I had worked for; scholarship, my medical studies, I who wanted so much to be a doctor . . . I was going on a journey *to* a war, and no one could tell me why, and now even I wondered why, I had forgotten why. But I pushed on. I would not look back.

"But you do know why" (said that other self in me). "Because you cannot live without China, you dumb so-and-so. Maybe you cannot live *in* China, maybe you are only a Eurasian, a dirty half-caste, as some people say, but you cannot live *without* China. For without China you die. *I* simply die, inside of *you*. Like that famous Greek giant Antaeus, who had to touch the Earth his mother, you can't do without China. Here you've been three years in Europe and have had everything you wanted and all you feel like is a stinking pool of dead water. You've got to go."

And yet this too was not the complete answer. It would take years and years to find the answer, which was not so simple. I had to learn that there is more to the human being than material comfort, more than success, more even than national spirit or patriotism. That in any being worthy of being human there is also a demand for justice, for liberty, and *that justice needs the evidence of all our lives, liberty is one and indivisible and collective*, and no one can talk of justice solely for expediency's sake, nor of liberty while human beings, anywhere else on earth, are still in bondage.

"You are an idiot, yes, a fool."

Attacks of weeping; another attack during lunch with Hers, which annoyed him. I upset my coffee upon my new suit. Now I wept, wept silently, tears running down my face. But still we proceeded southwards, proceeded although several times a day Louis would suggest turning off, to see a memorable medieval church, to visit a famous museum. A day in Nice, toasting in the sun upon the rocks; in the streets, near the piazza, flanked by pastry shops selling marrons glacés, I was suddenly hailed. It was Minette, in a bikini which revealed almost everything (but at that time they were called two-pieces). "Where are you going?" She walked a little with me on the sun-baked sidewalk and I told her I was going to China. "Ah," she was absent-minded, then, "You know I have met a man . . . he is marvellous . . . oh he is incomparable." Engrossed in her love, suddenly beautiful, she was golden with sun, glittering with love's effluvia. She shook hands gaily: "Do write to me, send me postcards." Does one send picture postcards of a war?

Marseilles was cold, blustery. The wind whipped out with malice, a vicious cat-claw at one's cheeks. We walked about, wandered in the Old Port . . . The women tore at Louis, wanting us to go in, to see a film. Only fifteen francs, ten francs, only five francs. Business was bad. "Let us try, it's a local product, it's typical of Marseilles." We are tourists, after all. We must not miss the local product. We are the only two in a small room, smelling of enclosed mould. The woman who has dragged us in puts on the film. I don't quite understand it, and anyway it is immensely sad, immensely boring and ugly. Something like the anatomy hall in the Medical School with its corpses laid out, staring at the sky, oozing lysol and grease and the humours that were life and are now death; only here in the film the corpses move about, assume postures, but it is really the same thing; it is death, walking, moving, performing gestures so completely without meaning, it is boring. We go out, Louis says: "It was quite amusing, wasn't it?"

hesitantly, for he is really ashamed, now, and I weep, weep silently but do not say a word for what can I say? There is nothing I can say except that it really does not matter, after all I am a medical student, I am not shocked. And Louis says, as we drag from café to café: "I love you so much, I will wait for you ... I did not want to tell you, but I love you with my soul, all my soul." The formless night sky is silent, is indifferent to all words.

The next day I climb on board ship, my cabin is a four-person one, my trunk is stowed away, I have a suitcase in the cabin. And I am right, there are other Chinese there: one of them is in fact Dr. Yu, my friend Yu. He tells me there are four other Chinese on board. "They are cadet officers returning from England." Dr. Yu is beaming, he has been offered a job, a good job, in the Army Medical Corps. "Perhaps I can get you a job too," he says grandly. Already the future is taking shape, presenting itself to me, accepting me. Hers was wrong, so wrong, to say no one was going back to China ... although it is true that many other students in Brussels will not budge until the Germans come in 1940 and send them home, yet here is Dr. Yu. The siren hoots, the gangplank is raised, the quay where Louis stands begins to slide away. I stare, already changed, already no longer the me going away from what I had wanted, but the me that is to be, amorphous voiceless, but already born, and of course born in pain, but childbirth is pain. In front of the ship, wide open lies the sea, the grey amorphous muscled sea. And I don't know quite what I will do and I don't know exactly where I shall go; but I have sixty pounds with me and I am going back, going back, going back, and now I know that there is no love, no other love, that there will never be any love stronger than this, which has no name, which I did not know was in me, stronger than anything else. For now it seemed that I had slept awake, and wakened to know that never would I find it enough merely to live to be happy, to find a man, a life all answered, faultless. And so I turn to look, not behind, but forward, at the sea with its slow, passionate pulse – the sea.

BIRDLESS SUMMER
Volume 3 in the China: Autobiography, History series

In the third volume of her masterly autobiographical history, Han Suyin reconstructs the events of Chinese history between 1938 and 1948, a time of terrifying confusion and corruption in China, and the period that witnessed the culmination of the revolution that finally catapulted China into the modern world.

'Han Suyin's third volume, in her combined autobiography and history of modern China, makes it plain that a masterpiece is in progress ... vastly illuminating'
The Observer

'Han Suyin's autobiography will, I fancy, be re-read two generations hence as one of the key documents of the twentieth century. A monumental achievement'
Daily Telegraph

£2.50

Han Suyin's History of Mao Tsetung and the Chinese Revolution

THE MORNING DELUGE
Volume 1: 1893–1935

This volume covers the period from the childhood of Mao Tsetung to the Long March, when the Red Army retreated to the barren wastes of Shensi Province to prepare for the inevitable clash with the Kuomintang forces of Chiang Kaishek.

'Han Suyin has on any estimate an extraordinary and epic tale to tell, and tells it with elegance and skill. Especially useful is her stress on the continuity of Mao's thinking, and the pre-echoes of recent struggles, particularly the Cultural Revolution, in much earlier days ... an absorbing account'
The Observer

Illustrated £1.75

THE MORNING DELUGE
Volume 2: 1935–1953

This second volume of Han Suyin's history of the Chinese Revolution describes the Revolution at war – at war with the Kuomintang, with the Japanese, again with the Kuomintang, and finally with the American forces in Korea.

'*The Morning Deluge* will surely be the most detailed popular account of the subject in English ... an important, enjoyable ... excellent book. Han Suyin has an instinctive sense of structure, paces her narrative and analysis very evenly and makes a huge amount of rare topographical and ideological matter perfectly accessible to the Western reader'
The Times

£1.25

WIND IN THE TOWER
Mao Tsetung and the Chinese Revolution 1949–1975

In *Wind in the Tower*, Han Suyin concludes the epic story of China's long march towards social and cultural revolution under the visionary leadership of Mao Tsetung. Starting in 1949 with the Red Armies poised for victory just before Liberation, she presents a comprehensive view of China's transformation, its achievements and its importance for the future of the world.

'It is sometimes austere, often very much alive, always enthusiastic; it is the final touch to the picture, by an admirably dedicated witness of twenty-five years which shook half the world'
Sunday Times

'Her book may be compared to Snow's celebrated piece of reporting *Red Star Over China*'
The Economist

'Miss Han is resolutely and insistently putting the case for Mao. She does it skilfully and has had many advantages in her frequent visits to China, her access to ministers ... as well as to unpublished documents. *Wind in the Tower* will be a mine of information for students of China'
The Times

£1.75

OTHER TITLES BY HAN SUYIN
IN TRIAD/GRANADA PAPERBACKS

CHINA: AUTOBIOGRAPHY, HISTORY series

1 The Crippled Tree	£2.50 ☐
3 Birdless Summer	£2.50 ☐

NON-FICTION

The Morning Deluge (Volume 1)	£1.75 ☐
The Morning Deluge (Volume 2)	£1.25 ☐
Wind in the Tower	£1.75 ☐
Lhasa, The Open City	£1.25 ☐

NOVELS

... And the Rain My Drink	£1.25 ☐
Destination Chungking	£1.25 ☐
A Many-Splendoured Thing	£1.25 ☐
Cast But One Shadow and Winter Love	60p ☐
The Four Faces	£1.25 ☐
The Mountain is Young	£2.95 ☐

All these books are available at your local bookshop or newsagent, or can be ordered direct from the publisher. Just tick the titles you want and fill in the form below.

Name ....

Address ....

....

Write to Granada Cash Sales, PO Box 11, Falmouth, Cornwall TR10 9EN.

Please enclose remittance to the value of the cover price plus:

UK: 40p for the first book, 18p for the second book plus 13p per copy for each additional book ordered to a maximum charge of £1.49.

BFPO and EIRE: 40p for the first book, 18p for the second book plus 13p per copy for the next 7 books, thereafter 7p per book.

OVERSEAS: 60p for the first book and 18p for each additional book.

Granada Publishing reserve the right to show new retail prices on covers, which may differ from those previously advertised in the text or elsewhere.